Wealth,
Waste, and
Alienation

———————————

Wealth, Waste, and Alienation

Growth and Decline in the Connellsville Coke Industry

Kenneth Warren

University of Pittsburgh Press

Copyright © 2001, University of Pittsburgh Press
All rights reserved

This paperback edition, 2019

Cataloging-in-Publication data is available from the Library of Congress

ISBN 13: 978-0-8229-6621-0
ISBN 10: 0-8229-6621-2

For Jean

Contents

List of Illustrations ix
List of Tables xi
Preface xv
Acknowledgments xix

1. The Foundations of the Industry 1
2. The Maturing Industry 25
3. Organization in the Coke Trade 77
4. New Districts 120
5. New Technology 157
6. The Physical and Social Implications of Beehive Coke Manufacture 195
7. Peak and Decline 229

Appendix A. Statistical Tables 261
Appendix B. Biographical Notes 267
Notes 271
Bibliography 287
Index 293

Illustrations

Maps
Coke works built before 1870   27
Coke works built 1871–1880   33
Coke works built 1881–1900   42
Growth of the H. C. Frick Coke Company, 1871–1901   49
Iron smelters known to be using Connellsville coke, 1879   60
Coke-producing districts or works of central and western Pennsylvania, 1886   124
Development of the Lower Connellsville coke region   128
New coke districts of West Virginia and Virginia   147
Coke works built in the "old basin" after 1900   177
Byproduct ovens making furnace coke, 1914   188
Plan of Leisenring, Fayette County, 1886   196
Coke and mine settlements in the "old basin," 1910   199
The new pattern—river coal and byproduct coking   240
The H. C. Frick Coke Company in the Connellsville region, 1937   253

Photographs
Derelict ovens   xvii
Henry Clay Frick, A. A. Hutchinson, Andrew W. Mellon, and Frank Cowan, 1880   37
H. C. Frick, ca. 1890   55
Thomas Lynch   84
J. V. K. Thompson   109
Morris Ramsay   115

Hauling coal underground, ca. 1893   121

Coke workers at South West No. 3   127

Locomotive pulling charging larries and hand-drawing of ovens, ca. 1893   159

Ovens at Star Junction, early twentieth century   198

Leisenring No. 1 mine, ovens, and settlement, ca. 1893   210

Leisenring No. 2 mine, ovens, and pollution   213

Tenements at Valley works, ca. 1893   215

Superintendents' houses at Trotter, ca. 1893   216

Union Supply Store at Summit Station   219

Workers and supervisors outside the Leith Mine, 1893   220

Early company town, or "coal patch"   227

Union-organizing parade   227

Early byproduct ovens at Dunbar, ca. 1905   230

A battery of the Clairton coke works, ca. 1930   237

Leisenring No. 1, ca. 1946   256

Remains of the Allison ovens, 1982   259

Chart

Output of byproduct coke and shipments of Connellsville coke, July 1929–December 1930   248

Tables

1.1. Increase (decrease) in output of iron according to fuel, 1855–1880   6
1.2. Output and productivity of various furnace fuels, 1890   6
2.1. Pig iron production by fuel used, 1860, 1864, 1869, 1873, and 1880   26
2.2. Iron-finishing trades of Pittsburgh, 1863 and 1871   26
2.3. Connellsville coke, 1870–1879   32
2.4. Weekly iron capacity of blast furnaces using coke, 1878, 1885, and 1895   38
2.5. Production of Connellsville coke and U.S. coke-made pig iron, 1880–1900   39
2.6. Coke and pig iron average prices and freight rates on Connellsville coke, 1887–1913   45
2.7. Production and prices in the early 1880s   47
2.8. Oligopoly in the Coke Region, 1882, 1894, and 1900   48
2.9. Connellsville coke prices at ovens, 1882 and 1883   51
2.10. H. C. Frick Coke Company major acquisitions and new controlling interests, 1889   56
2.11. H. C. Frick Coke Company production assets, 1882, 1890, and late 1900   57
2.12. Operations and production costs at H. C. Frick Coke Company plants, December 1882   61
2.13. Ovens incorporated in the South West Coal and Coke Company, 1882–1900   64
3.1. Increases in wage scales at H. C. Frick Coke Company, 1895   103
3.2. Sample wage rates in the Coke Region, 1894–1912   103

4.1. United States pig iron and Connellsville district coke production, 1895–1902   122

4.2. Coke output of Connellsville "proper" and other Pennsylvania districts, 1898–1902   125

4.3. Coking coal and coke ovens controlled by Carnegie Steel and major rivals, December 1900   130

4.4. Coke shipments by Connellsville and Lower Connellsville, 1900–1911   136

4.5. Coke works and ovens of Lower Connellsville, 1901, 1906, 1908, and 1914   136

4.6. Selected companies in Connellsville and Lower Connellsville districts, 1914   139

4.7. Plants, ovens, and coal used in Connellsville and Lower Connellsville, 1900–1929   139

4.8. Iron output and fuel consumption in selected furnaces, 1885–1892   142

4.9. Chemical composition of selected coking coals   146

4.10. Coke output of Connellsville and West Virginia ovens, 1880–1907   151

4.11. Chemical analyses of coke from Connellsville, Pa., New River (Pocahontas), W.Va., and Pineville, Ky., 1889–1891   151

4.12. Appalachian states' coke production, 1880–1905   154

4.13. Coke shipments from Connellsville, the Flat Top region, and other districts, 1895–1897   154

4.14. Coking assets of expected steel consolidation, December 1900–January 1901   155

4.15. Populations of leading coke and coking-coal counties, 1890–1940   156

5.1. Estimated capital costs and performances of beehive and byproduct ovens, 1896–1898   169

5.2. Comparative estimated average production costs per ton of Bessemer pig iron in selected world districts, 1897–1898   176

5.3. Coke production, 1900, 1910, and 1913   179

5.4. Estimated plant and expenditures to produce 118,800 tons of coke annually, beehive and Otto-Hoffman ovens, 1904–1905   181

5.5. Estimated relative costs of coke made in beehive and byproduct ovens, 1906   181

5.6. Average annual prices for beehive coke and selected labor costs, 1900–1913   182
5.7. Byproduct ovens by location, 1899–1913   188
5.8. Byproduct ovens in major iron and steel centers, 1899, 1903, 1906, 1913   189
6.1. Populations of Fayette and Westmoreland Counties and Pennsylvania, 1840, 1880–1920   197
6.2. Foreign-born males in the Coke Region and elsewhere, 1880   197
6.3. Population of Connellsville and Uniontown, 1840, 1880–1920   200
6.4. Range of manufacturing in coke district settlements   201
6.5. Headquarters of coke firms working the Connellsville and Lower Connellsville regions, 1914   201
7.1. Output of beehive and byproduct coke in peak pig iron production years, 1907–1920   232
7.2. Beehive coke works and ovens, Connellsville and Lower Connellsville districts, 1914 and 1919   233
7.3. Byproduct ovens at major iron and steel centers, 1914 and 1920   234
7.4. Source of coal used in Illinois and Indiana byproduct ovens, 1917   235
7.5. Annual changes in total coke production and that by the beehive and byproduct processes, 1913–1920   236
7.6. Production of bituminous coal in southwestern Pennsylvania counties, 1900–1920   243
7.7. Production of leading Appalachian coking-coal counties, 1906 and 1920   246
7.8. Capacity and output of the beehive and byproduct coke industries, 1910–1930   249
7.9. Byproduct and beehive coke industries, 1939   250
7.10. Mines and coal outputs of selected Appalachian coking-coal districts, 1923 and 1929   251
7.11. Pig iron shipments and coke output, 1936–1940   252
7.12. H. C. Frick Coke Company in the Connellsville Coke Region, 1910, 1920, 1930, and 1938   254
7.13. United States, Pennsylvania, and Connellsville coke production, 1915–1940   254

Preface

Away from the sprawling, built-up area of greater Pittsburgh, much of southwestern Pennsylvania consists of pleasing if unspectacular rural landscapes, a rolling countryside of woodland, small farms, and a few not noticeably bustling towns. Two hundred years ago this section lay on the pioneer fringe of the nation: farmland and sites for new settlements were carved out of what seemed to some of its early white inhabitants an earthly paradise. Looking at the area from either a contemporary perspective or, in the mind's eye, the decades around 1800, one finds it hard to realize that it was for many years home to one of the nation's greatest and most distinctive mineral-based economies.

Coke manufacture was highly concentrated in time. In less than three-quarters of a century it grew from slight beginnings, mushroomed, and fell away. Peak levels of production were reached by a vast multiplication of fairly standard units of plant supported by an influx of capital and workers. Many of the latter were foreign-born members of the "new" immigration of the late nineteenth century from central, eastern, and southern Europe. Operators fought a series of violent, often bloody battles with these workers before settling for an uneasy and, as it now seems, rather mean paternalism. Decline of the industry and the society that directly depended on it was speeded by the profligate manner in which the resource base was exploited and by the rapid advance of a new technology that altered the whole nature of production.

The industry was an extreme example of localization in space, the areal concentration of a large part of a national economic activity. In 1913 a district stretching roughly thirty miles north and south from the small town of Connellsville made about 47 percent of America's metallurgical coke and some 18 percent of the global output. It was the leading supplier of fuel to the nation's blast furnaces. But the iron and steel industry lay well away from the coke field so that when its resource-based activities declined, this once pulsing, noisy, grossly polluted district settled slowly into a postindustrial phase.

Compressed into a handful of decades of mineral-based activity, industry and area passed through a whole development sequence—recognition of possibilities; the building of links to distant markets; the influx of enterprise, capital, and labor; the construction of plant; and then, after massive expansion of these facilities and their output, a gradual unwinding of the whole complicated structure. Growth and decline alike were accompanied by the wholesale reshaping of the district's material and social fabric. Together natural resources and human effort yielded wealth to individuals, companies, and to some communities, but there was also social alienation, appalling waste, and despoliation of the physical environment. Even now a good deal of the decaying legacy of these earlier phases of development can be seen as relict features in the region's landscapes.

The pleasing countryside of low rolling hills stretching out to the northwest of Chestnut Ridge is covered by a close network of country roads connecting a scatter of small rural settlements. There are a handful of rather bigger centers, such as Smithfield, Scottdale, and Mt. Pleasant, and two larger towns, Connellsville and Uniontown, with ten and under fifteen thousand inhabitants respectively. The land is widely farmed, but the agricultural scene indicates a satisfactory rather than marked fertility, with little sign of any rural affluence. In a few places on the margins of the area, strip mines still produce small tonnages of coal. There are various manufacturing activities on the outskirts of the main settlements and a few more recent industries in open countryside near highway intersections. Yet traveling this apparently unexceptional area, the visitor also becomes aware of other features of its landscape. Here and there by the roadside are half-hidden structures overrun by wild vegetation. One may see, ghostlike behind bare winter branches or a patch of scrubland, a strangely located, long, straight, and obviously man-made embankment, its top and side pierced by a regular pattern of holes. In exceptional cases there are great ramparts of brickwork, curving to fit the contours of the land surface, sometimes with abandoned loading gear, tools, and even railroad cars strewn along their length. Nearby, often in what appear to be anomalous positions, is a small group of houses or the empty shell of a settlement of perhaps a score or more rundown, clap-boarded homes. The surface of the road is here and there broken by what was obviously once a railroad crossing; in various directions the alignments of former tracks may be made out in the scrubby woodland. Some places have piles of waste in which may be

Preface xvii

Derelict ovens, half-hidden by shrubs. *Courtesy of Eugene Levy*

found large blocks of hard fibrous material with a distinctive blue-gray metallic glaze. Gradually, one recognizes being in the midst of a widely extending old mineral district, its relict features silently but relentlessly rotting away, a largely unremembered yet priceless part of America's industrial heritage. The processes of growth and decline that produced this unique present-day landscape are the subjects of what follows.

Considering its key importance throughout the decades in which the United States was becoming the world's leading economy, the Connellsville coke industry has received scant attention. There are two fine studies, John Enman's 1962 research thesis and a comprehensive Historic American Engineering Record survey of 1995. (I particularly appreciated Enman's encouragement to embark on this work.) As will be clear, I have made use of both works, but my aims have been different. Above all and throughout, I have tried to set the industry within its wider context of time, space, technological change, and connections with iron manufacture. In researching the industry and region, I used the excellent trade journals and a few good secondary sources. I was particularly fortunate in being given access to primary source material, especially the minutes and letters of the Carnegie Steel Company, the United States Steel Corporation, and the archives of the industry's leading entrepreneur, Henry Clay Frick.

Acknowledgments

For help in locating and for granting permission to use photographs, I thank Eugene Levy of Carnegie Mellon University; Warren Hull of USX; the Frick Art and Historical Center; Pamela Seighman of the Coal and Coke Heritage Center at Pennsylvania State University, Fayette; Julia Allen of the Connellsville Free Library; Marjorie J. Laing; Christy Fusco of the Uniontown (Pennsylvania) Public Library; Sister Eleanor Soroka of the Sisters of the Order of St. Basil, Uniontown; Pat Trimble, mayor of Dawson, Pennsylvania; and Charles M. Lynch, who made available the photograph of his great-grandfather Thomas Lynch. Publication of the photographs and maps was generously assisted by a grant from the Eberly Foundation of Uniontown. I have much appreciated the help over the years of Martha Frick Symington Sanger, great-granddaughter of Henry Clay Frick. Finally, I am especially grateful for the encouragement, generous hospitality, and very practical help of Frederick A. Hetzel.

Wealth, Waste, and Alienation
---

1 The Foundations of the Industry

The Nature, Use, and Early Development of Coke in the United States

Coke is the residue produced when great heat is applied to coal kept out of direct contact with air. The process is conducted either by covering the coal with a more or less impermeable layer or, more effectively, by enclosing it in an oven. Volatiles are driven off, leaving a product that is largely carbon. There are various types of coke. That made as a byproduct of gas production is derived from coals fairly high in volatiles and is rapidly processed in retorts at relatively low temperatures. The resulting coke is dull, spongy, and burns readily. In contrast, low-volatile coals produce insufficient gas to complete the coking process. Between these extremes are the so-called caking coals. "Burned" at higher temperature and with a long continued heat, the best caking coals—which should also have only a low ash and sulfur content—produce a coke much harder and denser than gas coke, a coke that is strong, fibrous, and silver-gray in color and has a semimetallic luster. Its hardness means it is resistant to abrasion and therefore free from fine particles. This kind of coke is porous, its structure vesicular—that is, having minute holes formed by the release of the gases that it once contained. Because it is admirably suited for use as a fuel in furnaces provided with a strong draught, this product of a limited, special group of coals with these highly distinctive properties and striking appearance is known as metallurgical coke.

Coke has been employed in a wide variety of metallurgical processes. In the nonferrous sector it was a major provider of heat and a reducing agent in the earlier stages of processing such important minerals as copper, lead, and zinc. It is used in steel making when high temperatures and chemical reactions with carbon are required, but it is essential not to risk the presence of the wider range of impurities so often present when raw coal is used. In quality steel making coke was for many years a fuel and source of pure carbon for the furnaces in which broken blister steel was heated, melted, and refined. The cupola furnaces, which melted pig iron and scrap for making iron castings, used coke. In the nineteenth century it was also burned in cupolas to remelt cold pig iron for the Bessemer converter, which itself was heated to make it ready for its first blow by burning coke within it. Collectively, these activities provided a considerable outlet, but far and away the major use of metallurgical coke, the category of consumption that transformed its provision into a great industry, was and remains the smelting of iron in the blast furnace. In the operations of this type of furnace, good quality coke is as important chemically as iron-bearing materials, and it is second only to the latter in tonnages consumed. In 1957, for example, the American iron and steel industry consumed 70.44 million net tons of coke. Of this total 0.13 million tons were used in foundries, 1.6 million for various purposes, and 68.69 million tons by blast furnaces.

In blast furnace operations coke performs an impressive range of functions. From its combustion is derived the thermal energy required to melt the huge material load, a mixture of iron ore, flux (the limestone that converts into slag such impurities in the ore as silica and alumina), and the coke itself. Chemically, the carbon in the coke acts as the reducing agent for the oxides of iron, which in a variety of chemical combinations and in differing degrees of iron content constitute the commercially usable iron ores. The porous structure of the coke provides an extended surface for chemical reactions, and its hardness enables it to support the huge column of mixed minerals as they slowly descend into the furnace's reduction zone. The large, blocky shapes of the coke keep open the ways for the passage of the heated air blown through the "tuyeres" into this lower part of the furnace. In short, iron smelting draws on a remarkable range of properties in the metallurgical coke. Given these functions, it is not surprising that it is now universally the main blast furnace fuel. However, in the United States coke was not the leading fuel in iron making until the mid-1870s, and before that its manufacture was not a major industry. Other abundant sources of energy were available but eventually proved inferior to coke. For a time, though, they too offered ironmasters a number of attractive features.

Raw coal, anthracite, charcoal, and—only as an energy-rich supplement to solid fuels within recent decades—oil have all been employed as sources of carbon in iron smelting. Even peat has been tried as a reducing agent. For century after century, through the long history of iron making in the western world since the introduction of the blast furnace, charcoal was the standard fuel. It was widely available, chemically pure, and, though rather soft, well suited for low-shaft furnaces. Until the first years of the eighteenth century, all pig iron made in Europe used charcoal. Long before that time, clearing of the continental forests meant that the large areas needed to provide furnace timber were becoming scarce. In Britain, where destruction of wooded areas had created serious problems as early as the Elizabethan Age, numerous attempts were made to substitute mineral fuel, coked or uncoked. As early as 1589 a patent was granted for making iron with "cooked" coal; a century later Dud Dudley claimed to have produced pig iron using uncoked Staffordshire coal. A technically and commercially successful breakthrough was at last achieved in the early eighteenth century. Even such a generally well-informed American authority as Joseph Weeks, author of the 1880 Census report on coke, was vague about the time of this breakthrough, citing either 1713 or 1735.[1] It is now known that it was in 1709 that Abraham Darby of Coalbrookdale, Shropshire, succeeded in smelting iron using coke made from local coal, an achievement that legitimately gave this small district its reputation as the hearth of the industrial revolution in metals. At first Darby's innovation spread relatively slowly even in his own country, partly because he had been producing special irons and partly because it was found that coke suitable for blast furnace use could not be produced from all coals.[2] In the second half of the eighteenth century, the pace of adoption of coke smelting in Britain increased, helped toward the end of the period by the new blowing power provided by the introduction of the Watt steam engine. A century after Darby's initial innovation, only a little over 6 percent of British blast furnaces were still using charcoal. In sharp contrast, until the 1830s United States furnaces, though already producing a quarter as much iron as those in Britain, remained wholly dependent on charcoal.

This difference between the two national industries in no sense indicated a lack of either knowledge or enterprise on the part of American ironmasters, but rather reflected the fact that their natural resource endowment was far greater. The efforts of such bodies as The Friends of Domestic Industry, the Franklin Institute, or various other organizations sponsoring economic development in the individual states and the easy routine transfer of knowledge of innovations in technical papers between two societies with the same language ensured there was no lack of information about the technical improvements being made in Europe. Indeed, some of the new processes pioneered there were adopted in the New World with remarkable alacrity. For example, the Scot James Beaumont Neilson patented the hot blast in September 1828; by 1834 his process was in use in a New Jersey blast furnace. In short, when commercial benefits could be anticipated, the American iron industry showed itself well able to accept new methods. For a number of reasons, as far as furnace fuel was concerned, there seemed to be little urgency to follow trans-Atlantic practice.

The forests extending from Ohio eastward over a huge area meant that charcoal could be procured for furnaces located near almost any of the widely scattered deposits of iron ore. Use of charcoal as a fuel meant low furnace outputs but, apart from a few large urban-industrial areas on the eastern seaboard, the United States was as yet mainly a rural society with widely spread and rarely intensive levels of demand. It is well to remember that as late as 1830, no city other than New York and Philadelphia was larger than 100,000 in population; of the rest Baltimore, Boston, and New Orleans alone exceeded 40,000. Even so, iron consumption was rising rapidly through the 1820s and 1830s, and although much of the metal supply was imported, home output too was increasing—later American Iron and Steel Association estimates put 1820 production of pig iron at 20,000 tons, rising to 130,000 tons in 1828 and 200,000 tons by 1832. A few years later the beginnings of iron-rail production provided a large, localized demand for pig iron to be processed in puddling furnaces. Such new mills at last made bigger blast furnace outputs desirable. The higher levels of production required more iron capacity, which in turn involved the hauling of charcoal supplies from ever-wider catchment areas, pushing up procurement costs. Under such circumstances, although additional charcoal furnaces were built and their output largely increased, many established iron works found fuel supply so difficult that they had to blow out furnaces and wait for a regrowth of their timber. In the longer term iron made with charcoal was unable to meet increases in demand. From 1854 to 1856 the average annual output of pig iron was 715,000 tons and from 1867 to 1869 1,482,000 tons; between these two periods charcoal furnaces raised their output only from 314,000 to 329,000 tons a year. In reality, their failure to keep pace was only in part due to raw material supply difficulties; it was largely because charcoal furnaces were less competitive than a new generation of ironworks using mineral fuel. The hot blast, introduced to the United States soon after its first application in Scotland, provided the blowing power necessary for the use of new, less easily fired but more concentrated sources of energy.

The first real successes in the use of coke in American blast furnaces were gained in the 1830s. Coke was tried in a furnace on Bear Creek, Armstrong County, Pennsylvania, as early as 1819, but at that time the air blown into the furnace was unheated and the blowing power available was too limited. A decade later, iron consumption was growing rapidly, technical resources for the use of mineral fuel were more favorable, and already charcoal was sometimes difficult to procure. In 1835 the Franklin Institute offered a prize for the first iron made with coke. By that year some ironworks along the Little Juniata River were having to haul charcoal ten to twelve miles; they apparently resolved to try coke when railroad extensions made it available. Some even reckoned that by coking the coal and using local iron ores, both minerals being carried by canal, it should be possible to make pig iron in the Hollidaysburg area for as little as ten dollars a ton as compared with over seventeen dollars in South Wales, then a major source of finished iron for the United States. As so often happens, proposing an idea on paper proved easier than realization. In 1835 for a short period—perhaps only a month—coke made from Broad Top coal was used by Mary Ann furnace, Huntingdon County. Two years later a furnace at Fairchance, Fayette County, made some iron with coke before reverting to charcoal. That same year the Lonaconing furnace in the Frostburg coal basin of western Maryland became the first important user of coke, to be closely followed by Mount Savage Ironworks in the same area and Brady's Bend Ironworks on the Allegheny River in northwestern Pennsylvania. However, these furnaces were not consistently successful in their pioneering. Sometimes there were problems with the quality of coke made from local coals, which meant the output of furnaces and mills was not of an acceptable quality. At Lonaconing transport costs proved a handicap. By 1849 not one coke furnace was at work within Pennyslvania.[3]

A vitally important reason for the slow take-off of the coke iron industry and therefore of large-scale coke manufacture was the powerful rivalry of another mineral-based iron industry. This competition was moderated for a time by distance, which provided for two distinct market areas for iron, one east and another west of the Appalachians. It was because of this division that Overman, writing in 1850, confessed himself unable to understand why coke smelting had not been able to succeed west of the Allegheny Mountains.[4] In the east, use of anthracite as a furnace fuel had only become possible with the introduction of the hot blast. Anthracite iron manufacture began a year or so later than the coke iron industry but established itself firmly and expanded much more rapidly. The first technically and commercially successful furnace operations using anthracite dated from 1839. By the following year there were six anthracite furnaces, all within eastern Pennsylvania. By spring 1846 Pennsylvania and New Jersey contained forty-two; ten years later these states had ninety-seven blast furnaces using anthracite, and twenty-four were in other eastern seaboard states. Production of anthracite iron reached 341,000 gross tons in 1855, for the first time exceeding the output of charcoal iron. At that time the tonnage of iron made from either coke or raw coal was only 56,000 tons, or 8 percent of national production.

Though long overshadowed, from the late 1850s coke iron began first to improve its position and then to overhaul the other furnace fuels. As with anthracite earlier, its advance accelerated. From an 1859 share of slightly over one-tenth, five years later it approached one-fifth of iron production. By 1869 the tonnages smelted with coke and raw coal exceeded that made with charcoal, amounting to almost 29 percent of national production (compared with 51 percent for anthracite iron). Within another

Table 1.1 Increase (decrease) in output of iron according to fuel, 1855–1880 *(gross tons in thousands)*

Years	Bituminous and coke	Anthracite	Charcoal
1855–1860	53	123	(55)
1860–1865	60	(36)	(15)
1865–1870	340	402	92
1870–1875	337	(19)	41
1875–1880	895	803[a]	113

SOURCE: Based on P. Temin, *Iron and Steel in Nineteenth Century America: An Economic Enquiry* (Cambridge, Mass.: MIT Press, 1964), 266.

a. From 1875 onward some coke was also used in anthracite furnaces.

Table 1.2 Output and productivity of various furnace fuels, 1890

Plant	Furnace height (feet)	Iron output per month (gross tons)	Avg. iron content of ore used (%)	Fuel used per ton (lbs)
Ashland, Wisc. (charcoal)	60	3,379	55	1,815
Secaucus, N.J. (anthracite)	65	2,698	55	2,244
Penna, Pa. (anthracite/coke)	80[a]	3,844	60	2,520
E. Thomson, Pittsburgh (coke)	90	10,536	59	1,737

SOURCE: J. Fulton, "Physical Properties of Metallurgical Fuels," *American Manufacturer*, quoted in *BAISA*, 24 November 1894, 267.

a. 1892

six years they were ahead of anthracite iron. Most impressive of all, though the pace varied, bituminous coal and coke iron proved able to sustain the advances they made whereas the production levels of charcoal iron and even those for anthracite iron were less consistent. By the mid-1870s the large outputs possible in furnaces fired with coke had conclusively proved that this was the fuel best suited to the increasingly common practice of hard-driving a blast furnace; that is, using the maximum blowing power in order to gain the largest output in the shortest time.

As coke became the prime furnace fuel, capacity to make it had to be extended. Though widely procured, it eventually came above all from a very small area. Some thirty years after the mushroom growth of anthracite coal mining set in train the transformation of a handful of eastern Pennsylvanian counties, coke manufacture began to make an even smaller area within its southwestern section into another of the nation's outstanding and most distinctive mineral districts. Before the middle decades of the nineteenth century, this area was largely agricultural, though for a short period it had also played a part of some significance in the iron trade.

Southwestern Pennsylvania before the Coke Age

The Connellsville region was opened by European pioneers, the military, and then by settlers a century before it became renowned for coke making. Fort Necessity, on the east side of Laurel Ridge, was a control point established by George Washington. Following the French and Indian Wars, settlers reached the Youghiogheny Valley. After a period of frontier settlement, southwestern Pennsylvania became a zone of passage and source of supplies for those moving farther westward. A route from the Potomac led northwest by a narrow portage to the Youghiogheny and from there to and beyond the Monongahela, a course that with further improvement became the National Road. Along this route Uniontown, settled in 1767, was one of the first small communities, nuclei that would grow into towns, and so become fixed points through the various stages of economic development. Connellsville and Greensburg were established two or three years later, Brownsville was laid out in 1785, and Mt. Pleasant in 1797. Westmoreland County was formed in 1773, and Fayette County ten years afterward.

Life in such frontier lands was hard in the last quarter of the eighteenth century. In 1791 the Reverend Thornton Fleming was assigned to Methodist service some way farther up the Monongahela Valley in the Clarksburg circuit of what was to become West Virginia. More than forty years later, he looked back on his early days in the area: "When I came to my appointment this whole country appeared as a howling wilderness. Settlements were quite thin, quite remote from one another in many parts, and little cultivated. In many places the living, manners, state of society and morals of the people seemed to correspond."[5] The fact that Fayette County was one of the centers of the Whisky Rebellion of 1794 was a sign it shared both the remoteness and some of the human characteristics of Fleming's Clarksburg.

A decade after the Whisky Rebellion, Thaddeus Harris, traveling in the areas west of the Alleghenies, found a happier situation. Along the valley of the Monongahela, economic development and diversification were underway: "The settlements on both sides of the Monongahela river are fine and extensive, and the land is good and well cultivated. Numerous trading and family boats pass continually. In the spring and fall the river seems covered with them. The former, laden with flour, whiskey, peach-brandy, cider, bacon, iron, potter's ware, cabinet work, etc, all the produce of the country, and destined for Kentucky and New Orleans or the towns on the Spanish side of the Mississippi. The latter convey the families of emigrants, with their furniture, farming utensils, etc, to the new settlements they have in view."[6] The region was becoming agricultural, but, though contemporaries such as Harris described the soil as fertile and well farmed, there is evidence—admittedly from many years later—that farming in this area was in fact not very prosperous. By 1850 the proportion of improved land in farms throughout Pennsylvania was 57.8 percent, and the value of implements and machinery per acre of improved land was $1.71; at that time the respective figures in Fayette County were 53.8 percent and $1.40. As a local paper recalled much later, during the 1830s the area was characterized by poor farmland.[7] By 1840 the population of Fayette County was 33,574 and of Westmoreland County, 42,669; though established seventy years, Connellsville was a diminutive town of 1,436 inhabitants, and Uniontown was populated by 1,710 people. Long before this some had realized that the natural wealth of the area could be found beneath rather than within its soil. The earliest of its mineral-based developments were in iron.

On 1 November 1790 the first blast furnace west of the Appalachians—though owned by a Philadelphia partnership—was blown in on Jacobs Creek, Fayette County. The Alliance Ironworks also included a forge. Five months later the Union furnace was at work on Dunbar Creek four miles south of Connellsville. In 1792 a forge was built along George's Creek south of Uniontown and five years later a furnace was established along the same stream. Plumsock Forge had been built in Menallen Township, Fayette County, by 1794. Two years later a sixth part of Laurel furnace, its ore bodies, and forests lying within two miles of the Youghiogheny was advertised in Pittsburgh.[8]

These furnaces and forges supplied a variety of markets. There was local demand in the expanding needs of the rural economy, soon a more concentrated and rapidly increasing consumption in the region's central point of Pittsburgh, and the requirements of the extensive areas to the west made accessible via the National Road and by water through the vast outlets of the Mississippi lowlands. Indeed, as Thaddeus Harris had recognized in the early years of the nineteenth century, southwestern Pennsylvania occupied an important position in a great system of exchange that, as far as possible, employed water transportation around the outer edges of the landmass of the whole eastern half—at that time the only economically "effective" part—of the United States. Nearly three-quarters of a century later, long after this pattern of commerce had been superseded by others, E. Pechin, the manager of the Dunbar furnace, vividly recalled the trade. In the early days the castings and forge products of ironworks between the Youghiogheny and Monongahela had been hauled in teams for fifteen to as much as thirty miles across country to Brownsville. From that river port the goods were taken on flatboats down the Ohio and Mississippi and traded in frontier communities for corn, pork, whiskey, and other products, which in turn were carried on to New Orleans and there exchanged for sugar and molasses. These were sent by sea to Baltimore, where they were disposed of for groceries, dry goods, and other items that, loaded on Conestoga wagons, were hauled some three hundred miles over the Appalachians to the furnace or forge communities from which the iron products had been dispatched. Barter was the basis of the whole system according to Pechin, who quoted an old furnaceman who conducted business continually for three years and in that time saw only ten dollars in money.[9]

The natural resources for the iron trade that helped southwestern Pennsylvania gain the various necessities of life were its numerous small deposits of iron ore and the cover of forests, which yielded fuel for the furnaces. Between 1794 and 1815, thirteen blast furnaces were built in Fayette County, most of them in the latter half of that period. In all about nineteen were built in that county, and others were constructed in Westmoreland County. The productive lives of these establishments were relatively short. By 1837 the area that later became the coke region contained four forges, rolling mills, and numerous foundries but only nine operating blast furnaces. Each of the latter made some five hundred tons of pig iron a year. Eventually, a swathe of idle furnaces, outnumbering those still at work, extended from east of the Youghiogheny through to the Monongahela. They had suffered from unreliable access to market due to the uncertainties of river movement, but the main reason for failure had been the exhaustion of supplies of readily accessible charcoal, partly as a result of their own past successes as well as the further advance of cultivation at the expense of forest. Estimates of the amount of charcoal required per ton of pig iron vary widely, from as little as ninety bushels to as much as twice that, but in any case the demands on the forest resources were large. Some years later Birkibine suggested that every thirty-five bushels of charcoal required the use of one cord of wood, an amount roughly representing the annual growth of one acre of woodland. In short, by his rough and ready generalization and utilizing the lower figure of charcoal use per ton of pig iron, the nine active furnaces in the region in 1837 would have used, if worked to their full capacity, the timber from about 11,600 acres of forest—one year's growth covering eighteen square miles.[10] Deforesting the area surrounding them, the furnaces increased their own costs and often had to be blown out to await regrowth of woodland, but in fact were never reactivated because trading conditions changed. By 1840 about three-quarters of all the furnaces built in the area had been abandoned; in the late 1850s only four were left.[11]

The charcoal iron industry played an important part in the peopling, settlement, economic growth, and landscape-shaping of many parts of Pennsylvania, a role eloquently summarized by John Birkibine at the first meeting of the Association of Charcoal Iron Workers: "To the charcoal iron-master we are indebted for the discovery of many superior iron mines. The business which the charcoal furnaces and forges drew about them encouraged the building of highways, canals, etc. They formed the nucleus for some of our most flourishing towns, and thousands of acres of the best farm lands were first cleared to make charcoal for iron works." These words were more applicable to the lowlands of the far east of the state or to the Appalachian uplands than to southwestern Pennsylvania. His valedictory for the industry seemed more appropriate for the latter section: "Many of the old-established sites are now abandoned. The ruins of a furnace stack, a coal-house utilized as a barn, or perhaps only a pile of cinder marks the place where years ago there was a thriving iron industry."[12] Indeed, traces of charcoal iron making persisted in those parts of the region that had been affected by especially heavy calls for wood: the uplands that remained unsuitable for cultivation, especially Chestnut Ridge and Laurel Hill. Half a century after the passing of the age in which charcoal iron manufacture was an important activity in southwestern Pennsylvania, one observer noted: "these mountain sides from base to summit are dotted with the old circular charcoal pits which yet lie as bare and barren almost as on the day of their abandonment."[13] In the second half of the 1850s, state geologist J. P. Lesley, compiling his magnificent guide to the ironworks of the whole United States for the American Iron and Steel Association, had visited the Ross cold-blast furnace on Laurel Hill in Fairfield Township, Westmoreland County. He recorded it had been abandoned in 1850 "for a second growth of timber or for bituminous coal."[14] The failure of this furnace as well as the collapse of the iron industry throughout Westmoreland and Fayette Counties for want of fuel was ironic, for underneath the farmlands stretching between their two main rivers lay the nation's greatest deposit of first-class coking coal. Exploitation of this incomparable resource began as the charcoal furnaces, one by one, reached the end of their working lives.

In 1836 the *American Journal of Science* published a long article on the Ohio basin.[15] After sketching the area's endowment in forests and fertile land, it turned to mineral wealth. The article quoted the opinions of a practical engineer and geologist, R. C. Taylor, on coal resources. In the upper portions of the region coal was being used by salt works along the Conemaugh River and in the steam engines of Allegheny County. Taylor also looked to other avenues of advance: "The coaking process is now understood and our bituminous coal is quite as susceptible of this operation and produces as good coak as that of Great Britain. It is now used to a considerable extent by our manufacturers in Center County and elsewhere." The essential complement to mineral availability was industrial demand. Together, natural wealth and favorable local and wider circumstances of consumption would promote around the headwaters of the Ohio a closely integrated network of industrial districts, developing the area into one of the world's greatest industrial regions. Already by the 1830s perceptive observers had vague anticipations of these exciting future prospects.

By the second quarter of the nineteenth century, Pittsburgh already was acknowledged as the natural source of iron supply for the nation's interior. As Grenville Mellen stated in 1839: "The situation of Pittsburgh is as advantageous as can well be imagined; it is the key to the western country, and excepting New Orleans and Cincinnati, is the first town of the whole valley of the Mississippi." The area's mineral wealth had "converted [it] into a vast workshop and a warehouse for the immense country below."[16] Three years earlier Taylor had recognized that coal "constitutes the life spring of western Pennsylvania, the pedestal of our great manufacturing emporium [Pittsburgh]." Hildreth added to this that the promise of coal and iron could "open to the imagination a long vista of power and greatness which the utmost stretch of the imagination is hardly able to equal."[17] Soon, conditions became favorable for this new, mineral-based iron industry. Its growth would transform economic and social life as well as the landscape of the district through which the Youghiogheny and Monongahela meandered down toward Pittsburgh.

Factors of Production

In the classic terms of the factors of production, the future coke region of southwestern Pennsylvania possessed the one outstanding asset that made it commercially attractive to bring together other essential inputs—a physical resource of exceptional quality. Capital, labor, managerial talent, and entrepreneurship were equally essential for building a great industry, but whereas its natural wealth was fixed, these other assets were mobile and were partly procured from outside the region. The essential technology, at least in the early stages, came wholly from elsewhere.

The modern commercial world commonly regards human ingenuity as the ultimate resource. To a large extent this is understandable, indeed incontestable, for without the know-how, efforts, and organizations of mankind over many generations, none of today's almost infinite diversity of material goods or range of services could exist. But whether in genetics, high-technology farming, or space research, the amazing inventiveness of humankind can only take place through the manipulation of matter—in other words by changing earth "stuff" into forms that supply human needs and go some way at least in meeting never fully satisfied wants.

Critical to this situation is the existence of suitable natural conditions. Another vital consideration, and one that society, in its headlong rush to produce wealth, has all too often ignored, is wise and effective resource management to maintain the natural systems on which human life ultimately depends. The life history of the Connellsville coke region provides more than a century of thought-provoking insights into many aspects of the whole, complex business of resource-development issues.

A mineral resource exists when a portion of the earth's surface is found rich enough in a concentration of a particular desired material to justify application of the other factors of production to its exploitation. Without these favorable conditions a mineral deposit is not a mineral resource. When such a resource is opened, the length of its working life is determined by the level of production, which in turn reflects the proportion of total demand the deposit is able to supply. If working becomes more difficult, perhaps due to increasing depths of operation or greater amounts of waste, costs will rise. This may price the product out of the market, encouraging the opening of new areas or the introduction of an alternative technology. On the other hand, if there are no or few rival sources of supply, rising prices may make it practicable to work less-rich deposits of the mineral, involving tracts and depths previously considered uneconomic. Sometimes there may be a knife-edge situation—prices must rise to extend the life of the mining operation, but if they rise too quickly, consumers will turn to other suppliers.[18]

Geological facts and growing knowledge of them clearly demarcated the core area of the Connellsville coking-coal region, but beyond it, north and south, were coals of very good, if slightly poorer, coking quality. Still farther away were large deposits of acceptable coals, though often in less accessible locations. Lurking in the wings through much of the history of the region was another method of making coke. It could use mixtures of poorer coals procurable over a much wider area and offer cost savings derived both from lower transport costs and from credits for valuable byproducts not available to the Connellsville industry. In addition, the life expectancy of the core coking area was limited by the tonnage of high-grade coking coal available and by the amount of it worked annually. In fact, demand rose rapidly on this strictly limited resource base. Tonnages available were reduced by waste in mining, though over the years this was gradually reduced. During the fifty-six years central to its most important period of production, the Connellsville region—both the "old basin" and "Lower Connellsville"—produced 500 million tons of coke requiring the extraction and processing of about 770 million tons of coal. In six peak years annual coal consumption exceeded 28 million tons. Both the coal and the mines from which it was procured provided exceptionally favorable conditions for the massive industry that mushroomed in this small area.

Bituminous coal is found over huge areas of the Appalachian plateaus from Ohio to Alabama and from the western counties of Virginia into western Kentucky. This is in fact one of the world's great energy stores. The quality of its coals varies considerably from place to place. In the west, where folding of the strata was much less intense than farther east, the coal is generally high in volatiles and has a relatively low carbon content. It often contains sufficient sulfur to create serious problems for those who try to coke it. Eastward toward the Allegheny Front, the coals were determined too "dry" to produce first-rate coke, their volatile content being very low and fixed-carbon content higher than in the west. The ideal coals for coking by the technology available in the mid-nineteenth century lay in the southwestern counties of Pennsylvania and in neighboring or not far distant areas of West Virginia and Virginia. Because of the tectonic structure and subsequent erosional history of the plateau, the finest and most accessible coking coals were found in a narrow basin running roughly north-northeast to south-southwest, straddling the Youghiogheny River. This area became the Connellsville coke region.

The Connellsville coal seam is part of the famous Pittsburgh bed, which when opened averaged seven feet in thickness and was persistent over a very wide area, extending into neighboring states. It was classed as a high-grade gas coal in the Irwin basin of Westmoreland County, a good steam coal in Allegheny County and the western parts of Washington County, and was later to prove an excellent coal for new methods of coking in southern Washington, Greene, and the western parts of Fayette Counties. Above all, it proved to be an outstanding coking coal in Fayette and Westmoreland Counties.[19] The long axis of the coke basin in these counties stretched for fifty to sixty miles—depending on the basis of definition; east to west its width was only two-and-a-half or three miles. When working began it contained some eighty thousand acres of coal land. The coal seam outcropped on the western side of Chestnut Ridge, but over much of the area it lay 60 to 150 feet below the surface. As the country was dissected by a network of streams—locally called "creeks" or "runs"—from the early days of settlement the coal had been worked where exposed by stream erosion in "country bank" mines. Later drifts and slopes were opened on the valley sides. Under such physical circumstances entry to the coal trade was relatively easy. As a local chamber of commerce account breezily put it in the mid-1880s, "while it takes from $300 to $400 thousands in the old world to reach a vein of coal whose thickness frequently does not reach over 1.25 to 2 feet, mining here requires no outlay whatever, or only an insignificant sum, since the coal crops out on the flanks of the hills and the banks of the rivers, the investment being simply that for transportation facilities from veins to carrier or market." Gradually, as the operations became bigger and more sophisticated, extraction by shaft was added. By 1892 there were thirty-six drifts and thirty-two slopes in the basin, but the coal was also worked at greater depths in twenty-one shaft mines, the deepest of which reached 542 feet. The workable seam, eight to ten feet in thickness, produced a coal that was generally of a resinous luster, though some of it was bright, shiny, and "crystalline." It was soft and clean, usually almost free from slate and sulfur, and generally of uniformly high quality. Because its extraction required neither powder nor machinery, the overhead costs of mining were low. In fact, the coal here could be so easily worked by the pick that in the mid-1880s as much as 10 tons could be cut and loaded in ten hours by a man and a boy, the miner's productivity being double that of his counterparts working the thinner, harder seams around Pittsburgh. At that time the cost of digging coal was about $.25 a ton: in the four years to 1887, the selling price of Connellsville coke averaged $1.37 per ton. In the differential between those two figures lies the clue to the wealth the region would yield to its enterpreneurs.[20]

In addition to outstanding advantages in the quality and workability of its raw material, this area possessed in high degree favorable conditions of what used to be called the economies of place. Coke is a commodity that is bulky and heavy in relation to its value. For the thirty-four years before 1914, its average price at the ovens was $2.078 a ton. Averaging only 2.93 million tons over the first five years of this period, the amount of coke shipped increased irregularly to reach an annual average of 18.58 million tons over the final five. Throughout the industry's long history, the growth of activities consuming its product within the immediate area was slight, but the resource was so advantageously located within the northeastern United States as to serve not only regional but also both western and eastern markets. All that was needed to underpin a highly localized growth of the industry was the provision of facilities to transfer very large tonnages of low unit-value products from the small area of production to the main areas of consumption, eventually spreading throughout the manufacturing belt. Transportation costs determined the ease with which the coke could be delivered to consumers and therefore how effectively it could compete with coke from other areas or with alternative fuels. Connellsville-area producers had good access to early outlets by water, and later suppliers were favorably located in the evolving rail systems of the manufacturing belt. The points at which transport routes entered the region and the course they followed within it closely influenced which sections of the coal field were developed at a particular time. Over the decades the progressive filling out of the railroad network was accompanied by a sequence of additions to the area of production until the whole of the geological basin was provided with rail facilities. Other aspects of freight movement that eventually became important in regional economic development were its physical equipment, particularly the provision of the necessary car capacity to handle an output that might vary drastically from month to month, and the charges made for railroad services.

The other essential prerequisites for the growth of the industry were enterprise, backed by technical expertise and capital, and a suitable labor force. In the early stages of the industry both were locally available; later, large contributions to each came from outside. The first entrepreneurs were farmers or tradesmen who ventured their usually meager capital along with slight technical ability, scant knowledge of markets, and therefore a great deal of dependence on good fortune. Their other lines of activity gave them the necessary security to meet the collapse of any hopes placed in coke. Though this local emphasis to investment applied particularly in the earlier stages, there were later examples as well, sometimes involving local bank capital. After the value of Connellsville coke had been proved, private individuals and iron firms from other areas came in either directly as new producers or by acquisition of interests in existing coke makers. Most were from Pittsburgh, but eventually distant centers were also involved, including the Valleys and Chicago iron districts and major sources of national capital in New York, Philadelphia, and Boston. Managers and overseers were initially procured within the area, but requirements for various kinds of technical expertise later caused an increase in recruitment from elsewhere. Even so, until a surprisingly late date many of the leading men in this sector of the coke trade were local.

In the early 1840s the provision of manual labor could scarcely be separated from that of the capital for the industry, the partners in the first firms taking a part in building and operating the ovens and in undertaking the transportation and sale of coke. As expansion occurred unskilled labor could be recruited from farming or the small service settlements. Presumably workforces, small as they would be, were only partially employed in coke making and largely worked in agriculture or other local jobs. As late as the 1850 Census, only one person in Connellsville, Silas White, chose to identify his occupation as that of "coaker." At that time too the enumerator listed only 51 persons born outside the United States in the township's population of 1,507. Then and later, no apparent evidence of large-scale inward migration of "native" American workers from other districts exists, certainly not on a scale to support the industry as it moved into its period of large-scale expansion. As the local supply of workers proved insufficient, it was supplemented by a significant influx of immigrants, particularly from eastern Europe. Over the next few decades, this gave a new, distinctive character to labor relations, social structures, and the reputation of what was now commonly referred to as the Coke Region.

Technically, nineteenth-century coke manufacture was fairly simple. In the earliest stages it was made like charcoal by merely heaping the raw material into a pile, covering it with a relatively impermeable layer of sod or clay, and setting it alight. Manufacture in such "ricks," or "meilers," continued for some time after improved methods were introduced, older processes occasionally going on side-by-side with newer ones, especially during periods of unexpectedly high demand. However, the exceptional reputation of Connellsville coke was built on the so-called beehive oven. It became a rule of thumb in the industry that each oven required two acres of coal lands from which to draw its supplies. With this, each oven in a typical battery of the style built about 1900 could be supported for twenty to twenty-five years, producing some seven hundred tons of coke per oven annually. But the life of the actual oven—

rather than the coke-making capacity that it represented—was only about five years. In the early decades of the industry, the beehive was commonly eleven to twelve feet in diameter and from five to seven feet in height; later its dimensions were often slightly larger. In the 1890s construction of the average oven required some 2,500 ordinary bricks and about 1,150 firebricks to provide its inner lining. These and the specially shaped bricks for arch blocks, jambs, and so on were made in the district. The coal was dumped through an opening—the "trunnel"—about two feet in diameter in the top of the oven and spread evenly over its floor to a depth of two to two-and-a-half feet. The top was then closed. There was a door in the side that, when the process was underway, was nearly closed with brick, "luted" with loam or clay. Heat from the previous charge started the coking process, and as it went on access for air through the door aperture was more and more completely closed off. An average charge of coal amounted in the early years to 100 bushels, but by the late 1890s ranged from about 120 to as much as 165 bushels. The coking process took about 48 hours for furnace coke; "72-hour coke" was also produced for foundry use. Because of the swelling that went on in the oven during the process, there was an increase in volume, every 100 bushels of coal making about 120 bushels of coke, but the expulsion of "byproducts"—at this time entirely waste products—also meant a sharp reduction in weight, from 1.6 tons of coal charged to 1 ton of coke produced. When the coking process was finished, the door was removed and the coke was cooled by water sprayed on it from a hose before being drawn from the oven with a scraper, a long metal rake with a curved head. Access to a large supply of water was essential for success, five hundred to eight hundred gallons being used at each oven every time it was drawn. Finally, the coke was either forked into or carried by wheelbarrow to the railroad car, in early days an ordinary boxcar and later an increasingly specialized item of rolling stock. The typical furnace coke dispatched from these yards contained few impurities, was cellular, had a silvery luster and almost metallic ring, and was described as "tenacious" as well as porous. As the coke expert John Fulton emphasized, to a greater extent than the product of any other district, the Connellsville district's product possessed the essential four properties of the finest coke: "hardness of body, well-developed cell structure, porosity, [and] uniform quality of coke."[21]

Each beehive-shaped oven in the coke region was linked with its next-door neighbor in a covering or outer coat of brickwork, which made a battery or row of ovens look like a continuous embankment. These were arranged in two distinct ways, both according to local topography. Those built against a hillside were in single rows and known as "bank ovens." Where there was more space, ovens were commonly placed back to back to form double rows, or "block ovens." In the former the railroad that carried away the coke ran along the front of the row; in the latter a rail yard would lie between two blocks. In the few years before World War I, the "rectangular" oven was introduced. Though different in shape and mechanical procedures, its operating principles were otherwise the same as conventional beehives.[22]

The processes of development in a coal and coke-making operation were relatively simple compared with those in many nineteenth-century industries. Even so, because the area in which the industry concentrated was rural, it was often necessary to provide facilities that in an urban context would already have been in place. In short, what elsewhere would have been external costs in this setting had to be provided by the enterprise. However, these investments often became additional sources of profit. An instance of the range of considerations involved was provided in 1891, when Chicago iron and steel interests requested information about the costs of large oven plants. An experienced coke superintendent provided estimates under the headings preliminary engineering, sinking the shaft, buildings necessary for the operation, ovens, yard and track, and equipment and tenements for workers.[23] An additional common cost was that for a company store. In total these ancillary expenditures exceeded the cost of the ovens themselves. Three hundred dollars per oven was then a common figure used in assessing the value of the beehive industry, but because of these additional considerations this was a deceptively low figure; other estimates placed costs at up to over twice that level.[24] In 1899 the president of the largest company made a valuation of his own enterprise and that of an associated firm. According to his reckoning each oven and the necessary outlay for shafts, tipples, bins, mine wagons, locomotives, railroad sidings, haulage, engines, boilers, electric light plant, larries, livestock, other equipment, tenement houses, and other buildings cost seven hundred dollars. He pointed out that the region's last large new plant had required eight hundred dollars per oven. In the late 1890s the manager of this plant had estimated that, in addition to construction costs, each oven required maintenance and repair work amounting to about twenty dollars a year. In 1895 the editor of the *Connellsville Courier* put the aggregate capital in the coke industry at sixty-five million dollars; a few years later the leading firm alone was valued at over forty-five million dollars.[25] Even though by this time coke manufacture represented a huge capital outlay, it had begun only a half century before as a small, uncertain business.

Origins of Connellsville Coke Production

The antecedents of a successful coke manufacture in western Pennsylvania are indistinct but may be traced back to the time of the second war with Britain. The conflict caused an interruption to imports of iron, and as a result the United States had to make about 80 percent of the bar iron it consumed in 1814. Prices were higher than in the early years of the century, and production too was probably at a record level—unfortunately there are no reliable estimates. This seemed a propitious time for innovation. In April 1813 a British immigrant addressed an advertisement in the *Pittsburgh Mercury*, "To the Proprietors of Blast Furnaces." Notwithstanding an antique style, his message was clear enough: "John Beal, lately from England, being informed that all the blast furnaces are in the habit of melting iron oar with charcoal, and knowing the great disadvantage it is to proprietors, is inducted to offer his services to instruct them in the method of converting stone coal into coak. The advantage of using *coak* will be so great, that it cannot fail to become general if put into practice. He flatters himself that he has all the experience that is necessary in the above branch to give general satisfaction to those who feel inclined to alter their mode of melting their oar. John Beal, *Iron Founder.*" Despite the apparently commercially favorable circumstances, no one apparently took advantage of the offer of a new technology, presumably because charcoal supplies were judged more than sufficient to meet the fuel needs of the industry even at high levels of activity. On a number of occasions over the next quarter-century, there were further inquiries into coke making or reports of experiments with coking based on advice from experienced former British coalfield workers, but all of these trials had no firm, long-sustained commercial outcomes.[26] A few coking experiments, however, did occur in southwestern Pennsylvania.

In 1818 coke was used in the refinery at Colonel Meason's Plumsock Ironworks near Upper Middletown on Redstone Creek, Fayette County. After about two years, the colonel returned to the use of charcoal. Through the 1820s a large increase in iron production occurred, but the old fuel sufficed. The early 1830s saw new stirrings in the use of coke. There was a short-lived, small-scale output of it at Plumsock and in Connellsville under the guidance of a man called Nichols, who was said to have had some experience of beehive coke in Britain. By now commercial circumstances were becoming more favorable: Between 1820 and 1837 output of pig iron seems to have increased from twelve to fourteen fold; iron prices were again at fairly high levels. Large scale, localized production and further processing of iron began to grow in importance in association with railroad construction, though for many years most railroad iron was imported. Meanwhile, failure continued as the common fate of the pioneer. In 1834 Lester Norton bought the Plummer Farm for thirty-seven dollars an acre in the hope of building up a coke and iron business; nothing came of his vision.[27] According to F. H. Oliphant, iron was made with coke fuel at Fairchance near Uniontown in 1837, three years after a rolling mill had been built there. Oliphant was so proud of his success that he took specimens of the iron to the Franklin Institute, Philadelphia. After that, as with Meason at Plumsock, Fairchance reverted to use of charcoal. At both of these works, it is likely that, as later commonly reported, the coke was made on the ground in open piles, or ricks. However, over sixty-five years later, one man who had worked in the Plumsock yard claimed that some coke made there came from a stone-built oven holding forty-eight bushels.[28]

The first reliably recorded ovens were built during summer 1841. Again they were the outcome of local enterprise, this time from individuals lacking connection with the iron trade, without industrial experience, and possessing even smaller resources than some of their predecessors. Given such circumstances, it is perhaps not surprising that the time they chose was also not a favorable one. Following tariff reductions in the 1830s, pig iron output and prices were both falling. Perhaps it was just as well that the partners undertook the work as a speculation. Provance McCormick and James Campbell were both carpenters, though McCormick had also been a teamster leading goods between Philadelphia and Pittsburgh. With William Turner, they resolved to build a coke plant. McCormick drew the plans for the ovens, and a fourth man, John Taylor—who combined farming with the trade of stone mason—built two small ovens for the three entrepreneurs on his own land at a place, which was later known as Sedgwick Station, near the outlet of Hickman Run into the Youghiogheny River. Four other local men were engaged as coke workers.[29] This venture suffered a variety of setbacks, some reflecting its promoters' ignorance of the principles of coking. Their ovens were small, with a crown flatter than in later practice. The charge was about sixty-five bushels, which proved insufficient to make good coke. At last, in early winter 1841–1842, they succeeded in producing a tolerably good coke with regularity. By next spring they had made enough of it to load about eight hundred bushels (some 10.5 tons) onto two boats, or "arks," built by the two carpenters as their material contribution to the enterprise. At the first main rise of the river, they and their cargo traveled down the Youghiogheny into the Monongahela and along the Ohio to Cincinnati, where their product was unfavorably received, allegedly being denigrated by local foundrymen as "cinders." Apparently, it then had to be hawked around the area in coffee sacks before a sale was secured from a Mr. Greenwood, a foundryman, for 6.25 cents a bushel, or $4.70 a ton. (Many years later the *Connellsville Courier* suggested the price was 8 cents a bushel.)[30] Payment for this cargo was made half in cash and half in old mill-iron. Some of this coke was then later traded by Cincinnati parties to a foundry in Dayton owned by a Judge Gebhart, who had moved to that area from Pennsylvania and who, in contrast to the skeptical Cincinnati iron founders, was satisfied by its quality. Some reports state that Gebhart later traveled to Connellsville to ask Campbell and McCormick to make more coke for him, only to find that, disillusioned by their general experience as operators and salesmen, the partners were unwilling to try again. Yet despite their own scant commercial success, McCormick and his colleagues were the pioneers of a great industry. Nearly half a century later, in an official report, Edward McCormick of Greensburg (possibly a relative of one of the 1841 party, though unknown) was eloquent in the florid way of his time in celebrating their achievement: "The stones of these old ovens are long since torn asunder and scattered, the mortar in their old joints has crumbled away and mingled with the earth, but the fire lighted that day.... burns now in thousands of ovens, multiplying millions of capital, and supporting one of the chief of Pennsylvania's excelling industries."[31] That advanced stage of industrial development was only reached after many more, and initially at least, slow steps.

Coke was again made in the first ovens during autumn 1842, this time by the initiative of the Cochran brothers, Mordecai, James, and Sample, members of a family that would remain involved through the maturity of the industry. After coking about 1,300 bushels, they too boated their product to Cincinnati and sold it to Greenwood. By now he had recognized its value in foundry work, but even so seems to have paid only seven cents a bushel. Sometime that fall, Richard Brookins began to mine coal just across the river from the Cochrans and built five ovens. In 1844 the coal operator Col. A. M. Hill bought the Dickerson farm and put up seven coke ovens. These were bigger, with an increased diameter and raised crown, so that the charge of coal was increased to ninety bushels.[32] By 1845 there were three works and fourteen ovens in this core area of what would become the coke region. Far to the south near New Geneva on the Monongahela, the Shaler brothers, owners of a local foundry, built an oven of ordinary brick that they operated for some years.[33] During the mid-1840s Stewart Strickler, long engaged in boating agricultural produce downriver to Pittsburgh, put up six beehives at Jimtown, their output marketed by the Cochrans. Growth continued to be extremely slow, and as late as 1855, fourteen years after the first ovens were built, there were reportedly only about twenty-six ovens "above Pittsburgh." At that time the rest of western Pennsylvania probably contained nearly three times as many coke ovens as the Connellsville region.[34]

Before the mid-1850s the market for coke in iron smelting was limited by consumer resistance, by the relatively slow growth in the production of finished iron— and therefore in demand for pig iron—and by transport difficulties. The latter part of the decade was marked by changes in these and other circumstances that, taken together and working out over the course of only a few years, transformed the situation and set off a sharp spiral of growth.[35] The first two decisive developments altered the relationship between Connellsville and Pittsburgh. Louis Hunter pointed out how use of coal changed the iron trade from scattered, small-scale operations to a business conducted in bulk by a few great agglomerations of plant: "It was pointed out about 1850 that, whereas from 2,000 to 5,000 acres of timber were required to supply an ordinary charcoal furnace, a coal mine with a 6-foot seam, covering half an acre, would furnish a sufficient supply. The centralization of the iron industry was made possible by coal."[36] This was no doubt true, but the same principle worked in reverse—growth in a major, concentrated iron capacity like that of Pittsburgh justified the large investments of enterprise and capital that created the Connellsville coke industry. Growth in either location was impossible without reliable, all-season bulk transport between the two.

On first consideration it seems remarkable that the sales efforts of coke-region pioneers were directed to distant Cincinnati rather than to the much nearer metallurgical center. This was because Pittsburgh already had its own coke ovens dotted along the Monongahela that obtained their coal from "city" mines and served both the foundries and forges, which worked up charcoal-smelted pig iron brought in from country districts, and the city's crucible steel works. Cincinnati was a major foundry center lacking comparable local supplies. As far as blast furnace operations were concerned, the chief impetus to change to coke came from an increase in scales of production. In Pittsburgh this was delayed and when it came was largely due to a general extension in demand for finished iron products; in other instances it was often associated with large-scale production of wrought-iron rails, an activity requiring big and regular deliveries of pig iron of a consistent quality. In the East, anthracite could support such major operations, as for instance at the Lackawanna works in Scranton, established in 1846. Charcoal proved too dispersed and unreliable a fuel to sustain the tonnages needed for puddling furnaces and rail mills. Understandably, therefore, "western" iron-rail makers, distant from anthracite, were pioneers in using coke in blast furnaces. This happened at Mount Savage and Brady's Bend in the 1840s. However, construction of these iron-rail mills was not followed by a steady upward trend in coke consumption. After the reduction of import duties in the Tariff Act of 1846, production was so deeply depressed that by late 1849 only two of fifteen rail mills were still in operation, and even they were working well below capacity.[37] An interior location, which gave at least some extra protection against imports, a widened sphere of marketing provided by new railroad links, and higher blast furnace productivity derived from the use of coke were the basic assets of a new generation of rail mills, which began with the establishment of the Cambria Ironworks, Johnstown, in the mid-1850s. When coke made there from local coal proved inadequate, the management found Connellsville coke a superior alternative.

The transfer to coke was speeded by a new boom in iron. After highs in 1847 and 1848, national pig iron production fell in the early 1850s, but after 1855 there was a strong general revival, though this was interrupted by recession in 1858. A large part of this increase in iron production was taken by furnaces using mineral fuel, especially coke. At the end of the 1840s, not one coke furnace was in blast in Pennsylvania; by 1856 there were twenty-one, however, except for Johnstown, probably all were using local rather than Connellsville coke.[38] Though coke iron was mainly replacing the output of charcoal ironworks, it was already making headway more rapidly than anthracite iron. In 1856 raw coal and coke furnaces provided only 8 percent of national output as compared with 50 percent from furnaces using anthracite; during the next four years production from the latter rose 17.2 percent and from coal and coke furnaces by 75.8 percent. In Pittsburgh the breakthrough came a few years later than at Johnstown. At first it seemed less spectacular, but eventually the success of coke smelting there was seen to have provided the turning point for the coke region. Though it was to be a key player in rail manufacture, Allegheny County had been a late entrant to that trade. Not until late summer 1853 was its first rail rolled at the West Pittsburgh works of Bennett, Marshall, and Company.[39] This new business, but still more the growth in output of other finished products, meant increased demand for pig or forged iron. Previously, this had been satisfied by long and sometimes difficult hauls from distant points of production; now at last it called into being a local furnace industry. In 1859 the rolling-mill firm of Graff, Bennett, and Company built a blast furnace near the Point, in which they smelted the first pig iron produced in the city since a short-lived operation in the Shadyside district over sixty years before. This pioneer "Clinton" furnace used Connellsville coke. After its initial success, the owners tried to economize by substituting local coke. In spring 1860, recognizing this fuel as inferior, they reverted to coke from Connellsville.

This first use of Connellsville coke carried overland for some fifty miles was a practicable proposition because the relative isolation of the coking-coal district had now been broken by improvements in transport. In its earliest stages the coke districts' transportation facilities had depended on partially improved natural routes, specifically the rivers. Under those conditions coke consumption was largely limited to outlets at locations on or near the riverside, and the choice of sites for coke works and mines was similarly confined. There were only two substantial streams in the coking-coal area of southwestern Pennsylvania: the Monongahela beyond its western extremity and the Youghiogheny, which in the short stretch of its course below Connellsville cut across the coke region's middle section. Within Pennsylvania, the Monongahela was generally free from islands, bars, rocks, or rapids. It was improved, indeed effectively canalized in the 1840s, but was too far from the main area of what were in early years considered the best coking coals to have any significant impact on the coke industry until about sixty years later. Unfortunately, there were much greater physical difficulties on the Youghiogheny, including rapids and low falls. The Connellsville and West Newton Navigation Company was incorporated in

1841 to make the river navigable between the two towns but failed in this task. In contrast, by 1850 the Youghiogheny Navigation Company had "slackwatered" the river below West Newton by construction of locks and dams, making it navigable by steamer from there to Pittsburgh. Presumably as a result of the earlier experiences, no effort was made to extend these improvements above West Newton. Instead, a rail portage was planned between Connellsville and the head of navigation. Then, during the break up of heavy ice and a period of high water in 1855–1856, the log and stone dams and their accompanying locks along the lower part of the river were swept away. Until then the district's small and slowly growing output of coke had been confined to both banks of the Youghiogheny in the narrow belt in which it cut across the coal basin. Now it was to be freed from these constraints.

Rail transportation was far less subject to the vagaries of the seasons, could provide ease of movement, eventually to a much wider range of destinations, and by making major extensions of both areas of consumption and of production possible, could service a greatly increased output. The railroad thereafter would dominate transportation throughout the life of the main area of the coke field. A rail connection between Connellsville and West Newton was opened in 1855, at a time when there were about twenty-five ovens in the region. By 1857 it reached Turtle Creek and four years later, when completed into the city, the Pittsburgh and Connellsville Railroad linked the coke region into the commerce of a much wider commercial world. Promoters had anticipated that agricultural produce and local iron would be the main sources of railroad business, and the first goods carried were in fact from district farms, but coke soon came to dominate its freight schedules. The first, excessive charge of twenty-two dollars for a rail car of coke—six dollars more than the cost of carriage by river—brought pressure from the industry and resulted in a reduction to a carload rate of nine dollars. Thereafter access to a railroad was a prerequisite for the success of any coke works. Almost immediately extension of track began. In 1857 the Fayette County Railroad was organized with local finance, and within three years had opened a 12.7-mile line along the eastern outcrop of the Connellsville seam from Uniontown to a junction with the Pittsburgh and Connellsville. In the first five years of railroad operations, the number of ovens in the region increased from about twenty-five to seventy. Most of this expansion was at existing coke works, but there were new plants as well. In 1855 Strickler bought eighty acres of coal on the Taylor lands near his Jimtown works and two years later opened the Sterling works on this tract. Its ovens and the tramway he built from them to the Pittsburgh and Connellsville tracks were impressive signs of a new scale of thinking. At about the same time, Philo Norton and two partners bought coal lands near Davidson station north of the Connellsville town limits from Norton's father, sank a shaft to about eighty feet, made large tonnages of coke in ricks, and built four ovens. Before the end of the 1850s, the coke works of A. S. M. Morgan below Broad Ford station was making a reported one thousand bushels of coke a day and was shipping by the Pittsburgh and Connellsville to a large number of destinations in the interior of Ohio and Indiana as far west as Indianapolis. Coal land that had sold a few years before for thirty-five dollars an acre now fetched one hundred dollars.[40]

It was during the mid-1850s that there occurred another, apparently irrelevant but ultimately decisive, influence on the coke iron industry. In late summer 1856, far from the scene of these developments in Pennsylvania, Henry Bessemer announced his process for bulk manufacture of steel. The full impact of his discovery was delayed for many years, but eventually output of Bessemer steel would require the support of pig iron production on a scale almost beyond the imagining of furnacemen—and coke makers—at that time. The long-term implications for Connellsville would be far more dramatic than any that could have been anticipated by those who were then rejoicing in the convenience provided by a new railroad or, a few years later, in the enterprise of Graff, Bennett.

2 The Maturing Industry

Expansion, Boom, and Crisis—the Coke Industry in the 1860s and 1870s

Despite the trauma of the Civil War, the United States rose to a preeminent position in the world's industrial production within twenty-five years after 1860. At the beginning of this period, its output was about two-thirds that of the United Kingdom and also lagged behind France and the German states; by the early 1880s it accounted for 29 percent of world production as compared with the United Kingdom's 27 per cent.[1] Given the fact that this national economic growth involved opening half a continent, it is not surprising that infrastructure building played a prominent part. One result was the spectacular advance of the iron industry. The years 1860 and 1880 were times of record production for pig iron both in the United Kingdom and in the United States. Britain's output doubled from 3.8 to 7.7 million tons while American production was 821,000 tons in 1860 but 3.8 million twenty years later. Shortage of timber and the unceasing urge for greater furnace productivity ensured that much of this increase was derived from furnaces using bituminous coal and coke, above all the latter. Connellsville was now the unquestioned center of the rapidly growing national coke production. As late as 1860, and despite the expansion following the opening of the Pittsburgh and Connellsville railroad and the start of iron production in Pittsburgh, the district contained only about 70 ovens; ten years later it had at least 550. Over the following few years, the district experienced the first of its frenzied booms, and by 1873 there were more than 3,600 ovens. There followed years of stagnation or depression before demand strengthened again in 1878 and developed into another boom the following year. By 1880, when the first reliable statistics appeared, the coke region had 7,211 ovens.

The pioneering example of Graff, Bennett in smelting iron in Pitts-

Table 2.1 Pig iron production by fuel used, 1860, 1864, 1869, 1873, and 1880

Year	Total (th. gross tons)	By fuel (% of total)		
		Charcoal	Anthracite	Raw coal/coke
1860	821	30	57	13
1864	1,014	21	60	19
1869	1,711	20	51	29
1873	2,561	20	46	34
1880	3,835	13	42	45

SOURCE: P. Temin, *Iron and Steel in Nineteenth Century America: An Economic Enquiry* (Cambridge, Mass.: MIT Press, 1964), 266, 268.

Table 2.2 Iron-finishing trades of Pittsburgh, 1863 and 1871

	1863	1871
Number of rolling mills	27	43
Puddling furnaces	262	562
Nail machines	408	508
Metal used by mills (th. tons)	132	350
Number of foundries/machine shops	45	75

SOURCE: *Pittsburgh Commercial*, quoted in *BAISA*, 27 December 1871.

burgh was soon followed by others. Within two years Jones and Laughlin had built the two Eliza furnaces, each with a capacity twice that of the Clinton stack. The two Superior furnaces were erected in 1863 and those of Shoenberger two years later. At full capacity, these seven furnaces required 85,000 tons of coke annually, about 85 percent of the total then being used in iron production.[2] These developments were accompanied by a new round of extensions in the Connellsville district. Already there were signs that coke manufacture was becoming big business. In 1860 the newly formed Pittsburgh and Connellsville Gas Coal Company, backed with $300,000 of capital, built a forty-oven plant on the Davidson site, which Philo Norton had started developing five years earlier. At about the same time, the Connellsville Gas Coal Company put up Wheeler works and Cochran and Keister constructed the thirty-oven Fayette plant on the site of Turner, McCormick, and Campbell's first operations at Sedgwick. Together with Strickler, the Cochran and Keister Company supplied Clinton furnace. By 1864 the latter firm had also built the forty-oven Jackson works farther from the Youghiogheny; for some years delivering its product to the main line by tramway. From 1865 the nation began to regain its peacetime economic momentum. Output of rolled iron increased 43 percent in the four years from 1865; pig iron

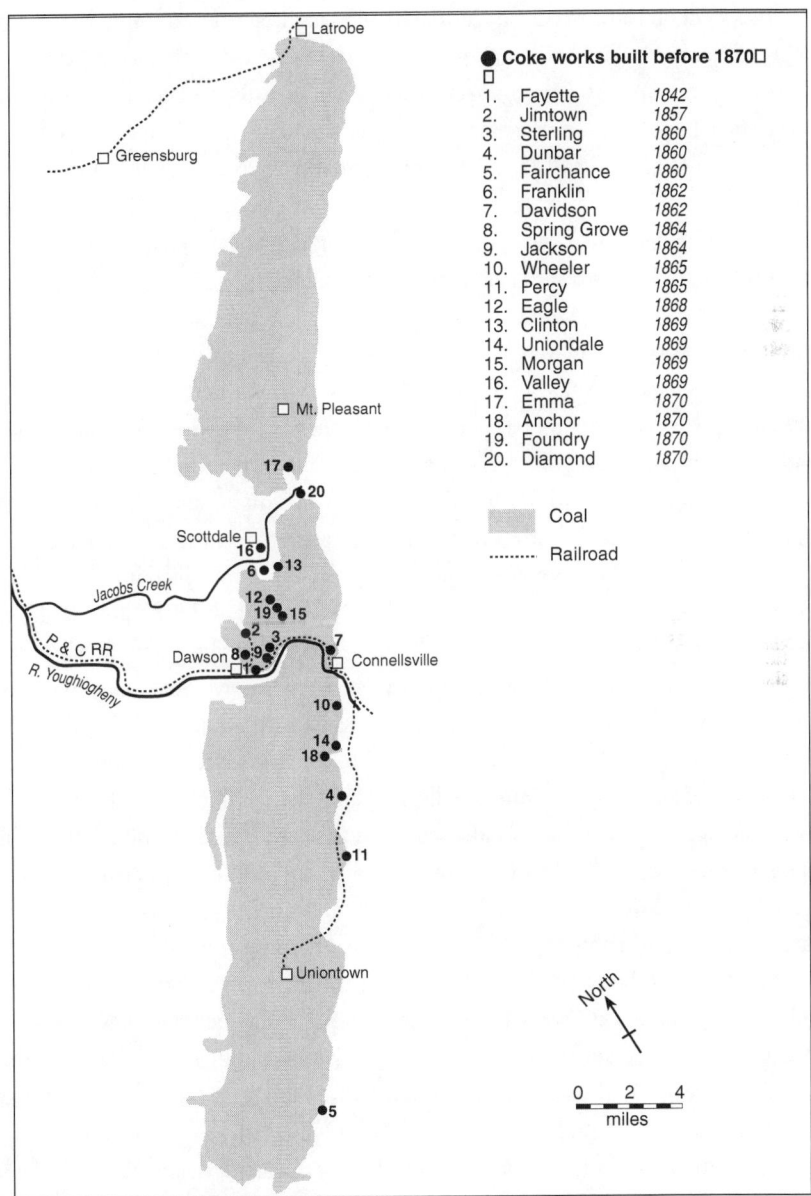

Coke works built before 1870.

tonnages went up 106 percent. As the metal trades of Pittsburgh continued in a headlong expansion, and as their own product began to replace competing fuels elsewhere, coke region entrepreneurs kept pace either by extensions or new works. In 1868 John F. Dravo took charge of and largely extended the Davidson works. By 1870 annual production in the district was running at about 180,000 to 200,000 tons of coke.[3]

In fact, growth on the scale of the late 1860s marked the early stage of a completely unprecedented expansion. The boom was maintained into the early 1870s, output of pig iron in 1872 and 1873 being well over three times that of 1865. More furnace operators also began switching to coke. At the end of 1869, all twenty-four blast furnaces in the Shenango Valley of northwestern Pennsylvania were still using raw coal as their predecessors had done when surveyed by Lesley more than ten years earlier. Within three years at least one was using coke, the start of a trend that over the years eventually saw them all transfer to a fuel that provided higher furnace outputs. The 1873 tonnage of iron made with coke or raw coal was 76 percent above 1869 figures.

Railroad extensions had now widened out the areas within which mines could be profitably opened and ovens built. In 1871 the Mt. Pleasant and Broadford Railroad opened the eastern edge of the coal basin north of the Youghiogheny much as the Fayette County Railroad had done for the area south of the river four years previous. A branch line up Hickman Run improved access for operations in that valley. The Pittsburgh and Connellsville (P&C) was linked to the Baltimore and Ohio (B&O) by completion of a track from Connellsville to Cumberland. Four years later the B&O leased the P&C and its local subsidiaries. Until the early 1870s all traffic out of the region had been controlled by the latter company, but with coke demand spiraling up, Col. David Davidson of Connellsville, ousted from the P&C's board in a dispute during negotiations about the B&O takeover, tried to interest the Pennsylvania Railroad (PRR) in building a track into the region. The PRR was initially unresponsive, and Davidson along with some coke region entrepreneurs, including J. K. Ewing, S. Dillinger, B. F. Ruff, and other Westmoreland County families, formed the South West Pennsylvania Railroad Company. It was, however, largely PRR money that they drew upon in order to build from the mainline at Greensburg to Scottdale, and by 1873 the South West Pennsylvania was controlled by the Pennsylvania Railroad. That spring, the line's construction reached Davidson and was held up for two years by controversy over rights of way with the Baltimore and Ohio. Getting over this obstacle, the South West Pennsylvania bridged the Youghiogheny, extended to Uniontown, and by 1876 had reached Fairchance. This southern extension "annexed" to its tracks a number of coke works that until then had been served exclusively by the Fayette County Branch. The South West Pennsylvania became a very heavily used line and paid high dividends. Not surprisingly, its success and profitability along with that of the Baltimore and Ohio eventually attracted new competitors.

In this period of expansion, the iron, coal, and coke industries of the United States were visited by two foreign experts, each familiar with at least one leading European coke district. A German, Gustav Klupfel, came in spring 1870. Rather surprisingly he concluded that St. Louis offered the "soundest foundations in the country for all branches of the iron manufacture, from pig iron to Bessemer steel." Iron was then being made there using two-thirds noncoking coal from Indiana and one-third coke from near Pittsburgh. It was Klupfel's opinion that coke production was "astonishingly backward in America"; he reckoned he had not seen in the whole country a "rational" plant to compare with those in the Westphalian coalfield. Yet there were exciting possibilities. Improved plant near Pittsburgh could be "lucrative" or even "enormously profitable" since small coal suitable for coking was being thrown into the river. In that district coke "made from the purest coal" was being sold in large quantities for three dollars a ton, from which Klufel concluded: "we can judge how cheap it would be if the present waste of raw material were stopped and a healthy competition established among rational coking establishments, constructed on Belgian-German systems." His account seems to indicate that he did not visit Connellsville.[4] It would be two decades before the first example of the sort of "rational" system of production he recommended was in operation.

Four years later Lowthian Bell, a distinguished ironmaster from northeast England, then the world's biggest iron district, which in that year alone produced iron equivalent to 84 percent of the whole United States output, traveled through the American coal and iron regions. Bell was also a leading coal owner and coke operator in County Durham, whose best coals were at least equal in coking quality to those of Connellsville. Whereas Klupfel had emphasized the high prices paid for coke and the scope for cost reduction, Bell was above all impressed by the low cost of the Connellsville coke, notwithstanding what he thought were not particularly careful methods of production and a product he reckoned "greatly inferior" to that in his home area. Coal was wastefully used—he estimated anything from thirty-two to forty hundredweights were burned per ton of coke—"and yet coke was put into wagons at the pits at 5 shillings [about $1.20] per ton, or not more than half the price which Durham coke commands at the present time."[5] (The Dunbar ironmaster, Pechin, in 1875 put the loaded price of coke at $1.37 a ton.) Such low costs reflected the extraordinarily favorable mining conditions.

Rapidly increasing iron production, the transfer of more furnaces to coke, and that fuel's low costs of production in relation to the prices it commanded, naturally encouraged yet further extensions. Though sketchy, contemporary statistics provide some evidence of the scale of the industry. It was also at this time that the first efforts were made to ensure that competitive production did not unduly lower the price for coke. In mid-July 1873 representatives of thirty coal and coke producers met in the Yough House, Connellsville, to form an association named The Coal and Coke Exchange of Southwestern Pennsylvania. The importance already reached by their industry was indicated by the estimate that the interests present at this meeting had a combined capital of at least $7 million. Officers were elected, and the group decided to hold regular meetings in the town on the first Tuesday in every month at which, one of the joint secretaries optimistically recorded, "everything pertaining to the coal and coke trade will be considered and acted upon so that cooperation and unanimity may be secured."[6] It was a vain hope. There seems to be little or no record of the achievements of the Exchange; for a time such cooperative action seemed unnecessary since the state of business justified wholesale expansion. When difficult times followed, cooperation, however desirable, would prove difficult to secure.

In the early 1870s there was a particularly rapid extension in Pittsburgh-area pig iron output, though for a long time production fell far short of being able to satisfy the demand from local puddling furnaces and foundries. This margin provided some protection for blast furnace operators when demand for finished iron fell. Until 1872 the area had a weekly capacity of about 1,000 tons of pig iron. Early that year four new furnaces were added, increasing capacity by 1,700 tons. By midsummer a total of twelve blast furnaces offered a 3,600 tons per week capacity. At the national average rate of about 1.4 tons of coke per ton of iron, there must have been during 1872 alone an increase in annual coke consumption in Pittsburgh from about 70,000 to 250,000 tons. Pittsburgh mills and foundries consumed about one-quarter of the 1872 national pig iron production of 2.8 million net tons. The nine furnaces operating early that year could produce only about one-quarter of the area's pig iron requirements.[7]

The financial panic that began in the second half of September 1873 heralded the beginning of a depression. By 1 November 1874 nearly three hundred of the almost seven hundred blast furnaces in the nation were out of blast. But even in these generally difficult times, the iron trade of Pittsburgh suffered less than that of any other leading center. Many firms even enlarged their works, and blast furnaces there were almost constantly at work because of the large local deficit in pig iron. In November 1874 Isabella furnace established a new American record; Jones and Laughlin pulled down one of their Eliza furnaces to erect a larger one in its place. The national production of pig iron in 1876 was 73 percent the 1872 level, but locally expansion was still underway, with the capacity of Pittsburgh-area blast furnaces increasing by roughly one-third between summer 1872 and spring 1876.[8] In turn, as the main source of fuel for these favored furnaces, Connellsville did not suffer as large a contraction as might otherwise have been expected.

The impact of depression on the coke region was also reduced because the transition from other fuels was continuing. In 1872 coke and raw coal furnaces accounted for 34 percent of national pig iron production; four years later their share was 47 percent. Until this time increases in anthracite iron output had kept pace with the overall increase in the nation's iron production. But though a good fuel by virtue of its purity and strength in the furnace, anthracite was in other respects increasingly viewed as unsatisfactory. Iron makers striving for larger outputs in order to increase their share of normally expanding production and to reduce unit costs began to "drive" their furnaces harder in order to get greater tonnages in a shorter time. The slow rate of combustion for anthracite made this difficult. Moreover, each ton of iron required more anthracite than coke—Fulton later calculated that to make one ton of Bessemer pig from Lake ores required 2,200 pounds of anthracite but only 1,800 pounds of Connellsville coke. As a result, though still increasing in tonnage, by the early 1870s anthracite iron was lagging behind the growth of raw coal and coke iron. With the onset of depression, its share continued to fall. Then, at this critical time, serious labor troubles occurred in the anthracite coalfields. The disruption of their regular supplies forced many ironmasters to supplement the local fuel by mixing it with coke, and in doing so they soon recognized that the tonnages made by their furnaces were increased. On the other hand, coke had to bear heavy extra costs for haulage. In March 1875 coke on rail cars in the Connellsville district cost $1.50 per net ton. One calculation put the freight charge from there to furnaces near Harrisburg at $2.60 and to the Schuylkill Valley at about a dollar more than that; later it was admitted that these estimates might have been too low. The Thomas Iron Company, using one-quarter coke to three-quarters anthracite, reckoned the overall cost of coke delivered in the Lehigh Valley was $6.50 a ton. At this time coke was also mixed in the same proportion in New Jersey furnaces 285 miles from Connellsville. Among others, the Connellsville Gas Coal Company, finding its trade westward "almost entirely cut off" after the 1873 panic, built up new outlets in eastern furnaces.[9] When the results from part use of coke were analyzed, some of the evidence proved inconclusive. In 1874 the thirty-five-year-old Catasaqua works of the Crane Iron Company made about 1,200 tons of pig iron each week using 2,100 tons of mainly Lehigh basin anthracite. During the strike it used some of the best Connellsville coke and found that in some furnaces—though not in all—yields increased. The iron quality was poorer, but the company secretary attributed this not to the coke but to the "miserable" quality of the anthracite they were then having to mix with it.[10] When the strike was over, it was possible to make more balanced judgment of the comparative merits of the two fuels. John Fulton, who, as mining engineer for the Cambria Iron Company was perhaps not a completely disinterested observer, concluded: "The testimony of furnacemen in relation to the use of coke as a mixture with anthracite is harmonious. One-third to one-half of coke not only produces an economy of fuel per ton of pig iron, but also improves the working of the furnace in every way."[11]

Raw coal was less important as a furnace fuel than anthracite but was employed in furnaces along the Mahoning and Shenango Rivers—the "Valleys" district—in the Hocking Valley of Ohio and in parts of the northwest. One disadvantage of raw coal was the large amount used per ton of iron—about twice as much as with coke. Inevitably, though only gradually, the superiority of coke became more fully recognized in these districts. Brier Hill coal was the exclusive fuel in the Youngstown area until 1869, but after that increasing amounts of coke were mixed with it. By 1875 a Milwaukee blast furnace was using one-quarter Brier Hill coal and three-quarters Connellsville coke. One computation suggested that between 1874 and 1879, 246 new blast furnaces were built, of which 24 used raw coal, 68 charcoal, 75 anthracite, and 79 coke.[12]

In short, expansion in those large works, which combined iron and steel making with rail-mill operations; the buoyancy of the general market for pig iron in Pittsburgh, both the nearest and biggest iron center in the nation; and the headway coke was making at the expense of other furnace fuels all combined to help cushion Con-

Table 2.3 Connellsville coke, 1870–1879

Year	Number of ovens	Coke capacity (th. tons)	Coke shipments (th. tons)	Operating rate (%)
1870	550 [a, c]	214	n.a.	n.a.
1873	3,673 [a]	1,432	n.a.	n.a.
1875	3,673 [b]	1,432	666	46.5
1876	3,578	1,395	770	55.2
1877	3,620 [b]	1,412	869	61.5
1878	3,668	1,430	1,075	83.9
1879	4,200	1,638	2,014	122.9

SOURCES: *Connellsville Courier*, 16 June 1888, quoted in *Iron Age*, 21 June 1888, 1013; F. Quivik, *Connellsville Coal and Coke Region* (Historic American Engineering Record. Washington, D.C.: Department of the Interior, 1995), 17. Coke shipments from 1875 to 1878 are from W. P. Shinn, "Pittsburgh: Its Resources and Surroundings," *TAIME* 24 (1879–1880); the 1879 figure is from J. Fulton, "Coal Mining in the Connellsville Coke Region of Pennsylvania," *TAIME* 13 (1884–1885).

NOTE: The average annual capacity per oven is taken as 390 tons. In 1879 the number of available ovens increased substantially during the year.

    a. Indicates estimate.
    b. Even more approximate measures.
    c. Other estimates for 1870 vary from as few as 300 to as many as 790.

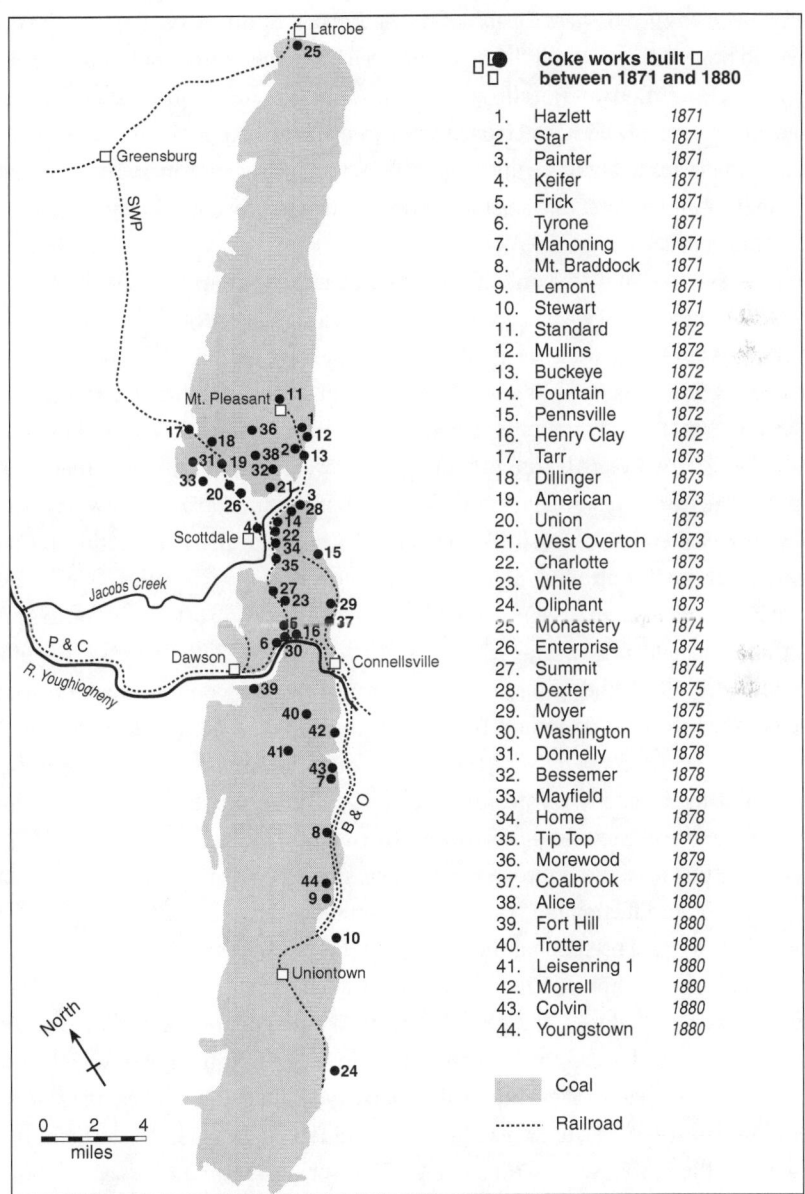

Coke works built 1871–1880.

nellsville from the harshest aspects of the depression of the 1870s. Even so, the district did not escape serious difficulties, financial problems, and some failures. Henry Clay Frick long afterward recalled the mid-1870s as "an awful time."[13] Nevertheless, there had previously been generous profit margins; Lowthian Bell had put the cost of coke at the ovens at about 54.5 percent of the selling price. Such margins might narrow sharply in the worst times but were wide enough to provide considerable protection against collapse.[14]

In the summer of 1875, Franklin Platt made an extensive survey of the coke region as part of the second geological survey of Pennsylvania. He recorded forty-five coke works, 3,455 ovens, and 2,279 employees. Capacity was 1.49 million bushels, roughly 27,000–28,000 tons a week.[15] For a few years after this, the industry seemed too large for its markets. From its 1872 peak, the output of iron with coke and raw coal had fallen for two years before beginning to recover, slowly at first and then more rapidly. The works were still greatly underused, but shipments rose year by year from 1875. That September, only a little over two years after the abortive meeting in Connellsville, owners controlling more than two-thirds of the ovens gathered in Uniontown intending to form a "combination" with a board of control to divide orders pro rata and regulate prices. The scheme seems to have had little success, for nine months later yet another combination was formed of those controlling about 2,000 ovens. Its aim was to cut production and regulate prices.[16] Such associations were harbingers of the cooperative action that became important a decade later, but revival during the late 1870s owed more to the general rebound from the depression and the particular buoyancy of coke iron, especially in Pittsburgh.

During this period the recovery quickened and then ripened into a boom. Coal and coke iron production in 1878 was 21 percent more than in 1873; capacity to make coke seems to have been about the same as in the earlier year. However, the experiences of 1879 were unprecedented. Coke iron production increased 46 percent above the level six years before and more coke was being used in anthracite furnaces. One estimate suggests that capacity to make coke at the beginning of the year was some 14 percent greater than in 1873; production outstripped it. In the darkest days of the decade, the price of coke had fallen to as low as ninety cents a ton, but during 1879 it rose to $2, then to $3, $4, and even higher. That spring one company's costs of production were reckoned to amount to $1.15 a ton; the selling price at the ovens was $1.30. By the year's end prices ranged up to as much as $5 per ton of which, as the biographer of the head of the firm quietly recognized, "three-fifths was net profit."[17] Those who survived the bad times were now very amply rewarded for their endurance. Predictably, mushrooming prices brought not only frantic activity, but also called forth major extensions to existing plants and the construction of additional coke works.

For years few new ovens had been built. Fulton later calculated that the district contained 3,576 ovens in 1876; at the end of 1878 there were 3,668. But by late summer 1879, the *Uniontown Republican Standard* reported: "A run through the coke country about Mt Pleasant develops the fact that every coke oven in the district is ablaze. Works which have been lying idle for years are now in the full tide of prosperity and the outlook is certainly encouraging. New ovens are being erected on every hand." It was no exaggeration. A later state report spelled out some of the implications of the almost revolutionary change in the situation: "New plants sprang up everywhere, thousands of workmen were employed as rapidly as they came. Operators burned slack upon the ground and sold the product at fancy prices. In one year after the boom came, coke jumped to $5.00 per ton, and there were 8,000 ovens in the region. This was the most prosperous season the trade has ever seen." (The figure for ovens was an exaggeration—in late November 1879 a trade journal noted that 4,200 ovens were running day and night; thirteen months later 7,211 ovens existed in the district.)[18] Established concerns expanded existing works and built new ones. A. R. Overholt put up 62 ovens at West Overton in 1873; he added another 74 after the depression. Boyle and Hazlett operated 182 ovens near Mt. Pleasant; by August 1879 they were building 100 more. At John M. Cochran's Buckeye mine, 30–40 new ovens were almost complete by August. Of the wholly new plants, some of the biggest were in the northern part of the field. Among these were the large Standard works of A. A. Hutchinson, who already owned the Globe ovens near Broadford. Along the June Bug Branch Railroad, an offshoot from the Mt. Pleasant Branch, Cassius Markle of West Newton was breaking ground for a number of ovens. The whole character of the area was changed. As late as spring 1879, Mt. Pleasant was "a small inland town comparatively unknown in its quiet progress." A year later it was "surrounded by a belt of fire." Yet the biggest project of all from this period was located south of the Youghiogheny, where a huge coal tract was secured by the Connellsville Coke and Iron Company. Another aspect of this period of high activity and large-scale expansion was that by the end of the 1870s, coke making had ceased to be an adjunct of farming or a small-scale, chancy industry. Henceforth it was big business.

It was in this decade that the foundations were laid for the future unexampled successes of the H. C. Frick Coke Company. From as early as 1859, Abraham O. Tinstman and Joseph Rist had interests in coal and coke. In 1868 they were associated with Col. A. S. Morgan in a larger project that failed. In March 1871 they were joined by twenty-one-year-old Henry Clay Frick. Some time before, while employed in his grandfather's merchandise establishment, Frick had made clear his ambition to succeed to a relative who was a fellow worker. After things had been cleared up and put in good order for the next day, they set about cooking an oyster stew for their evening meal. As they did, young Clay remarked, "I see no reason why I should not become a millionaire during my lifetime."[19] Significantly, when the new company began trading, it was under the name Frick and Company. Even by the standards of that time it was a fairly small enterprise, controlling only 150 acres of coal and fifty coke ovens at Broadford. The next year, borrowing from relations and from banker Thomas Mellon, fifty more ovens were added and another one-hundred-oven works, Henry Clay, was built nearby. By early autumn 1873, when the nation's basic industries were laid low by depression, Frick and Company controlled two hundred ovens, a little over one in every twenty of the district total. Through the next few years the company struggled to survive. Already, though, Frick was beginning to play a larger part in the industry than seemed justified either by the size of his stake or by his age. In September 1873 he became joint secretary of the newly formed Coal and Coke Exchange of Southwestern Pennsylvania, and in June 1876 Frick was one of the five directors of the trade combination controlling two thousand ovens.[20] Trade during that year was still at a very low ebb, though as could be seen in retrospect, an upward movement had already begun. At this dull time Frick bought out his partners. His efforts to find outlets for the product of his two works were unceasing. Already, their market area was extensive. Frick delivered coke not only to nearby outlets such as Confluence on the Youghigheny in Somerset County by mid-1876 but also to consumers as distant as John Gilmore in Ironton, who was served by barge; to ironworks at Newcastle in the Shenango valley; to Wheeling and Benwood; and even as far west as the Milwaukee Iron Company.[21] In 1877, as coke shipments again edged upward, Frick bought the eight-year-old Morgan works, the White ovens, and leased from Wilson, Boyle, and Playford the 102 ovens of Valley works near Everson. Valley was idle when purchased, but Frick put the ovens to work and operated them throughout the year. That fall he took E. M. Ferguson into partnership, bringing in another 70 ovens near Dunbar on the Fayette County Branch. In spring 1878 Frick and Ferguson leased and put into operation Anchor works and later that year the Mullen ovens near Mt. Pleasant. During 1879 Foundry and Tip Top were bought, and on a number of former farms Frick began to build a planned 500 ovens at what became Morewood coke works. In three years Frick had increased his interest in the industry from two works to ten and now controlled 853 ovens. As a sober account of his progress later recorded: "When business revived his good judgement in these purchases was demonstrated by the fact that for a time the annual profits more than equalled the purchase prices."[22] Under such circumstances it was scarcely surprising that by his thirtieth birthday in Decem-

Henry Clay Frick, A. A. Hutchinson, Andrew W. Mellon, and Frank Cowan, 1880. *Courtesy of Frick Art and Historical Center, Frick Archives*

ber 1879, Henry Clay Frick had already realized his youthful ambition to be a millionaire. Over the next decade his company would push rapidly toward a preeminent position in the region.

The Course of Trade 1880–1900

In the last twenty years of the nineteenth century, coke became overwhelmingly dominant as a furnace fuel. There was an extraordinarily rapid increase in its consumption: 1.9 million tons of coke were used in blast furnaces in 1880, 8.2 million ten years later, and by 1900, 14.7 million tons.[23] Charcoal iron production made a considerable recovery during this period, but this achievement involved a migration to less accessible parts of the nation, notably to the upper Great Lakes states. By the latter half of the 1880s, use of raw bituminous coal alone in smelting had fallen off so much that it was now confined to a few furnaces in Ohio, Indiana, and Kentucky. Brier Hill coal, first used alone in Valleys furnaces and then for twenty years mixed with coke, was unobtainable by 1890 in adequate tonnages; coke had become their staple fuel.

Table 2.4 Weekly iron capacity of blast furnaces using coke, 1878, 1885, and 1895 *(gross tons in thousands)*

Region	1878	1885	1895
United States	21,735	43,943	130,372
Pittsburgh	3,980	8,130	37,776
Mahoning Valley	2,250	3,565	8,810
Illinois	1,250	4,300	13,564
Alabama	350	4,220	15,858

SOURCE: *Iron Age*, 23 June 1895, 1082.

That year there were thirty-eight furnaces in the two valleys. The type of fuel for two of them was not recorded, but of the rest five used a mixture of coke and raw coal and thirty-one coke.[24] Overall, the largest part of the increase in pig iron production using coke was west of the Alleghenies, and this as well as the superior product made in Connellsville ensured that it continued to receive the lion's share of the expansion. But coke was now also dominant in the East, use of anthracite dwindling as the superior fuel made its way into the stronghold of its old rival. In 1883, when first separated in American Iron and Steel Association (AISA) statistics, the tonnage of iron made with anthracite was 19 percent of the national pig iron output; mixed charges of anthracite and coke claimed another 18 percent; by 1900 no iron was made in furnaces using only anthracite and those using mixed anthracite and coke produced only 12 percent of the total. Shortly afterward, Fulton suggested that where cost of coke was not over 25–30 percent more than anthracite, it would be preferred by the operator. As a not unimportant, though very secondary part, of its wider market, from the early 1880s coke was replacing anthracite in East Coast foundries, resulting in a roughly one-third greater tonnage of iron handled per ton of fuel.[25]

The increase in Connellsville coke production, though large, was less than that in coke iron production. This was due to two main factors: the large output of coke from other coalfields and a reduction in the coke rate; that is, the consumption per ton of iron produced. In 1879 the latter averaged about 1.47 tons per ton, by 1889 it was 1.29, and ten years later 1.20; a fuel economy in two decades of over 18 percent.[26] By 1900 the Connellsville region contained almost three times as many ovens as twenty years before and its output was 361 percent greater. This expansion occurred almost exclusively within the district soon after referred to as the "old basin," or Connellsville "proper." By the end of the 1890s, this growth had more or less reached its peak; a further doubling of Connellsville production before the outbreak of the Great War in Europe would be almost entirely due to the opening of a nearby, geologically similar but separate district whose first coke was produced in 1900.

Table 2.5 Production of Connellsville coke and U.S. coke-made pig iron, 1880–1900

Year	Connellsville Coke Region			U.S. output of iron made using coke and raw coal (th. tons)
	Total ovens	Coke shipments (th. tons)	Avg. price	
1880	7,211	2,206	$1.79	1,741[a]
1885	10,471	3,096	$1.22	2,389
1890	16,020	6,464	$1.94	6,388
1895	17,947	8,244	$1.23	7,950
1900	20,954	10,166	$2.70	11,728

SOURCES: *Connellsville Courier*, May 1914; P. Temin, *Iron and Steel in Nineteenth Century America: An Economic Enquiry* (Cambridge, Mass.: MIT Press, 1964), 266–67.
  a. The small proportion of these totals made up of iron smelted with bituminous coal decreased sharply over this period, but precise measure of the extent is impossible.

The increase in number of ovens was much greater in the 1880s than the 1890s. Indeed, in relative terms 1880s expansion exceeded that of any other time period, at least subsequent to the early 1870s. Output too increased more in the 1880s, though only by a slim margin. Extension of the rail network and competition between the main railroad companies continued to shape the distribution of this expansion. Prices followed an uneven course but ended the twenty-year period at a higher figure than any reached within it. There was a strong movement toward a more oligopolistic organization during this time, which began without a predominant firm, but well before its end one company possessed an almost controlling power. The courses taken by both prices and company structure were closely related to a major influence from beyond the region, the ever-closer links with the iron and steel industry. There was a large investment of outside capital in coke and the first effective attempts at cooperation in order to reduce unprofitable price fluctuations. Finally, these two decades, particularly the years 1885–1895, contained the most violent confrontations between capital and labor.

Developments in Coke Region Transport

By the late 1870s the Vanderbilt group had acquired large interests in the Pittsburgh and Lake Erie Railroad, which had begun as an independent route from Pittsburgh to Youngstown, where by a connection with the Lake Shore and Southern it gained a through route to Chicago. When the coke trade boomed again, the Vanderbilts were eager to get their share of the increasing business. During the early 1880s production steadily increased but prices fell year after year. The coke operators looked for competitive freight rates to preserve their position and were therefore interested in plans for railroad extensions. The so-far unsatisfied ambitions of the Vanderbilts and Franklin B. Gowen, president of the Philadelphia and Reading, seemed to hold some promise. By 1882 the Vanderbilts along with a group including Frick; A. A. Hutchinson; David Hostetter; at least two principal members of the Carnegie group, Tom Carnegie and D. A. Stewart; and banker Thomas Mellon were reported to be planning a new coke district railroad.[27] By 1884 they had built a track from Pittsburgh to New Haven, the Pittsburgh, McKeesport, and Youghiogheny Railroad (by a play on the sound of its constituent parts afterward commonly referred to as the "Peemickey"). They intended this line to turn at the latter place so as to pass through southwestern Fayette County, tapping areas not served by the PRR or the B&O systems. Rather than see this happen, the other companies settled for new pooling arrangements to accommodate the newcomer. For instance after making a connection with the South West Pennsylvania at New Haven, the Vanderbilt line was allocated all the coke from south of Moyer. Through an agreement with the Youghiogheny Northern, it tapped the Morgan Valley plants of the H. C. Frick Coke Company.[28]

Time and again other projected trunk-line routes into the region were defeated or fizzled out. The grandly named Pittsburgh, Virginia, and Charleston had been conceived as part of a link from Pittsburgh to the South, but it had failed to achieve such a grand objective. In 1882 the company began work on a track from Brownsville to New Haven, along which it expected coke works would soon be established. After building to north of Uniontown, it fell into the hands of the South West Pennsylvania and was completed as its Redstone Branch.[29] Larger schemes were by then on the horizon. Though second to arrive, the Pennsylvania Railroad predominated in district movements, shipping 76 percent of all the coke in the record year of 1883.[30] By this time the Vanderbilts were further threatening this supremacy by reviving a project first mooted thirty years before. In 1854 the State of Pennsylvania had granted a charter to the Duncannon, Landisburg, and Broad Top Railroad Company to build westward from the Susquehanna to tap bituminous coal in Bedford County. By 1857 the plan had been changed to involve connections with the Allegheny Portage Railroad and with the Pittsburgh and Connellsville, perhaps at West Newton. Two years later the name was altered to the Pennsylvania Pacific Railroad Company and by 1863 to the South Pennsylvania Railroad Company. Capital was increased to $20 million. Despite these changes, no construction occurred; as one railroad journal reported, "the corporation slumbered peacefully on, being aroused only about once a year in order to go through the form of holding an annual meeting and keeping the charter alive." By the 1870s new surveys had shifted the proposed line to the Cumberland Valley, cutting the distance between Pittsburgh and Harrisburg to 229 miles.[31] In

1883 this little more than moribund scheme was transformed into a far larger threat to existing coke roads than the Pittsburgh, McKeesport, and Youghiogheny. Vanderbilt took a controlling interest in the South Pennsylvania and through his son in law, Hamilton McKown Twombly, began planning its development. A new trunk line could provide both a direct route to rapidly expanding outlets for coke in eastern furnaces and an alternative route to markets there or overseas for Pittsburgh steel. It was clear that the other railroads would respond. For a time it even seemed possible that the PRR might build a parallel line to protect its traffic.[32] Meanwhile, the South Pennsylvania had to chose a route within the coke region. As early as February 1883, Frick was suggesting to Twombly that, if he decided to reach the Youghiogheny at the mouth of Sewickely Creek, it was desirable to also acquire the Ligonier Valley Railroad.[33] By summer, a route had been chosen and Frick was urging the need for local branch lines. He wanted Twombly to visit Pittsburgh so that he could take him over the ground and join in coal and coke developments, writing him to take "hold of the several properties of which you are acquainted and on which we hold options, . . . feeling satisfied that, as an investment, it will prove highly profitable to you, to say nothing of the other advantages your interests will derive from it."[34] However, it soon became clear that the high politics of railroad affairs transcended the interests of even such an economic area as the coke region.

At the end of 1883, less than two months after regular coke shipments began on the Pittsburgh, McKeesport, and Youghiogheny and following "innumerable conferences" and "a good deal of dickering," the two established companies agreed to share the coke traffic with the Vanderbilts. From 1 January 1884 it was agreed that the Pennsylvania would get 55 percent, the Baltimore and Ohio 25 percent, and the Pittsburgh and Lake Erie/Pittsburgh, McKeesport, and Youghiogheny 20 percent. Their apparent concord was deceptive; the situation was an unstable, interim position, which in the words of one onlooker, "has the appearance of an armistice, during which the combatants will probably continue to manoeuver for positions favorable in a future fight." Indeed, the PRR was apparently dissatisfied with its share. In April 1884 another meeting was scheduled in Pittsburgh to try to hammer out a new agreement. It was postponed because of the nonappearance of the president of the Lake Shore and Southern, another line controlled by the Vanderbilts, who were reported to "want a larger share of the plum" and to be actively at work once more on the South Pennsylvania, which would either wrest traffic from the other railroads or secure it by negotiation.[35]

It later became known that when the Vanderbilts agreed to raise $5 million for the new main line (one third of the total capital), Andrew Carnegie and his friends had raised an additional $2.5 million or, according to some accounts, $5 million.[36]

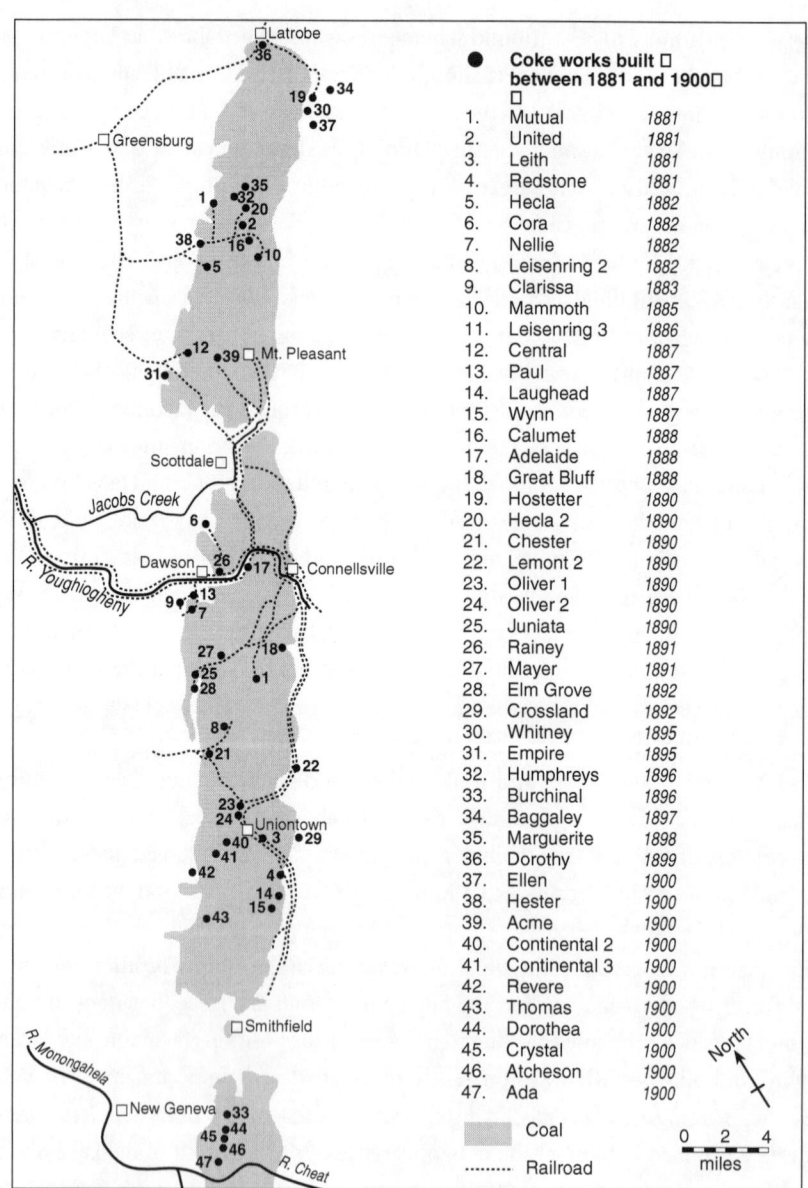

Coke works built 1881–1900.

Contracts were let for tunneling through the Appalachian ridges, Carnegie expressing hope that traffic would be moving on the new line by the summer of 1885. The PRR proved equal to this challenge to its supremacy. A first step was to improve services to coke operators. It reduced freight rates and in spring 1884 consolidated its position by buying the short Mahoning Branch Railroad, a switch line serving 360 ovens whose business was now transferred from the B&O.[37] A much more dramatic reaction to the South Pennsylvania project then began to take shape. Years before, Gould interests had built a track up the west side of the Hudson to threaten the main line of the New York Central. By summer 1884 this speculative venture was in receivership, and it was rumored that, in retaliation for the invasion of its "own" territory, the PRR would buy the West Shore and thereby put itself in a position to compete with the New York Central in upper New York State and New England. To avoid such a major disruption to business, in July 1885 J. P. Morgan engineered a meeting between the presidents of the PRR and the New York Central, George Roberts and Chauncy Depew. The West Shore was sold to the New York Central and work was stopped on the South Pennsylvania. The charter, rights of way, and work already done were transferred to the PRR, which allowed these items fall into disuse and decay. A few weeks later Carnegie had to deny that his party was to receive any advantages in coke rates as a reward for the removal of the threat of competition to the PRR. In fact, charges in some respects rose again.[38]

Ten years later the Vanderbilts briefly revived the idea of a major east-west line through Pennsylvania, this time in the form of the Pittsburgh and Eastern, projected to run across Clearfield and Indiana Counties to Saltsburg, cross the Pennsylvania main line at Latrobe, and from there join the Pittsburgh, McKeesport, and Youghiogheny opposite West Newton.[39] This too failed to materialize as did a scheme to use the long planned and slowly developed Western Maryland Railroad, running from Cumberland to the Youghiogheny, as a trunk route to the East for both Carnegie operations and the coke region.[40] A few years later the ill-fated Wabash project seemed promising for a time but then failed to deliver a new route westward. The existing main lines, especially the PRR, remained dominant in linking the coke region with other industrial districts.

Though much less dramatic than the great trunk line schemes, additional branches within the region opened wholly new sections for mine and coke expansion. In the north the Youngwood Branch encouraged investments in 1882. By late 1885 the PRR had already partially graded its so-called Texas Branch, linking Everson to Latrobe. Many expected that by the following spring it would open the Pleasant Unity section and that J. W. Moore, David Hostetter, and Ralph Baggaley, all of whom held coal land there, would build ovens.[41] This link was not completed at this time, but there was important plant construction in the area during the late 1880s. Farther south a planned link between Leisenring and West Leisenring fell short of its target. A Baltimore and Ohio "Short Line" from Connellsville to the Juniata and Elm Grove coke works on the western edge of the coal basin was not extended, as projected, to the Monongahela. The Youghiogheny Southern, planned in the early 1890s to run from the Peemickey through the valleys of the Leisenring country, also was not built. (Its intended route is shown on J. Paddock's map of 1892.) However, by the end of the century, a B&O extension southward to the Cheat River and on to Morgantown, West Virginia, had opened the southernmost parts of the basin and a small area on the very edge of Pennsylvania, which was soon to be known as the Geneva and Point Marion field. Of more significance, railroads were being extended westward into an area that in the early years of the twentieth century would become a major new source of coke.

Despite the track extensions, coke operators often felt ill-served by the railroad companies. In part this was dissatisfaction with physical provision; in part with the charges made for the services provided. Sharp variations in coke demand meant it was difficult for railroads to provide adequate carrying capacity. The author of an official Pennsylvania report summed up the cokers' dilemma: "When the demand for coke was brisk, there was a great scarcity of cars. The frequent depressions in the iron industry of course have brought disaster to the coke trade, and destinations were wanting when cars abounded."[42] In reaction to this situation, some coke makers acquired their own carrying capacity. By spring 1899, for instance, H. C. Frick Coke owned 2,500 rail cars. Later when the three main railroads appointed special agents to handle coke traffic, serious car shortages became much less frequent. Another factor by then making company ownership less usual was a change in the size and type of car. Early coke cars were wooden and fairly small. By the early 1880s most carried 15–16.25 tons, and this remained the average over the next ten years. At the turn of the century, the normal size was 20 or 21 tons. Steel gradually replaced wood, and by 1907 some steel coke cars carried 50 tons. By 1914 wooden cars and privately owned rolling stock had virtually disappeared from the region.[43]

Coke operators and iron makers commonly regarded freight charges on coke as unfairly high. Certainly there was a good deal of arbitrariness. Rate setting, as the *Connellsville Courier* once remarked, "had a fine contempt for equities. Discrimination lurked in every corner of the tariff sheet. If it was not written large and fair on the surface, it existed underneath in the shape of rebates and drawbacks. The rates on coke were seldom questioned, and when they were it was only to try to establish to the satisfaction of the rate-makers that the traffic couldn't stand the tax."[44] The editor of the *Pittsburgh Dispatch* particularized the problem: "It is within the personal knowledge of the writer that in the late '70s the Pennsylvania Company employed an expert to figure out how much of Pittsburgh's advantage in the cheapness of fuel the railroad could take in greater profits than charged to Cleveland and other points." W. Rowe, president of the Pittsburgh Steel Company, testified to the Stanley Committee that for a number of years the railroads set rates on ore, coke, and limestone so as to bring about more or less equality of costs of iron production in Pittsburgh, the Valleys, and at Wheeling.[45]

On the other hand, shippers and consumers alike did their utmost to squeeze concessions from the railroads. As prices fell in the early 1880s, transport costs pressed harder. Early in 1884 Carnegie was complaining to the PRR vice president and new general freight agent about freight rates, including those on coke. Seven years later he was outspoken in a public interview: "Well the Pennsylvania Railroad people heretofore considered coke a plum and have exacted rates for its transportation which bear no relation to rates upon other things. They have discriminated against western Pennsylvania, their own home traffic." Perversely, and against all the logic of long-haul rates naturally tapering with distance, Carnegie argued that the charge of 72 cents on coke to Pittsburgh "should be the same as it is upon coke delivered beyond Pennsylvania—52 cents per ton; the rates to the Valleys 1 cent per ton mile more."[46]

In 1885 a Vice President King of the Baltimore and Ohio wrote to assure Carnegie and Frick that the H. C. Frick Coke Company was getting rates as favorable as those of any rival. As he ruefully put it, "rates this past summer have been so low all round that there has been no room for favoritism." Shortly before, Frick had been in contact with Twombly on Vanderbilt rates. Again it was all rather secretive. Asked about

Table 2.6 Coke and pig iron average prices and freight rates on Connellsville coke, 1887–1913 *(in dollars per ton)*

	1887	1889	1899	1901	1907	1912	1913
Annual average prices:							
Connellsville coke	1.79	1.34	2.00	1.95	2.90	1.92	2.95
Pig iron[a]	20.92	17.75	19.36	15.87	23.89	13.90	14.77
Freight charges on coke to:							
Pittsburgh	0.55/0.65[b]	0.70	0.55/0.70[b]	0.75	0.75	0.80	0.75
The Valleys	1.65	1.35	1.10/1.20[b]	1.20	1.35	1.35	1.35
Cleveland	2.20	2.80	1.40/1.50[b]	1.50	1.65	1.65	1.65
Chicago	3.30	2.75	2.25/2.50[b]	2.50	n.a.	2.80	2.50

SOURCES: For annual prices, *Iron Age*, 21 April 1887; *EMJ*, 26 Jan 1889, 100; *Coal and Coke*, 15 December 1899; *BAISA*, 25 April 1901. For freight charges, *Iron Age*, 18 April 1907, 1226; and 19 June 1913, 1478–79; *Coal and Coke*, 26 December 1912, 46.

a. Rates per long ton; through 1907, No. 1 Foundry iron at Philadelphia; from 1908, basic iron, fob, at Valley furnaces.

b. Indicates old and new rates in the year.

these discussions some sixteen years later, Twombly replied cautiously: "As far as the Frick Coke Company matter is concerned, I would suggest that when you see Mr. Frick you ask him about the circumstances of the transaction. For myself, I would rather not talk about the matter anymore for the present." Writing to Carnegie a few months earlier, Andrew Moreland had been equally furtive: "Rates is a thing which don't want positive or strong records on."[47] In other words, freight charges were matters for negotiation in which bigger companies looked for concessions not available to smaller rivals. After 1887 much of the coke traffic became subject to the general oversight of the newly formed Interstate Commerce Commission. Sometimes the rulings of this body fell harshly on a coke-using district. In the summer of 1913, for instance, finding that existing rates on coke to the Mahoning Valley and to Cleveland were too high, the ICC reduced the charges by 5–15 percent. The Shenango Valley, for most purposes treated the same way by freight carriers as the Mahoning Valley, received no concession because it lay fully within the borders of Pennsylvania.[48]

Combinations and Price Management

Unfortunately for the well being of the coke industry, its growth was frequently out of phase with the levels of activity in its chief market. Booming conditions in iron in 1879 and 1880, with outputs respectively of 2.7 and 3.8 million tons—both unprecedented figures—not only brought the coke industry out of depression but also sparked a major expansion in response to record prices. In 1881 and 1882 the number of ovens increased 28.7 percent. The following two years were good for iron and steel, especially for coke pig iron, but the extensions in coke proved unsustainable. As a result, for the first four years of the 1880s prices slipped. By 1884, though output was almost 45 percent above the 1880 level, the average price for coke was 37 percent lower. Given the labor-intensive nature of the processes involved, reductions in production costs would mean either bringing in lower-priced labor or wage cuts for those already employed. Confrontation between operators and employees and a disruption of production would result. But there were other ways in which financial performances could possibly be improved. Operators could close ovens and slow down or stop building new capacity. However, it would be difficult to ensure that all firms followed suit, and in fact 1885 was the only year in which there was a decrease in oven numbers, and then only by 0.7 percent. A greater result might be gained by combining restrictions on new building with reductions of output from existing plants, this being achieved either by combination or by collusion. It was this sort of comprehensive approach, rather than the token reduction in ovens, that brought a small increase in prices in 1885. Even when it had some success, such a policy also had dangers.

Table 2.7 Production and prices in the early 1880s

Year	Production (th. tons)			Prices ($ per ton)		
	Steel	Coal & coke iron	Connellsville coke[a]	Bessemer rails[b]	Pig iron[c]	Connellsville coke
1879	935	1,285	2,014	48.25	21.50	n.a.
1880	1,247	1,741	2,206	67.50	28.50	1.79
1881	1,588	2,035	2,639	61.13	25.15	1.63
1882	1,737	2,177	3,043	48.50	25.75	1.47
1883	1,674	2,401	3,552	37.75	22.38	1.14
1884	1,551	2,272	3,192	30.75	19.88	1.13
1885	1,712	2,389	3,096	28.50	18.00	1.22

SOURCES: P. Temin, *Iron and Steel in Nineteenth Century America: An Economic Enquiry* (Cambridge, Mass.: MIT Press, 1964); *Connellsville Courier*, May 1914.
a. Shipments.
b. Price at works in Pennsylvania.
c. Foundry pig at Philadelphia.

Higher coke prices might be welcome to operators but were anathema to consumers, particularly when their own trade was falling away. In 1885 the price of Connellsville coke advanced 8 percent on the previous year, but the average price for pig iron fell 9.4 percent. Too much interference with free-market forces could encourage iron firms to integrate backwards by acquiring their own mines and ovens or to switch their purchases to other areas where costs of coal lands and labor might be lower. Moreover, if prices were kept artificially high this would likely induce other capitalists, not party to the restriction agreements, to extend their coke capacity or even enter into the trade for the first time. Finally, higher prices for beehive coke might encourage adoption of alternative methods of coking. In fact, a large increase in immigrant labor, strikes against low or reduced wages, extended control by iron firms, new entrants to the coke trade, expansion in other areas, and the advocacy of byproduct ovens were all leading themes in the 1880s.

At the beginning of the decade, there were important combinations of producers; the middle years were marked by attempts to regulate trade by collective action; after that there was a return to the processes of concentration into bigger companies. At a slower pace consolidation continued into the 1890s. The year 1880 ended with 7,211 ovens in the coke district. Next spring there was great activity as the iron trade boomed. Old blast furnaces, long idle, were blown in and new ones built. Smelting expanded rapidly in the west. Some 6,000 ovens were working and 1,500 to 2,000 more were under construction. Already there were signs of dangers to come, for coke prices were already barely half what they had been during the "spasmodic" advance a year or two earlier, and there was already surplus capacity. By July, 6,680 ovens were at work.⁴⁹ Two years later, output of coke iron reached new records, but by then producers of coke were obviously suffering from capacity outstripping demand. The average price that year was not much higher than those of the worst years of the 1870s when the tonnage of coke iron had been only one-third as high. By May 1883, operators were sufficiently alarmed as to plan restrictions of output and wage reductions. Next month repeated meetings were held to try to agree on collective action. Owners of 4,000 of the now 10,000 or so ovens signed a paper favoring a cut in production of 50 percent, but their agreement had no practical outcome. In fact, the meetings were not attended by owners of enough of the total capacity to make any decision effective. There was also an important division of interest between operators of drift and of shaft mines. For the latter a coke price of $.85 a ton at the ovens meant a loss of from $.08 to $.18 a ton, and therefore they favored restriction of tonnage in hope of strengthening the market and earning at least something on their investment. Costs were lower for drift mine owners and therefore they were less eager to make concessions. Later that year the iron trade passed into recession and began to reduce its coke consumption. By mid-December, Valleys furnaces were taking only half their normal tonnages, and in Pittsburgh the stopping of one of the Edgar Thomson furnaces and the two Lucy stacks had cut coke shipments by fifty cars a day—this alone amounted to a reduction of about 7.7 percent compared with the high activity of two-and-a-half years before. By the year's end prices were at "bedrock" at $.95 to $1 a ton. Members of the trade owning two-thirds of the ovens then at work decided to cut production by 15 percent, or 3,600 cars a week. They would neither load coal nor draw coke on Wednesdays. To reduce tonnages further they would concentrate on seventy-two-hour coke.⁵⁰

Table 2.8 Oligopoly in the coke region, 1882, 1894, and 1900

Ovens	1882	1894	1900
Total	8,438	17,613	18,942
H. C. Frick	1,022	7,102	8,343ᵃ
W. J. Rainey	313	1,422	2,231
McClure	53	2,213	2,065

SOURCES: F. Ellis, *History of Fayette County* (Philadelphia: Everts, 1882); A. Y. Lee, *Map of Coke Region* (Pittsburgh, 1894); S. G. Nelson, *Nelson's Biographical Dictionary and Historical Reference Book of Fayette County* (Uniontown, Pa.: S. G. Nelson, 1900).

NOTE: The total number of ovens in the district does not correspond with the *Connellsville Courier*'s figures (given in Appendix A, table A2). The discrepancy reflects the different time of the year in which each source calculated this data.

a. From 1895 H. C. Frick controlled McClure. Along with other ovens whose output Frick marketed, it was reckoned that by 1900 the company effectively controlled nearly 15,000 ovens.

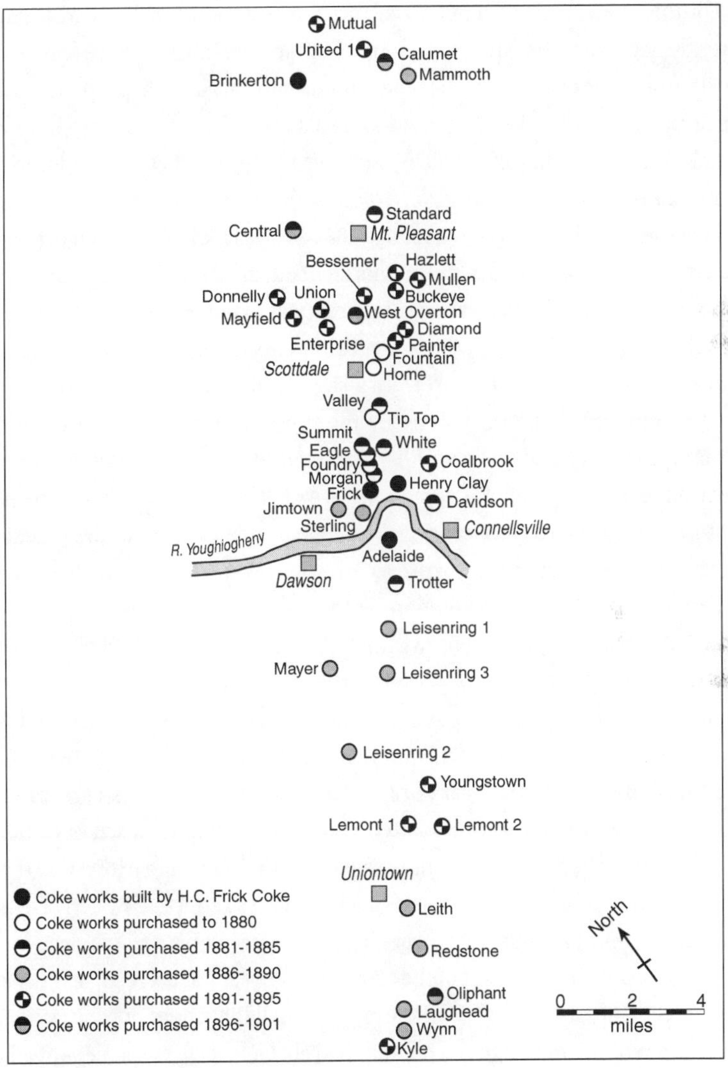

The Maturing Industry 49

Growth of the H. C. Frick Coke Company, 1871–1901.

Meanwhile, low prices had also encouraged important steps to consolidation, so that by the end of 1883 the H. C. Frick Coke Company had increased its share of the total capacity from roughly one-tenth in 1882 to over one-third. Its main acquisitions, made in September 1883, were of the properties of the Connellsville Gas Coal Company and of A. A. Hutchinson. The former brought in the 400 Trotter ovens, the latter gave Frick control of Standard works with 573 ovens at the northern end of the field. For this works and 185 acres of coal, Frick paid $700,000. A few weeks later he apparently negotiated for McClure, though at that time it was a much less attractive proposition than it would later become, and he summarized its properties as, "of a low order, and short lived, coke inferior." He also thought he had "closed up" a deal for a link with Schoonmakers, which "more nearly approaches ours in location etc, etc," but this too came to nothing.[51]

One of the trade journals characterized 1883 as a year "of exceptional depression," which "will long remain vivid in the memories of all interested in this great industry." In its course demand had decreased as capacity was extended, and there had been "a remarkable fall in values."[52] Reading such comments, a casual observer might easily have overlooked the fact that, apart from a slightly higher 1882 figure, more pig iron had been produced than ever before. By the time these jeremiads on the industry were published, Frick had taken another step toward remedial action. After consulting two other large operators, James Schoonmaker and the McClure interests, he wrote to a third, Edward B. Leisenring. The tone was confident but the urgency that prompted it showed through: "I write to ask you if you will meet me here at a very early date regarding the coke situation. From the fact of our four concerns owning and controlling about 6,000 ovens, we think there should be no difficulty in agreeing upon a plan of mutual benefit to take effect February 1st."[53]

The first plan for a controlling syndicate quickly failed as smaller firms refused to cooperate. By April 1884 there was another scheme under which the big operators agreed to sell the output of smaller operators at a commission of 2.5–15 cents, according to the state of the market, the latter in return binding themselves to build no more ovens and to reduce output at the request of the syndicate. Hope was reported of a price advance of 10–15 cents a ton as a result of these efforts.[54] By early December 4,513 ovens, 43 percent of the total, were idle; on 18 December the syndicate decided to shut down another 10 percent of the capacity. The year's average price for coke had been $1.13 as compared with $1.14 the year before. All that could now be claimed was that a collapse of prices had been checked. By February 1885, 60 percent of all ovens were out of production.[55] Soon after this a revival of trade began and by November 1885, 80 percent of district capacity was at work. The average price for the full year was $1.22. It was a modest victory, but it had been won in the face of a downward swing in iron and steel prices.

Although the Coke Syndicate seemed to have succeeded in bolstering prices, its actions and achievement had some counterproductive results. Those firms that stayed outside the agreement could benefit from the general firming of prices while avoiding restriction of their output. In May 1884, for instance, when the trade was "without a particle of change," three major independent producers, Rainey, Cochran,

Table 2.9 Connellsville coke prices at ovens, 1882 and 1883

	1882	1883
Early in year	$1.70–1.75	$1.20–1.25
February	n.a.	$1.15–1.00
March	n.a.	$1.05–1.15
June	$1.40–1.50	$0.85
September	$1.15–1.25	$1.05–1.10
November	n.a.	$1.10–1.05
Year end	$1.30–1.35	$1.00

and Moore, who together controlled 806 ovens, continued to cut prices and run full time while the syndicate reduced output by 20 percent. Another weakness was exposed early in 1885 when, in hope of eliminating some of this outside competition, the syndicate paid $150,000 to buy 313 ovens controlled by J. W. Moore and Company. Immediately, the Moores used the purchase money to extend their capacity once again. Presley H. Moore paid $17,000 for coal and surface land on the Clement farm one mile north of Uniontown with the prospect of building ovens there the next year. J. W. Moore began to build 300 ovens in the Pleasant Unity district at the northern end of the basin at what became the Mammoth works. A few weeks later another independent, James Cochran, sold a half-share of a 340-acre coal tract on the Dickerson Run Branch of the Pittsburgh, McKeesport, and Youghiogheny Railroad to Capt. C. S. Brown of Pittsburgh, and the two men built the large Nellie works. The new Atlas Coke Company, incorporated in Pittsburgh in May 1885, bought the Colvin works from the Dunbar Furnace Company and withdrew from the Coke Producers Association, a grouping of smaller producers subject to direction by the syndicate. In spring 1886, shortly after the Coke Syndicate was renewed for another year, rumors warned of a rival group forming, made up of all the independent operators and backed by Pittsburgh and Baltimore capital, including the Baltimore and Ohio Railroad. However, this never came to anything. Meanwhile, the syndicate continued to bear the burden of trying to hold up prices. In September 1886, responding to a drop in demand, it once more decided to close all coke works it controlled every Wednesday.[56]

Another result of coordinated control was to provoke a reaction by blast furnace operators, who were faced with increasing trading difficulties as iron prices began falling. Immediately after the syndicate was formed, Cambria Iron Company was reported as having "decided objections" to it and to be looking for more coke ovens of its own. The press warmed to the prospects of conflict: "If it gets them, it will not be the fault of the syndicate that controls the new dispensation." Before the end of

1884, the syndicate was accusing the iron masters, in their eagerness to break up the coke association and gain lower prices, of supporting outside coke makers.[57] Next year Cambria added the Mahoning coke works to its existing oven capacity.

As capacity increased the Coke Syndicate's ability to restrict output and hold up prices was undermined. The northern part of the coal basin was an area of particularly active expansion at this time, though the scale achieved was sometimes different from that initially announced. In 1887 the new Calumet Coke Company began to develop a coal tract of 5,000 acres, with the expectation that it would build up to 1,000 ovens; by 1890 it had completed only 225. Nearer to Latrobe, the Hostetter, Baggaley group built up by various purchases a holding of 4,300 acres of coal and planned a mine and 500 ovens. By 1890 they had two works and over 600 ovens. (Neither Hostetter nor Baggaley were members of the company, which instead took its name from a tract of coal; three directors were from Pittsburgh, one from New York, and another lived in London.) Even prominent members of the syndicate were unwilling to forego expansion. Early in 1887 the Connellsville Coke and Iron Company began to sink a third shaft, halfway between Leisenring 1 and 2, that would supply another 500 ovens. Schoonmaker was adding 130 ovens to the 320 already at Redstone works. J. W. Moore, who by then had works in both the northern and southern parts of the field at Mammoth and Wynn, several times refused to join the syndicate. They offered $1.5 million to buy him out for the second time, but Moore held onto his works.[58]

By the end of 1887 the syndicate was nearing the end of its life, weakened by internal dissension. Frick, controlling by far the largest capacity, was at odds with his colleagues over $90,000 they owed him. When his claim was settled and he pressed for a pool including all operators, Edward Leisenring opposed the idea of including Moore in their organization, "because he is such a man that makes trouble." Other important outsiders including Rainey and Cochran would not join. Pooling arrangements were abandoned in March 1888. That autumn an attempt was made to form an association of smaller coke producers, centered on Moore. It seemed promising for a time, but failed to make much impact. A return to a more certain way of achieving coordination, combination of companies, was soon actively underway.[59]

Though 1888 was a year of record coke output, the price was lower than at any time since 1884. In June, eighteen of the region's seventy-five plants were wholly idle and another sixteen partially so, putting nearly one-quarter of 13,047 ovens out of production. Yet the strong momentum for expansion remained, with an increase in total ovens of well over one-sixth during the year. By now some producers, and notably the Leisenrings, were becoming discouraged by the difficulties of the trade, their frustrated efforts to control output and prices, and unhappy experiences with labor relations. By the fall of 1888, Edward Leisenring was already trying to interest Frick in acquiring some Connellsville Coke and Iron stock, "with a view of our working together and helping one another in the trade."[60] He badly misjudged his man, who was not the sort to work with others on a basis of equality. In fact, over the next twelve months, H. C. Frick Coke once again became the nucleus of a series of major combinations of capacity. These moves proved the fine sense of timing of the man who directed its major decisions.

Connellsville coke averaged $1.34 in 1889, but the main acquisitions were made during summer when trade was dull and prices nearer $.90 than $1.00 a ton. H. C. Frick Coke then acquired three major operations, Moore, Schoonmaker, and Connellsville Coal and Iron, as well as a number of smaller companies, making what was already by far the biggest single unit in the region into the dominating firm. Schoonmaker, who controlled 5,000 acres of coal lands, 1,500 ovens, and 400 rail cars, approached Frick in early March with the suggestion that he should be bought out. At first Frick was reluctant, and he later explained his reason to Chicago business colleague Jay Morse: "There are so many more ovens built now than is really needed—and yet there are parties starting new plants—that I cannot see very much in the near future for coke men, and I have no doubt but what there will be some pretty cheap coke properties for sale within the next year or two."[61] Within fifteen days, though, the H. C. Frick board approved the purchase of Schoonmaker for $0.65 million. J. W. Moore controlled 579 ovens that were acquired despite the fact that Thomas Lynch seems to have had scant regard for their quality. However, Connellsville Coke and Iron proved harder to get. Leisenring asked $3 million. In turn Frick pointed out that Carnegie, as majority stockholder in "his" company, was reluctant to pay a high price and that, in the opinion of their own experts, $500,000 would have to be spent to bring these operations up to standard. An attempt to make the acquisition with bonds failed in May, but on 1 July 1889 the Frick Company paid the $3 million Leisenring originally had asked for—$500,000 down, five payments of $100,000 over the next year, and $2 million in bonds. Despite Frick's reservations, it was a price that was later recognized as barely covering the investments made and interest on them up to the time of sale. As the *Connellsville Courier* put it, "Mr. Frick got a bargain."[62] When organized in April 1882, the H. C. Frick Coke Company had been capitalized at $2 million. Acquisitions increased the company's value to $3 million in 1885 and $5 million by 1889.

As a result of these takeovers, by late summer 1889 H. C. Frick Coke controlled 57 percent, or 8,050, of the 14,060 ovens in the district; less than three years before they had held only 3,453 out of 12,918. Soon there were further acquisitions, though the pace of expansion slackened. In autumn Frick absorbed Davis, Garret, and Company and negotiated for the Mayer Coke Company west of Leisenring 3. Late in the year he was incorrectly reported to have purchased part of the three-plant Rainey enterprise. When asked to name a price for his properties, Rainey had replied that he would think the matter over and let Frick know, but nothing more was heard from him. There was speculation of negotiations with Cambria Iron for the 600 ovens at the Wheeler, Morrell, and Mahoning works, but no change of ownership occured.[63] Then during 1890 Frick Coke bought the coal lands of the J. A. Strickler Coke Company and half the capital of the much bigger Hostetter-Connellsville Coal Company. By that autumn it owned or controlled more than half the Coke Region's coal lands and almost 63 percent of its ovens, had a daily capacity of 1,100 cars of coke, and operated thirty-five miles of railroad. Its workforce was 11,000 men.[64] Though it was unrivalled in scale and comprehensiveness, there remained one or two other important, independent companies in the region, and the creation of new firms continued.

In 1886 the W. J. Rainey Company had controlled only two mines and coke works, Fort Hill with 144 beehive ovens and the Grace works at Moyer with 292. By 1890 major extensions had been made at both works, and two new ones had been brought in near Fort Hill, Rainey north of the Youghiogheny and Paul, originally built by James Cochran in 1887. The other major independent to survive this round of consolidation was the McClure Coke Company. In autumn 1886 McClure controlled ten works with 1,264 ovens. In September 1889 there was speculation that Frick would absorb McClure, but instead the latter began its own, though much smaller, expansion program. By 1891 it had made small extensions to three plants and acquired the Mullen works of Strickler and Company and A. C. Cochran's Buckeye works. These operations were concentrated between Scottdale and Mt. Pleasant, but in the autumn of 1889, McClure broke away from this area when the company spent a reported $131,500 to buy the 134 ovens, 175 acres of coal lands, and other properties of Robert Hogsett at Lemont in the southern part of the basin. Immediately, it planned to buy more coal and put up another 100 ovens. Within five years there were two McClure works and 534 ovens at Lemont. Its thirteen works and 2,153 ovens meant this company was now the second largest in the region, far ahead of Rainey's six works and 1,420 ovens.[65]

During the autumn of 1889, H. C. Frick and McClure were actively competing to buy their smaller rivals. These lesser producers considered banding together into a new 1,500-oven group as the only effective way of protecting themselves against unwelcome attentions from these predators and securing freight rates comparable with those negotiated by the bigger concerns. The smaller companies failed to make this link. In other instances sale of coal and ovens freed enterprise and capital to seek out opportunities elsewhere. For the Leisenrings this meant development of coal

H. C. Frick, *circa* 1890. *Courtesy of Frick Art and Historical Center, Frick Archives*

lands and the building of ovens in southwestern Virginia. In other cases, notably with J. W. Moore, it brought a search for further new possibilities in southwestern Pennsylvania.

After high activity in 1890, coke production fell sharply in 1891, revived in 1892, and then was even more seriously depressed in 1893. The following year output increased again, but the average price at $1.00 a ton was lower than in any year since the 1870s. During 1895 Carnegie tried and failed, partly because of his clumsiness, partly as a result of Frick's touchiness, to engineer a merger of the Rainey Company into Frick Coke. Frick dismissively but inaccurately remarked late in these negotiations, "Rainey is but a drop in the bucket." By 1895 production was higher than ever

Table 2.10 H. C. Frick Coke Company major acquisitions and new controlling interests, 1889

Company	Coal land (acres)	Coke works	Number of ovens
J. W. Moore	2,300	Mammoth Wynn	579
J. M. Schoonmaker	ca. 5,000	Alice Jimtown Redstone Sterling	ca. 1,500
Connellsville Coke and Iron	9,000	Leisenring No. 1 Leisenring No. 2 Leisenring No. 3	1,504
United Coal and Coke	n.a.	Mutual	ca. 150
Kyle Coke Company	n.a.	Kyle	ca. 160
Fayette Coke & Furnace	n.a.	Oliphant	ca. 130

SOURCES: H. C. Frick Company minutes, Frick Papers; *EMJ* (various issues as listed in the notes to this chapter).

NOTE: The "number of ovens" is the combined total for all works listed for a company.

before, but prices were again low and another flurry of merger activity occurred. H. C. Frick Coke took over the Youngstown Coke Company, and for about $4 million it also acquired McClure Coke, which brought in over 2,000 ovens. Although until 1903 McClure properties continued to be operated under the old company name, in the second half of the 1890s H. C. Frick Coke was effectively in control of two-thirds of the district's 60,000 acres of coal and 18,000 ovens. Much of Frick's coal was in the center of the basin and of the best quality, and its organization was generally superior to that of its rivals so that the real extent of its preeminence was even greater than these proportions suggest. As the head of the Pennsylvania Bureau of Mines wrote in 1898: "The officers and managers of this company from its distinguished founder down have been uniformly active, energetic, and progressive, and to these marked characteristics of management may in large measure be attributed the company's present commanding position." Others shared this high opinion, including Charles M. Schwab, the new president of Carnegie Steel. He reported on a visit to their associated H. C. Frick Coke properties in July 1898: "Our whole trip was indeed most interesting. . . . The operations of Coke making, while comparatively simple as compared with Steel, were carried on in an excellent manner, and . . . above all, the condition and equipment of all the works we visited were model in every respect."[66]

The approach to monopoly in the coke region in the 1890s was accompanied by generally higher prices than in the previous decade, with the exception of 1893–1894 and, to a lesser extent, 1895. On the other hand, until the decade's last three years,

Table 2.11 H. C. Frick Coke Company production assets, 1882, 1890, and late 1900

Year	Coal lands (acres)	Coke works	Coke ovens
1882	3,000	9	1,022
1890	35,000	42	10,046
1900[a]	38,010	41	10,473

SOURCE: H. C. Frick Company Papers, U.S. Steel Corporation Archives.
a. includes McClure Coke Company

there seems to have been more under use of coke capacity even than in the 1880s, though the capacity figures on which such an assessment depends were very much less certain than prices. Although 1896 was the best year for prices since 1890, by late summer and early autumn only about one-third of the oven capacity was being used. Carnegie felt moved to comfort Frick: "You must be sad when you look at the coke business; but do not be discouraged, Connellsville coal is a very good thing to keep; it will do to bank on." That year Carnegie also gave unqualified support to Frick's aspirations to control the whole industry: "We cannot go wrong now in securing all the Connellsville coke property we can, since we have so much." However, within a year of this dismal operating situation, another boom was underway: "New ovens are being fired up, production continues on the jump, while the shipments are limited only by the car supply. The production last week aggregated 140,000 tons, as compared with 56,000 tons for the corresponding week of last year."[67] The revival was no flash in the pan; each of the next three years turned out better than the last. The 1899 average price was higher than that of any for twenty years with almost three times as many ovens in operation. By now a quite different problem was looming. It was becoming clear that in future periods of high activity, especially if large-scale expansion in pig iron production continued, Connellsville would be unable to meet the calls made upon it. Extension of production to nearby areas, previously considered unsuitable; increased output from smaller, already established beehive districts in other parts of the Appalachian plateau; and investment in production by technologically more sophisticated methods would all be essential.

Control of Connellsville Coke Manufacture by Iron and Steel Firms

Development of the coke region began with local entrepreneurs. Sometime later men from as far away as the "city"—Pittsburgh—began to invest the modest amounts of capital needed to enter what was still a small-scale and technically simple activity. There were occasional bigger outside interests whose money had been made in different lines of business as with Rainey or the Leisenrings. An important, increasing, and eventually dominant contribution came from iron manufacturers. As the making of pig iron became above all an adjunct of the steel and rolling-mill industry, it was more vital than ever to ensure that fuel supply was not a weak link in the chain of production. In short, as with iron-ore mining, coke production became an integral part of the iron and steel complexes that in the decades on either side of 1900 grew and spread across the northeastern United States. Though these mineral sectors provided the foundations for the whole industrial pyramid, the largest profits were made in the stages of manufacture that further processed the raw materials into capital or consumer goods. Such a connection brought not only expansion but also subservience to the coke trade.

Well into the twentieth century, unattached coke works—"merchant" ovens—remained important, but "furnace" ovens, controlled by the makers of iron, grew in relative significance. In the summer of 1881, of some 6,680 Connellsville district ovens, *Iron Age* reckoned that 4,800 were merchant and 1,880, or 28 percent, were furnace ovens. Eleven years later 61.2 percent of all ovens were subsidiaries of iron companies or were owned by the H. C. Frick Coke Company, which in many ways was the same thing.

For a number of reasons ironmasters desired to control their coke supply even if it lay fifty or perhaps as much as three hundred miles from their furnaces. First, the quality of coke was an important factor in determining the quality of pig iron. It affected the productivity of their furnaces. Even when separated by distance, ownership or large financial interest gave some hope of control over the character of the fuel delivered to the furnace. Second, although economy in the use of fuel was going ahead rapidly in the latter part of the century, the cost of coke remained an important factor in the price of iron. Control of ovens made it possible to avoid at least some of the short-term oscillations in fuel prices. The furnace operator might even benefit permanently from reduced prices for coke in return for his contribution to the initial capital outlay in building or buying oven capacity. Third, assured delivery was itself important. When the trade was stretched to meet demand at times of high activity, ownership or part interest might mean that supplies could be guaranteed when rivals were compelled to dampen down their furnaces for want of fuel. In terms of quality, price, and availability alike, the ironmaster could buy increased security by controlling at least some of his coke supply. The uncertainties resulting from a lack of such control were well illustrated in the plea for help from J. G. Butler, general manager of the Brier Hill Iron and Coal Company, to Frick during fall 1890:

I think it time that some move be made in the direction of a lower price for coke. . . . We are confronted with Southern pig iron which is now being sold on the basis of $9.00 per ton on cars in the South. [That year the average price per gross ton for no.1 foundry iron in Philadelphia was $18.40, and Bessemer pig in Pittsburgh cost $18.85.][68] This valley is being flooded with it. More than ten thousand tons have been sold here within a week past and I think that you will find that large blocks of it are being taken in Pittsburgh. The Southern people are aided by the railroads. The freight from Birmingham to Cincinnati is $2.75 per ton and from Cincinnati to Chicago $1.25. Our western trade is gone. I hope you will consider the matter seriously and I will call and discuss it the next time I am in Pittsburgh.[69]

A first phase of iron trade investment occurred during the 1860s, when the tonnage of iron made by use of bituminous coal and coke increased by 350 percent and Pittsburgh iron production began to grow rapidly.[70] Shortly after the big price rises of 1864, Pittsburgh ironmasters began moving into the coke industry. Graff, Bennett, and Company had obtained almost all their coke supplies since 1860 from the Sterling ovens of Stewart Strickler. They now paid some $35,000 for a one-third share in his coke works. A few months later Shoenberger bought the other two-thirds. During 1865 Shoenberger also acquired one-third of Cochran's Fayette Coke Works.[71] The Laughlin interests, whose first Eliza blast furnace had been built five years before, followed a different line to the same goal, putting up coke works at Tyrone near Broadford. In 1875 Tyrone contained 105 ovens, and by 1879–1880 the number had increased to 141.

Perhaps surprisingly, Valleys ironworks, which originally used raw coal, were among the early firms to establish their own ovens. In 1879 John Stambaugh, Henry Bonnell, Augustus Cornell, and Thomas Kennedy, each managing Youngstown area blast furnaces, joined to form the Youngstown Coke Company, which built the Stambaugh coke works between Dunbar and Uniontown. By 1882 this contained 240 ovens whose whole output was shipped to Youngstown. Nearer Dunbar was the Mahoning coke works of Brown, Bonnell, and Company, also of Youngstown. In 1885 a syndicate of Valleys furnaces was reported to have been formed to buy a large block of Connellsville coal with a view to making its own coke.[72] The rapid expansion of Bessemer plants and rail mills, representing a large investment, and the fact that they were subject to pressure from railroads to ensure speedy delivery for new construction, made it essential for them to do everything possible to prevent a break in iron production. Large assured coke supplies became essential. The Cambria Iron Company was the first major steel maker to take the initiative. It began to make Bessemer steel in 1871. By 1875 the managers realized that coke made from Johnstown area coal, previously used in their furnaces, was unsuitable for large-scale smelting of Lake ores to produce Bessemer iron. Though pure and with little ash, the locally made coke was too soft for the bigger furnaces, which became too hot in their upper parts and

60   The Maturing Industry

Iron smelters known to be using Connellsville coke, 1879.

not hot enough below. Daniel Morrell, Cambria's general manager, asked John Fulton to look into the matter, and he proved that the harder, more cellular Connellsville coke possessed the qualities their own coke lacked. During 1879–1880 Cambria built the Morrell Coke works midway between Dunbar and Connellsville. In spring 1884, when the Coke Syndicate was trying to push up coke prices, it bought the Connellsville Gas Coal Company's Wheeler ovens. That summer Frick made an unsuccessful attempt to form an association with Cambria, offering to buy their coke works and in return give them a controlling interest in his Morewood coal and coke properties "at a fair price." Early the following year Cambria was said to be negotiating for ovens at Cokeville, near Blairsville, but instead in November paid $35,000 for the one-hundred-oven Mahoning coke works, which had passed to the control of the National Bank of Fayette County at the time of the failure of Brown, Bonnell.[73] By 1886 the Cambria Iron Company controlled six hundred ovens.

The Carnegie interests, involved first with iron and from 1875 also in steel manufacture, took many years to find an acceptable supply of coke, then becoming at a stroke the controllers of the largest capacity in the region. Their first blast furnace,

Lucy, was blown in during early summer 1872. Already they had decided to invest in a coke works at Larimer station, some twenty miles away along the PRR mainline. Eighty ovens were put up there in 1871, forty more in 1872, and another twenty in 1874; that same year they also built fifty ovens farther east at Monastery. At both works, in contrast to the situation in the main part of the coke region, coal had to be washed before it was charged. In 1877 a second Lucy furnace started work, and in 1878 and 1879 three blast furnaces were built to supply iron to the Edgar Thomson Bessemer plant. To meet some of these fuel requirements, sixty more ovens were built at both coke works in 1880. Even together, they were unable to satisfy long-term needs, and the Carnegies began to search for a suitable connection in the coke region. Early in 1880 they secured an option on half the capital in the A. A. Hutchinson Globe and Standard works for $190,000. The next year they contemplated a variety of options to meet their supply needs: acquiring eight thousand acres of coal lands, purchasing coal from W. J. Rainey or entering into a possible cooperative development with him, acquiring Morgan's plant at Latrobe, or buying the Davidson works. At the beginning of 1882, they again negotiated for half of Hutchinson's interests. None of these efforts came to fruition, but by the end of this period the Carnegies had agreed in principle to a close link with Frick's coke operations.[74]

In December 1881 Andrew Carnegie and Henry Clay Frick agreed on an association of their iron/steel and coal/coke interests. The formal arrangements were completed in April 1882. By that time Frick controlled 1,026 ovens at nine plants, the effi-

Table 2.12 Operations and production costs at H. C. Frick Coke Company plants, December 1882

Plant	No. of ovens	Coke made (tons)	Cost of coal at ovens per ton (cents)	Cost of coke making per ton (cents)	Total cost per ton manufactured (cents)	Net cost of coke after extras & deductions[a] (cents)
Henry Clay	100	3,759	n.a.	n.a.	n.a.	n.a.
Frick	106	3,417	38.91	65.62	104.53	91.13
Morgan	168	5,841	36.16	57.19	93.35	89.67
Foundry	74	2,520	35.57	59.73	95.30	95.33
White	148	5,274	42.00	52.21	94.21	93.21
Eagle	80	2,681	40.05	55.34	95.39	90.47
Summit	142	4,846	35.67	63.89	99.56	96.57
Tip Top	56	2,003	41.12	53.03	94.15	96.93
Valleys	152	5,237	40.00	54.90	94.90	74.51
Monastery	208	7,650	42.53	76.80	119.33	121.40
Total	1,234	43,232				

SOURCE: H. C. Frick Coke Company cost sheet, Frick Papers.

a. Extras include superintendence and overheads; deductions include store profits, house and farm rents, coal sales, and car service.

ciency and costs of which varied widely. Carnegie's Monastery works—but not Larimer—were transferred to H. C. Frick Coke. From this time the Carnegie furnaces took a large share of the Frick coke, but a still greater tonnage was sold to others. For instance, in the fourteen months prior to the end of February 1883, the first period in which the two operations were operating together, the coke company made 596,000 tons of coke and sold an additional 350,000 tons on behalf of other makers. Of this 946,000-ton total, the Lucy and Edgar Thomson furnaces took only 302,000 tons, 628,000 tons was railed east and west from the coke region, and 16,000 tons were shipped by river.[75] The Carnegies initially acquired a large share of the coke company's capital; within two years they owned more of it than its nominal head. In turn Frick ensured that much of their increasing capital involvement was used to finance further acquisitions among the fifty-seven coke works outside his control in 1882. By November 1888 only 12,611 of the 60,000 fifty-dollar shares in H. C. Frick Coke were owned by Frick; Andrew Carnegie held 14,950 and Carnegie Brothers, 14,208.

Henry Oliver was at the center of another, though much smaller, Pittsburgh group that bought its way into coke. He had long had interests in that region's affairs: in 1875 he was an active promoter of the Pittsburgh and Lake Erie Railroad and seven years later was involved in the Pittsburgh, McKeesport, and Youghiogheny. Oliver organized the company that in 1891 leased coal lands near Uniontown and built the three "Oliver" coke works. By 1897, with William P. Snyder, he had formed the Oliver and Snyder Steel Company, which in addition to two blast furnace plants, steel works, and the Oliver coke ovens, also controlled coal lands in the Unity section of the region.[76]

Outside Pittsburgh, the greatest concentration of steel and supporting iron capacity was in Chicago. Into the 1880s Chicago was indeed more important in steel making, though growing less spectacularly—between 1875 and 1882 Illinois production of Bessemer steel increased from 136,000 to 397,000 net tons, while that of Allegheny County went up from 15,500 to 258,000 tons. The three major Illinois companies were Union, Joliet, and the North Chicago Rolling Mill Company. In efforts to control an important part of their coke requirements—a move that would also give them power to influence conditions of supply for others—they proceeded, like Carnegie, through a combination of independent construction and association with established coke makers. The Leith coke works south of Uniontown was built in 1881 by the Chicago and Connellsville Coke Company, controlled by Joliet Steel. Initially provided with 106 ovens, it had 284 five years later. At the beginning of 1886, the North Chicago Rolling Mill Company reportedly spent $250,000 on one thousand acres of coal land near Uniontown and planned 700 ovens for the site.[77] This huge coke project for the so-called Revere tract—which contained a relatively small coal reserve—did not come to fruition because all three Chicago firms became involved in a major collaborative venture in the form of the incongruously named South West Coal and Coke Company. Though the motivation came from their own trading position, the basis on which the coke company was built was again shaped by the ambitions and drive of Henry Clay Frick.

In 1879 Frick acquired a farm midway between Mt. Pleasant and the Greensburg to Scottdale section of the South West Pennsylvania Railroad. He then organized the Morewood Coke Company to work a mine on the northern extension of the June Bug Branch of the railroad. The coke works built there was the most thoroughly equipped plant of its time. By 1882, with 470 ovens, it was also one of the biggest in the region, shipping about one thousand tons of coke daily.[78] Soon afterward, coke prices fell as expansion of the industry outstripped that of its markets. By autumn 1883 Frick was pressing Carnegie to buy Morewood and also offered to bring in the Hutchinson works, the South West ovens at Tarr Station, and the old Stoner Hitchman works containing one thousand acres of coal. His suggestions were coolly received. As Carnegie's cousin George Lauder put it: "I do not see why we should wish to take these properties into the Frick Co. . . . Let Frick worry with them is my verdict." Having failed in this direction and in an attempt to interest Cambria Iron, Frick approached his friend Andrew Mellon. He indicated that the operation was making profits on coke, houses, and store sales equal to about $50,000 a year, even though only about 60 percent of its ovens were then at work. Again he failed to secure a buyer. Then in September 1885 an agreement between South West and a combination of Frick and the Ferguson brothers brought Morewood into the South West group, which also included the former Warden operations north of Stonerville, a plant by then renamed the American works. Three months later South West Coal and Coke paid $85,000 for the Dillinger and Tarr plant just south of Tarr Station. This gave the company 2,400 acres of coal and 668 ovens. In November it became part owned by the Joliet and Union steel companies, with a minority share owned by Frick as president, who, as the experienced coke maker, made operational decisions. The capital of South West Coal and Coke was $1 million; Frick's share was $200,000. Under the initial agreement the Chicago companies were to pay $1.10 per ton for coke when the syndicate price was $1.20. Four years later, when the properties of J. M. Schoonmaker were acquired by H. C. Frick Coke, the opportunity was taken to concentrate operations geographically. Through a rearrangement of ownership, Leith works became part of the H. C. Frick Coke Company and Schoonmaker's Alice works were transferred to South West Coal and Coke. Together the four South West works made up a

Table 2.13 Ovens incorporated in South West Coal and Coke Company, 1882–1900

Work	1882	1886	1890	1894	1900
SW 1. Morewood	470	470	620	620	625
SW 2. Alice	200	250	251	251	251
SW 3. Dillinger and Tarr	66	130	180	180	205
SW 4. American	74	72	100	151	151

SOURCE: H. C. Frick Company Papers, U.S. Steel Corporation Archives.

major block of coal and oven capacity at the northern end of the main coke district. In addition, there was an agreement between the Chicago iron and steel companies and the H. C. Frick Coke Company for supplementary supplies.[79]

Although formed to provide Chicago with assured supplies of good coke at reliable, reasonable prices, and no doubt advantageous in these respects, over the years the South West operations faced numerous problems, their severity being exacerbated by the distance that separated coke production and consumption. There were recurrent disputes about coke quality and price, labor, and freight charges. The steel companies now and again considered whether they should turn to alternative sources of supply.

The coke supplied was not of a consistent high standard. Frick was often at a loss to explain these deficiencies. Sometimes he was made impatient by the criticisms from his business colleagues, and one occasion he seemed confused. Early in September 1886, before the North Chicago Rolling Mill Company joined South West Coal and Coke, its president, Orrin Potter, complained about the coke his company was receiving. The next day Frick dictated a reply, which he marked "Confidential." He tried to explain away the problem, even attributing it in part to conditions at the furnaces, but was forced to recognize there had also been deficiencies at his end. "There has been more or less complaint, generally, since the strike in the Connellsville coke region. All the manufacturers of coke have, since the strike, had complaints from furnace companies about the quality of coke; and I have given the manufacture of it at our Works close attention, and from the appearance of the coke I cannot see but that it is fully as good as any we have ever made." After citing problems with other makers, he asked Potter, "Don't you think the extremely warm weather we have had this summer has had much to do with the poor results from coke, which cooler weather may remedy?" Then, before ending with a promise of care and an admission that things did go wrong, he added what to a man of Potter's background might have seemed a very provocative remark: "We have had little if any complaint from Messrs Carnegie Brothers and Co., and I am sure the general run of coke sent them is not better than that sent some other customers of ours who have complained. On January 1st next, when we commence shipments to you, it will be our endeavor to please you, and we hope we can. I am very sorry to say, however, that, not having as good control of labor as formerly, even with closest attention to our business, Furnace Companies often have reason to complain."[80] In 1888 W. R. Stirling of Joliet pointed out that the sulfur content of their coke was higher than "the average first class Connellsville coke." Six months later a letter from H. A. Gray of Union showed how irritating such a flow of complaints could become: "I have already suggested to Mr. Stirling that we send some man to the South West works to inspect the coal and coke and manner of mining and coking, but he says he does not know of any one who would be suitable to do this. Later however, we may act on this." In March 1888 Thomas Lynch of H. C. Frick Coke referred to a Mr. Clark, representative of the North Chicago Rolling Mill Company, as: "the greatest 'busy body' I ever saw and it seems to me is attending to everything in this region except that which I understand he is paid for—inspecting coke."[81]

Correspondence often reveals Frick trying to hold the center ground between his works managers and his Chicago business partners. For instance, in April 1889 he told Morris Ramsay at Mt. Pleasant: "We are getting quite a number of complaints of coke being loaded by you at your various works. Please look into the matter, and see that you load nothing but a first class article of coke and that it is loaded clean and free from dirt and ashes." A few weeks later, responding to another complaint from Stirling about high sulfur figures, he sent the South West secretary and treasurer, F. W. Haskell, to look into the matter. He either failed to understand why their coke was not good or denied that this was the case. Saying Lynch had assured him that some coke shipped to Union works by H. C. Frick Coke was as good as could be made in the region, he made clear his frustration by yet again attempting to teach the ironmakers their trade: "The trouble with you people, I am afraid, is that you are trying to get along with too little coke per ton of iron."[82]

Disputes over quality highlighted the chemist's role in the industry, and thereby provided another cause for disagreement between coke makers and furnacemen. To coke makers it must have seemed the iron works were preoccupied with chemical analyses, whereas Frick had the practical manufacturer's scant regard for careful research into his product. Again, distance added color to both complaints and responses. Stirling's unfavorable comparison of their coke with the general run of Connellsville coke exposed these differing points of view: "Your letter of the 17th received. I am not prepared to accept Mr. Sweeny's statement regarding the quality of coke or correctness of analysis. It at any rate has no bearing on the present question, as the chemist who was employed at Leith works is not employed at Joliet." He pointed out their own results had been checked by chemists including Otto Wuth. However, a few months after this, in a vividly reported incident, Wuth made clear how little faith could be placed in his analyses. Haskell reported the situation to Frick:

Last Saturday (9th inst) Dr. Otto Wuth, the Chemist who has been analyzing coal and coke for us, called at this office and told me that the results of his analyses depended entirely upon ourselves, that he could help or hurt us as we might ourselves decide, that he never asked work from anybody but that we had better let him make things all right. The above was not said at once and was enveloped in a great mass of other words, but such was the meat of his discourse, and was so understood by Mr. Ramsay, who was present, as well as by myself. Aside from the unpleasantness of dealing with a man who holds our business integrity so lightly I feel that future results from this man cannot be relied upon. I therefore hope that you will concur with my opinion that our future work in this line should be placed elsewhere.

Frick wrote across the head of Haskell's letter: "Answered verbally not to have anything further to do with the Dr."[83] Understandably, such an episode reinforced Frick's low opinion of chemists. In July the Chicago interests, now combined as the Illinois Steel Company, sent another chemist, named Julian, to Morewood to make daily analyses of coal and coke. Frick seemed constructive, instructing Morris Ramsay, "Please furnish him every facility required and see that he is comfortably located in a good boarding house or hotel." But by the following summer, when yet another chemist was pressing South West Coal and Coke for a higher salary, Frick's prejudices were once more made plain: "I would not pay Mr. Carr the increased salary. If he is not satisfied I would leave him quit. I cannot see much use in a chemist anyway." By autumn Carr had indeed resigned and Frick's response was predictable: "We will endeavor to get on without a chemist for the next few months." Chicago thought differently, and in less than three weeks Frick informed Ramsay: "Am surprised that the Illinois Steel Company should have sent on a chemist. I have written them that I think it a useless expense. Please economize in every way you can." He made no attempt to conceal this opinion. To H. S. Smith, Illinois Steel's second vice president, he plainly spelled out his attitude to the new man, Mr. Hutzel: "If I thought it would be of the least good I would not object, but it looks to me like a waste of money."[84]

The cost and nuisance value of chemists were minor irritants in the relations between Connellsville and Chicago as compared with labor issues. Chemists monitored factors affecting furnace performance; the efforts of miners and coke men decided whether the furnaces operated or not. As with the better-known case of the Carnegie interest in H. C. Frick Coke, the Chicago firms proved to be more interested in ensuring regular supplies to enable them to meet orders for finished products and keep their works running than in paring wages or social expenditures in the coke region to a minimum. Naturally, such a division of interest between coke and steel was a fruitful source of policy differences. The agreement that produced South West Coal and Coke was approved at the beginning of November 1885; within twelve weeks the company was involved in its first clash with labor. On 18 January, writing to Morse, Frick recognized the pressures that might result, though by reference to their main competitor rather than explicitly to their own circumstances:

We are considerably mixed up just now over labor trouble in the Connellsville region. Since the first of January the men have been very uneasy, and at a number of works would come out one day and go back the next. We did not experience any trouble until last Wednesday at Morewood when the men quit work without making any demands. . . . If the Edgar Thomson trouble is adjusted this afternoon, it may put us in an awkward position, as I fear that Mr. Andrew Carnegie would insist upon us running without regard to what damage it might do us in the future. There is no question but that this strike should be defeated and no advance paid under the circumstances. If we are compelled to give in it only means more trouble in the future, while if we win it will be smooth sailing the balance of the year; and if trade justifies it, we can give them an advance along about the first of April or first of May.

In the course of two months in the middle of 1886, strikes cost South West $14,437.[85] By September, Morse was worrying about the effect demands made at Leith might have on other coke works and thereby on the rest of their business: "You cannot afford to have a general racket without proper notice is given us all. We certainly cannot stop our Works nor can other Mills until the winter. The Railroads at present are pressing for rails that are under contract. They require them promptly for the next ninety days as they are under obligations to the contractors who are grading new tracks for them, and I cannot see how we can stop the wheel rolling for at least four months to have a fight with your men. Don't fail to give us plenty of notice if there is any danger of this occurring." A few weeks later as they seemed to be sliding into crisis, he wrote, "You certainly are in a mighty bad shape and it is liable to place us in one equally as bad." In December he urged, "Do not let a strike occur—If it has got to come let the steelmen get together and decide when they will have it."[86] The following summer brought the dramatic incident in which Carnegie forced Frick to grant the wage demands of their coke company men in order to ensure that his mills should not be forced to close. In contrast, the Chicago companies allowed South West to stand firm with the other main coke firms against the workers. Even so, time and again they counted the cost of their loyalty and emphasized that they were looking to an early settlement that might allow them to keep at work. Before mid-July, Morse reckoned the strike had cost Union Steel alone at least $150,000. He and Stirling pressed for more coke, but otherwise the messages they sent were mixed: sometimes hard, more often conciliatory. Morse was prepared to endorse police protection for men who were willing to work and deplored as a sign of weakness "the present policy of waiting to see what they will do at Leisenring and Schoonmaker's." Frustration with both the problem and their remoteness from the point of action came out as well: "It has been disappointing from the beginning to the end, Carnegie's action, first, and the hopeful delay, since, but which seemed to us, here, as a sort of paralysis among the managers in which they neither shot or threw away the gun, but tinkered away, and they may have the best of reasons for that. We do not claim to be better judges than they are, but in conversation with Mr. Porter, today, we have made up our minds that we must have coke or we must disappoint all the railroads that we are under contract for our rails." Stirling too emphasized the urgent need for coke deliveries so that their works "should be kept absolutely running." He communicated ideas for a labor policy that, however wise, must have been galling to managers who held a much less idealistic view of relations with their employees and had to struggle with day-to-day problems on the spot: "It is my strong desire that we should constantly be selecting our men at the South West during this depressed time and while we are paying better wages than our neighbors, so that we may have the pick of the region working for us, and that we should treat them better than the average treatment in the region, that when rates advance and labor is in demand these picked men will appreciate what we have done for them and will stay with us. I do not like to see wages reduced to a starvation point as I think they were the last time coke was at its lowest price, and if we can hold our own at our works, or make a small margin in these times, I am willing to pay labor a fair rate, expecting that I will reap some benefit from so doing."[87] The strike dragged on, while the Carnegie works, having forced Frick to give way, obtained the coke they required—as H. A. Gray complained in late summer: "Our principal competitors have not only been able to obtain a supply of coke while our furnaces were idle, but they also obtained it at lower prices than we have had to pay."[88] (Yet, these circumstances notwithstanding, 1887 was a remarkably good year for the Chicago firms. Nationally, Bessemer production was up 29.4 percent on 1886. In Pennsylvania the increase was 16.2 percent; for Allegheny County, including a small tonnage of open-hearth steel, 35.5 percent; but Illinois managed a rise of 60.1 percent.)[89]

In summer 1889 another interesting sidelight was thrown on the way in which distance insulated the majority owners of South West Coal and Coke from everyday realities. At a time of renewed labor troubles, Frick wrote in exasperation to Carnegie: "To say that this coke strike was a surprise to me, and in fact to everyone, would but faintly express it. It leads me to lose almost all faith in men employed at the coke works. The Illinois Steel Company were hot for coke. I, however, soon got Morse here on the ground, and before he left he was a coke—in place of a steel—man, and if I had been governed by his advice, am afraid the settlement would not yet be made, although he was getting telegram after telegram from his people urging the starting of coke works on any terms."[90]

The availability of sufficient rail cars to carry away the coke and the charges for carriage were perennial matters of concern for a major consumer far from its ovens. Both iron production and shipments of coke varied widely from year to year. In 1889 the tonnage shipped was almost 1 million tons, or 19.7 percent, more than in 1888. The 1891 figure was down from 1890 at 1.7 million tons, or only 73.6 percent of the previous year; 1892 was almost back to the 1890 level; and 1893 was 24 percent below 1892. Pittsburgh had a major advantage in access to its coke supplies, and bit-by-bit it was also reducing its disadvantage in haulage of Lake Superior iron ore. In the increasingly keen competition in steel products, the comparative costs of iron manufacture became such an important concern that saving a few cents per ton on the delivered price of ore and coke was an important goal. There were numerous Chicago complaints about railroad services from Connellsville. They were a major factor encouraging furnace operators there to consider possible alternative sources of supply.

Only seven weeks after their business association began, Frick wrote to Morse about the freight rates on coke for Chicago in 1886. That day he had met King of the Baltimore and Ohio Railroad at the Duquesne Club. In response to his expressed hope that coke rates to Chicago should not rise, King had replied that they must. Frick then pointed out this would help build up rival coke production centers and flows of supplies from, for instance, the Reynoldsville coalfield in Jefferson County, the Broad Top coalfield in Huntingdon County, and outside Pennsylvania the New River district of West Virginia, the latter served by the Chesapeake and Ohio Railroad. Frick informed King that he was going east, where he would see the Pennsylvania Railroad management: "The argument that I shall use with the PRR people is that it will build up the Meyersdale district [thirty-seven miles northwest of Cumberland in Somerset County], . . . which is essentially B and O. This point, together with the promise that can be made to the PRR, that they can call for a larger percentage if they want it—I think it will do the business." In fact, the Pennsylvania Railroad became a particular object of criticism by the Chicago firms, and before the end of 1887 Morse was stressing the need to obtain coal lands in Virginia as a means of protection against the high rates they were paying from Connellsville. By the following spring Morse and his colleagues had become outraged by the issue, declaring that they were "willing to do almost anything to protect ourselves against the railroad that has obliged us to pay more than they agreed we should pay when coke was considerably higher than it is today." Later that month Gray and Morse responded to a plan for a two-mile link to the Baltimore and Ohio to free them from dependence on the Pennsylvania. Gray recognized that "if the Pennsylvania Railroad people do not do what is right voluntarily, we must be in a position to compel them." Morse assured Frick nothing would be done without consulting him, but followed up this promise with a tirade: "You say, you think the B & O people are treacherous and unreliable, and have I not the right to the same opinion of the Pennsylvania people? You cannot I think, for a moment, suppose they are anything else but treacherous and unreliable, and until they can satisfy me that hereafter, we are to be taken care of in every respect as well as any other company shipping coke, and that hereafter when they agree to do a thing, it will positively be done as per agreement, I shall continue to seek some means to protect our interests"[91] In June 1889, writing to Frank Thomson, first vice president of the PRR, Frick emphasized the size and importance of South West Coal and Coke and pointed out how easily they could find an alternative carrier for more of their shipments. Only a short line was needed to connect the ovens with the B&O and through that railroad to the Pittsburgh, McKeesport, and Youghiogheny. An alternative was for the PRR to "make some arrangement by which you [Thomson] could permanently secure a large proportion of all of this Chicago business." The next day Frick sent Illinois Steel a tracing of a previously mentioned short track—the Sherrick Run Railroad—to connect to the B&O.[92] High freight rates seemed to pose a serious threat to the long-term position of Connellsville coke in Chicago. On at least two occasions, Morse stressed to Frick that he should take an interest in West Virginian and Virginian coal because the quality of the coke made there, and by implication its freedom from control by northern railroads, seemed to promise an important future in supplying Chicago: "I should like you, through your men, to be familiar with this district, and if after your man has made his report, you want to take an interest in the lands we are buying, we shall be glad to have you do so. I am very much inclined to think coke from W.Va. and further south in the Pocahontas district will find its way North and North West in large quantities. The coke made from these districts is certainly first class in every respect. I think you had better take this matter under consideration and have it looked over, so that you may, if there is a change in the locality from which coke is made for the West and North-west, be ready to take advantage of it."[93]

The various strains affected the relationship between Frick and his Chicago colleagues. During the 1889 strike he tried to calm their fears: "Be patient. You are not hurt yet and not likely to be." But when asked why his men were taking a leading part in the strike, his impatience boiled over. It was not the fault of the coke company management, Frick argued: "If it is anybody's fault it is making a large interest like the coke interest subservient to the steel interest. Poor unfortunate coke has to take the blame when anything goes wrong at the furnaces or steel works." In 1888 and 1889 he was asked about the possibility of supplying additional furnaces in the northwest—the Calumet Iron and Steel Company and two Wisconsin blast furnaces at Maysville and Milwaukee. Replying to Gray, Frick pointed out that their contract provided for them to supply certain furnaces at certain works "located at certain places." "It seems to me that it would be very unfair that you should ask us to supply coke for furnaces and works located at any other points than those mentioned in the contract." Once more exasperated by his partners, he then asked: "You know quite well that there has not, ever since you have been in the coke business, been any particular profit in it; and don't you think the time has about arrived when coke men should make a little money?"[94]

Through the 1890s, South West Coal and Coke remained a major operation, but its freight-rate problems continued. Frick now tried a new device to obtain concessions from the railroads. Earlier, before it joined with the other major Chicago firms in the South West Company, the North Chicago Rolling Mill Company had bought the so-called Revere tract of coal near Uniontown. For a decade this lay undeveloped, but the possibility that further investment might be made there could always be used as a counterweight to the employment of coke from mid-Appalachian fields. In May 1892, writing to James McCrea of the Pennsylvania Railroad, Frick indicated that South West had contemplated putting ovens on the lands, now totaling 2,500 acres, but that "owing to the difference in freight rates Illinois Steel would rather not," but would instead possibly develop coal properties in Virginia. "It might be well for you to give this serious consideration. If, by a reasonable reduction in freight rates to all points in the West you could discourage the development of coal lands in Virginia, it would seem to me to be a wise move on your behalf." He told Gray that he had sent McCrea this letter on Virginian coke: "I think, just at this time, it will assist very much in securing what we are after, namely, lower rates on coke to Chicago, and all points in the West." PRR officials visited Frick. They had cut some freight rates—to the Valleys by 10 cents and to Cleveland by 5 cents a ton—but they had not so far made any other reductions. He urged a 25-cent cut in the Chicago charge, Frick wrote his partners, "but they are a hard lot to handle. Will stick to this and hope they can be brought to time soon." However, when he took it up with McCrea months later, saying that the $2.75 per ton Illinois Steel was paying for freight was too high, he discovered Morse had not fully explained the situation: "So you see that I entered into the discussion with him somewhat handicapped." In fact, with the concessions the PRR was making for Illinois Steel's Blue Island Railroad, that steel company was getting coke via the PRR for only $2.40 a ton, which Frick agreed was a fair rate.[95] But the sense of grievance persisted. During the 1893 depression, national pig iron production fell by over two million tons, and the average price of Bessemer pig at Pittsburgh was only 68 percent the level of four years previous. In June of that year the Illinois Steel directors resolved: "That this board of directors earnestly protests against the action of the railroad companies operating between the Connellsville district and Chicago in making their tariff on coke to Chicago higher relatively than to other points, and it is the judgement of this board that they should either increase their rates on finished iron and steel coming into this company's market in competition with it, or else reduce the present rates on coke to Chicago, so as to do justice to this company."[96] In September 1894, after the great labor dispute of that year, there were new signs of tension in Frick's relations with Morse: "The strike has been a very expensive one to this company, and more so by its desire to keep your furnaces fully supplied." He hoped that for the rest of the year, Illinois Steel would be able to take all their output—probably implying by that remark that they should not further extend their contact with mid-Appalachian coke districts.[97] Morse was now succeeded as head of the Illinois Steel Company by John W. Gates.

Concern about the freight charges persisted. Though 1897 was a good year for steel tonnages, especially keen competition meant very low prices. The average market price of Connellsville coke fob ovens was $1.65. By December Illinois Steel had acted to reduce its fuel costs by increasing use of mid-Appalachian coke after making special arrangements with railroads from that area. After some negotiations with the Virginia Coal and Iron Company (the transferred Leisenring enterprise), Illinois Steel came to an agreement with the Pocahontas Company for 35,000 tons of coke and an option of up to 50,000 tons a month at a rate of $1.16 at the ovens. Arrangements were made with the Erie Railroad for this coke to come up through Columbus to Marion, Ohio, from which point the Erie would carry it to Hammond and on then to its destination by the Chicago, Lake Shore, and Eastern Railway. The delivered cost was expected to be 77 cents less than for Connellsville coke.[98]

During the late 1890s Frick disentangled himself from South West Coal and Coke and therefore from these sources of vexation, but the manner of his going showed how complicated the connection had become. As a result of very different business pressures, by December 1895 he was clearly laboring under great strain. On the same day that he wrote a vital letter to Carnegie in an intensifying quarrel that would lead a few days later to his resignation from the Carnegie Steel chairmanship, Frick was also in contact with Gates. In part, this concerned a visit he was to make to Chicago to settle coke prices for 1896, but it also contained an offer to sell his stock in South West—a proposition made at the request of the steel company. This question of sale lingered on for more than a year, with a fair price as the key issue. In November 1896 he offered his 6,000 shares for $125 a share, or $750,000—little over seven years before he had told Frank Thomson that his financial involvement in South West was $200,000. Illinois Steel declined. The matter became disputatious and had to be taken to arbitration under Mark Hanna in Cleveland. Eventually, Frick was paid for $600,000 of stock by receiving 1,250 acres of the undeveloped Revere tract—his own valuation of this was $1 million. South West now became a wholly owned subsidiary of Illinois Steel. As a parting shot, late in 1898 Lynch sent Frick a brief comparison of South West Coal and Coke and the H. C. Frick Coke Company. The latter had 10,640 ovens and 38,774 acres of unused coal; the former not only lacked comparable ancillary plant but possessed only 1,210 ovens and 2,920 acres of unused coal.[99] In that inferiority, by no means fully cancelled out by Illinois Steel interests farther south in the Appalachian plateau, lay part of the incentive that, within only a year, caused the Chicago firm to become a leader in opening the Lower Connellsville district. Meanwhile, Carnegie Steel had made a bid to become a complete iron and steel operation by not only largely controlling all the mineral supplies it required, but also the means for their delivery. This involved the idea of a privately owned railroad to the coke region.

By the late 1890s not only had the American steel industry achieved world leadership in terms of both size and economic efficiency, but its leading companies were rapidly making their way toward the comprehensive and fully linked operations that were to be a characteristic feature of the twentieth century. Control of reliable supplies of coke played an important part in these industrial complexes. Through 1896–1897, Carnegie Steel had been completing the remarkable integration of all its operations, making it virtually impregnable to competition. Either by ownership or lease it had secured ample Upper Lake ore. The company was building a specially designed mineral line from Conneaut, Ohio, to join with the Union Railroad that linked together its Pittsburgh area plants. Through Conneaut it hoped to secure better rates both east and west for finished products, either by the railroads with which the Pittsburgh, Bessemer, and Lake Erie Railroad made connections or by lake movement. From this position it was inevitable that Andrew Carnegie's fertile brain would think of further improvements, including access to the coke region. In fact, his earliest ideas in this direction preceded those for a railroad to the Lake Erie ore ports.

Early in 1890 H. C. Frick Coke was dissatisfied with the service given by the Pennsylvania Railroad, which was very much overcrowded. In the first half of January, Frick learned that Carnegie had authorized a survey for a possible railroad to enter the coke region from the north. For his part, he believed this might be useful but did not want his company publicly associated with it, for he thought this might be detrimental to their interests.[100] Six years later, when his company was busily making arrangements for the ore road, Carnegie had more fully developed ideas about a coke railroad. Any railroad company building to the coke region probably would be attracted by the prospects of agreements with existing carriers. If Carnegie Steel took up the task itself, things would be different: "The one thing we can do and make a great deal upon is to build a railroad from Bessemer and Duquesne Furnaces to our Coke and run it as a freight railroad.... As we are at a great disadvantage in Pittsburgh over competitors on the Lake Shore, some day, I think, we shall have to do this in self-defense—40 ton cars and heavy rails, slow speed, no passenger traffic, will enable us to transport at less than two mills per ton."[101] In a June 1897 letter to Harry Phipps, Carnegie wrote: "The Chairman [Frick] is right—our new Road [the P&LE] will help coke, but extended to coke it would make our coke property a mine of wealth, let that be our next year's expenditure, I say." Forwarding this to Frick, the rather slower-moving Phipps added his own note, "This matter will bear keeping in mind—important." But Carnegie was not the sort of man to just "keep it in mind." He was in a euphoric mood when he contacted Frick from Cluny Castle in the Scottish Highlands early that autumn: "We leave on 19th for London, Paris and Cannes. Am getting a yacht to lie in the harbor, subject to my orders so that the family can have sea air every fine day." He was also expansive about their business, touching on progress with the Pittsburgh, Bessemer, and Lake Erie Railroad: "I am happy knowing that we are now secure in our ore supply. This was the only element needed to give us an impregnable position. We can now figure costs within a trifle and take contracts ahead without danger.... Since we have the ore mines on our shoulders, and coke, and the railroad, we cannot afford to do anything that will restrict us from taking the business of the country and running full." There were still chinks in their armor, though: "I hope our friends are quietly attending to that remaining vital step, which taken, we can then rest. Do get everything necessary secured and be ready. We have probably undertaken quite enough for this and next year but for 1899 we should do the one thing lacking. I am more than ever satisfied that our great coke estate cannot be made to yield its harvest minus that indispensable appliance."[102] Their railroad from Conneaut had cancelled out some of the cost disadvantage on their ore deliveries compared with Chicago; their own tracks to the coke region could not conceivably be countered by any steel-owned coke railroad to Chicago. In short it would give them immediate overall reductions in freight charges and longer-term security from the power of the railroads to charge high rates for the immense tonnages of coke now being hauled to Pittsburgh.

Attention centered on the eighteen-mile Monongahela Southern Railroad, which Andrew Mellon was building toward the coke region that fall. There was good coal along this line that Mellon would ship onward by railroads now controlled by Carnegie Steel. The latter anticipated that Mellon would be willing to lease or sell his railroad, which could be connected to the Union Railroad at the Pittsburgh end and extended to their ovens from its southern extremity. Frick wanted to proceed slowly, but Carnegie as usual was impatient: "When we get our own railroad through from mines to connection with trunk lines we can control matters, not till then." For Lauder, Carnegie filled out his vision of complete control of all the steps in steel production: "We are very near that, and when Mr. Frick gets our railroad extended from Duquesne to the coke, then is only left the transportation of ore and finished products on the lake. . . . The greatest saving that can be effected now is in the cost of transport. . . . We shall never get full benefit from our railroad until it is part of a rail and lake route. This seems to me the most important question now before us."[103]

Mellon offered to sell his line, surveys, and rights of way to them for $50,000—independently it was valued at $100,000. Supporting the purchase—which went through—Frick again expressed an opinion that they should not rush into development; they could gain all they wanted by the threat of going farther without actually spending more: "Can see no reason why we should want railroads to reduce their rates generally, to everybody. So long as our arrangements are satisfactory, it is far better to keep their published rates as high as they please." A few days later he summed up his thoughts on the matter. "It seems to me we are in the railroad business just as far as it is necessary for us to go—far enough to control the situation."[104] Apart from recognizing that the railroads would respond favorably to a threat, another argument for caution was the fear that if this threat was realized, the main roads might then retaliate in other ways. Both themes were present in Carnegie and Frick's relations with the Pennsylvania, though the threat of retaliation appears to have been implied rather than spelled out. Early in December 1897 Frick saw Frank Thomson, with whom they had negotiated the previous year for lower rates on coke. He told him about the eighteen-mile line, "a feeder to the Bessemer [the Pittsburgh, Bessemer, and Lake Erie]." Frick estimated the cost of such a line as $1 million but reckoned it would mean they would be able to deliver coke to the main line for as little as 14 cents a ton. Thomson replied that the PRR could offer better grades and more attractive charges. He followed this up with a letter offering to open new lines "on fair and equitable terms." Then came a request for cooperation and the railroad's own veiled threat: "In the light of these facts, may we ask you to reconsider your proposed construction, upon which, in view of our friendly relations we cannot be expected to look with favor, and to take up the question of our offer and determine whether you are not willing to accept the same."[105] Although by May, Frick was suggesting they might obtain control of their own coke railroad by buying or leasing the

Vanderbilt system's "Peemickey" line, because this railroad system now regarded its route along the Monongahela as its own main access to the coke region, it began to recognize that the mere suggestion of building or acquiring railroads would indeed secure lower rates. By this time Carnegie agreed: "We have the railroads just where we want them. We have gone far enough in railroad building now." Before the end of that year, Mellon had confirmed his willingness to buy back the rights of way for his railroad. The problem of coke rates and the possible remedy of building into the region was to recur, but Carnegie Steel proved able to meet all comers even without a coke road of its own.[106]

3 Organization in the Coke Trade

Labor, Labor Disputes, and the Era of the Great Strikes

Labor conditions in the Coke Region were hard, and there was a great deal of what a later generation would describe as oppression, though conditions were not worse than in much of the manufacturing economy of the time. Small, isolated communities with a dearth of alternative employment provided conditions ideal for exploitation, especially when populated by recent immigrants with lower expectations than native Americans and often having severe difficulties communicating in English. Although the area was much less remote and more open to outside observation than some of the mid-Appalachian coal settlements whose appalling management/employee relations have been analyzed by Corbin and others, the ten years from 1885 was a period of serious labor troubles. There were various minor disputes and three great strikes in 1887, 1891, and 1894. The first of these illustrated the divisions in the ranks of both labor and capital; on the one hand two competing unions, on the other the ironmakers always pressing on, and at critical times overruling, coke operators. The 1891 conflict highlighted the intensity of violence that could occur even in this country district. In fact, it achieved an intensity as great as that of the Homestead strike of the following year without receiving anywhere near a comparable stature in the collective memory of working people or the same prominence in labor history. The struggle of 1894 contained elements of both the others—violence, large-scale mobilization, and anger on the part of the workers, targeting of Connellsville as a key sector by central union organization—but also for the first time provided a reasoned, persuasive presentation of the grievances of the men, a public relations exercise on the part of the owners, and the beginnings of a realization that better conditions for workers might be in everyone's best interest.

The Labor Troubles of 1886–1887

Based as it was on a cheaply worked natural resource and using relatively unsophisticated plant and equipment, beehive coke manufacture was, technically, a relatively simple industry whose main variable cost was labor. Apart from a small managerial, administrative, engineering, and sales staff, most of its work force was unskilled. Platt in the summer of 1875 put the number of employees at 2,800. By 1881 there were 7,000 and in 1887 12,000–13,000.[1] The importance of labor costs and the characteristics of those employed provided both incentive and opportunity to pay low wages. Unceasing pressure from the iron industry gave an increased impetus in the same direction while importation of workers to the region increased the size of the pool from which day labor could be drawn. Though delayed until the early 1880s, a massive increase in the recent immigrant proportion of labor ensured there were usually men willing to accept rates of pay that, high though they might be by the standards of their home country, were low by most American scales. By 1887 one-sixth of the workforce was reckoned to be Hungarian or Polish, one-sixth Bohemian or German, one-third Irish, and one-third "native."[2] Because of the laborers' cosmopolitan nature and the fact that they proved to be highly mobile, migrating from one mining area to another or even returning to Europe if conditions of work became financially unattractive, workers as a whole were difficult to organize in order to press for improvements in pay and conditions. Normally, the resentments of the coal and coke workers in the region were hidden under a sullen exterior; now and again they broke out into violent strikes, destruction of property, and attacks on individuals. This gained for the workers a reputation for brutality. In turn, mine and coke operators showed themselves well equal to the challenge of an effectively harsh response. The relative remoteness of the area from alternative employment opportunities not only made it still more difficult for labor to combine to force up wage rates but also gave operators exceptional powers to dominate their workers. There were still wider effects. Cheap, generally tractable, and sometimes explosively aggressive labor and inflexible managements operating within a rich but limited and wasting resource base were circumstances unfavorable to openness to new ideas of organization or of technology. Eventually others, working with poorer natural resources but improved processes, conducted on a larger scale and with smaller but better paid labor, were able to produce an acceptable coke at lower overall cost. When this was achieved the decline of the coke region industry, though delayed, was inevitable. With such a change were lost both exploitation and jobs alike.

Until the early 1880s labor in the Coke Region was undertaken by American workers or recent immigrants from northwest Europe. From early years there had been periodic labor disputes. In 1848 there was a strike over wages. Eleven years later another disturbance had been caused by the miners' wish for scale rather than bushel measurement of their output.[3] Inevitably, depressed conditions through the mid-1870s decreased worker opportunities for action. Then, as the recovery passed over into a boom, there was a general though very short strike in March 1879 in which the men tried but failed to secure a 5 cent, or 20 percent, increase in the rate for mining a wagon load of coal, and 10 cents, an almost 17 percent rise, for drawing and leveling each oven.[4] Expansion of output and of workforces continued after the spiraling prices of that year, but then, for reasons considered elsewhere, coke prices began to fall. The scene was set for bigger confrontations.

A short strike in February 1880 ended with work resumed at the old rates. A larger confrontation in June 1881 involved fifty-four establishments and 5,055 men. This was a good year for production, shipments at 2.6 million tons being 19.6 percent up on the previous year, but oven numbers had increased 13.8 percent, and the average price received for coke on the open market fell from $1.79 a ton in 1880 to $1.63. The labor dispute began in early spring at the recently completed Morrell ovens of the Cambria Iron Company. By June the confrontation had become general. Facing difficult marketing conditions, the owners refused an increase; after a twenty-day closure their men returned, defeated. As an official report airily put it: "There was no violence, and with the exception of evictions from company houses, no trouble, whatsoever. Those who were evicted formed themselves in to camps along the Mt. Pleasant Branch near Everson, and lived pleasantly enough." Before long it would no longer be possible to present strikes as little more than camping holidays. This short dispute was reckoned to have cost the workers $133,000 and operators under $37,000. Over the next two years, six smaller disputes, spread throughout various west Pennsylvanian coke districts including Connellsville, cost working men more than three times as much as the operators.[5] Future differences over pay were also colored by racial or rather ethnic prejudices. The movement of "Hun" workers into the region was soon becoming a flood. Though the effect was not immediately apparent, this change would strengthen the tendency for violence on all sides in future disputes. The content and tone of reports on or discussions of labor disputes over the next few years indicate that as elsewhere in the nation there lurked deep fears about the implications of the "new immigration" and consequently prejudice against its individual members. There was a good deal of truth, some gross exaggeration, and a dangerous bias in the words used when, a generation later, the *Connellsville Courier* looked back on this troubled time: "The foreign element, fresh from the galling yoke of oppression in their own country, had not been in America long enough to distinguish between liberty and license, and were willing tools in the hands of labor agitators. Once aroused they were controlled with difficulty, or not at all." In 1882 and again in 1884, English-speaking miners and coke drawers struck against employment of Hungarians.[6] Meanwhile, the average price for coke was drifting downward; by 1884 it was only 69.3 percent the 1881 average. There was clearly a case for some reduction in wages, but it was not until shortly before mid-winter 1884 that monthly rates for Connellsville workers were cut by one-third. The *Connellsville Courier* recognized how weak the men were to offer any resistance: "Nine out of ten had little or nothing coming to them on pay-day after their store bill and house rent had been deducted. They had been compelled to live a sort of hand to mouth life, and are in no condition to strike or offer any resistance to the reduction, were they ever so willing."[7]

In the bigger disputes of the mid-1880s, it became clear that not only were there irreconcilable differences between operators and men but that each side also was riven by internal dissension. These clashes and divisions worked their way out in the setting of a rapidly extending industry, itself shaped, conditioned, and restricted by a range of external factors. Operators were finding it all but impossible to depend on earning an acceptable, reliable level of profit. It seemed attractive to try to improve margins by holding down wages, but the large increase in the workforce and its changing composition made for more explosive conditions on that side of the production system. The 1886 and 1887 disputes illustrated how complicated the situation had become. Two unions were involved, the local branches of the Knights of Labor and the more radical, locally based Miners and Laborers' Amalgamated Association. In the ranks of the producers, the biggest operations were organized as the Coke Syndicate, others were in the Coke Producers' Association, and some, including one or two firms of considerable size, remained independent. Cutting across these categories, coke works were either "merchant" producers or controlled by iron and steel companies whose prime concern was to safeguard their supplies of good quality, but whenever possible, low-priced fuel. In fact, these strikes showed conclusively that, though it had grown so big, coke manufacture was becoming functionally part of the iron and steel industry and that those who controlled this market for coke would always put the well being of their industry before that of Connellsville operators. The Pennsylvania state legislature was also increasingly interested in coke-labor conditions.[8] Finally, there were pressures from local interests and those representing official concern for recent immigrants. It was often difficult to get at the truth about disputes as they took place in a rural area pretty well controlled by the companies. Occasionally, investigative journalists did manage to penetrate. Even so, *The Pittsburgh Commercial Gazette,* despairing of being able to sort out the issues, summed up the 1886 strike as "simply a conflict between money on one side and brute force on the other, with a seeming disregard as to the consequences." A few weeks before, from the side of the operators, Lynch had derided press reports: "I suppose it is useless to say that the reports in the newspapers this morning are entirely false and sensational in their character."[9] As always, the detailed course of events was shaped and colored by the interplay of individual personalities.

Although in tonnages shipped 1884 had been the second best coke year to date, the industry's capacity had been so largely increased by building new ovens that by August nearly half of the total lay idle. Many "Hungarians" were reported to be leaving the region, a good number being taken to the mining areas of the Hocking Valley, Ohio. Next year, there was a slight reduction in oven numbers, output was restricted by collaborative action, and prices strengthened slightly. That summer coke drawers complained they were being expected to work the new, bigger ovens then being built without a wage increase. A short strike of drawers was called before a return to work pending adjustment to the new conditions. At this time the state outlawed female labor in the industry, officially at least ending a common practice of immigrant women helping their menfolk even in very heavy work, especially in the coke yards.[10] In January 1886 a miner's convention in Scottdale demanded an across the board 10 percent wage increase, an apparently reasonable request in view of increasing output and strengthening prices. Sometime later the men added other demands—smaller pit wagons; consideration of the question of false weights, which meant they were not fully paid for what they mined; and abolition of company stores, a cause also fostered by independent shopkeepers. The men formed a local association in which recent immigrants were the majority, though its leader, Peter Wise, had been engaged in labor struggles since 1881. This dispute also involved a man whose position set him apart from direct interest, but who was always affected. In July 1879 Father M. A. Lambing had been sent to the Coke Region as Roman Catholic priest; he was to play an important part in its life for forty years. In 1886 he tried to act as a peacemaker, but his friendship with Frick sometimes made it difficult for him to avoid seeming an agent for the owners. Lynch was skeptical as to his power to influence their men.

A month-long strike caused the idling of up to three-quarters of the ovens. There was some destruction of property, including the burning of the tipple at Henry Clay mine. Greater violence threatened for, as Lynch reported, "arrests were made yesterday after both sides had met seeming determined to fight. When the rioters were within shooting distance of the Sheriff and his posse their leader drew his revolver and urged them to move forward but the uniformed men stood firm. . . . After the flight of the rioters the only trouble was to catch the men we wanted." This dispute ended with wages back to 1884 levels; the weights and company store issues were deferred. Hopes were expressed that one result might be to rid the region of the Hungarians, but such expectations proved completely misplaced since the operators could no longer manage without their labor. More concessions were made during the following months in response to a number of smaller strikes. The interests of the iron and steel companies that had invested in coke were aired, and although this was not of key significance (as already indicated), Frick for one was already well aware of the pressure for compromise that might come from that quarter.[11] In April the syndicate posted notices of salary advances from 5 percent to 16 percent.

After the strikes were over, production reached record levels in 1886. It was not a time for head-to-head confrontation, but quiet assessments could be made for future action. As Frick put it to his Chicago business colleagues, he had conceded some of the men's demands and they had withdrawn some, but in the near future he would "weed out" the bad men at Morewood.[12] The average price for coke that year was $1.36 a ton, well above the previous three years, though even then only 76 percent of the 1880 level. At the year's end there were 52 percent more ovens in the region than in 1880, and output was 89 percent higher. Gross revenues had been just short of 51 percent more than in 1885. Meeting on 18 October the Coke Syndicate decided not to increase prices further but to run all ovens at full capacity. The price for coke was rising to $1.50, and there was a shortage of cars to carry away the output. The workers decided it was time for them to share in this prosperity. The dispute that now began to take shape was to be much more significant than earlier clashes.

During November 1886 new wage demands were formulated. They were accompanied by a request for the weighing of coal and for a two-weeks' pay regime (payment twice rather than once a month). A union conference revealed labor was divided. The Amalgamated Association forced the issue; the Knights of Labor opposed strike action. On the side of the operators, an apparently unconnected event in December was the purchase by Carnegie Brothers of the large interests of the two Ferguson brothers in H. C. Frick Coke, increasing their already controlling interest. By now Carnegie furnaces consumed about 40 percent of the Frick coke output. After weeks of negotiations, strike action was expected to start on Christmas Day, but at a Pittsburgh meeting between operators and men on Christmas Eve, a compromise seemed to have been reached, the men receiving much of what they demanded. The owners offered an advance of 5 cents a hundred bushels but turned down the suggestion of payment twice a month on the grounds that they themselves were paid monthly by the furnace operators. The men rejected this offer. At another meeting in Pittsburgh on 16 February 1887, the syndicate met a workers' committee, refused its demand for a 20 percent wage increase, and in return offered 5 percent more to all classes of labor. This was not acceptable.[13] The two unions disagreed over arbitration, but eventually resolution of the dispute was referred to John B. Jackson of Pittsburgh. At the beginning of May, Jackson gave his decision against the men. After the long, drawn-out negotiations at last came decisive action. On Tuesday, 3 May, a joint meeting of the Knights of Labor and the Miners and Laborers' Amalgamated Association at Everson resolved to suspend work immediately and to remain on strike until an advance of 12.5 percent was received. Next day labor was withdrawn from all works, and within three or four days 11,000 ovens were out of production. As many as 12,000 men participated, about one-third of them "Huns." At the end of the first week, the press reported everything was quiet and that no trouble was expected unless attempts were made to bring labor in from outside.[14]

The impact on the iron industry of the wholesale ending of coke production was severe. On 1 May 1887, 148 bituminous and coke furnaces were in blast throughout the United States; by the beginning of June only 98 remained at work. The effect was greatest in Pittsburgh and the Valleys district. Major consumers could be expected to press for an early settlement even if this meant making concessions to the men. The operators were tempted to try to regain their previously booming business by introducing strike breakers. Meanwhile, as always, the resolution of the men was gradually eroded by their loss of pay. Within a week there were signs of a break on the side of labor when 200 workers at Leisenring offered to resume at old rates. Other plants also reported plans for return so long as those doing so could be protected from violence. Before the end of May, W. J. Rainey, the largest independent producer, was planning to concede the men's demands and start up again. For its part, the syndicate was taking action to "break the backbone" of the strike. During the weekend of 28–29 May, a large number of men were expected from the East. A New York labor bureau was said to be offering to furnish from 150 to as many as 1,000 men a day. There was some violence. Between 2:00 A.M. and 3:00 A.M. on 31 May, strikers attacked the shaft house at Davidson. Three watchmen were inside as stones were thrown. One went out and was severely beaten. A dynamite charge exploded but failed to cause significant damage. G. Harvey, describing this phase of the dispute in his biography of Frick, shows how easily one party could be presented in a favorable light and the other demonized when he wrote of "the operators standing their ground firmly and unanimously behind a small committee of which Mr. Frick was the leading spirit, and with the miners and their sympathizers brutally assaulting non-union men who wanted to work, destroying machinery and blowing up the works with dynamite."[15] On 31 May Robert Ramsay, Frick's superintendent of mines, reported that the conservative portion of the men in the Mt. Pleasant district—"not the ones that take any part in the strike"—felt the confrontation would go on for a long time and that their hopes of victory were slight. He also reported that at the

Thomas Lynch. *Courtesy of Charles McKenna Lynch*

same time: "The Committee men at Standard, with one exception, spend their time in drinking and fighting. Can you wonder that unreasonable strikes take place with such men in the front." He concluded that it was very evident "the leaders of the Amalgamated and the Ks of L are not sailing in the same boat." Ramsay argued that so long as William Mullen, the leading force in the Amalgamated Association, "is the little autocrat of the region, just so long will there be no end of trouble." Even if there was a settlement, he did not think Mullen could be trusted.[16]

Two days after Ramsay's letter and its evidence of weaknesses on the side of the men, with Frick's encouragement Lynch made contact with Mullen. Lynch reported that he had boarded the same rail car as two of the Amalgamated leaders, Mullen and his colleague Joseph Welsh, and two of the local leaders of the Knights of Labor, John R. Byrne and William Holsing. Mullen was asleep before the train reached Braddock. At this point Lynch took the seat next to Byrne and pointed out that five of the Edgar Thomson blast furnaces were smokeless, banked for want of coke. He mentioned the remaining two furnaces would be banked the next day: "He winced a little at that and remarked that 'it looked as if we had a long and hard struggle before us.' I agreed with him and added that it was a bad state of affairs for anybody but more for the men than for the operators." Byrne wished he could get out of the situation and told Lynch the two unions were to meet next day in Scottdale. When the train reached Manor in Westmoreland County, Welsh awakened Mullen, and Lynch went across to talk with them. Welsh implied the owners were trying to win public opinion by hiring men to plant explosives on their own works, "imitating the English soldiers in Ireland." After referring to a riot at Jimtown and an explosion at Davidson, Welsh discussed the arbitration award. He blamed "that Col. Schoonmaker" for breaking faith with his men. Mullen admitted there had been wrong on the men's side, at which point Welsh remarked that he also blamed Mullen. After this Welsh left Lynch alone with Mullen, who explained he could not get the workers back without an inducement. Lynch's response to this was that if they resumed work and then submitted a plan for a sliding scale for wages, he (Lynch) would resign and fight the syndicate if it refused to accept it. Mullen "brightened up at this," but Lynch warned they must act at once because he had "heard Carnegie Bros. tell [Frick] today that they would bank their last furnace tomorrow and the rail mill would shut down on Saturday [the following day] and if they had to shut down would remain idle until after the hot season and by that time the coke strike would be over." The upshot was that Lynch and Mullen were to see each other next day to arrange a scale that Mullen was to try to have adopted when the men met on Saturday. The hope was that work might be resumed on Monday, 6 June. After his conversation with the opposition, Lynch traveled on to Connellsville. Reporting these events to Frick, he revealed how insincere his own attitude had been: "I gave him a good deal of toffy on both yours and my own account, told him how much you admired his calm, earnest manner and predicted when he got his men well-disciplined that he would be the head of an organization which would be a benefit to the business, but they had to be disciplined."[17]

A rift in their ranks now threatened to undermine the men's position. Early in June, after its General Executive Board had decided to personally investigate the dispute and work toward an amicable settlement, the Knights of Labor declared the strike illegal. At this point, just when things seemed to be going against the workers, the balance of advantage dramatically altered. The apparently fairly united front of the operators was shattered when, in response to what was effectively a command from Andrew Carnegie, the H. C. Frick Coke Company granted the 12.5 percent wage advance. Two other big operators, Cochran and Rainey, also conceded. On 15 June the other producers, meeting in Pittsburgh, unanimously resolved not to give way. As Edward Leisenring had earlier put it to Frick, the members of the Coke Syndicate believed: "The battle must be fought out, no matter how long it takes. . . . There is no other way to prevent the continuous demands and unreasonable and petty strikes that have constantly occurred during the past year, which has made the coke business so annoying. The men, flushed with success heretofore, must be whipped if we want any peace hereafter."[18] That same day, also meeting in Pittsburgh, those furnace owners who were not also involved in rail manufacture, pressed for a price reduction on coke to $1.50 a ton—29 cents below that year's average. They felt strongly that they were discriminated against by coke makers, getting merely "scrapings" as compared with the big integrated concerns. On June 16 false reports circulated that Hungarian workers at the Sterling and Jimtown works of Schoonmaker had resumed at old rates. The strike dragged on for a few more weeks. On Tuesday, 5 July, 150 or so Pinkerton men arrived in Pittsburgh and "took early trains" to the Coke Region, where they were posted to protect employees wanting to work. However, though they had reopened, at no plant was there a large return to work, and as one trade journal was bold enough to remark, "It is reported that the real purpose in bringing Pinkerton men into the region is to evict the men from the company houses who have signed iron-clad leases."[19] On 21 July, Knights of Labor men returned to work and the Amalgamated members went in next day, at the old wage rates. The last fifty Pinkerton men left the Coke Region on Monday, 1 August.[20] During that month a joint committee of the Knights and of the Amalgamated Association in conference with the Frick Coke superintendent agreed on a sliding scale for wages. The base price for coke was taken as $1.35 a ton. An advance of 10 cents would bring the workers a 2.5 cent increase per hundred bushels of coal mined, 1.5 cents per hundred bushels of coal charged to the ovens, and an increase of about 2 percent for other labor. Other companies were not party to this agreement.[21]

The wider context and implications of the 1887 strike deserve comment. By the time the strike ended, the state had already passed a law requiring payment of wages every two weeks. Bitter feeling persisted between the Miners and Laborers' Amalgamated Association and the Knights of Labor. In October the former proposed another strike but the latter refused to join in. A few weeks later the Knights demanded a 6.5 percent advance, and this time Amalgamated withheld support. Ironmasters began to hedge against further interruptions of supplies. It was noticeable that expansion of coke capacity, though still going ahead rapidly, was also spreading to other areas where production might be expected to be freer from possible interruption. Within a few months proposals or plans for new coke ovens were announced for Hammond, Indiana (using Connellsville coal), in the near neighborhood of Pittsburgh at McKees Rocks, and by the Carnegie interests at Scott Haven on the lower Youghiogheny.[22] Above all, a legacy of suspicion and animosity meant continuing uncertainty.

Labor Relations, 1887–1891

The major labor confrontation of 1887 was followed by a quieter period, neither all-out warfare nor peace but rather a state of "constant disturbance," as a local newspaper put it.[23] Trade conditions in 1888 were unfavorable for the advance of labor's interests. The average Pittsburgh price for Bessemer pig was $17.38 per gross ton as compared with $21.37 in 1887. Connellsville expansion at least temporarily overshot that in the iron centers. Coke capacity had increased only slightly when iron production grew quickly, now iron tonnages fell back but more ovens were built. In 1887 slightly fewer than 1,000 new ovens were added, with a net increase the following year of 2,052. Shipments went up, but from the high 1887 figure of $1.79 a ton, which had sparked off the new round of extensions, the average coke price fell to only $1.19, the lowest in four years.

Operators and labor were regrouping. At the beginning of 1888, L. R. Davis succeeded J. A. Trimbath as president of the Miners and Laborers' Amalgamated Association. Two months afterward his union accepted a 6.25 percent wage cut. Later in the year attempts to combine the Amalgamated and Knights of Labor failed. All the time the various managements watched the men closely. One may sense something of the atmosphere of suspicion, conspiracy, and tension in the letters sent to Frick from the Coke Region by Morris Ramsay during the spring and summer of 1888. Early in April he wrote: "I see notices posted up that there will be a meeting of the Amalgamated in Mt. Pleasant on Wednesday to be addressed by Mullen, Davis and others to strengthen up the organization. They have printed bills all around posted on buildings, shanties and trees. . . . There is a good many Huns asking for employment just now but we will not hire many of them." He reported two meetings in August. Davis spoke at one gathering attended by only twenty-seven men. Ramsay also wrote of an evening during which there had been a meeting at Morewood School House. About a quarter of their men were there, but the organizers had to struggle to get a decent turnout: "They had to ring the school house bell until dark when the men came. The meeting was to be at 6.30 and only a few was on the ground at that time. The leaders sent over to the houses for the men."[24]

Early in 1889 the Amalgamated called a strike but were once more frustrated by the refusal of the Knights of Labor to join in. Those who did withdraw their labor were so badly beaten that the workers at Standard even had to pay for coke ruined because the ovens had not been drawn.[25] That April wages were reduced by another 6.25 percent. (In effect, the men were being forced to bear the impact of the bad trade; at this time H. C. Frick Coke distributed a dividend of $2 million on its capital of $3 million—Carnegie received $498,333 and Frick $420,367.)[26] In July the Knights of Labor, temporarily dominant in the region, called a conference to consider scales. On 1 August about one-third of the miners came out and within a week the strike was general.[27] Frick tried to make Carnegie recognize that giving way in summer 1887 had "demoralized" their men but reassured him about the present dispute. Yet Frick was puzzled that McClure and Schoonmaker, who had no agreement with their men, nonetheless had all of them at work, whereas about 2,000 of his own, notwithstanding their agreement, were striking. That they should "be the first and at present really the only ones is inexplicable.... I do not propose to let this continue beyond the danger line, but I do hope to get our men back without giving them an advance in wages."[28]

Carnegie affected to be sanguine about the prospects of standing firm. That year peace had been bought in a strike in their own works by giving way rather than risking violence. Despite his loud protestations of support for the rights of workingmen, Carnegie had disapproved of that action. He now encouraged Frick to stand firm: "Glad you are going to fix strike in coke. It is too bad but we must expect 3 years or so of trouble now. The surrender or compromise at Homestead may be right in itself, but the effect at Beaver Falls, coke works, Keystone etc. must be great and not favorable. Must do best we can." Now as the iron and steel trades boomed and coke prices advanced, it would be unprofitable to resist their men for long. An increase carried the industry through to February 1890, at which time a new scale should have been adopted for the next twelve months. The agreement was not renewed, and there were desultory troubles including small strikes at the Pennsville and Standard works in which "socialist" agitators were for the first time recognized in the region. Even so, the operators were obviously on the offensive. The steel companies stored coke. H. C. Frick Coke filed a suit for $100,000 against seven of the labor leaders. Again, Harvey put a favorable gloss upon the events.[29]

One of the bitterest strikes occurred in 1891. Indeed, in many aspects—the negotiations, violence and damage to property, injuries, loss of life, and wider implications—the conflict that raged through the region during late winter and spring of that year was fully comparable in stature with the 1892 Homestead strike. The latter is renowned as one of the great events of American labor history; except locally, the fourteen-week Connellsville strike is forgotten. The difference must be largely because the coke dispute was spread over a wide area and not concentrated at one place. In addition, being conducted in a country district, the violent strike was much less exposed to newspaper publicity.

From November 1890 the spreading impact of a commercial decline that began with the Baring financial crisis was marked by contraction in the iron trade, falling demand for coke, and the idling of capacity. Many coke ovens had been banked by December; in mid-January half the Frick ovens were out of production. The price of furnace coke, held since early February 1890 at $2.15 a ton, was cut to $1.90 on 1 January 1891. Ironworks in the Valleys were pressing for further reductions. On 2 February Frick sent Carnegie a bland message: "Conference is being held in the Coke Region today between Mr. Lynch and the Knights of Labor. It will drag on for several days." In these discussions the operators proposed a 10 percent reduction. Surprisingly—in "a spirit of utter perverseness," as one trade paper put it—the men asked for a variety of improved conditions, including an eight-hour day and an advance of 12.5 percent in wages.[30] Under such circumstances, failure was inevitable. As of 9 February, some 10,000 men were on strike.

By the end of the first week, only 833 of the region's 16,119 ovens were in operation, and these belonged to three of the four works of W. J. Rainey and Company, a nonunion firm. Press reports of the early stages of the dispute were varied, one local paper praising the "peaceful, even-tempered manner in which the strike has been inaugurated" and deploring "a great deal of sensational stuff printed in Pittsburg papers about riotous demonstrations on the part of the strikers which is wholly without foundation."[31] However, from the start Rainey brought in Pinkerton detectives and sheriff's deputies to protect those men still at work. This show of force had led to violence the day before the men withdrew their labor. George Levingston, a union miner from Nellie, accompanied by a former yard boss from Fort Hill, went to a boarding shanty at the latter place to ask the "Huns" if they would strike. The local newspaper reported what followed—ironically, on the same page offering its praise of the "peaceful, even-tempered" nature of the strike—"Receiving a negative answer he [Levingston] became very angry, and, it is charged, called them vile names and flourished his revolver. Both he and his companion were ejected with scant ceremony, whereupon Levingston opened fire on the door. When he had emptied the five chambers of his revolver, and before he could reload, the Huns sallied forth in force, beat him severely with shovels and coke forks, and threw him more dead than alive in the river. He crawled ashore only to suffer the same experience."[32] A few days into the strike a large meeting was held at Vanderbilt. Threats of force caused many men at Fort Hill and Paul to join. Large numbers of Hungarian and Polish miners were soon leaving the region.[33] On Monday, 23 February, the tone of the dispute hardened.

Some 4,000 men armed with clubs and revolvers gathered at Dawson. A group of about 1,500 drove some of the Rainey men from their work at Fort Hill. Deputies and Pinkerton men did not intervene. Soon after this there were further instances of assault and of acquisition of rifles from those who were attacked. In March labor leaders were arrested and charged with attacking Rainey officials who had obtained injunctions against interference with their operations. By the end of the month, the men's resources were dwindling as hunger, cold, and sickness affected them and their families.

By mid-March a break in the strike seemed likely, not as the outcome of discussions between the two sides but because of an agreement by operators to offer a sliding scale. But not all of the owners were confident or happy. Frick informed Carnegie on 17 March: "Reports from the Coke Region indicate that the strike will be settled on our terms before many days, but you know how uncertain these labor matters are." Carnegie too was cautious, though full of ideas. He seems to have failed to recognize the stark realities of Coke Region labor relations: "To announce terms and try to start ovens is a very serious step to take. It should be postponed until the last day possible, as everyday's idleness will render starting easier. I should not think of making a move this month. Cannot Lynch get some of the men to suggest a sliding scale, and you offer one in compliance with the request. This is the shape to get it in, and I think Lynch could lead up to that subject and get enough from the men to base your action upon. I do not like your idea of thrusting it upon them. It would show too clearly your desire to start." In fact, Frick had wider hopes, as he revealed in a letter to George Lauder: "If we succeed in winning on the terms proposed, organization in the Coke Region is killed. And if we adhere to our policy of keeping at all times good stock of coke at Edgar Thomson and Lucy we will be in position to take a strong stand any time our employees show a disposition to be unreasonable, and fight it out then and there."[34]

Notices of a new sliding scale with a base price of $1.75 for recognition by miners' committees were put up on Wednesday, 25 March. The next day sixteen coke works reopened. The turnout was mixed but on the whole disappointing. McClure had a full complement of men, as did that portion of Mutual works controlled by Frick, but Leisenring 2 and Morewood each attracted only twenty, Redstone thirteen, Leith twelve, Jimtown ten, White four, and Henry Clay two.[35] Even so, on 27 March the *Connellsville Courier* declared, "The great coke strike and lockout is broken." The announcement was tragically premature. Alleging bad faith on the part of owners in creating the impression that the dispute had been called off, the men's leaders rejected the agreement. The strike became more violent.

On Sunday, March 29, information surfaced of a plan to attack South West Coal and Coke's Morewood works and to murder the general manager, Morris Ramsay. Very early the next morning, Morewood was raided by four bodies of strikers, 1,200 or so in all, approaching from the villages of Alice, Standard, Bridgeport, and Bessemer. About twenty deputies defended the works under the direction of Sheriff Clawson. Having orders not to fire, Clawson withdrew his small force as the horde of strikers approached. A Pennsylvania official document described the havoc that followed: "The coke-oven doors were battered down for the purpose of destroying the coke which was in process of manufacture, tools were thrown into the ovens and destroyed, wheelbarrows piled up and burned and the railroad was rendered useless by numbers of the men seizing the ties and overturning the tracks, iron wheelbarrows were filled with the burning coke by the strikers for the purpose of firing the mine shaft and store houses, but they were saved from the general destruction by the counsel of the more moderate of the strikers; brick bats and rocks were thrown at the buildings however, and the doors and windows smashed." Lynch reported rioting and disorder at a number of works.[36]

In response to a request for help from Harrisburg, the National Guard company based in Mt. Pleasant was sent to help the sheriff. Under the command of a local dentist, Captain Loar, it was posted at Morewood. On Wednesday, 1 April, there was a near confrontation between these guardsmen and the strikers. Replying that day to a letter from Carnegie, Frick considered the coke situation and its relation to their steel business, once again seriously threatened by fuel shortages. On the whole he was optimistic: "All parties here feel just as you do, that now is the time to settle all difficulties in the coke region. . . . This strike certainly cannot last much longer. Please remember that when we closed down on the 10th of February there were only 50 percent of the ovens running. The men, or a large majority of them are very anxious to go to work, and it certainly will not require many days for them to see that we mean exactly what we say, and are offering to pay them most liberal wages. I expect Mr. Lynch at my house tonight, and will be able to give you quite full information on the subject tomorrow."[37] The meeting with Lynch did take place, but before morning arrived the situation had taken another dramatic turn, not because of decisions taken at Frick's quiet home in the outskirts of Pittsburgh, but as a result of events in the Coke Region.

Soon after midnight on 2 April, two columns of strikers, each containing about five hundred men and led by bands, moved from the areas around Mt. Pleasant toward Morewood. Those leaving from Standard cut the telephone wires as they left so as to prevent any advance warning of their movement, but the line was repaired and a message sent on. After threatening the Morewood works, the crowd turned, apparently intending to assault the guardsmen sheltering in a barn near the stables, though afterward they denied this had been their aim. Loar ordered the strikers to disperse, shouting in Hungarian as well as in English. He and his men later denied he had given an order to fire, but someone did, and several volleys were fired into the mass of strikers, who soon retreated leaving badly wounded and dead men to be carried by the soldiers into the Morewood stables.[38]

Reports of this episode were at once conveyed in various directions. In Mt. Pleasant rumors spread that at least forty men had been killed. The streets filled with workers and their families, who surged in one direction after another, apparently in a daze, as a cold drizzle fell on the town. At 4:53 A.M. Robert Ramsay sent a telegram from Mt. Pleasant to Frick. It was delivered by a special Western Union Telegraph messenger to his house in the Homewood district at about 7:00 that morning. The message was short, slightly inaccurate, and startling: "An attack was made on Morewood this morning at 2.30. The deputies returned the fire killing eight men and dispersing the rioters. As a larger mob may gather and over-power the sheriff's men it is important that assistance be sent out from the city at once until other help is obtained." By 8:30 Frick had sent the message on to Jay Morse, president of Illinois Steel, which held the major interest in Morewood. Not being a man to allow death, injuries, or uncertainty to cloud his judgment, and apparently now remaining cool under conditions in which many others would have panicked, Frick added a short note: "I have no further particulars. This will likely have a good effect on the riotous element up there."[39] In the course of the day, he did his best to support Morris Ramsay, Robert's brother, who was in control at Morewood. Again he showed remarkable coolness as well as a puzzling detachment from the night's horrors: "It looks to me as if the fight is over. Very important for you to make first sign of aggressive action by arresting all of last night's rioters that can be identified and got hold of. They are no doubt stunned and a blow just now will tell. It will not do to let up now. Keep your works running. It was unfortunate that it had to come to this, but the strikers got nothing but what they deserved. From this time on you certainly will have all the protection needed and your men can feel safe and secure."[40]

An inquest was held that day into the deaths of the seven men killed. Labor leaders entered a suit against Loar and some of his soldiers. Meanwhile, the governor ordered the Tenth Regiment of the Pennsylvania National Guard to the district. On Saturday, 4 April, Frick wrote again to Morris Ramsay, reaffirming his message of two days before: "These labor leaders, I judge from the paper, are endeavoring to make as much of this riot as possible. The scoundrels have no one to blame for it but themselves, and you should, as soon as possible, get men to work; stand on your dignity and insist that the whole cause of this trouble was the action of the leaders. Now that the soldiers are there in charge, your men should have no fears, as they will not be troubled in the future."⁴¹ That day about 10,000 people gathered in Mt. Pleasant for the funerals of the men shot down two days before.

The subsequent days were marked by moves in various directions, a few hopeful, most of them deepening the dispute. On Sunday Frick contacted R. J. Linden of the Pinkerton Detective Agency in Philadelphia, who at once sent T. C. Campbell, a man he characterized as "reliable and competent," to Pittsburgh "for detective work." (Whether or not Campbell was responsible for the many pages of penciled reports on affairs in the coke district, which seem to reveal an elaborate espionage system, and are held in the Frick records, is unfortunately not clear.) It took a week before Campbell confidentially told Morris Ramsay that he was a detective sent in by Frick and that two or three other men of the same nature were in the area. In the meantime work resumed at some of the plants. On Sunday sixty-one of the sixty-five newcomers brought into Mt. Pleasant the previous day went to work; the other four decided to stay out. "Old" men were said to be coming in "very slow." Then tension was heightened by the issuing of arrest warrants on both sides, the strikers wanted the deputies who had been on guard at Morewood, and the operators sought those who had seemed to be about to attack the plant's defenders—even including members of the brass band that had led the march. Hundreds of immigrant workers who had been on strike began leaving the coke district, and confusion was made worse by the serving of eviction notices on strikers in company houses. A week after the shooting, yet another element was added from outside when the United Mine Workers of America (UMWA) for the first time issued rations to the most deprived families of strikers. In fact, destitution among coke workers' families had often been acute for weeks. It now became clear that fear of retaliation from those remaining on strike was an important factor prolonging the stoppage. Lynch reported that at Painter a Polish priest had dissuaded men who might have returned. Frick was complaining that the short telegrams Ramsay sent him did not keep him fully informed; for his part, he remained in favor of vigorous action: "I would throw those huns out of the houses the moment their time is up, without any ceremony."⁴² From the other side of the dispute, the power of intimidation was proved when the National Guard was withdrawn on 17 April. Men who had returned to their jobs in Morewood left again. There was further rioting in the southern part of the coke field, and in Scottdale dynamite exploded near the homes of men considered willing to work. Two days after this, the coroner's jury delivered an ambivalent verdict on the Morewood deaths, finding the men had been killed by the deputies but without a ruling on whether or not the shootings were justified. A Pennsylvania state report highlighted another aspect of the prevailing bitterness: "The principal trouble about this time was caused by the striker's wives resisting the deputy sheriffs, who were engaged in turning them out of the companies' houses. These women, mostly Huns and Poles, fought savagely against the evictions, and the deputies received very rough handling and in some cases were severely injured in the discharge of their disagreeable duty."[43]

For a few days longer, desultory violence continued from both sides as the level of suffering in the families of strikers intensified. At Leisenring 2 riots broke out when evictions were attempted and more or less continued for some days: "The works are surrounded by the mob day and night. Explosions of bombs, firing of guns, blowing of horns and beating of cans can be heard at all hours. The whole community seems to be dazed, and no one knows what moment the worst may come." Through the pressure some managed to remain cool. On Saturday, 4 April, Linden looked into the situation at West Leisenring, the village that housed Leisenring 2 miners and coke workers. He concluded it would be unwise to decrease the force there because a number of men introduced into the area were living in houses from which families of strikers had been evicted. Protection was needed for property and for those who were working. A few days later Frick asked Linden for one hundred men, and these soon arrived under the command of "Captain" Foley, said to be "a man of great experience in matters of this kind." He had been in charge of private guards at Leisenring on behalf of the syndicate some years before. Morris Ramsay wanted protection for South West Coal and Coke men, but Frick did not want to go so far as at Leisenring, though as he made clear, this was not from any scruple: "Ramsay wanted me to order into Morewood 100 Pinkertons. I would much prefer getting along without them, if possible, as it is a very expensive proceeding."[44]

Within less than three weeks after the Morewood shootings, things seemed under control. Frick wrote to Carnegie in much the same resolute—though not always consistent—tone he would adopt fourteen months later during the Homestead strike. They had taken necessary steps: "We landed the hundred Pinkerton men at Leisenring No. 2 about 1:30 today, and they were immediately sworn in as deputy sheriffs. A special with 50 Italian miners, secured in the Punxsutawney Region, left here at 4 o'clock for the same place. I trust with this protection, and this number of men to start with at that works, we may succeed in running them full before long. We are holding our own at all other places, and giving a little at some. We must keep at this persistently and patiently and I am satisfied we will, before many days, get in pretty good shape." He reported in much the same manner to Morse.[45] The next day Carnegie sent him more gratuitous advice: "It is probable the Fabian policy would have been better had Lynch not acted in posting scale, but now we have to go ahead to the end. My idea of treating in a dispute with men is always to shut down and suffer, let them decide by vote when they desire to go to work. Say kindly: 'All right gentlemen, let's hear from you, no quarrel, not the least in the world. Until a majority vote (secret ballot) to go to work have a good time—when a majority vote to start, start it is.' Such an approach will mean no long stoppages and not much ill feeling."[46] A week later Frick sent in more strike breakers. This time the replacement force took an unusual form. "Have arranged to send up about 10 families from Braddock. Each family has generally from 10 to 15 boarders. This will probably give us 150 men in a body. They go fully understanding the conditions and situation in the Coke Region. These families and men will go to Adelaide." Sometimes this "scab" labor brought into the region was unaware of local circumstances, and when the men learned what these were they occasionally refused the work. Even so, as usual Frick was looking beyond the immediate situation, for he ended on an upbeat note: "This coke strike out of the way, and we ought to do a very prosperous business the balance of the year." Early in May Ramsay sent one of their Polish men to Pittsburgh on a Saturday night to recruit yet more men: "If he gets about thirty or forty they had better be sent around in a car to Morewood by themselves."[47]

Generally, Frick's lieutenants in the Coke Region seem to have encouraged him to stand firm; in turn he provided them with strong moral support. At the end of the month, he received expressions of frustration but also of resolution from Lynch and the Ramsay brothers. Morris wanted a purge of disturbing elements: "You can really see which kind of statements these labor agitators make. They care nothing about the truth. It is all for gaining their unjust ends. We cannot get clear of those kind of people too soon." Robert was equally adamant: "I feel we must win this fight. . . . Although the horizon may seem a little dark just now, I feel that the victory is ours if we remain firm." Replying to Morris the following day Frick wrote: "It is gratifying to see that the Hungarians are very angry about the new men coming in." He added: "Do not fail to keep most careful watch on all buildings that you think might be set on fire by some evil disposed person."[48]

Even now the workers seemed determined. What were described as "violent and incendiary" circulars were being distributed through the region by "the socialistic element" among the strikers. C. M. Parker, secretary of the district of the UMWA, did his best to check the drift back to work in a powerful letter published in the local Slavonic paper. The operators had it translated in order to advance their own purposes. Parker made some points that seem to have been valid, but he set them in a much wider, more threatening context. Indeed, his vision of the future was cataclysmic: "There will in a short time be a war between Labor and Capital. Don't you go to work and you will gain by it. We warn you not to go to work with the Blacksheeps. You have seen what trouble and bloodshed there has been in the region. Your life is not safe and you hinder the strikers from gaining their point. Don't believe the

Agents which fill their pockets with money and who don't care for your lives. They have already spilt lots of Slavonic blood and we don't want to see any more of it."[49]

As late as 29 April, there seemed little hope of an early end. By now Lynch was impatient with some of the moderating influences. They had only two men at work at Summit. "This is in Father Lambing's parish." Later in the same letter, he observed: "Father Lambing's influence in the neighborhood of Valley is just about as much as it is in the region inhabited by the Sioux Indians." Lynch continued, "I am afraid you have a wrong impression of this strike; I never seen anything like it, and talk will not change the situation—force is what is required." A willingness to continue the conflict and reluctance to return were still the dominant themes. As Lynch put it a few days later: "The situation now seems to have reached the point of braggadocio—a sort of feeling 'that we have been out for three months and can stay out so much longer; that is the kind of good men we are.' That, I think is the prevailing sentiment now; but at the same time there are hundreds of fellows who would like to go to work; but who will not as long as the majority of the men are idle."[50] That week Samuel Gompers visited the Coke Region pledging financial support if the men became associated with the AF of L. He was unsuccessful. Meanwhile, the national convention of the UMWA decided to drop its general struggle for an eight-hour day in order to concentrate on Connellsville.

Despite the confusing outward appearance of things, the position of the strikers was in fact crumbling, partly because of their need for work and wages as well as the importation of large numbers of strike breakers, especially Italians. Even so, the dispute dragged on for a few more weeks. In mid-May the case against Loar and his deputies came before a grand jury. Ramsay informed Frick of a suggestion that the latter sit in on the closing arguments: "It would be a good thing for you to come out a short time this afternoon and hear Mr. Moorhead make the closing address. He thought that your presence in the Court Room would have a good effect even for only a short time."[51] In the course of one day in the middle of the month there were three fights at Leisenring 1 between men wanting to go to work and those trying to prevent them. On Wednesday, 20 May, Frick telegrammed Morse that though a convention in Scottdale had resolved to continue the strike, the employers were making small gains. The following day, just over fourteen weeks after walking out and in defiance of their leaders, a large number of men resumed work. Over the weekend the strike collapsed. By Saturday Morse had sent his congratulations: "You have had an awful hard battle and I have often thought of the load you were carrying. I hope the trouble you have had will not occur again very soon. Is it not your opinion that this strike will probably be the last one for two or three years? Has not this taught the men a lesson that they will not soon forget? I return you Mr. Ramsay's letter. I hope he will get rid of any of his old men who have hitherto been the cause of trouble."[52] In fact, as always when restarting, the owners weeded out those they regarded as troublemakers. Many labor leaders were discharged, but otherwise "such of the men as had not by their prominence made themselves objectionable to their employers were permitted to return to work." Some of those blacklisted were unable to get jobs anywhere in the district.[53]

Again, the cost of a major strike had been high. Plant had been damaged. There had been the deaths and injuries at Morewood. About two thousand evictions had occurred and the men had lost about $4 million in wages. Loar and the deputy sheriffs were tried and acquitted; when fifteen rioters came before the court they were convicted, though in eleven instances the sentence was suspended. Gradually the region resumed the appearance of peace. On 25 May Frick ended a cable to Carnegie: "Coke victory complete."[54] In the euphoria of the time, it must have been all too easy for operators to believe this. Some remained more coolly realistic than others about the situation and the future; not surprisingly, despite his pleasure in "victory," Frick was one of those thinking ahead. A month after the return to work, in a note to Morris Ramsay he asked, "What have you done with all of the Winchester rifles, pistols etc. purchased and sent you during the strike?"[55]

The violent events of the 1891 strike had helped stir up deep feelings of ethnic fear and prejudice. A report from the Pennsylvania Department of Internal Affairs concluded with a damning reference to the nature of the new immigrant workers who had been prominently involved, although it also criticized their employers: "The operators themselves are not blameless in this matter. Desire for cheap labor seems to have influenced them in employing men utterly unacquainted with our laws and customs, unfitted in many respects to be associates of the better class of citizens, and who, in time, acquired a knowledge that led them to be breeders of discontent and trouble. Excited and infuriated, unable to reason or to be reasoned with, the only course seemingly left to them was the destruction of property. This affair clearly shows that there are considerations besides cheapness of labor in employing men—the peace of society, the safety of human life and property, which cannot be safely overlooked."[56] Two days after the Morewood shootings, the *New York Tribune* had been far more inflammatory: "This unhappy situation calls public attention to the fact that a great proportion of these people now awaiting sullenly a chance for revenge are absolutely unfit for citizenship and ought never to have been admitted into the country. They are densely ignorant, brutal by instinct, incompetent to form an intelligent, independent judgement, passionate in temperament, and submissive only to superior force. They and those like them everywhere are a constant menace to the peace of the country, as they are totally incapable of comprehending its institutions. . . . They are samples of the refuse which is pouring into the country from the Old World in a tide which is fast submerging parts of the United States in vice and ignorance and stupidity."[57] It was scarcely a good augury for future harmony.

The Great Strike of 1894 and Afterward

As after the 1887 outbreak, two fairly quiet years followed the labor troubles of spring 1891. Then changing conditions in the iron and steel trades helped bring on a new confrontation. Steel output in 1892 was only 72,000 tons short of 5 million tons, almost twice the record of six years earlier. The following year, though, brought a sharp recession, with output down by 18.4 percent on the previous year and pig iron 22.2 percent less, a fall of over 2 million tons; Connellsville shipments decreased by 1.5 million tons. Coke prices had drifted down since 1890; in 1893 the average was almost 18.5 percent below the 1892 figure. Again, capacity extensions were out of line with the state of trade. Few new ovens had been built in 1892; the next year's figure was much higher. In summer 1893 wages were cut.

It was in this apparently favorable setting for their efforts that the United Mine Workers again targeted Connellsville for attention. The trade press pictured the union as breaking an accord in which, the men "have worked under agreements made with their respective employers. . . . The professional agitators and mischief makers who are the curse of all labor organizations could not let this peaceful state of affairs to continue any longer if they could prevent it, and they decided therefore that the men must again be organized, an increase in wages must be demanded although coke has been selling at the lowest prices ever known, and if not granted then a strike must follow."[58] Some Coke Region newspapers did present the workers' point of view, but only an exceptional working man was able to make a case directly in a manner persuasive to the general public. The vast majority of laborers were inarticulate compared with the spokesmen of the operators, and even more important was the unwillingness of most of the press to report their arguments. Fortunately, one document from the early stages of this new dispute put across their case with reason, moderation, and clarity. On 12 April 1894 Matthew J. Welsh wrote from West Leisenring to the editor of the *Pittsburgh Times*. The editor published his letter two days later.

Welsh wrote asking "correspondents of certain newspapers to refrain from publishing matter made known to them through the operators or their officials without consulting some workingman." He revealed the deep alienation of laborers in mines and at the ovens and outlined their grievances.

The workingmen, and especially the Hungarians, of the coke region are represented as an ignorant class of men. Certainly we are to a certain extent or we would not be toiling our lives out with work that former day slaves never dreamed of on a coke yard or in the mines. Ignorant as we are, we know that it is time to quit work and die of starvation rather than be trying to work and starving at the same time. The public can easily see that the leaders of organized labor are hounded and put to jail at the least possible chance. This is done in order to check the workingman's chance to organize. A house divided against itself cannot stand, so the workingmen cannot get along without organization. It's a necessity. Now is it a proper thing to discharge a man because he belongs to an organization for the betterment of existing labor? It is being done in this region at the present time and superintendents won't be content with that, but will conspire to murder a man and his family by blacklisting him, depriving him of a day's work and bringing him and his family slow death—starvation."

Welsh singled out the H. C. Frick Coke Company as rather better than most employers: "It must be admitted that the Frick wages are about the best and their stores the most reasonable, and if a man had any money coming to him he got it regularly every two weeks. Other works, and especially Rainey's, have not been doing this. At Mt. Braddock cokers received no pay eight months, but were compelled to draw it all out in store orders." But even at Frick works there was much that was wrong: "The present Frick scale, which seems to be satisfying the men so much, is one made by the company itself to suit it. The men were compelled to sign individually or get work somewhere other than at any of Frick's numerous works." Moreover, working arrangements meant published scales were deceptive: "For digging coal the men are paid 78 cents per 100 bushels mined, which is 39 cents a car supposed to hold 50 bushels, but in reality holding 70 bushels with the hump on. Why don't the men see about getting the cars measured etc? Simply because if a man opens his mouth about such a thing he is discharged. Many men go into the mine for one wagon of coal a day, and the coal sheets show the average run to be between two and three wagons per man. Deduct from the amount made the cost of oil and a lamp for use each day, the price of tools etc. and then behold your day's wages after being in the mine 10 or 12 hours, in danger all the time. Little as this leaves, the companies want it again in enormous rents and store orders." For his part, each coke drawer was "forced to do that which the operators seem ashamed to specify in their so-called scales. . . . He ought to wheel his coke the length of two to five ovens, but sometimes was made to move it past 12 or 13 without extra pay . . . and must not say anything about it either under pain of discharge." Welsh added: "The company says it is paying him 43 cents per 100 bushels for drawing, but as there is no checkweighman he must pull the coke that was humped on the wagon and is given what the company wishes to give him—60 cents for drawing 175 bushels. Is that 43 cents per 100? No. The operators do not even live up to their own scales. It's time for organization. No one knows the hardships of a coke yard or mine but those whose fate compels them to work there." Operators maintained they were not making money on coke, but he pointed out their "financial standing" proved they made a great deal. They opposed organization of the men but did not want orders for coke to pass to West Virginia as had happened during the previous dispute.[59]

A new strike began on 3 April 1894. It was to be the biggest confrontation in Coke Region history, lasting six months. From the start there was violence as bands of from five hundred to one thousand men "marched" about the region, intimidating those remaining at work. On the third day the *Connellsville Courier* was already writing of "a Reign of Terror": "Workmen have been beaten and driven from their posts, and the region from Fairchance to Scottdale so thoroughly intimidated that only three plants were in operation yesterday. Two lives have been sacrificed. Joseph H Paddock, Chief Engineer of the H. C. Frick Coke Company was foully murdered, and retribution swiftly overtook one of the brutal assassins." In fact, though the sheriff's deputies had been instructed not to shoot the retreating rioters, at Broad Ford they had fired across the river, and one of the "Huns" had been shot in the back and had died instantly. Welsh too condemned "riotous conduct," keenly regretting the death of Paddock, "a well-known and respected citizen," but contrasted reports of that tragic event with those of the shooting of the Hungarian: "That is all we hear of that act though. And why? Because he was a poor man; and it is safe to say no more will be said about him."[60]

By mid-April seven plants from Uniontown to Fairchance, active when the strike began, had been shut by threats from a very large crowd—reported as 2,000 men. The result was that 1,200 ovens closed and 1,000 men were thrown out of work. There was a brief hope of settlement before the situation flared up again. On 2 May, Frick wrote to his general superintendent at Mt. Pleasant. His letter revealed the extraordinary lengths to which operators would go in order to break a strike and the more than commercial motivations for their actions: "It would seem that by the judicious expenditure of even a considerable amount of money you ought to be able to reach some of the leading Hungarians, or others, and get them to make a break looking towards the resumption of work. Do not hesitate to spend some money if that will accomplish a decided break. Of course the money would better not be expended, or payable rather, until the goods are delivered. There is not anything in running coke works at present, yet it is annoying to see our trade going to some of our competitors, and to other coke districts." A few days later, he received an ill-written letter from a man who had been disabled digging coal at Standard, stating that he had suffered "so much bad luck that I am Broken up." Asking for money, he offered to provide 50 to as many as 300 nonunion men.[61] Four persons were killed in a riot in May and the coke towns were "terrorized" by strikers. In June the governor decided to prohibit further marches. From a strike, the dispute now developed into a lockout.

W. J. Rainey imported black laborers primarily from Roanoke, Virginia. The men who were out tried every method of persuasion to get the strikebreakers to quit.[62] Locked out, by September some of the Slavs were leaving the region, which was then said to be "running normal."

After the men had been defeated, other approaches were tried to undermine the workers' position. Action was taken to diffuse discontent within the district and to improve the area's public image. From spring 1895 wage scales were increased—for mining and loading coal by some 15.4 percent. The government of Austro-Hungary, having received "exaggerated" accounts of the killings and evictions in 1894, requested that the conditions of the approximately ten thousand Slavs should be investigated. Early in October 1895 an impressive group came to the region to carry out this inquiry. Accompanied by Lynch, a representative from Carnegie Steel, and local Slav banker and editor A. Fail were the Austro-Hungarian consul in Pittsburgh, Mr. Dessewil, and Baron Hengelmuller, Austro-Hungarian minister to the United States. They visited Trotter and then moved on to Leisenring, where they went down the shafts. They "examined" many individuals, Slavs and others, who were said to know about the Slavs' situation, looked into housing, and enquired about wages, savings, and general living conditions. Reporters wrote that the Baron was, "surprised when taken into Slavs' houses to see pianos in the parlors, carpets on the floors, curtains at the windows, and good furnishings generally. He was visibly impressed with the fine condition of the miners." In light of this favorably shaped perception of the area, it was satisfying, if scarcely a matter for surprise, that the visit produced an uneventful outcome: "Baron Hengelmuller will send in a favorable report to the Austrian Government." Fortunately, some purposeful steps were now taken toward the amelioration of general conditions of life in the region. Frick, for example, presented five acres in the center of Mt. Pleasant for a park for the use of school children.[63]

After the 1894 strike the Coke Region often seemed to be teetering on the edge of a new outbreak. In late summer 1895 there was more unrest. Frick reported to his colleagues at Illinois Steel that Lynch was "quite nervous over the labor situation . . . and rather favored posting notice of an advance in wages." But labor was plentiful and the "only reason advanced for giving an advance now was fear of a demand for it, and if that should be refused, a strike." Frick continued by observing: "You are aware, however, that it does not take much to bring about a strike these times. Had hoped, however, and still hope that we will be able to avoid any trouble, and any further advance in wages, this year." Lynch meanwhile attributed the nervousness to other managements rather than to himself—"The Cambria Iron Co. . . . call me up two and three times every day from their works at Morrell and from Johnstown."—and he assured Frick that reports of meetings at one of their works and on the Mt. Pleasant Branch were untrue, "At least if there were meetings, we can not find out anything about them, and I do not believe it would be possible to hold meetings at either of these places without our getting on to it."[64] However on Friday, 27 September, miners, coke drawers, and coke workers generally at H. C. Frick Coke were informed wages would be increased 6 percent. Despite what Frick had revealed to his Chicago partners, the press reported this rise as planned some time before: "It transpires that an advance was contemplated several weeks ago, but was not announced because of the strike agitation. The operators did not wish to place themselves in the position of having been frightened into doing that which they intended to do." In any event, the increase had a favorable effect. As Lynch reported on 9 October, the efforts of the *Merchant and Miner* in calling on every works to be represented at a delegate convention of miners and coke drawers the previous day had been a complete failure. Only six men turned up—the president, vice president, two Hungarians from Oliver, and two others from Lemont.[65]

The operators could well stand the 6–7 percent increase of October 1895, for the average price for coke that year was 23 percent higher than 1894; because much larger shipments were made, gross revenue was almost 86 percent more. In the first quarter of the year the list price remained at $1.00, though a good deal of coke was then sold for $.90 or even $.85. On 1 April the official price was advanced 35 percent and on October 1 by another 18.5 percent. Increases in Frick scales were considerably less. Some twenty years later the *Connellsville Courier* looked back to the move to higher wage rates as a decisive step in ending the labor problem: "There has never been any necessity for organized demand for fair wages in the Connellsville coke region since that time. The operators have made it an unwavering rule . . . to anticipate the justice of advanced wages, and to reduce them only under stress of great necessity." This was too favorable a judgment. Relative to coke prices, labor costs first fell, and later they were still generally well below their relative level at the time when the 1894 strike broke out. In 1896 H. C. Frick Coke kept the coke price at $2.00 a ton; though smaller firms sometimes sold for a good deal less and the district average was $1.90. Again, wage scales lagged behind, but the men took no purposeful action. A critical press authority put its own interpretation on their failure: "A futile attempt was made by some of the old strike leaders to revive the organization upon which they fed and fattened in 1893."[66]

In a striking indication of the general nature of the hostility of the owners to the aspirations of their workers, the Carnegie Steel Company proved no more amenable after Frick's removal than he had been to the miners and coke workers. Early in 1900 Carnegie's president, Charles M. Schwab, discussed the labor situation with Lynch. It was afterward considered by the Carnegie Board of Managers. Men from Ohio and

Table 3.1 Increases in wage scales at H. C. Frick Coke Company, 1895

	1 April 1895 over 10 February 1894	1 October 1895 over 1 April 1895
Mining and loading 100 bu^a room/rib coal	15.4%	6.0%
Chargers, per day	7.1%	6.0%
Leveling, per oven	12.5%	5.6%
Drawing coke, per 100 bu charged	16.3%	6.0%
Forking cars, over 60,000 lbs	33.3%	6.0%

SOURCE: Based on *Connellsville Courier*, May 1914, 30.
a. bushels

Table 3.2 Sample wage rates in the Coke Region, 1894–1912
(as percentage of year's average coke price)

Period	Mining/loading 100 bu^a room & rib coal	Charging per day	Drawing per 100 bu
February 1894	78.0	140.0	43.0
April–October 1895	75.4	125.6	41.9
March 1900	46.3	70.5	26.7
June–December 1903	40.8	62.6	23.3
March 1907	46.5	69.0	26.5
January 1910	64.3	95.2	37.1
April 1912	75.0	112.0	42.7

SOURCE: Based on *Connellsville Courier*, May 1914, 6, 30.
a. bushels

Indiana were reportedly trying to organize the Coke Region. A meeting had been held at Adelaide where ninety-five of the four hundred men employed attended. Lynch feared they might demand an eight-hour working day, which would reduce output 20 percent. The Carnegie managers supported "active" opposition to these moves. Schwab's brother, Joe, was more direct: "I think we ought to go ahead and break up the organization and assemblies wherever we find them springing up, or do what we can with that end in view." Andrew Moreland's advice to Lynch had been, "Find some excuse to discharge the organizers, if employed by us, and do so promptly." A week later Schwab reported Adelaide had been closed as a result of dismissals made there; there was no trouble at other works. When asked if they were getting fair treatment from the newspapers, Schwab replied: "Yes, the newspapers are all against the men.... My idea is not to publish anything at all respecting the matter in the newspapers. I think our policy should be to remain quiet."[67]

Through scale adjustments to January 1903, the wages of all classes of labor in the mines and coke yards advanced progressively. In the summer of 1902, quoting the *Connellsville Courier*, the *Bulletin of the American Iron and Steel Association* entitled an article "Contented Connellsville Miners." A few years later, celebrating the centenary of Connellsville town, a group of local authors were almost euphoric concerning labor relations and the general felicity of the men: "The workmen in the region, numbering about thirty thousand, are paid wages according to the 'Frick scale,' which fixes the prices paid for mining coal, drawing the ovens etc., according to the selling price of coke. Although this scale may not be followed accurately, the workmen's wages have steadily advanced since 1894, till now they are receiving the highest wages ever paid in the district, and the relations between capital and labor are so genial and happy that conditions have excited the admiration of the world."[68] In fact, as always, the benefits from the business continued to be strongly skewed in favor of the owners. This had been clearly revealed in an assessment made by Lynch. By summer 1899 H. C. Frick Coke owned 40,000 of the estimated 55,000 acres of mineable coal in the Connellsville basin. Though paying the highest wages ever in the region, costs of mining were not over 25 cents a net ton. Coke fob the ovens was $1.50 a ton. At this price it would yield a profit of $3,500 per acre over and above interest, taxes, and other overheads. Every 10-cent increase in coke prices would increase profits per acre by an additional $700. Even at current values Frick's coke holdings should provide profits of $140 million.[69] Income from company stores would add further large revenues derived from the everyday needs of their workforce and dependents.

After six advances in wages since February 1894, amounting in all to an increase of 63 percent, in mid-December 1903 H. C. Frick Coke followed the lead of independent operators by cutting rates, in its case by an average of 17 percent. After this wages again rose. There was an increase in March 1905 and then, on 18 February 1907, Frick Coke announced additions for the various grades of its 18,500 employees in the Coke Region ranging from 8 to 12.5 percent, increasing its wage bill for the year by about $1.5 million. Production was at capacity levels and coke prices in the early months were abnormally high at $3.40 to $3.50 a ton. For the first forty weeks of 1907, shipments averaged 400,000 tons. However, that autumn there was a sharp recession, shipments in the last twelve weeks of the year averaging under 200,000 tons. Many ovens were taken out of production and prices ended 1907 at between $2.25 and $2.00. Slackening activity and hard prospects for the winter were causing many men to move out of the Coke Region. As early as 12 November a "solid trainload" of Italians, Hungarians, and Slavs left Pittsburgh via the Baltimore and Ohio Railroad for New York to embark for Europe. Some of these individuals came from Pittsburgh mills, but most were from the mining districts. Many took considerable savings with them. The promptness of their response to the depression evoked grudging respect.

As one trade authority put it: "The remarkable fact about the sudden departure of foreign working people is that, although they are the most ignorant class of workers in the country, they were able to discern the trade depression ahead of almost anybody else and acted promptly for what they considered their best interest."[70] By early January 1908 H. C. Frick Coke was offering coke at 20–25 percent below previous levels and had removed the wage increases granted ten months before. Early in 1910 it returned to the February 1907 scales, or for some lines of work to slightly higher rates. In March 1910 a strike began in the peripheral Irwin-Greensburg coke district. This ended in failure for the workers after more than fifteen months.[71] Beyond the disturbing times of World War I lay more labor disputes, but they were conducted under radically different conditions in both coke production and marketing.

Dealers, Operators, and Managers

The basis of the whole, massive economic development of the Connellsville region was its first-rate coking coal. Control of ample acreages of coal lands was the essential prerequisite for a successful enterprise in coke. When the industry began, much of the lowland was in farms; it became a never-ending concern of the owners to buy from farmers lands underlain by favorably disposed portions of the Connellsville seam or to obtain them from speculators or smaller rivals. This was often difficult as there were large numbers of originally separately owned tracts. The first task was to persuade the owners to sell so that a large, and if possible continuous, tract of coal land could be pieced together. Sometimes ovens were bought less for their own value than in order to gain control of adjacent coal lands. For the long-term future success of a coke works, it was vital that it should be able to draw upon a large enough acreage of coal acquired at reasonable cost. In turn, the size of the coal tract determined the size of the oven plant built to use its output. Prices paid for coal lands varied widely, partly reflecting the character of the coal—depth, thickness, coking quality—and in part in relation to the proximity of railroads. Because the coal would have to support the oven capacity over a long term and could not in any case contribute to production immediately, the value placed on coal land could not be expected to reflect the short-term ups and downs of coke prices. Given such circumstances, successful buying and selling of coking coal land required skill, could be a source of disagreement, sometimes of exploitation of weaker parties, and conversely might yield great profit to the discriminating dealer. As time went on some individuals found it worthwhile to speculate in these lands, holding on to what they bought in the expectation that eventually growing demand for coke would bring them an opportunity to sell at great profit.

Acquisition of a very large tract of coal lands such as the 8,000 acres with which the Connellsville Coke and Iron Company began business was exceptional. The origins of this venture may be traced back to the "panic" that began in 1873. At that time Frick's older cousin, Abraham Overholt Tinstman, was in financial difficulties and sold his interest in their joint business to Frick. By 1876 Tinstman seemed to have lost everything but within about a year had sufficiently regained his powers so to acquire an option on 3,500 acres of coal lands west of the South West Pennsylvania line between Connellsville and Uniontown. He sold this large tract to the chief engineer of the Pittsburgh and Connellsville Railroad, Edward K. Hyndman, who added to it 4,500 acres of contiguous coal acquired from other parties. The 8,000 acres were reported as purchased at the very low average price of $20–30 an acre, though other sources put the figure much higher.[72] Hyndman and a group of his east Pennsylvania friends, led by John Leisenring, incorporated the Connellsville Coal and Coke Company on 5 March 1880 to develop mines and build ovens on this tract. Given the large area involved, they planned two coke works of 500 ovens each. When their first annual report was issued on 10 February 1881, the directors acknowledged how fortunate they had been in the purchase: "The Board desire to congratulate the shareholders on the possession of so fine a property in Fayette County; doubtless it is among the best tracts of coking coal land in the State and probably in the world. Its value has already appreciated to nearly or quite double its original cost."[73] The transaction with Hyndman had also put Tinstman on his feet again. In 1880 he established in Pittsburgh the firm of A. O. Tinstman and Company to engage in coke manufacture. The next year he bought the Mt. Braddock Coke and Pennsville Coke Companies. A few years later he sold them and thereafter continued buying and selling coal lands until he retired.[74]

Another long-term holder of coal was Andrew Mellon. Already, before the end of the 1870s, his family controlled large portions of the Pittsburgh bed downriver from the Connellsville basin on the left bank of the Youghiogheny. A few years later the family made their way into the coking coal districts. Early in 1886 Mellon was reported to have bought about 750 acres in Hempfield and East Huntingdon Townships from Henry Croushour and M. L. Painter, paying a total of $150,000, or $200 an acre.[75] A few months later he and Frick spent $60,500, much of it shared equally between them, for coal, mining rights, and land.[76]

Naturally, as his company grew to a dominant position in the district, Frick had to become a major purchaser of coal and ancillary lands. Predictably, he took great care with the process. This came out well in instructions given to Lynch about negotiations in fall 1882: "Some time ago I told Mr. Jas. R. Stauffer that we would like to buy all of that flat or bottom land near Valley Works, from Mr. Sherrick. We had some negotiations with Sherrick but it did not amount to anything. I would like you to call upon Mr. Sherrick on Monday and get the option on that land near Valley on the best terms you can. He may want to include his entire farm. If he does and insists upon it, and you cannot get the option on the other without that, take the option on the whole thing. His price heretofore has been $300 per acre for the flat land. You can probably do better with him. If he should say that he has given Mr. Stauffer the refusal of it, go and see Mr. Stauffer and get him to give you a letter to Mr. Sherrick waiving any right to it." In the spring of 1886, Frick displayed his subtlety in dealing with hopeful farmers in instructions to Robert Ramsay: "We intend to accept the Myers option, but this is between you and I, but would prefer to have it extended as per enclosed option, for reasons not necessary to give. See him and tell him I have been so busy could not get out to see his farm and avoid this extra time. Won't suppose you will have any trouble getting him to extend. If he won't extend, advise me in time."[77] Such provision for all eventualities identified an acute negotiator, but even he could not avoid some disappointments.

In 1883 the H. C. Frick Coke Company paid $700,000 to A. A. Hutchinson for the 573 ovens of the Standard coke works and a 185-acre coal tract extending northward from it, a relatively small holding. In May 1885 Frick filed a bill in equity in Pittsburgh against Hutchinson, Peter Rumbaugh, and others alleging Hutchinson had failed to convey to him 85 acres of coal land, part of this tract he had contracted to purchase from the other defendants.[78] Hutchinson's own experience showed that to be a successful coke operator required the keenest appreciation of long-term prospects. At one time he held large options south of Uniontown, had numerous tests made of the coal in adjacent ovens, but then gave up the opportunity to buy it. At that time the option price was from $25–40 an acre. Before the outbreak of war in Europe in 1914, the same land was worth between $2,500 and $3,000 an acre.[79]

Big companies sold as well as bought. Sometimes this was because a particular tract was ill located, and in other cases because they could exchange it for something better suited to their needs. In July 1886 Frick corresponded with John G. A. Leishman, a man who was to be a close colleague at Carnegie Steel a few years later but was at this time a broker. It seems that Leishman had inquired about two properties. The main one was the John K. Ewing farm of 157 acres fronting on the Youghiogheny and served by the Pittsburgh, McKeesport, and Youghiogheny Railroad. The upper end of the property was, Frick indicated, well suited for a mining village and other colliery buildings, and there was room for two hundred ovens (or twice that number if block ovens were built) and the necessary sidings. He adopted the generously expansive tone of the salesman: "To a party such as you represent we would be willing to sell an undivided one-half interest in that farm, together with an interest in as much coal adjoining it as they might want, upon as fair terms as they could purchase from any one in that locality. There would be no difficulty in obtaining connection with either the Pennsylvania or the Baltimore and Ohio Railroads, which would give us the advantage of three (3) railroads. If your party mean business, we would be very glad to meet them personally, and show them over the ground. Think we could suggest an arrangement that would be mutually beneficial." The other possibility was farther north and inferior: "In regard to the property near Mt. Pleasant, we could sell it at a very much less price per acre than we could this property, for the reason that the latter is nearer a good supply of water and the vein is somewhat thicker."[80] The sale did not go through, and shortly afterward H. C. Frick Coke itself chose the Ewing farm as the site for its large Adelaide coke works.

Illinois Steel in the second half of the 1890s provided an example of another motivation for selling. Under the leadership of John W. Gates, it was trying to raise capital to modernize its operations in order to better meet the very keen competition it was then suffering from Carnegie Steel. At one stage the company was reportedly willing to sell off some of its Connellsville district properties as a means to this end. A few years later its successor company, Federal Steel, was pioneering new developments in southwestern Pennsylvania.

Beyond that region speculative investors acquired some big coking coal tracts long before they became of practical interest to coke makers. During the 1880s the Leisenrings purchased very large areas in the western parts of Virginia. When they sold their Fayette County coal and ovens to Frick in 1889, they turned to the development of these properties. However, though richly endowed, they were much less favorably located than those they had sold in Pennsylvania. A decade and a half later, the United States Steel Corporation became deeply involved in coke developments in the Pocahontas district. It was disappointed in at least one of its proposed large coal purchases. In 1906 U.S. Steel's Finance Committee discussed the question of purchasing 105,000 acres of coal lands in Preston, Barbour, Taylor, and Marion Counties in the valleys of the Monongahela and Cheat Rivers. This tract had been acquired over the years by James McClurg Guffey, a man whose fortune had been made in oil and who had recently, with the Mellons, established Guffey Petroleum, the predecessor of Gulf Oil. It was said that this coking coal section could be acquired for forty dollars an acre. The matter was regarded as of such importance by U.S. Steel that its president, William Corey, was authorized to negotiate for a six-month option to investigate and explore the property. Guffey refused them an option.[81]

By far the most important and distinctive speculator in coal lands in southwestern Pennsylvania was the Uniontown banker Josiah Van Kirk Thompson. The wealth that could be made from dealing in coal was indicated by his fortune, which once reached $70 million; the vulnerability of those depending on this activity was high-

J. V. K. Thompson. *Courtesy of The Sisters of the Order of St. Basil, Uniontown*

lighted by the fact that he had lost most of it before he died. Thompson was born in the Uniontown area in 1854. His father, Jasper Markle Thompson, was then a cattle farmer and buyer. In 1864 J. M. Thompson started the First National Bank of Uniontown and soon afterward became its president. He was involved with development schemes for the area, including a proposed Uniontown and West Virginia Railroad, which would have opened coal areas south of the town, but was not built. Thompson also acquired some coal land. In 1886 Frick and Mellon together bought some small tracts from Jasper and his wife.[82] In 1871 Josiah joined his father's bank and on the elder Thompson's death in 1889 succeeded to its presidency. Like his father, but on a much larger scale, J. V. K. Thompson traded in coal lands. From as early as May 1890, Frick bought coal from him, at that time paying $56,000 for 622 acres of the "Beeson Coal" south of Uniontown.[83] He made a few more but smaller purchases during the 1890s and substantial ones in later years. Thompson's major impact was on the development of Lower Connellsville. His father had owned some land there, but Josiah did not become a large investor until the coking quality of its coal was proved at the end of the 1890s. At this point he sold some of his holdings in the "old basin" in order to buy his way further into the promising new area. In July 1899 he sold 5,000 acres of this new coking coal land to J. W. Gates for the benefit of the American Steel and Wire Company. The price was $170 an acre. Eight years later, when buying an adjoining tract, Thompson had to pay ten times as much.[84]

In Lower Connellsville Thompson also interested himself in the wider processes of economic development. He proposed a new railroad, the Uniontown and Wheeling Short Line, which would cross the field, delivering its coal or coke to important markets. The idea was taken up by the promoters of the Wabash extension to the Pittsburgh and southwestern Pennsylvania areas but died with that ill-starred project. Eventually, Thompson also became a coke operator. The Thompson-Connellsville Coke Company was organized to develop one of his coking coal tracts. Two coke works were built, Thompson 1 and 2, for which the highly experienced John P. Brennen was hired as president and manager. In November 1906 Thompson sold 2,000 acres of coal to the newly formed Tower Hill Connellsville Coke Company at $1,700 an acre, making the sale worth $3.4 million. Tower Hill came into production in 1908 with two coke plants, and J. V. K. Thompson took the presidency himself. All four of these works and their coal supply areas were south of Merrittstown. He was also associated with the Rich Hill Coke Company, whose works were at Outcrop, five miles north of the Cheat River in the Geneva and Point Marion coke field.

Although he also invested in coal in West Virginia, Thompson above all played an important role in the opening of the coking coals across the Monongahela River in Greene County. By early 1914 he held title to coal in seventeen of that county's eighteen townships, a tally of around 120,000 acres. Worth probably an average $200 per acre, Thompson's assets there totaled $24 million.[85] Thompson was years later described as a man who "doubtless has more intimate knowledge of the coal lands and coal values in the Connellsville coke region and in West Virginia than any other man identified with the business."[86] Gradually, he sold to steel companies as they built byproduct coke plants as part of their integrated operations and shipped coal from the area. For instance, in December 1913 he disposed of 5,000 acres of coal lands in the eastern part of Greene County to the Youngstown Sheet and Tube Company. Despite the huge coal holdings and the high reputation he had built up, it was soon afterward shown that he could be outmaneuvered by more ruthless men. He had bought some tracts of land in the Dunkard Creek area at prices ranging from $50 to $280 an acre. Early in 1914 the H. C. Frick Coke Company expressed a wish to buy some of this coal. When Thompson arrived to negotiate he was received not as he apparently expected by Frick but by Lynch, president of the coke company. Unwisely, he asked to see Frick, which seemed to offend Lynch. In February he sold about 10,000 acres of the coal to Frick, apparently for the latter's personal investment and probably at about $600 an acre.[87] A few months later Frick was encouraging Gary to acquire as much as 50,000 acres of coal in Greene County, which he was sure "would prove very valuable in the future." The lands he had bought had been very satisfactory in quality and had proved a good investment. He thought they would appreciate still more, for "good, clean coal of about 8 feet in thickness, so accessible as this will grow in value very rapidly." He went on to say, "Mr. Lynch will know how to go about securing options." Frick then made clear that he was aware of the weaknesses of Thompson's current situation: "Mr. JV Thompson, with whom I traded, is a large holder and some people say is hard pressed financially, and if anything should happen to him, think there would be a large amount of good coal for sale cheap; but if a low price could be had now and long time, I don't think I would wait."[88] Sheppard suggests that somehow word got around that in the course of negotiations with its coal and coke subsidiary, Thompson had displeased U.S. Steel and that this, together with the 1914 recession, helped cause him serious financial problems. In spring 1915 he offered some of his best coal lands to U.S. Steel for $40 million; they were only prepared to pay $19 million. Thompson dropped his price to $34 million but the corporation would not raise its offer over $21 million. That July he was reckoned to own 141,413 acres of coal lands, but by the early autumn creditors were descending on him "like a flock," many wanting "some of his highly valuable and unduplicatable coal-bearing properties."[89] By December 1915 a Creditors' Association had been formed to sort out his financial affairs. Before the close of the following year, Frick had acquired 12,000 acres of Thompson's finest Greene County coking coal for $6 or $7 million, $550 an acre. Much of the coal was eleven feet thick and situated near to the Monongahela, making it ideal for transportation to the new byproduct ovens U.S. Steel was by now engaged in building at Clairton. There was a feeling that the price paid had been favorable to the buyer. Despite his huge holdings, worth according to some estimates anything from $110 million to a figure twice as large, Thompson proved incapable of escaping his immediate problems. By September 1917 he was declared bankrupt.[90] Even the largest independent control of rich coking coal had proved no adequate defense against the superior power of the predominant coke company or the giant integrated mineral, iron, and steel concerns now dominating the coking coal and coke industries. Coal dealing was obviously no longer a job for amateurs, however talented.

Operators and Managers

A rich resource base, the large-scale influx of entrepreneurship and capital, and the assembling of an ample workforce were essential conditions for the success of the coke industry. However, it was untypical for an operator to choose to live in the midst of the confusion, pollution, and noise that were an inevitable part of the operations he had built up and that generated his wealth. There was a need for a chain of command in which mine bosses, engineers, general managers, and superintendents played essential parts. Each of the bigger companies depended on more-or-less complicated control structures of this kind. Some officers became important innovators, one example being Thomas J. Mitchell, brother-in-law and general manager for Rainey, and the pioneer of the rectangular coke oven. A few years earlier John Brennen, formerly McClure's manager, played a central part in the proving and opening of the Lower Connellsville district. By far the best-documented insight into managerial structures is found in the records of the H. C. Frick Coke and South West Coal and Coke Companies (on which the following discussion is based). Like their head, many though not all of Frick's managers were locally born. In building his own great and uniquely successful steel operations, Carnegie often claimed, and has subsequently commonly been credited with, a talent amounting to genius in choosing men who could serve his purposes. Though a leader of very different personality, Frick too usually chose top men well, maintained close contact with them, and gave them remarkable support and sympathetic understanding.

In 1875 the twenty-five-year-old Frick, struggling through the long depression, engaged a twenty-one year old from the southern part of the Coke Region to act as clerk in his Broadford store. This young man would become his trusted chief lieutenant and eventual successor as head of the H. C. Frick Coke Company. Thomas Lynch was born in Uniontown in 1854 to Irish immigrant parents. At eighteen he left high school, became a clerk in the Dunbar Furnace Company store, and later in the nearby store of the Atlas Coke Company. After this he worked as yard boss in the Atlas coke works before, like Frick, spending a short period in Pittsburgh retailing, in his case about eighteen months in the wholesale grocery store of Allen Kirkpatrick in Liberty Street. Returning to the Coke Region as store clerk for Frick at Broadford, he soon afterward again transferred to the production side as superintendent of the Anchor mine, in 1877 of the Tip Top mines, and then the recently leased Valley coke works and store. Five years later and at twenty-seven years old, Lynch became general superintendent of all H. C. Frick Coke Company operations. By 1890 he was general manager and in 1896 became president, retaining this post under United States Steel, for which he was a director. In later years Lynch was also president of other coke and mineral companies and a director of banks both in the Coke Region and in Pittsburgh, including Mellon National Bank and the Union Trust Company.

Lynch seems to have been a wholly reliable man. Soon after his death, appreciations apart from those offering the usual fulsome tributes to "keen and well balanced judgement" and "indomitable will and resistless energy," recognized other qualities that, being less conventional subjects for praise, seemed likely more accurate representations of the truth—his faithfulness, modesty, and general care for the company's employees, "leading them along paths of thrift and economy to higher and surer footings in their struggles upward." After the 1891 Mammoth mine disaster, he had played a leading part in pushing through improvements in mine safety, his care for this element of their operations over time having an impact far wider than merely on the company and industry in which he introduced it. Lynch helped upgrade the coke villages with better houses, schools, social provisions, and incentives for gardening. Inevitably, the promotion of the long-term interests of his company was mixed in with disinterested goodwill. It does not require a Marxist philosophical standpoint to recognize this; even a highly laudatory biographer incidentally did so: "He believed that attractive homes and home surroundings, and the best possible sanitation, with satisfactory pay, made contented workers." The evidence, considered elsewhere, shows that conditions remained hard until well after Lynch's death, but there is no reason to doubt that, within the often very narrow constraints he was allowed and the assumptions of his times as to what were acceptable working conditions, he eventually administered a relatively humane regime.[91]

For many years Lynch kept Frick well informed about conditions in the Coke Region, negotiations over coal land or oven purchases, labor relations, and new technology. In the whole extensive correspondence between them there is no sign of dissension. In two respects, however, their relationship seems to have had unfortunate results. Evidence suggests that around 1890 Lynch was slightly more receptive than Frick to the idea of technological innovation, specifically to inquiry into new types of ovens. Later, perhaps learning that such openness to new methods was unwelcome, he became a conservative, apparently always pleased when he could pass on news of failure in the operations or commercial results of byproduct coke operations. (There is also at least circumstantial evidence that he helped bias the attitude of the United States Steel Corporation against early large-scale involvement in Lower Connellsville.) Less widely important there was, in the early years at least, a measure of sycophancy in their relationship; Lynch's eldest child was named Clay Frick Lynch.

Frick was sufficiently generous with gifts for Mrs. Lynch and for Clay, that on Christmas Day 1885 Thomas was moved to write, "We want Clay to feel as he grows up that we gave him your name as an evidence of my gratitude to you for past kindnesses and for that sentiment alone."[92] (Young Clay Lynch became assistant general manager at H. C. Frick Coke in the first decade of the twentieth century. In January 1915, during the managerial shakeup that followed his father's death, he was brought back from work in the Illinois coalfield to become general superintendent.)[93]

When Lynch became president of the coke company in 1896, he was succeeded as general superintendent by an almost exact contemporary, Orran W. Kennedy. After sixteen years as a clerk for the Pennsylvania Railroad in which he rose to the post of freight office chief clerk, in 1890 Kennedy joined Frick's Pittsburgh office and a year later went to Scottdale as Lynch's assistant. In about 1904 Kennedy left the Frick organization. His successor was an engineer, a profession that in the 1890s had begun to make its way into more prominent positions in the Frick organization. Walter H. Clingerman had worked for the Pennsylvania Railroad and in 1895 was given leave by his employers to build car shops at Everson for H. C. Frick Coke. He joined the coke company and in 1897 became assistant general superintendent. On Lynch's death Clingerman took over as president.[94]

In many ways the most interesting insights into management in Frick Coke can be derived from the relationships between Frick and three members of the Ramsay family, Robert, his brother Morris, and William, Morris's son. Born into a poor family near Dunfermline, the brothers learned the skills of machinists and engineers before immigrating to the United States with their parents in 1863. When the parents returned to Scotland, the sons remained behind. Robert started work at the Hays coal mine on the Monongahela above Pittsburgh. Two years later he became hoisting engineer at Shafton, Westmoreland County, the first shaft mine west of the Alleghenies. He was engaged by Carnegie, Phipps, and Company in 1881 to operate their Monastery coke works, but two years later, following the merging of Monastery into the H. C. Frick Coke Company, was transferred to Mt. Pleasant as superintendent at Standard works. There in the late 1880s, in a technical culmination of his early American experiences, he controlled the nation's largest shaft-mining operation. He made some innovations to increase efficiency, for instance using waste heat from a few of the ovens in a boiler to generate motive power. Another development at the same works four years later was for a very different purpose, worker surveillance. The company installed the first electrical "watchman detector" in the Coke Region. A clock with a round sheet of paper revolving in place of the hour hand was connected by wire to ten stations around the plant: "On reaching each of these stations, the watchman turns the box with his key and the time he does so is punched through the sta-

Morris Ramsay. *Courtesy of Marjorie J. Laing*

tion's number on the office dial." Robert Ramsay died in 1899 at the age of fifty-nine.[95]

The younger brother, Morris, was originally a miner, then in turn inspector and engineer before joining Frick in 1882. In 1886 he became head of the engineering corps at H. C. Frick Coke, and after that directed the extensive mining operations and four coke plants of South West Coal and Coke, first as superintendent and then as general manager. His correspondence with Frick reveals the strain under which managers sometimes operated in the midst of communities overwhelmingly made up of workers or their sympathizers. In turn, Frick showed not only a remarkable capacity in supporting him but also an impressive concern for his physical well being. These aspects of their relationship were shown most clearly during the 1891 strike. On Thursday, 16 April, two weeks after the Morewood shootings, Frick replied to two letters he had received from Ramsay that morning whose "tenor" he concluded confirmed newspaper reports of his fears that the militia would soon be withdrawn: "However you may feel, I think that it is bad policy to show so publicly that you are frightened. That feeling will certainly be communicated to the men that are working for you. You should put on a bold front publicly, no matter what you may say to me, or to General Wiley [of the Pennsylvania National Guard], and thus inspire confidence in men working for you. This is the way the thing strikes me. . . . We are going to fight this thing through; it does not make any difference how long it takes. . . . Be aggressive. Our side of the question is right as you know. . . . Any hopes and fears you may have, express freely to me. We will consult together. I know you are doing the best you can, but present a bold front to the public and the enemy."[96]

Even before this time of extreme tension Ramsay, formerly a strong and powerful man, had been unwell, and Frick suggested he should go to the seaside or to the then fashionable winter resort of Lakewood, New Jersey, "within 11 miles of the seashore and in the pines; but of course your Doctor will be able to tell you the best thing to do."[97] Then, a year after the strike, disturbances, and violence of 1891, Ramsay was struck down by an illness that proved difficult to diagnose. At first it was attributed to overwork. Again, Frick was solicitous, though obviously tempted to try to over-organize the life of the sick man. In May he was quite exceptionally familiar in his form of address: "My Dear Morris, . . . I think that your health demands that you should make arrangements to take a six weeks trip to Scotland, leaving here about the middle of June, returning early in August." In fact, in early June it was arranged that Ramsay would be off work for only a few days; at the same time his annual salary was increased by $1,000. During his illness he was sent to a sanitorium in the mountains, at which time it was said that he had a kidney problem. In late July Frick again encouraged him to arrange for a break: "It seems to me you should take at least 10 days. I would try Atlantic City, if I were you."[98] Instead, Ramsay spent two to three months in Europe. When he returned home on about 20 October he had to take to his bed. Frick wanted a good doctor to examine him, and, as he indicated to Robert: "All this will not cost Morris anything. Would like you to say to him that we would be perfectly willing to provide the best medical attention in the country, if he is willing to have it." A few days later he paid a Dr. Sutton $105 for two visits made to Mt. Pleasant to see the sick man.[99] On 29 December Morris Ramsay was operated on and found to have cancer of the pancreas. He died the same day; he was only forty-four. After a service in his home on Monday, 2 January 1893, attended by Frick, Lynch, and the general managers of the McClure and Hostetter-Connellsville Coke Companies, he was buried in Irwin Cemetery.[100]

Frick acted with great consideration to Morris Ramsay's family, a mark of his high regard for the general manager he had lost. On the day following the funeral, reporting the situation to Jay Morse, his partner in South West Coal and Coke, Frick wrote: "We buried Mr. Morris Ramsay yesterday. He was a most faithful man in the interests of this Company and leaves a family of nine children [four others had predeceased their father], seven of whom are small; leaves an estate which will amount, I think, to about $18,000.00. I think we should pay his widow a sum equal to his salary for one year." The death also prompted ideas for reorganization. Frick proposed that the company should appoint a chief clerk at the works, since "a great deal of Mr. Ramsay's time was taken up by routine office work, which could have been devoted elsewhere to better purpose, or at least given him more rest." Morse was asked to reply promptly if he agreed to the change. In the meantime Frick appointed the twenty-two-year-old son, William Ramsay, acting general superintendent. William had been in the company engineer corps for several years and for the last, difficult year of Morris Ramsay's life had been his father's assistant so that he was familiar with everything at the works; "Is very much like his father in temperament and disposition, and I feel will get along very well with the men." A local paper gave its own endorsement: "He is an apt student, industrious and energetic. He will succeed."[101] For a time all went well under the new management, but eventually William proved much less satisfactory than his father, and Frick became less patient. Above all, experience over the short time in which the son was in charge confirmed the great pressures under which those on the spot worked.

The coke trade had a bad time during 1894. Prices were low, at $1 per ton average for the year, less than at any time since the end of the long 1870s depression. Labor relations were at low ebb, the United Mine Workers actively working for a confrontation since March. Frick busily urged all-round economy and bombarded his superintendent with advice on various possible savings. Late in March he stressed: "You must not allow any organization to get a hold at any of the South West works. . . . Discharge anyone that you think is trying to form one." Ten days later he asked why the company needed two watchmen: "What changes you do make, leading towards more economical management need not be made with a rush, but be done quietly and intelligently." Then he returned to labor relations, urging William to "stick at it," adding "take good care of yourself and keep cool." A few days later he wrote: "Glad you succeeded in capturing the dynamiters." Soon he was advocating evictions of strikers, expressing pleasure with Ramsay's stand, and finally inviting him to see brighter prospects ahead: "You are certainly doing very well, and are no doubt keeping a bright look out for any flank movements of the enemy.... When this strike is once over, we will have peace for a long time." Early that autumn William managed a short vacation but soon afterward had to contend with accidents, including fatalities at the plants he controlled. Frick again stressed the need for economy: "Would like you to get along with present heating facilities in Morewood store for this winter. Do not care to expend any money now that can be avoided." After this he even engaged in a correspondence on feed for the animals at their mines: "Is it ground or fed as whole grain? What is it costing you? Having as many mules as we do, it seems to me, if close attention is not given to the stables, a great deal of money can be wasted." Soon afterward he returned to the same theme. "You don't give me any reason why you should not use wheat, which costs so much less per pound than oats." Later he was still pushing cost savings: "Am much pleased to see that you are introducing all the economies you can from time to time."[102] Meanwhile, other pressures were mounting. In June 1895 Frick sent William a letter that seemed to point to nepotism: "I get a good many anonymous letters about you. Rarely pay any attention to them. I, however, would like to have you furnish me with a list of your relatives, either by blood or marriage, employed by the South West Company, state the positions they occupy and the salaries they receive. See that this list is absolutely correct." From one cause or another in the middle months of 1896, the health of the young manager began to break down, and he had to withdraw from his post. James A. Cowan, an older man and superintendent at Tarr since 1893, was put in to replace him. Some of the effects of the severe strain under which William Ramsay had been working were disclosed in the content and tone of letters he wrote to Frick the following fall. In mid-November William mentioned that, after talking with friends the previous night, he had decided to try to secure the American consulship in Glasgow under the new administration. He wanted Frick to ask Senator Quay to take an interest in the matter. Six weeks later he had moved in a different direction. Until he was well again, William would try to get a living by handling a variety of jobs—fire brick business for the Eureka Fire Brick works of Mt. Braddock, acting for the Hurst Coal Company, and working in real estate and fire insurance. It seems surprising that this could be regarded as a suitable work load for a sick man, but he was optimistic about the prospect: "I believe combining the above together it will enable me to earn enough until such time as my health is all right."[103]

In the middle of 1897 William approached Frick again. He reminded him that in 1894 he had kept the South West works in operation during the strike and had succeeded in getting his men to accept the scale wages. By his reckoning his action had so far saved the company $300,000. South West mines he claimed were acknowledged to be in better condition than any others in the region—a claim that Lynch was shortly afterward to point out was groundless. Yet, despite all this, he had received little more than half the salary paid to his father. He ended, "Now Mr. Frick to sum it all up I lost my health so that at present I am not able to go into my old line of business and I wrote you asking if you could advance me $3,000 so I could start into business conducive to my health in order to earn a living." Not until he had written three times did he receive a reply. Haskell, South West's secretary, asked to provide "data" to enable him to respond, pointed out that William's salary had increased by almost 200 percent in little more than three years following his appointment, and reminded him that his salary had been higher than what his father had received in 1887 "after many years of valuable service as a man of matured judgement." More recently, Cowan had succeeded in making coke at 8 cents a ton less than in Ramsay's last quarter at the works and had made more of it [which presumably may have helped cause the fall in costs]. Frick wrote to Ramsay the next day in a tone that was a mixture of impatience and continued willingness to help, even if not financially: "I note your favor of the 1st. Your letter is ridiculous in almost every respect. I have been under the impression that we have treated you very well indeed. . . . I regret that your health is not good, and am quite satisfied that a loan of $3,000.00, to start into business, would do you no good whatsoever. I shall, however, be glad to have you call on me almost any time, and see if some way cannot be devised to assist you." Frick was contacted again early in 1899 when Ramsay was considering taking charge of the Crescent Coal Company of Gallup, New Mexico. The following year he offered Frick some coal lands and to build for him modern plant at West End, West Virginia. But by spring 1901, writing to ask for a job, he appeared to be without any strong sense of direction: "I would prefer to remain away from the Pittsburgh field, however will be glad to do whatever you say." There seems to be no later evidence of contact.[104]

4 New Districts

The Opening and Development of Lower Connellsville

Through the 1880s rising demand for coke was met by extensions of production in a district whose geological limits were already well known. There were 7,000 ovens by the end of 1880 and 16,000 a decade later. Development of other coking coalfields in Pennsylvania was relatively insignificant. During the 1890s there was a further rise in the number of Connellsville ovens, though under 5,000 in total; for the four years through 1899, the increase was only 1,338 ovens. One reason for this reduced rate of growth was the concentration of control in the region; acceptable prices could best be maintained by ensuring no further expansion than what was essential. There was, however, another, more fundamental limitation—the lack of undeveloped or at least unsecured coking coal lands in the original coking coal area, that which came to be known as the "old basin." Beehive production was expanding elsewhere, and byproduct oven tonnages were increasing, though as yet only slowly. The immense surge in pig iron production at the end of the 1890s required more coke. Those operating in Connellsville now took very purposeful action to boost their output, but their success was limited by the fact that they were pressing hard on the physical limits of the resource base. A major result was the opening and rapid growth of a completely new coking district in Fayette County. Before this could happen, though, it was necessary to overcome a number of obstacles—physical, commercial, and psychological.

The sharply rising output of iron caused a strong upward movement in coke production each year from 1896 to 1900; the total was not only a record, but 112 percent greater than only twelve years earlier. Prices were rising to levels unmatched for twenty years. An "immense boom" in coke occurred in 1899, and by the latter part of

Hauling coal underground in the Connellsville seam, *circa* 1893. *Courtesy of Frick Art and Historical Center, Frick Archives*

July shipments reached heights previously unmatched in the region's history. By this time the companies were bringing in more workers from wherever they could find them, and one journal reported, "All the abandoned ovens in the region that are worth it are being repaired and put into operation as soon as they are in shape." Except for twenty-four ovens at Sterling No.2, H. C. Frick Coke was said to have every one of its ovens at work.[1] That autumn existing works were being expanded wherever possible. Among other projects, H. C. Frick Coke was "rushing matters" with more ovens at Mutual, Adelaide, and Calumet as well as restoring those at West Overton. An additional one-hundred-oven block was going up at the Oliver No.2 plant, Rainey was extending Paul works, and new ovens were to be built near Greensburg. By the following spring previously abandoned capacity was being fired up even if it had to be supplied with coal from other mines because its own reserves had been worked out, as at West Overton and Morrell. Spring Grove works along Hickman Run had

Table 4.1 United States pig iron and Connellsville district coke production, 1895–1902

Year	Pig iron production (th. gross tons)	Bessemer pig iron price at Pittsburgh	Connellsville coke shipments (th. tons)	total ovens	price
1895	9,446	$12.72	8,244	17,947	$1.23
1896	8,623	$12.14	5,412	18,351	$1.90
1897	9,653	$10.13	6,915	18,628	$1.65
1898	11,774	$10.33	8,460	18,643	$1.55
1899	13,621	$19.03	10,130	19,689	$2.00
1900	13,789	$19.49	10,166[a]	20,954[a]	$2.70[a]
1901	15,878	$15.93	12,610[a]	21,575[a]	$1.95[a]
1902	17,821	$20.67	14,139[a]	26,329[a]	$2.37[a]

SOURCES: For pig iron, P. Temin, *Iron and Steel in Nineteenth Century America: An Economic Enquiry* (Cambridge, Mass.: MIT Press, 1964); for coke, *Connellsville Courier*, May 1914.

a. Indicates some output from beyond the "old basin" is included.

been closed years before because of the exhaustion of its coal, but Cochran Brothers now installed a new block of ovens there.[2] By the end of 1900, oven numbers in the whole Connellsville region were almost 1,300 more than a year before. Even then, demand exceeded both the full utilization of existing plant and the capabilities of these extensions, and some operators resorted to the old-fashioned manner of making coke in mounds. Pressures continued to increase and there seemed every likelihood of further rises ahead. An upward tendency in annual average prices was one consequence, with consumers at critical times paying handsome premiums even over these figures. In 1901 the highest price paid for Connellsville coke was $4.25, but by September 1902, at a time when contract coke was nominally $3 a ton, some purchasers were paying as much as $10–12 for prompt delivery; $15 was reported in one case.[3] Long-term prospects for sustained expansion of output, though, were not good.

The geological limits to the established coking coalfield were very well known. Already having to resort to rail haulage from other mines as an emergency measure, producers realized this was a clear signal of a coming wider crisis as local coal supplies failed. In short, as demand mushroomed, supplies tightened, prices rose, and the old basin was visibly teetering on the edge of decline. A 1900 correspondent of the *Engineering and Mining Journal* provided a roll-call of the early casualties in what seemed destined to become an old mineral district: "West Overton ovens are out because of the lack of coal. Hazlett mine, near Scottdale, once a great money-maker, is now nothing but a series of hollow pitfalls, and the ovens are burning coal from an adjoining pit. Uniondale, near Connellsville, has seen its finish. Two hundred ovens are out of blast at Morrell because of the lack of fuel, and more will go out as the months go on. The old Fairchance mine is abandoned and the ovens supplied with coal from Kyle. Frick mine at Broad Ford is in the same state. Jackson mine at Broad Ford has about one more year to run. Pennsville is close to exhaustion, and Bessemer mine, near Mt. Pleasant, has begun operations on the last block of coal. Five years at the most will see the end of all the mines on the Mt. Pleasant branch road."[4] The times called for alternative arrangements. There were a few possible lines of advance.

It had long been known that a second seam of coking coal lay below the Connellsville seam. However, as this was not only deeper but also little more than half as thick, extraction costs would be higher. Much active coke working took place via slopes, and even when shaft mining was necessary, the depth of operations ranged from 80 to a maximum of about 550 feet; working the new seam would require shafts from 900 to 1,500 feet deep. Despite these disadvantages, as demand reached unprecedented heights, the first steps were taken to mine this less suitable coal. Having worked out their coal at Uniondale, Reid Brothers began boring to the second seam, the rest of the trade reportedly looking on with interest. A year later Peter Tarr of Scottdale paid only $35 an acre for 50,000 acres of Freeport coal centered on Mendon, Westmoreland County.[5] In fact, there was an outside constraint on the scope for action along such lines. Given the existence of other, if poorer, coking coals elsewhere in the Appalachians and of byproduct coking, costlier mining in old basin seams was likely to be uneconomic.

Another approach was to extend still farther those parts of the old basin from which the coal for the ovens was derived. Entrenched prejudice among established coke makers and consumers alike had long delayed recognition that first-rate coke could be made outside the old core of the region. As late as the early 1890s, there had been general agreement that the best coke, having an ideal combination of structure, hardness, and chemical analysis, was made from coal worked between Mt. Pleasant and Uniontown. At that time many consumers insisted that the sulfur content of their coke should not exceed 0.85 percent. The coal of the Pleasant Unity district, the area stretching northward from Mt. Pleasant toward Latrobe, had not then been wholly acceptable. Later, the coals of the northern end of the Connellsville syncline in Upper Connellsville—north of the Loyalhanna River—and the Greensburg field were developed. Sulfur content was slightly higher, but this could be largely corrected by washing the coal before charging. In cases like this, early comers gained the advantage of cheap coal lands, which increased in value as they were brought within the limits of acceptability. For instance, by the early 1880s the Thaw family of Pittsburgh had some coal near Hunker in the northern district for which they had paid

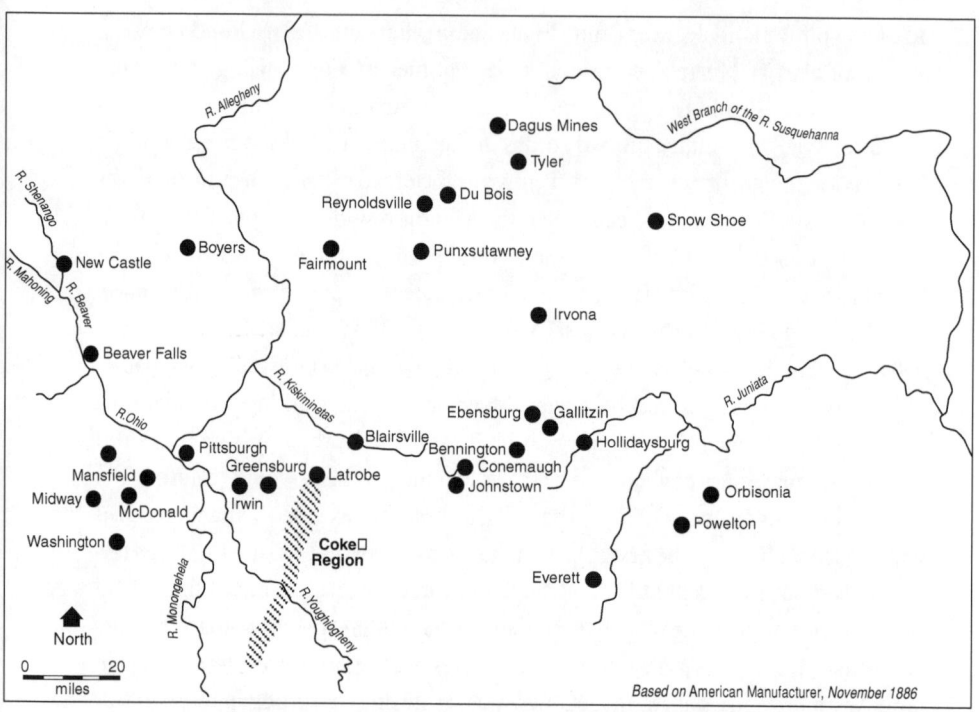

Coke producing districts or works of central and western Pennsylvania, 1886.

$80 per acre; by 1907 Boileau reckoned their holdings were worth at least $3,000 an acre. Similar changes affected areas south of Uniontown. It was here that A. A. Hutchinson failed to take an opportunity to buy coal lands at low cost before there was a shift of interest to this area at the end of the 1880s. By 1889 a combination of Pittsburgh, Philadelphia, and New York capitalists was reported to be planning railroad, mine, and oven construction in this section and had bought 793 acres of the best coal along Beeson's Run, four miles south of Uniontown and five from the South West Pennsylvania Railroad. A few months later, J. W. Moore, having sold out to H. C. Frick Coke, examined a 1,500 acre tract in Springhill Township even farther south. Three railroad lines had been surveyed into this tract, but only one, the State Line, had been built. Next year Mellon Brothers and Cambria Iron Company purchased large blocks of coal in the area, the latter paying $250 an acre for Bolton Farm in Springhill Township within four miles of the Cheat River.[6]

The Upper Connellsville and Greensburg districts lay only a little to the north of the old core area. There was some expansion here, but it was on a small scale and the

Table 4.2 Coke output of Connellsville "proper" and other Pennsylvania districts, **1898–1902** *(net tons in thousands)*

District	1898	1899	1900	1901	1902
Connellsville	8,315	10,390	10,021	10,236	10,418
Upper Connellsville	403	610	690	569	937
Greensburg	642	111	197	258	442
Reynoldsville	600	973	625	590	690
Allegheny Mountains	378	478	557	548	644
All other districts	1,019	1,129	1,078	1,297	1,910

SOURCES: E. V. D'Invilliers, "Estimated Costs of Mining and Coking and Relative Commercial Returns from Operating in the Connellsville and Walston-Reynoldsville Districts, Pennsylvania," *TAIME* 35 (1905): 44–59; *Mineral Statistics of the United States* for the years listed in table.

NOTE: Small tonnages of byproduct coke, and for 1898 and 1899 coke made in New York and Massachusetts, are included in the figures for other districts.

coke made was not so well suited for furnace use as to be a direct replacement. In fact, the produce of both districts was especially suited to the foundry trade. Other areas of Pennsylvania were already of some importance, and investments were made in Indiana, Armstrong, and Jefferson Counties. The results were slight in scale and still more in promise when compared with the looming problem of decline in the old basin.[7] Understandably then a very specific question was posed: "What will take the place of coke when the Connellsville region is merely a waste of ruined mines?" Some years before, the first steps had been taken toward finding a more satisfactory answer to the threat of change represented by that question. It involved an area nearby and long known to contain coal. Even more remarkably, this undeveloped region was, within only a decade, rapidly approaching parity in size with the older coke region, and its product was regarded as more or less equal in quality. The opening of this district had to some extent been delayed by physical and commercial factors, but the main deterrent was psychological.

In the mid-1890s well-informed operators in Connellsville still regarded the coal of the Pittsburgh seam beyond the old basin as a steam coal incapable of making acceptable coke. This had certainly been the attitude of those in control at H. C. Frick Coke as it expanded its operations in the mid-1890s. A boom year, 1895 witnessed district shipments at 8.24 million tons, 27.5 percent greater than in the previous record year of 1890, though prices were lower. In the middle months of the year, the company took over both the one-plant Youngstown Coke Company and the much bigger McClure Coke Company. In autumn it acquired Fairchance Fuel Company. Soon afterward, Lynch received an offer from W. H. Beckwith of coal land in Nicholson Township in southern Fayette County, part of a known field to the west of the old basin. Beckwith asked $200 an acre; at that time coal around Fairmont, West Virginia, could be had from between $15 and $60 an acre. Lynch was scathing about the proposition on other grounds. The seam offered contained "not over 5 feet of clean coal, such as it is" and was too high in sulfur. He added, "As I understand our policy, we do not want it at any price because it is not Connellsville coal, and we are not hunting cheap coals, or coals that make coke nearly as good as Connellsville." Next spring Lynch returned to the same theme when commenting on what he called "Monongahela River Coal," reserves near that river and thereby well-placed for shipment. An almost unlimited acreage of this seemed to be available in western parts of Westmoreland and Fayette Counties as well as over into Washington and Greene Counties. It could be had for between $25–50 an acre. Lynch was unimpressed by its quality, cost, or location, though once more his condemnation was rather weakly based on precedent: "We have never bought any coal outside the Connellsville basin."[8]

Lynch was not the only skeptic. In 1900 Fred C. Keighley, closely involved with the coke industry for twenty years, in the course of a short history of the district resorted to purple prose in asserting there was no rival to the mineral he knew so well. What began as an account became a eulogy:

There is no other coal as regular, as uniform, of as convenient thickness, as Connellsville coal and as easily mined. These are not mere statements, but facts; facts that have made Pittsburgh the steel center of the world; facts that have taxed the three great railroad systems of southwest Pennsylvania to their very uttermost; facts that have in thirty years brought up the output of blast furnaces from 35 tons to 700 tons per day [The latter would have been quite exceptional. In 1898 one of four furnaces at the recently built and outstanding Duquesne plant averaged 711 tons; two years later 155 tons was the national average.][9] and facts that are going to make the United States the greatest nation on earth. . . . I have time and again heard iron and steel makers explain that they have found other coke that answered their purpose, but I have always noticed that they were in the market for Connellsville coke when they had to make a fine grade of iron or steel. Every time a man or company found a new coal field, they came out with the glowing statement that it was as good as Connellville coal. Why, I have seen alleged Connellsville coal and coke from every section of Pennsylvania, Ohio, West Virginia, Virginia, Illinois, Indiana and even Pacific Slope. . . . The fact is, that every one is anxious to prove that he controls a field of genuine Connellsville coal, no matter whether it is located on the top of Pike's Peak or in the Dismal Swamp.

Yet Keighley was forced to recognize that at current outputs, Connellsville coking coal would be exhausted in fifty years; if production expanded at the rate of the last decade, it would be gone in half that time. Like others, he anticipated that as the Con-

Coke workers at South West No. 3. *Courtesy of Pennsylvania State University, Fayette, Coal and Coke Heritage Center*

nellsville coal supply's life expectancy shortened, the value of the remaining reserves would appreciate. He failed to recognize, at least in public, that this would encourage alternative technologies and the opening of other fields even if they contained poorer coal. He did mention, "Here is the latest Klondike right at our doors basing its future greatness on the reputation of Connellsville coal."[10] The field to which he made such brief, rather condescending reference soon won such a reputation that the *Connellsville Weekly Courier*, always jealous for the good name of the local product, found it acceptable to include its output with that of Connellsville "proper." Combined in this way, expansion in the new district disguised the slower growth and the later beginnings of absolute decline in the older region. Even then, some operators retained their prejudices, which meant they played a small role in the new area. For a number of years this continued to be the case with H. C. Frick Coke.

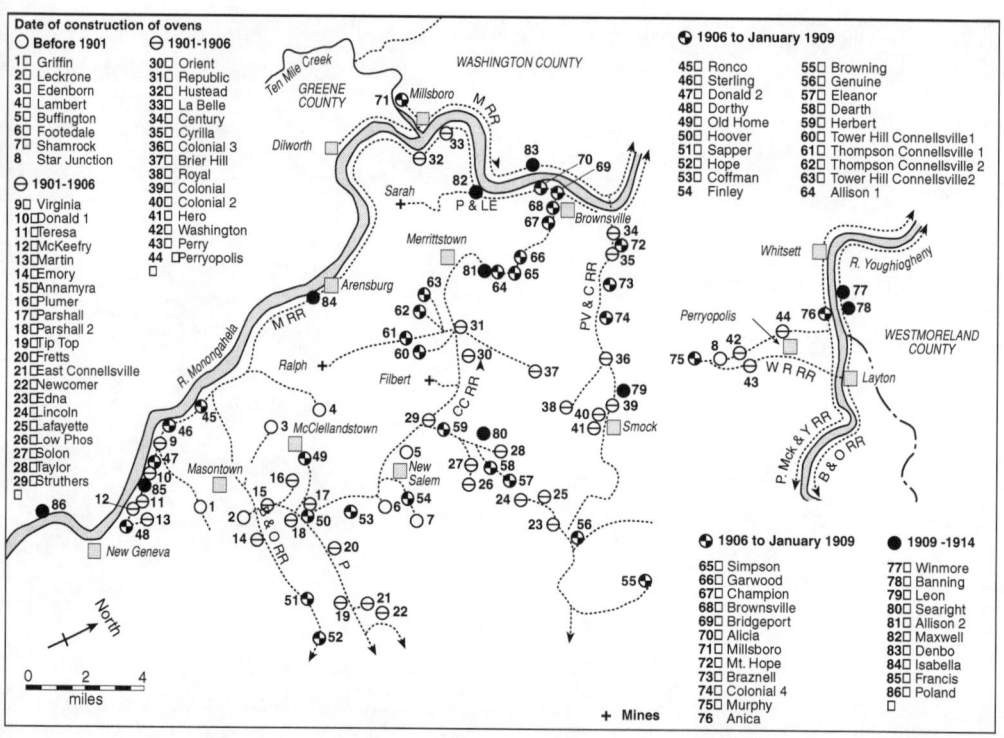

Development of the Lower Connellsville coke region.

The Lower Connellsville district occupied a narrow belt lying west of and subparallel to the axis of the main Connellsville field, separated from it only by an anticline from whose top the coal had been eroded—in other words, it extended between the old basin and the Monongahela River. Although it reached into Westmoreland County, its northern limit was normally taken to be Redstone Creek so that it was essentially a Fayette County field. Westward, coal of similar quality was found along the eastern edges of Greene and Washington Counties. To the south it extended across the state line into West Virginia, though in some definitions the area south of Jacobs Creek was designated as the separate Geneva and Point Marion Field. In a number of respects, the coal and the coke it produced were slightly less easily worked or as good as that from the old basin, but advancing technology helped improve the new district's competitive position. Lower Connellsville coal was much harder than that in Connellsville "proper"; an essential preliminary was to prove that it could make a furnace coke more or less as good. Eventually it was established that, though this coal was lower in phosphorus and slightly higher in sulfur, denser, and normally brought to the surface in smaller blocks than the old basin product, the coke made from it could be dealt with satisfactorily in the modern, more powerfully blown blast furnaces. Newer style mining operations—steel structures replaced wood and electricity was used from the start in mining operations for haulage and on the tipples—increased the operational efficiency. The new rectangular ovens, mechanically leveled, quenched, and drawn (and therefore cutting labor costs), were installed from 1900 in Lower Connellsville, whereas only two installations of this improved technology seem to have been made in the older field.[11] Together, physical and economic circumstances gradually made acceptance of the slight differences in product necessary. There were a few years of tentative approach before production began.

M. M. Cochran was a member of a family that had been associated with the Connellsville coke region from the earliest days. By the first years of the 1890s, he was involved in running 300 ovens north and south of the Youghiogheny near Dawson and with the Juniata Coke Company, formed in 1890 to operate between Leisenring and Vance's Mill. In 1893 he formed the Washington Coal and Coke Company to work coal already optioned some years before for as little as $20–30 an acre. The Washington Run Railroad Company was organized by the same interests, and soon thereafter mining began. This new company made its first coke in a plant at Star Junction in 1893, and four years later had 320 coke ovens there. Though on or somewhat beyond the northern edge of what was later to receive the name Klondike and soon after, and more permanently, Lower Connellsville, Cochran's company was essentially the pioneer venture in the new region. Two years later, in fall 1899, Andrew Carnegie threatened to acquire large coal holdings and build coke ovens along Washington Run if the minority stockholders in H. C. Frick Coke would not supply his operations at the low price he stipulated. These first steps, or projects, were all well north of Redstone Creek, but there had already been stirrings farther south. In the late 1880s the South West Pennyslvania had surveyed a route from Uniontown to the West Virginia line and up the Monongahela via the little community of Masontown. J. A. Nicholls, representing several large capitalists, apparently owned options on coal lands near this settlement and was expected to purchase as much as 2,000 acres at about $50 an acre to be held as an investment.[12]

By early autumn 1899 major iron and steel companies were reportedly planning to break the shortage and high prices for coke by opening new fields from Preston and Monongalia Counties in West Virginia northward into Greene and Fayette Counties, Pennsylvania.[13] Because it controlled such a large proportion of old basin coal and ovens, Carnegie Steel, through H. C. Frick Coke, showed no real early interest in these new areas. Indeed, at the end of 1900 Schwab's comparative statement of the resources and facilities controlled by their rivals and themselves proved how

Table 4.3 Coking coal and coke ovens controlled by Carnegie Steel and major rivals, December 1900

Company	Connellsville		All other regions	
	Coal (acres)	Ovens	Coal (acres)	Ovens (in Lower Connellsville)
Carnegie Steel	38,000	11,637	none	none
Federal Steel	1,500	1,200	6,000	1,200 (1,200)
American Steel and Wire	100	130	9,250	1,630 (1,000)
National Steel	2,000	900	850	400 (400)
National Tube	438	n.a.	500	n.a.
American Steel Hoop	130	n.a.	n.a.	n.a.

SOURCE: Based on C. M. Schwab, December 1900, January 1901, ACLC.
NOTE: Lower Connellsville figures added. For a somewhat different picture, see *EMJ*, 7 April 1900.

dominant they were in coke and, by implication, their lack of need to act as pioneers in extending the area in which it was made.

In contrast to its eastern parts, western Fayette County had been both undeveloped and relatively inaccessible. Away from the river, where the little port of Brownsville contained 1,552 inhabitants, its two biggest settlements were the banking post borough of Masontown and the village of New Salem, with 1900 populations of 466 and 200 respectively, and the county also included the community of McClellandtown with 100 people and Leckrone, a post village of 75. The Redstone Branch of the Pittsburgh, Virginia, and Charleston crossed the coal from Brownsville through the tiny post station of Tippecanoe and on to the southern part of the Connellsville field east of Vance's Mill, but most of the area had no railroads. Now its isolation was beginning to be eroded by construction of tracks from various directions. In 1895 the Baltimore and Ohio Railroad extended its Fayette County Branch to Morgantown, West Virginia. At the end of the 1890s, it built the Masontown and New Salem Railroad from Leckrone to New Salem, and in 1900 a branch from Smithfield into coal areas east of Masontown. The Pennsylvania Railroad opened branch lines from its main Connellsville-Uniontown-Fairchance route, including in 1900 the Coal Lick Run line from Uniontown to Leckrone. It also acquired control of the Masontown and New Salem Railroad. Having built a Belle Vernon to Fayette City branch in 1895, by 1900 the Vanderbilt system was surveying a line from the latter to Star Junction and on to New Haven with a branch into these new coal areas, but then instead joined the PRR in extending south from Brownsville, skirting the Monongahela to Martin. A link from Leckrone to Huron completed the circle of tracks around what was to become the early core of a new coke district. The lines jointly owned by the

PRR and the Vanderbilts were operated under the name of the Monongahela Railroad. In order to open further large tracts this new operator built a connecting line between New Salem and Brownsville. The scene was set for rapid development once other conditions were suitable.

The final, but vital, factor in opening the new district was the availability of men with technical and managerial experience of the old Connellsville coke trade, of others with wider experience of coking coals in other districts, and of firms having access to ample capital to back up these human resources. In the mid-1890s consolidation in the Connellsville coke region, and particularly increasing domination by the H. C. Frick Coke Company, had meant that excellent managers and engineers were displaced from top positions in once independent, but now subsidiary, companies. Some of them pioneered the new district.

Until 1896–1897, despite evidence from Washington Coal and Coke, it was generally believed that Lower Connellsville coals were noncoking. At this time John H. Hillman and John C. Neff acquired low cost options on some 6,000 acres of coal in this basin. Needing expert advice, they commissioned reports from a young mining engineer, Selwyn Taylor, and the long-established leading authority on coke, John Fulton. Both men assured Hillman and Neff that their coal had excellent coking qualities, but apparently they provided no direct comparison with Connellsville coke. For this, Hillman and Neff turned to John P. Brennen, who had been field manager for the McClure Coke Company until autumn 1895 when that company was absorbed by H. C. Frick Coke. Afterward, he had worked in the West, for a time surveying Indian Territory coal lands for the Pittsburg, Kansas, and Gulf Railroad. In 1897 Brennen concluded that Lower Connellsville coal could make a coke equal in quality to standard Connellsville grades. As a result, coal holdings there began to be recognized as valuable at the same time as the demand for coke was spiraling. During 1900 the first two coke works in the new district were completed; 100 ovens at the Shamrock works of the Fayette Coke Company on the extreme eastern edge of the new field near New Salem and 200 at Griffin on the edge of Masontown. The latter operation was owned by the Bessemer Coke Company, which already had two coke works near the northern end of the old basin. In May 1900 Griffin made the first coke ever turned out in Lower Connellsville.[14] The Fayette and Bessemer companies were closely followed by two new major steel groups searching for an assured coke supply.

The Illinois Steel Company had long controlled the coal lands and 1,227 ovens of South West Coal and Coke near Mt. Pleasant, which by the late 1890s turned out nearly 75,000 tons of coke each month. After Hillman and Neff disposed of some of their coal lands to an intermediary in Pittsburgh, these properties were sold on to Illinois Steel, which in 1898 began experiments in coking this coal. The Eureka Fuel

Company was organized to develop the resource. That year Illinois Steel and its properties were incorporated in the new Federal Steel Company. By summer 1899 Federal had bought nearly 6,000 acres of coal lands in German, Menallen, and Nicholson Townships, Fayette County. Charles H. Foote, head of Eureka, a man who a decade earlier had been open minded as to the virtues of West Virginia and Virginia coke, now hired Brennen as general manager and set him the task of developing the new field and justifying his opinion that it could make excellent furnace coke. Selwyn Taylor designed the ovens. A similar program was set in train by another of the recent steel consolidations. In October 1899 the American Steel and Wire Company (AS&W), which owned Baggaley and Dorothy coke works near Latrobe, decided to build 1,000 ovens in an area then identified as seven miles south of Uniontown but that soon turned out to be in the new coalfield.[15] AS&W hired as engineer Louis Fogg, who since 1892 had worked as a mining engineer in Latrobe. Within a year the AS&W ovens at Edenborn and Lambert and the first three drift mines and associated 1,200 ovens belonging to Federal Steel at Buffington, Footedale, and Leckrone were almost complete. In this year of the sudden emergence of the new coking field, little further extension occurred in Connellsville "proper."

The new mineral reserves were cheaply acquired by comparison with current levels in the older area. By early summer 1901 Connellsville coal lands were reckoned as generally worth $1,000 to $1,200 an acre; the large tracts acquired by Federal Steel cost about $300. American Steel and Wire purchases were even cheaper. It bought 3,100 acres southwest of the Federal Steel tract and then added another 5,000 acres west of this and near the Monongahela, paying $175 an acre for the first and $170 for the second. Inevitably, further growth caused increases in values. As early as July 1901, Republic Steel Company was reported to have sold 3,000 acres of coal land along Dunlap Creek near New Salem to A. W. Mellon for $1,300,000, or $433 an acre—apparently so that the Mellons could supply coke to the new Donora works, in which they had a large financial involvement. Early the following year a brother-in-law of Tom Carnegie's widow, Lucy, was courageous enough to refuse $1,000 an acre for coal lands near Perryopolis, believing he might later get as much as $1,500 for it. In fall 1902 Frank J. Hearne, the recently retired president of National Tube, sold 1,012 acres of coking coal land in the Masontown field to his old company. He had bought for $160 an acre but received $900 at the sale, netting him just short of $750,000. Time justified the patience of those who held on to what they bought. In 1900 Pittsburgh Coal Company purchased 500 acres near Redstone for $250 an acre; eight years later 200 acres, said to be the largest unsold parcel in that area, sold for $1,500 an acre.[16]

Shipments of coke from Lower Connellsville in 1900 amounted to a mere 3.8 percent of those from the older field. By 1903, with coke prices running at levels higher than at any time since records were first kept in 1880, its output was more than double the 1901 level; old basin output had decreased by 11 percent. Shipments in 1905 were 34.1 percent as large as those from the older field. Two years later, its 12,264 ovens meant it was already more than half as big as Connellsville "proper," although as a producing field it was still only seven years old. That year no new ovens were built in the latter, but 1,068 were constructed in Lower Connellsville. After another six years it had 17,000 ovens, and the number in the old basin was down to 22,000; its shipments were now 81 percent as large. Generally plant in the new district was superior to that in the old. Though the sulfur content in its coal was sometimes a little high, no washeries were put up during the early years.[17]

Given the short time involved, the emergence of Lower Connellsville as a major coke district was in fact more spectacular even than growth had been in the older field. Realizing there were good prospects, the railroads continued to expand their facilities. In 1903 the Pittsburgh and Lake Erie extended southward from Fayette City to make a connection with the Monongahela Railroad at Brownsville. In 1904 the short Connellsville Central was built with an easy grade up Dunlap Creek to serve four or five existing works in Menallen Township, with the expectation that within two or three years it would be "studded with as many more big works." By now there was a veritable flood of enterprise, capital—much of it from Pittsburgh—and labor, so much so that the 1906 writers of a centennial history of Connellsville were almost bowled over by what they had so recently seen. As soon as the first plants had proved the quality of their coke,

Fayette county went "coal crazy!" Farms that had been considered only heirlooms of dead fathers and grandfathers, suddenly blossomed into gold. Options were taken on every acre of coal land in the southern end of the county, these options were sold and resold again till, finally, the coal seam alone with mining rights brought as much as two thousand dollars an acre! Farmers, suddenly enriched by the sale of the coal under their farms, went into the coke business themselves in many instances, and every rank of the professions was depleted to fill up the ranks of "coal men"—men who shut their law offices to option the black diamonds under the hills, men who, not worth a penny to-day, by the turning of a deal were worth a hundred thousand dollars to-morrow.

Another writer was more concise, "Fortunes have been made that baffle description." As suggested above, a major source of the new wealth was the remarkable appreciation in land values. In the early 1890s $50 an acre for coal land was "considered an exorbitant price." By 1901 $400 was the prevailing level and six years later ten times that figure was offered in several instances, though $2,000 seems to have been a more normal figure. By that time it was reckoned that 95 percent of the coal lands in the Lower Connellsville region were already in the hands of coke operators. Consequently, there were no more important sales, and by 1912 only two tracts remained unsold, one of them owned by a farmer who, against the general grain of things, refused to listen to any offers.[18]

Growth focused first on one area in the new district and then on another. For instance, in 1906 the vicinity of Brownsville contained only two small coke plants having a combined total of 120 ovens. A year later there were three plants and 335 ovens and by January 1909 five with 512 ovens with two other works and 775 additional ovens proposed.[19] The sinking of mines and commissioning of ovens brought general economic expansion. Sparsely populated before, this portion of Fayette County and its main centers now grew rapidly. Between 1900 and 1910 the population of Westmoreland County increased by 44.41 percent, that of Fayette County by 51.66 percent. The urban complex made up of Brownsville, South Brownsville, and West Brownsville increased from 4,094 to 8,305. In particular, Uniontown made great headway, becoming as local enthusiasts put it "the Rome of this invasion into new fields."[20] A year later this small town of 10,000 was claimed—with what authority it is impossible to judge—as the wealthiest of its size in the world. Over the decade since 1900, 81.7 percent was added to the town's population, and though this was only slightly more than Connellsville—where the 1910 figure was boosted by its absorption of New Haven—Uniontown's growth contrasted sharply with the 28.04 percent increase for Scottdale and 22.49 percent for Mt. Pleasant in the northern part of the older field.

Some relatively small companies from the old basin played important parts in the new district. There were also many new operators with no experience with previous coke ventures. The Connellsville Central Company was established by one of the men who had laid the foundations for the district, J. H. Hillman. By 1906 it operated 232 ovens at Low Phos, and the next year decided to build the Herbert coke works just west of its first plant. In May 1906 a new firm, the Thompson-Connellsville Coke Company, bought 1,600 acres along Dunlap Creek in Redstone and Luzerne Townships. A connection was made with the Monongahela Railroad and two 400-oven coke plants were built.[21] At the beginning of 1907, a group from Pittsburgh, Boston, and Cleveland as well as from the local area formed the Consolidated Connellsville Coke Company to combine the operations separately conducted by the Sterling Coal and Coke, Masontown Coal and Coke, and Southern Connellsville Coke companies between Masontown and the Monongahela. A few weeks later Tower Hill–Connellsville Coke Company was established by a Cleveland syndicate with a capital of $8 million. Among its directors was Daniel N. Clemson, formerly a partner in Carnegie

Steel. Tower Hill had 2,000 acres of coal lands and planned 800 ovens. It was in operation during 1908 and by the year's end operated two works along the Central Connellsville line midway between Brownsville and New Salem. One thousand ovens were at first attributed to it, but as late as 1914 it had only 720 on site.[22]

All the above were and remained merchant coke plants; that is, operations selling on the open market. There were also a number of new plants controlled by iron makers. After the first flush of construction, these were in each case owned by companies in the Valleys. The Brier Hill Coke Company was a subsidiary of the Brier Hill Steel Company of Youngstown, Ohio. By 1907 it had 470 ovens southwest of Tippecanoe. In 1912 it shipped almost 290,000 tons of coke to Ohio. At Fairbank, northwest of New Salem, the Struthers Furnace Company had a smaller coke plant. By far the biggest operation was that geared to the needs of the Republic Iron and Steel Company, a combination formed in 1899 and by rationalization increasingly concentrated in the Valleys. Its first coke works was Atcheson, well to the south in the Geneva and Point Marion Field. Early in 1905 it began a 400-oven works on a 1,200-acre tract along the Connellsville Central Railroad. A year later 100 ovens had been completed. Their coke was destined for associated furnaces in Youngstown, Newcastle, and Sharon. Late in 1908 Republic also acquired the 196 ovens and 420 acres of coal formerly operated by the Bessemer Coke Company at Martin on the Monongahela. More generally, because of its later development and the different affiliations of its ovens, the market area for Lower Connellsville was very different from that of the old basin. In 1907, 40.7 percent of the coke from Connellsville was sent to Pittsburgh, 53.1 percent to western markets, and 6.2 percent to the East; for Lower Connellsville the respective proportions were 14.4 percent, 73.3 percent, and 12.3 percent.[23]

As in Connellsville there was some movement of managerial talent from one project to another. Louis Fogg directed the American Steel and Wire coke operations both before and after they were merged into United States Steel, but in 1907 he became general manager for the Tower Hill–Connellsville Coke Company. John Brennen provided a more striking instance of migration. After advising on the opening of Lower Connellsville, he managed the Ronco properties of Sharon Steel only to have them taken over by Frick Coke in 1903 when that company was brought into U.S. Steel. Some years later he managed the Connellsville Central Herbert works before building up and serving as manager and president of the Thompson-Connellsville Coke Company.

W. J. Rainey Company was late to enter the new field, and when it did so built up its capacity there on a smaller scale than was initially expected. Not until spring 1906 was Rainey preparing to develop 1,500 acres of coal lands. On this tract in the Brier Hill district southwest of Tippecanoe, it was then said to be planning three shafts and

Table 4.4 Coke shipments by Connellsville and Lower Connellsville, 1900–1911 *(tons in thousands)*

Year	Connellsville	Lower Connellsville
1900	10,021	386
1901	10,236	1,116
1902	10,418	1,899
1903	9,102	2,329
1904	8,883	2,887
1905	11,365	3,871
1906	12,058	5,188
1907	13,089	6,311
1908	6,808	3,892
1909	11,517	6,269
1910	10,880	8,000
1911	9,665	6,669

SOURCE: *Connellsville Weekly Courier.*

Table 4.5 Coke works and ovens of Lower Connellsville, 1901, 1906, 1908, and 1914

Year	Works	Ovens
1901 (January)	2 complete	300
	5 building	2,200
1906	55	10,690
1908	62	13,162
1914 (May)	88	17,341

SOURCES: *Coal and Coke,* 8 February 1901; J. C. McClenathan, et al. *Centennial History of the Borough of Connellsville, Pennsylvania, 1806–1906* (Connellsville, Pa.: Centennial Historical Committee, 1906), J. B. Hogg, *New Map of the Connellsville Coke Region and Adjacent Fields, Showing All Coke Works* (N.p., 1909); *Connellsville Weekly Courier,* May 1914.

700–800 ovens. (In fact, by 1914 its Royal works there contained only 372 ovens.) Late in 1907 Rainey bought 2,000 acres of coal and the properties of the People's Coal Company, and again a huge installation was projected; later they built Allison No. 1 and No. 2. By late 1908 it was anticipated that these two works would total 800 ovens, but by 1914 there were only 300.[24]

Although the formation of United States Steel and the consolidation of its coal and coke operations brought H. C. Frick Coke into Lower Connellsville, for some years this company's main expansion was concentrated elsewhere. By 1906 it operated five Lower Connellsville plants, the units that Federal and American Steel and

Wire had built in 1900. Despite the huge scale of developments since then in this district, three of these five plants had not been further extended. At Lambert, 68 fewer ovens were completed than had been scheduled in 1900. At Leckrone only 116 had been added since. There is at least circumstantial evidence to indicate that the old H. C. Frick Coke prejudice against other coking coal areas in southwestern Pennsylvania survived into the new century and therefore into the first phase of Lower Connellsville growth. Early in 1902, as president, Lynch announced plans to develop 20,000 of the 50,000 acres that USS had leased in the Pocohontas Flat Top region.[25] Once described as "a conservative man," Lynch may have made a strong, though indirect, recommendation against bigger developments in Lower Connellsville, though evidence of this came many years later in a letter from Frick to Gary, commending Greene County coal. Frick recalled that at one time it had been possible to get Klondike coal lands at from $50 to $100 an acre, "but some of our people reported against it and we did nothing and you know how values have gone up in that district."[26] Necessity eventually forced a larger, though briefly maintained, expansion. In the boom of 1906 and 1907, output and prices in the two fields reached new records, and Frick Coke was forced for the first time for many years into a program of greenfield construction with four new works. Two of them, York Run and Phillips, each comprising 400 ovens, were in southern, more recently developed parts of the old basin. The other two were in Lower Connellsville, namely the 250-oven Dearth plant on the Monongahela Railroad north of New Salem and the 350 ovens at Ronco on the banks of the Monongahela, the first Frick plant to occupy such a remarkably favorable location. Coal had been worked for some time at the latter place, whose mine, first developed by Sharon Steel, had been brought with that company into USS at the end of 1902.

Another dramatic change of direction took place during 1908–1909. As late as summer 1908, construction of additional major Frick Coke works in Lower Connellsville seemed inevitable. It was announced that contracts had been awarded for two plants near Gates of 500 and 300 ovens. There was even a report that the company was asking for bids for up to ten new coke-oven plants.[27] In fact, neither the Gates works nor the others were built. At Ralph, where 500 ovens had been projected, and at a proposed 300-oven Filbert works, coal mining was begun but there was no further processing. There seems to have been a number of reasons for this sudden and complete change of plan. In the first place, 1908 was a year of deep depression. At the beginning of that year 13,420 Frick ovens were idle. Throughout the region the number of ovens had increased by over 2,000 from the 1907 level, but shipments were down by over 8 million tons, or almost 44 percent. Less than half of H. C. Frick Coke capacity was employed. Prices had been $2.90 in 1907, but that year they averaged

$1.80.²⁸ Second, in these difficult circumstances it proved possible to boost capacity to meet future needs by buying other companies rather than by building new plants. Late in 1907 H. C. Frick, already largely interested in the Hostetter-Connellsville Coke Company in the old basin, gained full control of that enterprise. Although not a case of further expansion, Hostetter-Connellsville's capacity could now supply USS. Two years later the 100-oven Bridgeport works of the River Coal Company upriver from Brownsville and, in 1911, the three works and 965 ovens of the Colonial Coke Company on the long-established Redstone Branch were acquired. But even in Lower Connellsville, new purchases were now becoming expensive. A third factor was vital in bringing about an increasing lack of interest in any major new departures in the region.

By 1909, though still by far the largest company beehive coke producer in the region, U.S. Steel had made the momentous decision to begin to move more rapidly into byproduct coke manufacture. In January Clay Lynch, his father's assistant general manager; Austin King, Frick Coke's district mine inspector; and Edward O'Toole, who though employed by the same company had been involved in plans for the Gary works, traveled to Europe "to make an exhaustive study of coal-mining and coke-making methods." Later that year USS was reported to have definitely decided to build no more ovens in the coke region except in order to round out existing operations; future expansion even with Connellsville coal would be in the form of byproduct ovens at the point of consumption. Between 1909 and 1913 U.S. Steel's production of beehive coke in all parts of the United States fell by 7.0 percent, whereas its output of byproduct coke went up 230.7 percent.²⁹

The change to byproduct coke started a process of depreciation in values throughout the Coke Region, though as with earlier increases there were inevitably so many variations as to make generalization difficult. In summer 1911, when USS bought the 7,077-acre Colonial coking area from the Pittsburgh Coal Company along with all the improvements and the associated Franklin Township Water Company, it paid only $1,450 per acre of mineable coal. At the same time, it acquired almost 9,000 acres from the Monongahela River Consolidated Coal and Coke Company for $850 an acre. A few months later Thomas Lynch decided he could not recommend to the Finance Committee a purchase of 900 acres of coal and 600 acres of surface in Fayette County from Capt. Harry W. Brown at $2,000 an acre. *Iron Age* sensed that the coke region was at a turning point, commenting that the price paid to Pittsburgh Coal was "a shock to many Connellsville operators, and perhaps to others who have been impressed by their arguments as to the extremely great value of this field."³⁰

One outcome of its late start and its early decision not to make any more developments on virgin sites was that Frick Coke had never attained a position in the new

Table 4.6 Selected companies in Connellsville and Lower Connellsville districts, 1914

	Connellsville		Lower Connellsville	
Company	Works	Ovens	Works	Ovens
H. C. Frick Coke	47	14,517	11	3,960
W. J. Rainey	9	1,879	3	673
Bessemer Coke	1	145	1	395
Sunshine Coal and Coke	1	54	6	682
Whyel Coke	3	130	1	36
Newcomer Coke	1	50	1	30
South Fayette Coke	1	36	2	112
Puritan Coke	n.a.	n.a.	2	202
Republic Iron and Steel	n.a.	n.a.	3	764
Washington Coal and Coke	n.a.	n.a.	2	1,000
Consolidated Connellsville	n.a.	n.a.	3	872
Connellsville Central	n.a.	n.a.	2	460
Thompson–Connellsville	n.a.	n.a.	2	800
Tower Hill–Connellsville	n.a.	n.a.	2	699
Total all companies	91	20,800	88	17,341

SOURCE: *Connellsville Courier*, May 1914, 2–3.

Table 4.7 Plants, ovens, and coal used in Connellsville and Lower Connellsville, 1900–1929

	Connellsville			Lower Connellsville		
Year	Plants	Avg. ovens per plant	Coal used per oven (tons)	Plants	Avg. ovens per plant	Coal used per oven (tons)
1900	98	216	712	12(?)	169	285
1905	100	220	771	45	166	757
1910	118	207	703	73	203	819
1915	102	210	680	76	216	727
1920	81	238	558	64	237	501
1925	62	247	402	54	214	438
1929	46	219	223	32	246	506

SOURCE: Based on H. N. Eavenson, *The First Century and a Quarter of American Coal Industry* (Pittsburgh: Privately published, 1942).

field that even nearly matched the level it so long held in the old. In 1906 the company controlled 21 percent of the Lower Connellsville ovens and in 1914, 22.8 percent. At the latter date it owned forty-seven of ninety-one works and 69.7 percent of the ovens in the old basin.[31]

As it had been virgin territory until 1900, it was not surprising that Lower Connellsville peaked later than the older field. Both the number of coke works and of ovens were at their highest in "Connellsville proper" in 1910. Lower Connellsville achieved both its maximum number of coke works and its banner year for output in 1916; oven numbers were at their highest the following year. After World War I both regions declined rapidly. Until the mid-1920s the old basin produced more coke, but later that decade Lower Connellsville was ahead. Even so, after many more years of oscillating fortunes, superimposed on long-term shrinkage, the last of this newer district's ovens had been abandoned before the 1972 closure of Shoaf on the western edge of the southern section of the older field. Connellsville had enjoyed a full half-century of preeminence in coke and as one of the world's great mineral districts; the glory days of Lower Connellsville were confined within less than half that time. Meanwhile, major new purchases of coal were made both farther south in West Virginia and Virginia and westward within Pennsylvania beyond the Monongahela. These marked yet another new phase of the coke industry, superseding the beehive industry of both the old and newer Connellsville coke districts. This westward trend and the expansion of the byproduct industry not only brought a decline in the basic business of the Connellsville region, but also a decay of its coke-dependent society.

Coke Production in the Coalfields of the Mid-Appalachian Plateaus

During the late nineteenth and early twentieth centuries, the Connellsville region contained one of the nation's most highly specialized concentrations of economic activity. Although it never monopolized the production of coke, there could be no doubt that the region dominated the market. In 1880 just under 5.24 million net tons of coal were charged into beehive ovens nationwide; 64.3 percent of this was processed in the Coke Region. Twenty-seven years later the national figure for coal used in beehives had increased nearly eleven-fold to 61.9 million tons. At 19.7 million tons, the Connellsville output was still almost one-third the total. Even more important, in quality Connellsville coke set the standard that other districts aspired—and usually failed—to match.

Yet, as its reduced share of production indicated, despite massive expansion of mines and ovens, the district was unable to keep pace with the increase in demand for coke. Resort to alternative fuels was no longer a realistic possibility for most operators now requiring coke to enable them to drive their blast furnaces hard. As late as 1883, when Connellsville shipments first exceeded 3.5 million tons and the average price for merchant coke was at the low figure of $1.13, almost half the national output of iron had been made wholly or partly with other fuels—11 percent charcoal, 19 percent anthracite, and 18 percent a mixture of anthracite and coke. Twelve years later 84 percent of iron was made with coke, the share of the other fuels or mixtures being respectively 2 percent, 1 percent, and 13 percent.[32] At the end of the century, there was a revival in the use of charcoal, but this was for making iron for specially demanding purposes and in tonnages that were very small in comparison with those for coke iron. This charcoal iron industry was largely in remote regions, by then the only places that could provide enough wood. There was no possibility whatsoever of charcoal iron production on scales sufficient to meet the nation's huge and rapidly increasing needs.

As demand spiraled, a check on price rises for Connellsville coke was provided by competition and competitive expansion among rival coke producers in the region, but this was limited by their individual holdings of coal lands and ultimately by the size of the mineral resource they all worked. From an early date it was realized that the life expectancy of the field was short, and it diminished rapidly as annual demands increased. One acre of the eight-foot Connellsville seam was reckoned to yield 12,000 tons of coal. In the mid-1880s John Fulton wrote of a Connellsville district covering about two hundred square miles. At that time the annual coal requirements of the 11,600 ovens in this district, if fully utilized, was 8.1 million tons; at full work they would exhaust the known coal reserve when working began within about 190 years. Twenty years later, 21.3 million tons of coal were used by the 26.2 thousand ovens of the now two Connellsville fields. At these extended levels of consumption, and taking into account the coal already coked, the expectation of life of the district was dwindling. As early as spring 1901, in evidence to the Industrial Commission, C. M. Schwab, newly appointed president of the United States Steel Corporation, reckoned that if his industry grew in the future as in the past, this finest of all coking coal fields would be exhausted within thirty years.[33] The pace quickened further—between 1890 and 1900 steel output increased by 138 percent, and 1910 output represented a further advance of 156 percent.

Naturally, failure of this prime district to keep pace with the demand for coke would lead to price increases. There is evidence that in relation to pig iron prices, over the longer term the relative cost of coke did increase, though unevenly. One way to limit the freedom of the Connellsville producers to charge more was to use alternative methods of coking, especially as these permitted use of poorer coals, which would not only be cheaper but might perhaps be nearer the point of consumption.

Table 4.8 Iron output and fuel consumption in selected furnaces, 1885–1892

Fuel	Furnace height (feet)	Iron output (gts a month)	Fuel consumption (lbs per ton iron)
Charcoal			
Spring Lake, Mich.	45	1,488	1,844
Bay, Mich.	48	2,615	2,060
Ashland, Wisc.	60	3,379	1,815
Anthracite			
Secaucus, N.J.	65	2,698	2,244
Anthracite/coke (51.9/48.1)			
a furnace in Pa.	80	3,844	2,520
Coke			
Pocahontas Ivanhoe, Va.	60	2,108	2,020
Connellsville Braddock, Pa.	90	12,000	1,800

SOURCE: J. Fulton, "Physical Properties of Metallurgical Fuels," *American Manufacturer*, quoted in *BAISA*, 24 November 1894, 267.

As a result, from the early 1890s, the mushrooming output of beehive coke was supplemented by a small but steadily growing consumption of coke made in retort ovens. Finally, it might be possible to open new areas possessing coals suitable for coking in beehive ovens even if the quality of their coke could not match that from Connellsville.

There were some coking coal districts beyond the area of competition with Connellsville. The most important was in northern Alabama, where coke was produced in large tonnages, though it was of relatively poor quality. It served the growing iron industry of the Southeast, which unlike the local coke, did compete in the Northeast as well as in the West. But as the leading coke district apart from Connellsville, Alabama produced only a little over one-seventh the Pennsylvania state tonnage in 1894 and less than one-eighth as much in 1910. Coalfields in New Mexico, Utah, and above all Colorado had smaller coke industries and were not nationally significant. For the Pittsburgh and Valleys districts, Lake Erie shore furnaces, and those of the East as they switched over from anthracite to coke, Connellsville seemed the obvious source of supply. But, for one major northern ironmaking center, there were equally near and major bituminous coalfields. Hopes were entertained over many decades that it might prove possible for Chicago works to obtain their coke, or an important part of it, from mines in the major coalfields of the northern section of the Mississippi lowlands much nearer their furnaces. The outcomes of repeated experiments and a number of commercial attempts were disappointing; the coke made proved unequal to its task.

In the mid-1870s local block coal, claimed to be little different chemically from western Pennsylvania coking coals, was coked at Brazil, Indiana, in twenty beehives. This coke was mixed with four times its weight of raw coal for use in local ironworks, which accordingly dispensed with Connellsville coke. The block coal was $1.50 a ton and local coke $3 at a time when rail charges of $4.50 meant coke from Connellsville cost $7 a ton.[34] But the attractions of superior furnace operating conditions with better fuel were soon seen to outbalance those of lower assembly costs. Over thirty years since a first attempt in 1857, coke was made in various parts of the western Kentucky coalfield. It was supplied within a natural market area that included St. Louis, Chicago, Louisville, Cincinnati, and Memphis. In the late 1880s rates of freight to the main western smelting locations were $1.50 to $2.25 lower than from Connellsville, and for a time it was reckoned that this might more than compensate for rather higher production costs. As a result some claimed, "western Kentucky will yet solve the problem of cheap metallurgical fuel for St. Louis and other western markets."[35] Again, high hopes were disappointed; in 1901 Kentucky produced 0.46 percent of all coke used in the United States.

All Illinois coals were relatively high in volatiles, moisture, ash, and sulfur. Coke made from them had an acceptable physical structure but was defective chemically. The adverse effect of the high ash content could be reduced by crushing and washing before coking, but this increased costs. On the other hand, the sulfur content could not be reduced and this made Illinois coke generally unacceptable. The Vulcan Iron Works of St. Louis built its first two blast furnaces in 1869. Given its location it naturally turned to Illinois for fuel, but the coke made from these coals was found unsuitable to produce pig iron of high enough quality for the Bessemer process, which it adopted in 1876. It had to resort to Connellsville. In the 1880s other attempts were made to use some Illinois coal in this plant.[36] Between 1880 and 1900 a considerable number of beehive ovens were built to coke Illinois coal, including ones near Murphysboro in Jackson County and at Equality in Gallatin County. But these plants were three hundred miles from the blast furnaces on Lake Michigan, about two-thirds as far away as Connellsville. At South Chicago attempts to improve the coke made from Illinois coal produced a fuel suitable only for light industrial use.

In 1894 Illinois produced 0.6 million tons of pig iron, apparently all made using coke and amounting to almost 11 percent of the total tonnage of iron made with that fuel; that year Illinois and Indiana together produced 8,751 tons of coke, less than 0.1 percent of the national figure. By 1899 Illinois output of coke pig iron was 12.3 percent of the total, but whereas at the end of that year Connellsville output was at unprecedented levels, 126 of the 130 coke ovens in Illinois and 40 of 52 in Indiana were idle. The two Midwestern states made 2,370 tons of coke; Chicago alone received 516,000 tons of Pennsylvanian coke. Given the high freight charge on this imported coke, its delivered price was more or less double that at the ovens, so there remained a strong incentive to continue to search for methods that might make nearer coals usable. At the close of 1899, twenty-six Hemingway patent ovens were under construction in the Midwest with the expectation that they would make it possible to use "dry" (low volatile) coals, generally classed as noncaking, from the interior coalfields. By the early twentieth century a more careful classifying of Illinois coal and improved machinery for crushing and washing it before it was placed in the ovens once again raised hopes of a breakthrough. As Fulton cautiously put it, they seemed to "afford indications of moderate success"; but he also reported that "so far ... the efforts at coking the large bed of coal in southern Illinois has not met the expectations of the parties in Chicago that have made a series of experiments testing the coking properties of these coals."[37] In 1904 Illinois and Indiana together produced 47.4 million tons of coal but only 4,439 tons of coke, figures respectively 48.4 percent and 0.03 percent of those in Pennsylvania.

The advance of the byproduct oven was to bring new hopes of making metallurgical coke from Illinois coal. There was even talk of it being delivered to Chicago furnaces for about $2 a ton. This enticing prospect was accompanied by the suggestion that every $1 saved might widen the market area of local steel mills by 100–150 miles. Again achievement fell far short of hope. Between 1904 and 1907 extensive tests on Illinois coal made at the Louisiana Purchase Exposition held in St. Louis proved that coke could be made but that it would have an unacceptably high sulfur level. During World War I government experiments were made at Canal Dover, Ohio, using coals from Franklin County, Illinois, and Pike County, Indiana. Satisfactory coke was produced but it lacked what has always been regarded as most desirable by furnace operators, uniformity of quality. In the 1920s the works at Gary and at Granite City experimented with coke-oven charges containing 85 percent Illinois coal and 15 percent coal from West Virginia. These experiments were not long continued. In short, despite efforts stretching over many years and continued into the future, Chicago had to rely on coking coals from the Appalachian Plateau.[38] However, within that more generally favored region there were a number of alternative sources of supply, and in 1930 only 7.4 percent of Chicago's 12-million-ton consumption of coking coal came from Pennsylvania. Illinois mines supplied 4.7 percent, 55.6 percent came from West Virginia; Kentucky delivered 32.3 percent from mines in its eastern counties.

Coals suitable for beehive coking were found widely through the bituminous coalfields of the central and northern sections of the Appalachians, though, as the *Connellsville Courier* stoutly maintained, figures proving their chemical purity did not necessarily mean that the coke made from them measured up to the local product in the essential physical function of supporting the burden in the blast furnace. Some of these competing coke districts were in Pennsylvania. For instance, Joseph Wharton, who in the early twentieth century operated a number of large blast furnaces at Port Oram (later Wharton) in Morris County, New Jersey, acquired a medium-sized battery of coke ovens at Bourne west of Smithfield in the Connellsville Coke Region. He also opened mines and built three hundred modern beehives at Coral on Black Lick Creek and a branch of the Pennsylvania Railroad in Indiana County. Sometimes such plants cost more than ovens in the Coke Region; each of the patent ovens that had to be used in coking the dry coals of Elk County cost $675 each, compared with $250–300 for standard Connellsville beehives. Coke was made in the Irwin district along the Pennsylvania Railroad line toward Pittsburgh; it was here, for instance, that the Carnegies operated Larimer coke works before becoming business associates of Frick. East of this was the Greensburg field, though in the forty years before 1900 it had produced less coke than Connellsville did in a single year. Coke makers near Pittsburgh used coal either railed in from the coal districts or slack coal shipped down the Monongahela. Until after 1900 this was not very important—in 1899 Connellsville produced 10.39 million tons of coke and delivered 166,582 cars of it into Pittsburgh; only 0.64 million tons of coke were produced within the Pittsburgh district.[39] North and northeast of the city were other scattered, small, and only locally important centers of coke production. Occasionally, hopes were aroused that one or other of them might grow into something bigger. For instance, as late as summer 1899 a paper given at a meeting of the Engineers' Society of Western Pennsylvania drew attention to the fact that in the early 1860s there had been coal production at Verona, only a little way northeast of the city, and announced the rediscovery of a coking coal field six to seven miles wide, extending ten miles or more along the Allegheny River and containing 60,000 acres of coal lands. It was characterized as "quite as large as the Connellsville field [and] . . . very much nearer to the city and which by recent tests produces coke equal to the Connellsville product." Though so grandly heralded, the region never came to anything in coke manufacture, though the Harmarville area across the river was later to ship coking coal.[40] (West of the Connellsville coal basin was another field, whose much greater importance receives attention elsewhere.)

Southward, at Mount Savage and Lonaconing in the Frostburg basin, Maryland had pioneered coke iron manufacture in the 1830s. Much more important in later production was the coal and beehive industry built up in the course of a few decades around the turn of the century in West Virginia, Virginia, and later (for coking coal) in eastern Kentucky. On a national scale, this region and Birmingham were the only other important beehive coke districts. Unlike Alabama, coke made here was in

Table 4.9 Chemical composition of selected coking coals *(in percentages)*

Region	Fixed carbon	Volatiles	Ash	Sulfur	Moisture	Phosphorus
Pennsylvania						
Connellsville	59.61	30.12	8.41	0.78	1.86	0.024
Broad Top	71.12	18.40	7.50	1.70	1.28	trace
Bennington	68.77	23.68	5.73	0.62	1.20	0.017
Greensburg	61.34	33.50	3.28	0.86	1.02	n.a.
Armstrong County	52.03	38.20	5.14	3.66	0.96	n.a.
Johnstown	73.84	16.49	7.97	1.97	0.72	n.a.
West Virginia						
Pocahontas	72.71	18.81	5.19	0.79	1.01	n.a.
Fairmont	54.80	36.70	7.00	2.10	1.50	n.a.
Illinois						
Mt. Carbon	53.47	38.20	8.02	0.63	2.08	0.027
Alabama						
Birmingham	68.35	25.77	3.70	0.07	2.10	n.a.

SOURCE: J. Fulton, *Coke* (Scranton, N.J.: International Textbook, 1905), 7.

direct competition with that from Connellsville. Given the complexities of Appalachian geology, it is understandable that a number of separate fields were involved in this area's coke production.

In 1885 the exuberant Pennsylvania state geologist John Peter Lesley and the Reverend C. Gordon Ames of Philadelphia in a short but illuminating account extolled Pennsylvania's mineral riches, but felt compelled to recognize that other areas of Appalachia were also well endowed. Good iron ore and coal had been shown to extend throughout the mountains and plateaus down to Alabama "with no sensible difference of quality or quantity in either direction." From their perspective, early development above all had given their state its outstanding position: "Pennsylvania has the advantage over other states of a first plant, both in ironworks and coal mines, and in a consequent multiplication and concentration of capital for these industries, which must keep her facile princeps in this respect for a long time to come. Sooner or later she must take a second rank in iron, but never in coal and coke."[41] Despite the inertia they recognized, and the unquestionably outstanding quality of the coke that Connellsville produced, necessity and opportunity together helped bring about the opening of what were first secondary but eventually important sources of coke and coking coal farther south than Connellsville.

Two promising areas of West Virginia were fairly accessible. The Fairmont or Upper Monongahela district was based on an extension of the Pittsburgh coal bed across the state line. Coal and coke were shipped from it by the Baltimore and Ohio

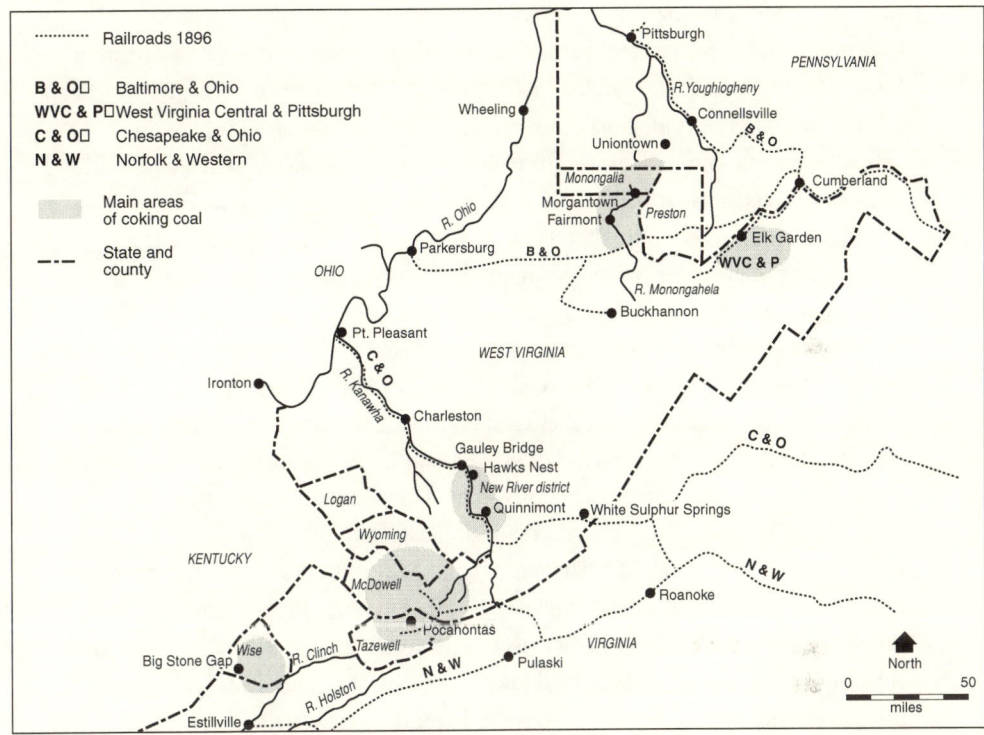

New coke districts of West Virginia and Virginia.

Railroad, with which in the late 1880s a syndicate led by a senator for West Virginia, Johnson N. Camden, made connections in the form of the Monongahela River and West Virginia and Pittsburgh Railroads. By late summer 1889 five hundred ovens were being constructed along the Camden syndicate lines. The intended outlets for their coke were in the Hocking Valley, Cincinnati, St. Louis, Chicago, and the Lake Erie shore. Further development was helped by improved navigation of the Monongahela.[42] Eastward, separated from Pennsylvania by the panhandle of Maryland, was the Elk Garden or Upper Potomac district, whose mines were developed along the Virginia Central and Pittsburgh Railroad. Much more important were areas farther south, the New River and Kanawha districts in the center of the state, particularly in Fayette County, and the Flat Top, or Pocahontas, region of Mercer and McDowell Counties, West Virginia, and Tazewell County, Virginia. Though separate districts, New River and Flat Top worked the same seam of coking coal. Some one hundred miles southwest from the little town of Pocahontas and centered on Big Stone Gap, Wise County, was what would prove to be Virginia's main coking coal deposit. Westward from there and across the mountains, major coking coal developments in Harlan County and other parts of eastern Kentucky took place during or shortly after World War I. In all these regions, coal lands and labor costs were usually cheaper than in Connellsville, but some other considerations were more expensive. In Connellsville the coal broke naturally into conveniently small pieces as it was cut and could be charged, unscreened, and unwashed as it came from the mine. Flat Top coal was produced in larger lumps that had to be broken and screened. By the early twentieth century, New River mines usually broke, screened, and washed their coal on site.[43]

To a greater extent even than with Connellsville, the pace of development and pattern of production in these coalfields were determined by railroad extensions. There were two main reasons for this: these locations were farther from major centers of consumption, and their general isolation was made harder to break by their topography and the consequent absence of other sources of potential freight. It was long recognized that West Virginia presented tremendous possibilities, but their realization was limited by inaccessibility. Three-quarters of the state was underlain by coal, nearly horizontal seams outcropping in the gorges of almost every large stream cut into the plateau country. Only adits were needed with gravity delivery to the riverside. Height and ruggedness declined toward the Ohio, but the better coals were farther away where the plateau had been eroded into "a network of narrow crooked ridges with deep gorges or narrow valleys."[44] The coal region in the extreme southwest of Virginia was also remote, difficult to access, and apart from coal offered few attractions for economic development. Even after World War I much of it was still a wilderness, "a mountainous region with ridges rising 300 to 1,000 feet above the very narrow valleys and except for some poorly kept farms along the tops of the ridges and the area occupied by the mining and coking plants and villages ... wooded throughout." At this time a vivid picture of the difficult environment, access problems, and strange combination of natural riches, human poverty, and exploitation in the Appalachian coal plateaus was provided by the geographer J. Russell Smith in his distinguished book *North America*.[45]

Before the Civil War, mineral extraction had scarcely begun in the middle Appalachians; even in 1873 West Virginia's coal output was no more than 0.6 million tons. Three years before that the state had only 387 miles of railroad. By 1890 its network amounted to 1,433 miles and ten years later 2,228, most extensions being made to open either or both lumber and coal. In the early 1870s the building of the Chesapeake and Ohio from Newport News, Virginia, through Covington, White Sulphur Springs, the valley of the Green Briar River, and on to the New and Kanawha Rivers opened the New River district. The coal here was shown to make a coke with 5 percent more carbon and only half as much ash as that of Connellsville. Sulfur content was variable but usually about the same as in the older district. Already by 1879 there were nine coking coal mines along the New River, four coke plants with 250 ovens, and plans for another 100 ovens. It was a surprise to some contemporaries that development had not been on a larger scale. One found an explanation in a slightly different direction from that of Lesley and Ames: "With all the mineral resources which the Virginias have, it is a matter of constant surprise to me that they are not the richest states in the Union. They can produce a good iron very cheaply and might in a few years take the coke trade away from Connellsville. . . . I can only account for their present poverty by the shortsightedness of their transportation companies and the want of energy of their people."[46] In fact, the distance of the region from any center of consumption even remotely comparable with Pittsburgh and the much more difficult relief conditions than in southwestern Pennsylvania must go far to explain what seemed to the writer a mere lack of enterprise on the part of mining entrepreneurs and railroad companies. By 1886 West Virginian coal production was already over 4 million tons.

Soon, the exertions of the managements of new or extending "coal roads" was breaking down more of the isolation of this plateau region. The Norfolk and Western Railway was formed in 1881 from smaller preexisting railroads, and over the next ten years the company built three lines into the coalfields of western Virginia and eastern West Virginia. By 1883 shipment of excellent steam and coking coals began from the Flat Top–Pocahontas region. Three years later 93,000 tons of the 640,000 tons of coal mined in Tazewell County, Virginia, was made into coke.[47] By then three coal operations on the Cripple Creek extension of the Norfolk and Western in the headwaters of the New River system were each planning 100 ovens, intending to ship coke as far as Alabama.[48] Virginia's coke output increased 383 percent from 1884 to 1887, though even in the latter year this equaled only one-and-a-half weeks' production from the Connellsville district. The Norfolk and Western was extended beyond the Ohio and by 1891 reached Columbus, Ohio, from which its mineral traffic was sent farther north and west by other roads. By 1899 government-financed work had completed locks on the Kanawha and Ohio Rivers making possible year-round water shipments of coal from mines along the former waterway. Three years after this the New River coalfield had sixty mines and some 3,000 coke ovens. (There were then 26,000 Connellsville ovens.) In 1909 the new Virginian Railroad was opened from the coal regions of West Virginia eastward to Norfolk, Virginia.

The final area of development was eastern Kentucky, though here it was largely to produce coal to be coked in byproduct ovens located at the iron and steel works. The eastern portion of the state is coterminous with the coalfield, but the name commonly given to part of it, the "Mountains," highlights its difficulties of access. The Louisville and Nashville had tapped it by 1892–1893 at Pineville, but as late as 1911 this state—including its western coalfield—produced only 13.7 million tons of coal. At that time Harlan County was still without a railroad. In this case inflated demand during World War I, labor problems elsewhere, and newly improved access—the Louisville and Nashville alone spent $30 million and built 333 miles of new track into the eastern coal region in the ten years after 1910—brought about remarkable increases in Kentucky's coal production to 25 million tons in 1916, 39 million in 1920, and 55 million five years later. By 1921 there was a railroad track the length of Harlan County along the Poor River and leading to the newly established U.S. Coal and Coke Company town of Lynch.

In two instances the strong attraction of these mid-Appalachian coal districts caused the involvement of those who were or had been large producers of Connellsville coke. The more important involved the iron and steel interests of Chicago. For them the West Virginia coking coal lands were nearly as far away as Connellsville, but Appalachan coke was believed to be comparable in quality, in addition to which coal lands there could be more cheaply obtained and were not already largely in the hands of powerful companies. Moreover, in the critical years of labor unrest in the late 1880s, West Virginia seemed likely to be a haven of relative tranquility. The three major Chicago steel companies, Union, Joliet, and the North Chicago Rolling Mill, were deeply involved in Connellsville through the South West Coal and Coke Company. The strikes of 1887 and subsequent years caused them great inconvenience. One means of mitigating the problem seemed to be to open other coking coal deposits farther south. In 1887 they examined Loup Creek, a west-bank tributary of the New River. Next January, mentioning the hope that it might also cause their current railroad carriers to lower their rates, H. A. Gray, secretary and treasurer of Union Steel, welcomed the fact that Frick was to send a man to look at the Pocahontas region. Sometime later Frick sent on a report from Robert Ramsay on West Virginia. Early in spring Gray himself went to examine the New River district. He reported to his president that the party had been shown a six-foot seam exposed in a river bluff. It was "without band or impurities of any kind in it, and is without doubt a coking coal of the best quality." This seam and another five-feet thick could be mined by drift along Piney Creek. Gray had been to the mines and ovens, 150 in total, at Caperton on the banks of the New River, and found them "fully equal, if not superior, to any that I saw in the Connellsville region." They had concluded that costs of production indicated that "if the freight rates continue proportionally as much lower," the area could compete for business in the northwest with Connellsville. Gray obtained options and strongly recommended purchase. Jay Morse, Union Steel's president, sending Gray's

Table 4.10 Coke output of Connellsville and West Virginia ovens, 1880–1907 *(net tons in thousands)*

Year	Connellsville[a]	West Virginia
1880	2,206	139
1890	6,464	883
1900	10,021	2,358
1905	11,365	3,400
1907	13,089	4,113

SOURCES: *Connellsville Courier;* E. W. Parker, U.S. Geological Survey, *Annual Report, 1899–1900,* part 6 (Washington, D.C.: GPO, 1907).
a. Shipments in the case of Connellsville. (Old basin only.)

Table 4.11 Chemical analyses of coke from Connellsville, Pa., New River (Pocahontas), W.Va., and Pineville, Ky., 1889–1891 *(in percentages)*

Contents	Connellsville "standard"	New River	Pineville
Fixed carbon	87.46	91.34	94.66
Ash	11.32	7.01	3.37
Sulfur	0.69	0.72	0.59

SOURCES: For Connellsville and Pineville, Fulton, Oct. 1891; for New River, J. Morse to H. C. Frick, 7 April 1888, Frick Papers.

report to Frick, added a scribbled note to explain a *fait accompli:* "Frick, we have accepted our options and paid for them. Enclosed please find copy of analysis of coke from this district we are now using." Within a few weeks the Union and Joliet furnaces had tried the new coke. Though it had not been carefully made, it performed well, giving a considerable economy in the coke and limestone used per ton of pig iron.[49]

In spring 1889 the Illinois Steel Company was formed by merging the three Chicago firms. It remained a major user of Connellsville coke but, like its predecessor companies, also looked for alternatives. Within a few months it had tested ten cars of West Virginian coke and proved that it was lower in ash than they were getting from the coke works Frick controlled on their behalf. In turn (as described earlier), Frick made use of their dissatisfaction to try to induce the railroads to cut freight charges, in the process tacitly admitting the other Appalachian districts could more or less match Connellsville coke quality. As he told the vice president of the Pennsylvania Lines West (a division of the PRR) of Pittsburgh: "It seems to me it is wholly a question of freight rate, in order to determine whether to open up and develop property owned by them in Virginia or extend their operations in the Connellsville Region."[50] In mid-1893 Illinois Steel placed orders for coke for the next six months with the Norfolk, Shamokin, Powhatan, and Lick Creek works in the Flat Top region. Their price was lower than that offered by the H. C. Frick Coke Company, and the new supply was made still more attractive by a decision of the Norfolk and Western to reduce freight charges, partly to promote its new line into Ohio and partly because of the large size and hoped-for regularity of the traffic.[51] Inevitably, there was an element of risk in these new areas. For instance, in mid-1894 coal lands were offered for sale in an area of Wyoming County, West Virginia, that were expected to lie along the line of a proposed extension of the Chesapeake and Ohio. The railroad was said to have paid $40–50 an acre for its coal lands, but a party in Parkersburg was offering 65,000 acres for $15 per acre. It pointed out that coal underlay just under two-thirds of the area but added: "'the bone must go with the meat' which is why we make this exceedingly cheap offer."[52] The railroad extension was not built, and it was not until the first decade of the next century that the county first had railroads and then only in its eastern parts. Before the end of the nineteenth century, Chicago furnaces were receiving coke from the New River district via the Chesapeake and Ohio and from ovens in the Flat Top–Pocahontas area over the North Western, but Connellsville remained their main source of supply.

The other instance of a dramatic transfer of Connellsville entrepreneurship to the new districts was given particular force because this same enterprise and investment had also been applied to the older coke region from outside recently and on a large scale. The Connellsville Coke and Iron Company, formed in the main by capitalists whose wealth had been made in the anthracite coalfields, had acquired the largest single tract of Connellsville coal at the beginning of the 1880s. During the next few years it built three major coke plants and by the end of the decade controlled 1,500 ovens, more than one in ten throughout the region. Then in 1889 Connellsville Coke and Iron sold all its properties to the H. C. Frick Coke Company and transferred its attention to the development of over 70,000 acres of coal and iron ore lands that, under the title of the Virginia Coal and Iron Company, it had owned for a number of years in the Big Stone Gap area of Wise County, Virginia; it was also interested in the Holston Steel and Iron Company some way to the east of Wise County. As the pioneering interests in the isolated county, they could hope to be free of the constraints that had troubled them in Connellsville.[53] Inevitably, the realization of any potential for this huge new mineral patrimony depended on connecting to larger markets and thus rail access. Early in the 1880s they had begun to build a railroad seventy miles long from Bristol, Sullivan County, Tennessee, to their mineral properties. By 1888 this line had reached beyond the little village of Estillville (later Gate City) to reach the Clinch River in Scott County, Virginia, half way to its destination. Although in 1890 Virginia Coal and Iron apparently had signed a contract for "an immense coking plant," as late as 1896 railroad extension seemed to have made no further progress. However, within another six years competitive building in order to gain a share in the expected development prospects of the Big Stone Gap coking coal area had ensured that this settlement of no more than 2,000 inhabitants had been provided with rail connections in three directions—the Atlantic and Ohio to Bristol and beyond; the Louisville and Nashville southwest to Cumberland Gap, Kentucky; and the Norfolk and Western northeast to the Pocahontas region of West Virginia.[54]

Though very much secondary centers of production, the coke districts of the Appalachian coal plateau south of Connellsville increased in relative significance. Before 1895 there were only two coke works in Virginia—one associated with the iron plant at Low Moor, Allegheny County, which used coal from the New River district of West Virginia, and the other at Pocahontas. During 1895 ovens were built in Wise County and two years later over 60 percent of the state's output of coke came either from there or from the upper valley of the Clinch River running southwestward from Tazewell County. In West Virginia there was more rapid progress, coke output increasing 173 percent in nine years from 1890. Not only was this proportionately a greater increase than in Connellsville, but in the mid-1890s there was a dramatic illustration of the limits it imposed on the ability of the Connellsville firms to exploit their leading position.[55] In 1896 a sharp fall in iron production from the level of the previous year took place, with a small fall in iron's average price. In this unfavorable setting Connellsville producers chose to increase their own prices. As a result their coke sales fell by one-third whereas shipments from the newer Appalachian fields and the rest of the United States increased. Having learned a painful lesson, Connellsville prices were cut in 1897. Even so, output there failed to reach 1895 levels, though it was higher elsewhere.

When the United States Steel Corporation was formed in spring 1901, its constituent companies controlled an acreage of coking coal lands in which Connellsville was over two-and-a-half times as important as all other coke districts; in ovens controlled it was over four times bigger. But its creation encouraged the remaining independent iron and steel companies to look to other districts for supplies as an antidote to a feared USS near-monopoly in Connellsville. Willis King of Jones and Laughlin explained their position to the Industrial Commission. When asked if USS would have an advantage over its competitors due to the corporation's control of Connellsville coal, he replied: "They would perhaps have an advantage in the coal of the Pittsburgh field, but there are other fields of coal in West Virginia and other places that are equally as good as Connellsville. Pocahontas coal is recognized as one of the best coals in the world." He emphasized that this covered its coking properties.[56] In the next few months, signs of a new direction of thinking about coking coal

Table 4.12 Appalachian states' coke production, 1880–1905 *(as percentage of U.S. total)*

Region	1880	1890	1900	1905
Pennsylvania	84.2	73.7	67.4	64.9
West Virginia	3.5	6.1	11.6	9.4
Virginia	n.a.	1.4	3.2	4.5
Tennessee	3.3	3.6	1.9	1.3
Alabama	1.5	10.5	9.1	9.3
Rest of United States	7.5	6.1	6.8	10.6

SOURCES: U.S. Bureau of Census, *Census of Manufactures 1905*, Bulletin 65, *Coke* (Washington, D.C.: GPO, 1906); for Virginia, 1890, U.S. Geological Survey, *Annual Report, 1899–1900*, part 6, (Washington, D.C.: GPO, 1900), 619.

Table 4.13 Coke shipments from Connellsville, the Flat Top region, and other districts, 1895–1897 *(tons in thousands)*

Year	Connellsville	Flat Top[a]	Other districts	U.S. total
1895	8,244	702	4,388	13,334
1896	5,412	1,000	5,377	11,789
1897	6,915	856	5,518	13,289

NOTE: Connellsville statistics from *Connellsville Weekly Courier*, May 1914.
a. Statistics compiled by the Norfolk and Western Railway as reported by *AISA*.

at U.S. Steel emerged. Three hundred thousand acres of coal belonging to the Pocahontas Coal Syndicate was sold to the Pocahontas Coal and Coke Company, in turn controlled by the Norfolk and Western Railway. Then one-sixth of this tract, or 50,000 acres, an area well in excess of one-third the original area of the Connellsville coal bed, was leased to constituent companies of USS, which thereby secured sufficient coal to provide "on the present basis of consumption for about 30 years." In these new coal lands, USS planned to build at least 3,000 of "the most modern coke ovens," a number equal to about one-sixth of the total of all the ovens it had controlled at its formation.[57] Work on this project was soon underway, and by summer 1904 the superintendent of the Trotter coke works had returned home after a long period of work in the new coal areas, during which he had supervised construction of 1,000 ovens. By that year another USS subsidiary, the United States Coal and Coke Company, had six mines in operation along the Tug River near Welch in West Virginia. Coke from Flat Top and the Tug Valley was said to compare favorably with that from Connellsville.[58]

Further mid-Appalachian development depended partly on growth in demand

Table 4.14 Coking assets of expected steel consolidation, December 1900–January 1901

	Coking coal land (acres)		Coke ovens	
	Connellsville	Other districts	Connellsville	Other districts
Carnegie Steel	38,000	none	11,637	none
Others[a]	4,168	16,600	2,230	3,230
All independents[b]	n.a.	n.a.	7,087	34,300[c]

SOURCES: Carnegie Steel Company papers, probably December 1900, ACLC; *Connellsville Weekly Courier*, May 1914; H. N. Eavenson, "The Pittsburgh Coal Bed: Its Early History and Development," *TAIME* (1938).
   a. Federal Steel, National Steel, American Steel and Wire, National Tube, American Tin Plate, American Sheet Steel, and National Steel Hoop.
   b. All others including iron and steel and coal/coke companies.
   c. Includes ovens in all parts of the United States.

for coke, but also on the fact that an increasing proportion of it was made in byproduct ovens, for which its coals proved ideal. Freight-rate policies played an important part in determining control of these expanding markets for coke or coking coal. By 1904, for instance, the Louisville and Nashville had cut the rate on coke from Stonega, Virginia, to Chicago from $2.65 to $2.25 a ton, a reduction that, along with good service, meant Wise County coke was reported as coming into both the city and the "Central West" in large tonnages, "much to the chagrin of the Connellsville representatives, who chafe under being forced to sit idly by while a region which they have been wont to ignore is making such a hole in their business." By 1910 there were almost 5,000 ovens owned by twelve companies in the Wise County coke district, but shortly after this, competition and the advance of byproduct coke were probably the causes of many of these coke works standing idle for months or even years.[59] Railroad extensions shaped the geography of future development. Thus in 1909, the most active area of coal development in West Virginia was along the new Virginian Railroad in Raleigh, Wyoming, and Mercer Counties, especially on the Windy Gulf Branch, along which all the mines produced low-volatile and coking coals. The Chesapeake and Ohio was extending into Windy Gulf to compete with the Virginian. To the southwest, Northern and Western branch lines were opening up McDowell and Mingo County coal.[60]

The opening and exploitation of these new districts brought an influx of workers, though, being remote, isolated, of unfavorable topography, and agriculturally infertile, in no instance did these towns or counties become as populous as the Connellsville district. For some of them it was the unprecedented level of activity during World War I that brought about the breakthrough. Together, Connellsville and Low-

Table 4.15 Populations of leading coke and coking-coal counties, **1890–1940** *(in thousands)*

County	1890	1900	1910	1930	1940
Pennsylvania					
Fayette	80.0	110.4	167.4	198.5	200.9
Westmoreland	112.8	160.2	231.3	295.0	302.8
West Virginia					
Fayette	20.5	32.0	52.0	72.0	80.7
Pocahontas	6.8	8.6	14.7	14.5	13.9
McDowell	?	18.7	47.9	90.5	94.3
Virginia					
Tazewell	19.9	23.4	24.9	32.5	41.3
Wise	9.3	19.6	34.2	51.2	52.4
Kentucky					
Harlan	6.2	9.8	10.6	64.6	75.2

er Connellsville shipped 21.6 million net tons during 1916, an outstanding year. While this was a record, it amounted to only 39.7 percent of the national tonnage of coke. The growth of other beehive coke districts explains a good deal of its shrinking share. Yet far more important was the fact that byproduct coke by then made up 35 percent of the national output at 19.1 million tons. Consideration of the delayed but eventual wholesale adoption of this new coke technology helps place the later history of Connellsville coke in context.

5 New Technology

The Introduction of the Byproduct Oven

The United States was superbly endowed with coal resources. It was this enviable situation that in large part accounted for her slowness both in adopting general practices for the conservation of energy and, specifically, the major advances in coking technology pioneered in Europe in the late nineteenth century. On the Continent—Britain was, or for long thought itself to be, in this respect well-favored and therefore cast more in the American than the continental mold—coals suited to the beehive process were less abundant; ovens of "retort" rather than beehive design made it possible to use such poorer coking coals. For some time retort ovens remained just that, a different shape of oven making possible an improved method of coking. Before long, though, most of them also became byproduct recovery ovens as the requirements of the chemical industries for tar, light oils, and other items—as well as those of agriculture for fertilizers, especially sulfate of ammonia—led to the development of means for recovering what previously had been an inconvenient joint product of the coking process and discarded as waste. In this industrial situation, what began as a necessity became a habit of efficiency. By contrast, America had first-rate coking coal, to a remarkably late date a relatively small chemical industry, and little demand from agriculture, except in the South, for artificial fertilizers. Together, rich natural endowment and lack of commercial outlets for byproducts helped induce and then long maintain a general lack of interest in new coking technologies. Though by then a major industry was already taking shape, it was not until World War I, when an unprecedented increase in coke consumption coincided with conditions in which the byproducts of coking were at last at a premium, that a wholesale switch to the new process took place. Only by this relatively late date were United States engineers making pioneering contributions to the technology of byproduct oven design and operation, predictably in the field of productivity.

As late as 1859 Frederick Overman foresaw little prospect for large-scale development of any kind of coke iron industry. At that time at least some, and possibly a fairly high proportion, of the small tonnage of coke was still being made in heaps rather than in ovens. In short, all but the prehistory of the American coke industry lay ahead. Yet already the first tentative steps to retort processing were being taken in continental Europe. The "Knab" oven built by a French engineer in 1856 was the pioneer. Twenty-three feet long, six-and-a-half feet high, and three-and-a-quarter inches wide, it saved some of the byproducts. The following year Appolt built a retort oven that used the gas it made for heating.[1] A few years later more direct ancestors of modern ovens were being built in both Belgium and France. In 1861 the Belgian Evence Coppee designed a retort oven in which heat was provided by burning waste gases in flues surrounding the coking chamber. Coke yields in the Coppee oven were 70–75 percent the weight of the coal charged as compared with the 55–65 percent common in beehive operations. Coppee did not recover byproducts. A year later the Pernolet oven, introduced in France, recovered tar, ammonia, and other byproducts, and again the gases produced were burned to heat the next charge. The Carves ovens built that year at St. Etienne produced high-temperature tar as well as furnace coke. By the early 1880s Louis Semet and his cousin, Ernest Solvay, had produced a byproduct-recovery modification of the Carves oven, above all in order to produce ammonia for use in the alkali process pioneered by the latter; Henry Simon in Manchester made the process more economical by a regenerative system of heating. At this time, under the impetus of its rapid industrialization, Germany had begun to contribute to technological progress in this field. Output of pig iron in the German Empire at the end of the 1870s was already as great as in Belgium and France combined; from 1880 to 1900 its increase was three-and-a-half times as large as those nations. Albert Huessener in 1881 built a successful recovery oven very similar to the Carves oven. The next year he installed the first byproduct recovery ovens in Westphalia. The regenerative principle was now applied to German ovens to improve their heat economy. Patents for these improvements were bought by C. Otto, who had been building Carves ovens and now began saving their byproducts. The first Otto-Hoffmann ovens were put up in the Ruhr in 1883. By 1897 coke oven plants operated by Otto and Company produced 7 million gallons of tar, 400,000 gallons of benzene, and 14,000 tons of ammonia products.[2]

Though it contained the world's biggest coking industry, in 1897 only 2 percent of United States coke output was from retort ovens. Even this very modest achievement had been due in part to enterprise from outside the coal, coke, and metallurgical

Locomotive pulling charging larries and the hand-drawing of ovens, *circa* 1893. *Courtesy of Frick Art and Historical Center, Frick Archives*

industries. Higher coke yields, the possibility of using poorer (especially lower volatile) coals to produce an acceptable furnace coke, and income from byproducts were the main attractions of these new ovens. The main material disadvantage was that byproduct coking required much larger capital outlay than beehive ovens. An additional but vital disadvantage, though it was largely psychological, was a conviction shared by coke makers and furnace operators alike that its product was inferior to beehive coke. It is important to emphasize that the physical resource situation, economic criteria, and the human perceptions that had been shaped by those conditions were each involved in the slowness of the United States adopting byproduct coking. Differences in natural endowment had largely accounted for the initial divergence between European and American coke oven practice. Continental Europe, particularly Belgium and France, had poor coking coals; the northern Appalachian Plateau, and particularly the Connellsville area, was extremely well endowed with coals of a quality that meant, in the case of the latter, it could make the finest coke in beehive ovens. In both continents years of experience conditioned attitudes, setting the patterns for further development. As a result technologies were not changed as soon as objective technical and commercial assessments might have indicated was desirable. In some cases habit even seems to have hardened into hostility to new ideas. These various human responses to the opportunities of technological change may be seen at three levels: those of the experts, the individual coke companies, and trends in the industry as a whole.

There were some undisputed points at which comparisons could be made between beehive and retort-byproduct ovens; the critical factor in deciding between them was the weight to be given to each of them. Retort ovens could utilize poorer coals. Although they required a larger capital outlay than beehives, their coke yield was greater. If the ovens recovered byproducts, the resulting revenue could offset some of the extra investment—but these byproducts had to command a market. Critical in any evaluation was the quality of the coke made and its acceptability to blast furnace operators. Precise costings were possible for some of these considerations, but other figures were open to dispute; the question of coke quality was largely a matter of opinion or even of prejudice. Given such complexities, it is perhaps understandable that before any new-style ovens were built, there were years in which a variety of schemes were mooted and the process of assessment was enlivened by protracted, and sometimes heated, debate among coke technologists.

From at least as early as the mid-1870s, Americans were experimenting with new forms of ovens. In some, the main emphasis was on improved methods of handling, while in others the focus was on recovery and use of some byproducts, if only to burn them at the ovens in order to improve fuel efficiency. Examples that never had commercial outcomes were the innovations of McLanahan and others at Hollidaysburg in 1875–1876, W. G. Merriman of Pittsburgh six years later, and John Green in 1884. There were complications and much skepticism. The coke made in any of the early experiments was later recognized to have suffered because no one realized that the proportions of a retort oven needed to be varied to take account of the type of coal used. Even more decisively, iron manufacturers remained convinced that beehive coke was superior to that made in "more modern appliances." But even this was contested; a leading trade paper pointedly remarked, "It does by no means follow that because Connellsville coke-makers condemn Belgian ovens, their experience ought necessarily to lay down the rules for the rest of the country." In order to test the matter, in the early 1880s the Iron and Steel Association of Virginia decided to establish eighty Soldenhoff modifications of the Coppee oven. Hawk's Nest coal from Gauley's Mountain, West Virginia, would be used. The builder guaranteed 95 percent of the carbon in the coal would be made into coke. The plant reportedly cost 35 percent more than a line of beehives of equal capacity.³ No conclusive proof came from this experiment, but four years later the old methods were questioned from the heart of the Connellsville Coke Region. This marked the start of a fierce controversy over new technologies versus established ways.

Through the columns of the *Engineering and Mining Journal*, R. W. P. Richardson of Scottdale put in a plea for more efficient use of the local coal: "It is a matter of extreme surprise to a scientific or practical mining engineer, on first visiting the extensive coke-producing region of Pennsylvania, to see the excessive waste of the valuable products incidental to and closely allied with the process of coking coal. It is so easily remedied, and does not require an expensive series of experiments, of the efficiency of which we have abundant proof in Europe." For the benefit of his readers, he outlined the various types of byproduct ovens and followed up with another attack on old methods: lack of luster in byproduct coke was not an indication of inferiority; there was a large saving from the higher coal/coke ratio and income from byproducts; with coke then at $1.25 a ton, revenue from byproducts could make the newer processes attractive to coke makers. Richardson ended on a hopeful note: "It will therefore appear to every thinking person that to allow a golden opportunity for economy like this to be neglected would be utter folly. . . . I am anxious that these facts should be made public; and if it does not warrant an immediate change, at least let it be gradual, and let us not constantly adhere to the present prodigal methods of coking coal."⁴ In fact, comparison of the two methods was more complex than Richardson admitted, and unfortunately not every "thinking person" was as conservation-minded as he. Soon the debate was taken up in more detail and more tendentiously.

In late 1886 and early 1887, a lively and illuminating controversy was carried on in a number of issues of the *Engineering and Mining Journal* over the deficiencies of old and the advantages of new coking processes. The protagonist for the byproduct oven was a mining engineer named F. Koerner. John Fulton, widely acknowledged as a coke expert, was his severe critic, though some years later Fulton would be persuaded by the evidence to change his allegiance. Interesting contributions also were made by Henry M. Howe, who a few years later presided over the mines and mining jury at the World's Columbian Exposition, and by one of the pioneers of the Bessemer process in the United States, John F. Winslow. Koerner began with a heavy indictment of the old method of coking, the words he chose unfortunately invited a similarly aggressive response. As he saw it, the coal, wastefully mined,

is dumped into coke ovens that are bad, cheap copies of the ovens in use in Europe thirty or forty years ago. In burning the coal 15 percent or more of the fixed carbon is lost. . . . When we see the imperfect, and in many cases, the slovenly means used to close the apertures of the ovens to prevent the access of air to red-hot coke after the gases have been expelled, we wonder that the loss of fixed carbon is not greater. The great length of the plant makes efficient supervision almost an impossibility. When the coke is finally done, a stream of cold water is turned into the oven to cool the coke; the heat of the oven accumulated during the burning of the charge, instead of being utilized for the next charge, escapes with the stream into the air. That the sudden contraction of the masonry consequent on the injection of the water, repeated every 48 or 72 hours, makes frequent repairs necessary, and causes loss of time, goes without saying. The coke is then drawn out by hand. If cars for transportation are at hand, it is wheeled by wheelbarrows into them; if not, it is wheeled to the edge of the cooling floor and piled up by hand. When cars come it is handled again.

He pointed out the coke industry had been built up in a hurry, mostly in the last ten years. As compared with the great progress made over thirty years in material handling in anthracite coal, with the exception of improved colliery hoist equipment, the Connellsville industry was much where it had been in the 1850s. Even more striking was the contrast with the mechanization and consequent labor economy then being so effectively pushed through in iron and steel works practice. With better ovens and machinery, Koerner estimated labor costs in Connellsville coking could be halved to 18 cents per ton. He even alleged that much of the coke produced so inefficiently was of poorer quality than was claimed on the basis of laboratory analysis, for such analyses were commonly confined to the best practice. Ash content of cokes was often far too high, reducing efficiency in the blast furnace; in surprising detail he had worked out the unnecessary extra cost of this to consumers at 14.62 cents per ton of coke. In operations he had seen in continental Europe, the ash content in coke was 4.5 percent compared with an average of 12.75 percent in twenty-nine specimens of Connellsville beehive coke; loss of fixed carbon was 0.75 percent against as much as 15 percent in the beehive. Coming to new technology, he suggested that if the industry installed byproduct ovens, it would cost 50–75 percent more per ton of coke capacity than to build beehives, but the cost of repairs would be only 10 percent as much. He ended as provocatively as he had begun, though this time with a challenge rather than a statement: "Is it not about time to call a halt and see whether we cannot do better?"[5]

Fulton responded from Johnstown. He disputed Koerner's claim that supervision was difficult because a row of ovens might be as much as 1400 feet long. Back-to-back ("block") ovens might be half that length. (Koerner made the obvious reply that a man inspecting operations still had to walk 1400 feet, but he seemed to ignore the fact that, in the case of block ovens, at the end of his route he would be in a position to begin his next round of supervision.) Fulton put the loss of fixed carbon at 6.1 percent rather than 15 percent, but his figure was challenged by another correspondent, quoting a letter from a coke operator whose ovens lost slightly under 20 percent. Under American conditions Fulton argued the time had not come for byproduct recovery. The most important consideration was that they should make the finest furnace coke rather than save a little here or there, and he believed that the internal, direct heat in the beehive produced a better metallurgical coke than heat conducted through the firebrick wall of a retort oven. He concluded that the case for or against the beehive as compared with the "Belgian family of ovens" was "an unsettled matter," but then allowed the partisanship of his opposition to Koerner full view: "We can only agree with the writer on one point, that it is 'about time to call a halt' [concerning] the 'enormous waste' of estimated losses that have no foundation in fact."[6]

In his contribution, Winslow recognized that better practice was needed, but he was open-minded about the new technology. Referring perhaps to the 1881 Virginia project, he mentioned that the Coppee oven had recently been tried on "a somewhat large and costly scale . . . but not with good results." Even so, Winslow continued: "A better oven and appliances are greatly needed and he who will give them to the country will be a benefactor." Howe, reviewing the evidence, was judicial but generally inclined to the retort oven: "In brief I believe that we may avail ourselves of the undoubted advantages of retort coking, its greater yield of coke, and the recovery of by-products, as the rest of the world has done, either by adapting the retort to the particular coal employed or by adapting the blast furnace working to the retort coke or by both means combined. I do not say that we will, but that we may. That we have not does not show that we cannot."[7]

The strong feelings aroused by this dispute were epitomized in a summing up from Koerner. He admitted there were some rational coke operations in the coke region, but generally reaffirmed his low opinion of them. He made caustic reference to Fulton's earlier reports for the Second Geological Survey of Pennsylvania: "Disinterested and attentive readers of these reports feel that Mr. Fulton's is a special plea, not for a better process and greater economy, but for a venerable abuse." Again, he reckoned the failures of Carves and other ovens had been brought up to "bolster an old abuse." Koerner noted that by some he had been accused of being a missionary, but he did not feel like one, "although it would be probably impossible to find an industrial field where a thoroughgoing missionary is more wanted than in Mr. Fulton's neighborhood." Finally, he passed on to his readers a reaction from an interested—but unidentified—party in Connellsville to whom, after spending almost a year working there, he had plucked up courage to point out the prevailing waste and loss.

He replied, "My dear fellow, I have not the slightest doubt as to the correctness of your observations, but put yourself in our place. You do not deny that the old ovens make good coke; it finds ready sale; we are making money, and our shareholders are perfectly satisfied; we, as well as all our neighbors, have hundreds of thousands of dollars invested in the old plant; it would take an equal or larger sum, not to speak of time and trouble, to build a better one." I remarked: "But somebody will after a while, when competition becomes sharper, start new and more rational works, and make more money or undersell you." To his own entire satisfaction, at least, he gave the coup de grace to my argument by saying: "Well, that will be hereafter. Our 'Syndicate' will attend to a man who goes fooling around trying to put us to an enormous expense." From his standpoint, this man was perfectly correct; so were the craftsmen of old. "Great is Diana of the Ephesians! Our craft is in danger!"[8]

For a few years longer, the controversy continued without any domestic experience with the new technology to give it real substance. In the early 1890s a Pittsburgh paper ran a highly critical article on "The Old Beehive Oven"; it was subtitled: "A constant reminder that American engineers have let coke-making remain at a standstill. What our foreign brethren gain by using improved ovens." The report quoted Bruno Terne of the Franklin Institute, who had acknowledged that each Simon-Carves oven cost $845 as compared with only $280 for a beehive and was more complicated and constantly needed repairs in order to save gases. But experience with the Simon-Carves ovens installed at the Besseges Ironworks in southern France had shown overall annual savings over beehives of $18,938, which worked out at $223 per oven or roughly 40 cents per ton of coal used.[9] Soon afterward, some firm evidence was gathered at last from the use of the new methods with American coal.

In summer 1893 eighteen tons of coal was taken from the Valley Mine of the H. C. Frick Coke Company to the Otto-Hoffmann byproduct ovens at Recklinghausen in the Ruhr, where they were coked in the presence of an experienced American furnace manager. The coke yield was 71.2 percent the tonnage of coal as compared with the 58–60 percent then common in beehive practice, labor costs were reduced, and coking time cut by one-third. The coke itself was described by American observers as of "most excellent quality, very hard, with metallic ring and silvery luster—impossible to distinguish from the original Connellsville beehive coke made from the same seam of coal." When a sample was exhibited at the Westphalian Mining Exposition in Gelsenkirchen, German furnace men pronounced it superior to the best coke made from their own coals. Early the next year, when the Cambria Iron Company and the Mather iron ore interests of Cleveland began to interest themselves in byproduct coking, another thirty tons of Connellsville coal were tried in Germany, again with great success. It was a matter for remark that by this time only two beehive coking plants survived in the whole of Westphalia. In the course of the same year the United States Geological Survey sent a commission to examine European, especially German, byproduct ovens. Its findings were reported to American manufacturers.[10] Even the general proposition that the United States provided a very limited market for the byproducts so attractive under European conditions was now shown to be less than conclusive. Tar superior to that made in gas works was at this time half as costly again as in Germany; in 1892 the United States imported 117,000 tons of that material. It also bought some, though not a great deal, of foreign sulfate of ammonia at an average price of $63.20 a ton. A byproduct coke industry could supply this and largely or wholly replace imports of Chilean nitrate.[11]

The inquiries and trials in Europe were now confirmed from experiments carried out under American conditions. In 1888 T. L. Johnson of Cleveland built a small street-rail mill near Johnstown. Six years later he began work on a larger steel works and rolling mills at Lorain. Contemplating an integrated works, in May 1895 he had a sample of 1,240 tons of byproduct coke made from Connellsville coal tested at the Buffalo Furnace; interestingly, these trials were conducted under John Fulton's direction. The resulting coke was more uniformly sized than beehive coke and loss from breakage was less; overall the results were encouraging.[12]

As Johnson's experiments suggest, in the early 1890s a byproduct coke industry had been successfully launched at last in the United States. However, the honor of pioneering fell to a company from completely outside the coal, coke, or iron and steel industries. Between 1891 and 1893, the Solvay Process Company erected Semet Solvay ovens at its ammonia soda works at Solvay, on the outskirts of Syracuse, New York. The main function of the plant was to produce ammonia for its soda ash columns. In 1895 this plant was doubled in size. Now the new process began to gain a footing in the iron and coal trades. For a time at least, it seemed that, like the beehive process, its center would be in western Pennsylvania. In 1894 the Otto Company, which had followed Semet Solvay to America, organized a coke and gas company, soon reconstructed as the United Coke and Gas Company, and began work on sixty Otto-Hoffmann ovens at Johnstown. The following year they built byproduct ovens at Sharon in the Shenango Valley and Dunbar in the southern section of the Coke Region. In 1896 a less-sophisticated plant was established in the Upper Connellsville region at Unity, not far from Carnegie's long established Monastery coke works, for Mathias Saxman's Latrobe Coal and Coke Company. To the northeast, byproduct ovens were also built at Bolivar on the Conemaugh River. By 1897 ovens were established at Glassport on the lower Monongahela. Apart from Dunbar and Latrobe, all these plants were situated away from, though fairly near to, their coking coal.

The evidence provided by these early installations as to the viability of the new technology under American commercial conditions was by no means clear. In part, at least, this was because the simple description of them as "retort" or "byproduct" ovens overlooked the fact that they differed widely in type and function. The Latrobe plant consisted of thirty ovens designed by Newton Chambers of Sheffield, England. They were "simply" beehives provided with apparatus for saving byproducts. A local locomotive tire works was able to use their surplus gas. Bolivar had three experimental ovens designed by Dr. Slocum of the Gas Engineering Company, Pittsburgh. This "Slocum" oven was a modified Carves type. Neither Latrobe nor Bolivar operated on a considerable scale in 1897 and were soon dropped from the lists of oven plants. Glassport, near the confluence of the Youghiogheny and Monongahela, could draw coal from either basin. A major function of its ovens was to supply gas through two large-diameter pipelines to domestic and industrial consumers in McKeesport, then suffering the adverse effects of decline in its supply of natural gas. Only Johnstown and Sharon were indisputably furnace plant locations. In the ranks of their beehive coke competitors, there was some satisfaction that the coke produced in early operations at Johnstown was said to be unsuitable for exacting uses.[13]

These first half-dozen plants confirmed a number of lessons that could have been learned from Europe. First, coke ovens were best located next to iron and steel works so that the coke required minimum handling and byproduct gas could find immediate use. Cambria, Sharon and, in part, Dunbar met these criteria. In other cases, as at Glassport and the very much larger installation a few years later at Everett near Boston, there was a nearby mass market for gas in domestic and industrial outlets, and the distribution of coke was a secondary consideration. Throughout a rural and small-town countryside only sparsely industrialized like the Connellsville region, no large demand for either coke or gas was immediately at hand. Second, it was recognized that the new processes permitted use of poorer coking coals and thereby opened up the possibility of shorter rail hauls on either coal or coke. Considering the advance of the byproduct oven in 1894, the *Iron Trade Review* traced further consequences: "The movement means, of course, increased independence of the Connellsville region, and hence, to a large extent, the elimination of the advantage enjoyed by steelmakers nearest that source of supply." A final sentence gave substance and direction to the general statement, though some of the assumptions on which it was based proved illusory: "If the coals of Indiana and Illinois, for example, can be successfully coked at the works of the Illinois Steel Company, the advantage Chicago now has over Pittsburgh in cost of ore will no longer be offset by the handicap of a long coke haul." By early 1895 Indiana and Illinois coals were being tested for their suitability for "German" methods of coking. The nearest coal was only forty miles from Chicago; it was noted that the freight rate on Connellsville coke was $2.65

a ton. Two-and-a-half years later, Illinois Steel reportedly arranged with Huessener for construction of a bank of byproduct ovens of modified design to be erected either in the Connellsville region or at their South Chicago works. There was some substance in these rumors. In November 1895 the executive committee of Illinois Steel approved a contract with Aktiengessellschaft fur Kohlendestillation of Bulmke, Westphalia, for the construction of Huessener ovens. The following spring it considered the location of what was by this time described as an "experimental" byproduct coke plant but deferred a decision.[14] The project aired at this time did not come to fruition, and by the time byproduct ovens were eventually built in Chicago, local sources of coal remained of negligible significance as contributors to their charges.

By the late 1890s not only was a new, improved coking technology available, but it also had been proved that its product was comparable in quality with that made by the established process. Byproduct coke output increased but to the end of the decade made up only a small part of the industry. At the beginning of 1898, 280 byproduct ovens were at work, though 680 more were under construction during the course of that year.[15] Between 1893 and 1900, coke output from byproduct ovens went up from 12,850 to 1,075,727 tons, but the latter was less than 5 percent of total coke production; and over the same seven years beehive production had increased by more than 10 million tons. Only recognition of the limited resource base for beehive coking seemed to hold out promise of a long-term future for the newer technology. Why was it advancing so slowly?

In the first place there had been instances of severe difficulties with the new ovens. A spectacular example of this was provided by the first of the major steel firms to install them. Cambria Iron Company had put up sixty Otto-Hoffmann ovens in 1895. The outlay, expected to be $250,000, was in fact $301,000. From 100,000 tons of coal charged it was projected that the ovens would produce 70,000 tons of coke, 3,530 tons of tar, 1,180 tons of sulfate of ammonia, and gas equivalent to 12,000 tons of coal each year. A German, Mr. Stammler, was put in charge. By early 1897 the extraordinarily high temperatures reached in the ovens—said to be up to 2,500 degrees Fahrenheit—had caused excessive contraction of the bricks so that one of the batteries, thirty ovens, had already required demolition to its foundations. In the other battery, eight ovens had been rebuilt, and of the twenty-two then being operated half had already been reconstructed and the rest were soon to follow. A rough estimate of rebuilding costs was $75,000. In short, along with the original cost overrun, this increased the initial outlay by 50 percent. A twenty-inch-diameter pipeline had been built from the ovens but had not yet been connected to the steelworks. Some coal was supplied from Gallitzin about fifty miles to the northeast, some from the same seam much nearer the works. Coke yield appeared higher than expected but, though varying a good deal, the coke produced had a higher sulfur and phosphorus content than that from Connellsville. As a consequence it could not be used alone either in Bessemer (because of its phosphorus) or in other grades of iron (because of the sulfur content). As a result, at the blast furnaces it was being mixed with Connellsville coke in the proportion of one barrow of byproduct to eight of beehive coke.[16]

Given the universally recognized excellence of Connellsville coke and evidence such as that from Cambria of difficulties with the new process, it was understandable that the iron trade was reluctant to give up a proven product. This was well illustrated at Jones and Laughlin. After exhausting much of the coal that had supplied their Tyrone coke works on the Youghiogheny, they built a new beehive plant on the north side of the Monongahela in Pittsburgh. Willis King attempted to justify their choice of the older technology in words that suggested an unwillingness to consider hard evidence from Europe but also identified some of the peculiarities of the American situation: "Coke made by the by-product process has hardly proved satisfactory for blast furnace use, although it may be successful when the requirements are not so great. Moreover the prices for tar and ammonia are hardly enough to warrant great expense in adopting the by-product system."[17]

At the end of the 1890s, coke production in the United States was in an interesting state. It was the world's largest producer. Output of beehive coke was still on the eve of its greatest-ever expansion. Yet the method of production and the Connellsville coke region that made up by far its largest unit were in many ways anomalous in an industrial economy given to innovation and an unceasing emphasis on increasing efficiency.

The economist Frank Taussig recognized how different the work and organization of this section of the great complex of the iron and steel industries was from that of iron-ore supply from the upper Great Lake ranges. In the coal mines, there had been not just "the same bold adventure in opening new sources of supply, the same conduct of industry on a great scale, the same firm organization in direct connection with the iron and steel industry," but also the use of cheap labor, "mainly pick and shovel work, requiring little handicraft skill or trained intelligence." This was even more the case at the ovens. In his report on coke in 1897 for the Division of Mineral Resources of the Geological Survey, Edward Parker had seen change as inevitable but anticipated it would be slow: "Coke making in the United States may be said to be at the beginning of a new era. But there is not going to be any revolution, nor any unsettling of existing conditions by the development of the by-product systems of coking."[18] To a large extent the events of the next few years justified his anticipations of gradual change, but Parker had failed to recognize how the pace would accelerate. Eventually indeed, even the word "revolution" would not seem so inappropriate after

Table 5.1 Estimated capital costs and performances of beehive and byproduct ovens, 1896–1898

Oven type	Capital cost per oven ($)	Coal:coke ratio	Yield of coke per oven/year	Capital cost per ton of coke ($)
Beehive	300	66.66%	600	0.50
Byproduct	3,896[a]	70.0%	1,166	3.34

SOURCES: For beehives, F. C. Keighley quoted in *Coal and Coke*, 2 December 1898, 15; for byproduct ovens, J. Fulton quoted in *BAISA*, 10 November 1896.
   a. Includes byproduct-recovery plant.

all. Before that, some very deep-seated predilections for old methods and antipathies to newer ones had to be changed.

A Case Study in Prejudice: The H. C. Frick Coke Company and Byproduct Coking

Throughout the 1890s, as the byproduct oven made its tentative way into coking, opposition arose to the new method of manufacture from the dominant enterprise in the coke region, the H. C. Frick Coke Company. Henry Clay Frick was not only the leading coke maker, but for many years he was a key decision maker in the concern that had a controlling interest in "his" coke firm, the Carnegie Steel Company. In iron and steel matters, he proved a strong supporter of technical improvement and was more willing than most of his senior colleagues to entertain possibilities of change in the location of production. In stark contrast to this, he remained until after the turn of the century implacably against the new coking technology and development of new centers of production. His highly conservative approach was adopted by his chief lieutenant, Thomas Lynch. At first it seems Lynch was induced to look for deficiencies in byproduct coking, knowing that Frick was against the new methods; later his opposition seems to have come from personal conviction. Eventually, Frick became more open minded, but Lynch continued to be skeptical. For both men, their attitude seems not to have been due to lack of knowledge of other coking coals nor even of the technical superiority of the byproduct oven, but rather to a realization that its widespread adoption would lead to a depreciation of the investment in beehive coke works as well as of the immense capital asset of Connellsville coal. By narrow, commercial criteria they may have been right, but the result was a continuing, immense, and increasing waste of energy resources. Considered from a perspective that would have been alien to them but eventually recognized in the new century as more relevant, the long-term, wider public good was being sacrificed for short-term company interests.

At a very early stage in their close business association, Carnegie pressed Frick to be receptive to new coking methods. During 1882 the major British coke firm of Pease and Partners built the first byproduct ovens in the Durham coke field. That November a leading Teesside ironmaster, Lowthian Bell, himself a firm skeptic about the quality of byproduct coke, sent a rather vague letter to Carnegie: "I am interesting myself in a very important invention consisting in the obtaining of petroleum oil and ammonia from coke ovens. Would you be inclined to take up the discovery in the United States? Some wonderful results have been obtained from some kinds of coal here." Carnegie sent this letter on to Frick, having scribbled at the bottom: "I have written Mr. Bell that we should be disposed to take up anything he thought well of. He is a large coke manufacturer. Scientific and sound."[19] Carnegie's tone cannot have endeared the message to a young, independently minded, and prickly cokemaster; in any case Bell's interest in byproduct coking was short lived.

Seven years later H. C. Frick Coke was given the opportunity to build the first byproduct ovens in the United States. Evidence suggests refusal to play the pioneer was determined by prejudice not confined to the head of the company. (However, in mitigation, it must also be remembered that this was a time at which H. C. Frick Coke had made huge acquisitions of major Coke Region rivals and was inevitably preoccupied in integrating them into the parent company.) Apparently, Frick's custom was to send visiting "experts" out to see their current practice in the Coke Region. In mid-November 1889 he directed a Mr. Jacobs, a man promoting the Simon-Carves oven, to see Lynch, then his general superintendent in the region. Lynch reported back promptly: "Had him to stay with me last night to hear what he had to propose and what he can do." The rest of his letter was an interesting combination of objective reporting and statements that not only revealed his own preferences for well-tried methods but were cleverly designed to reinforce those that he must have known were already firmly entertained by his superior. He recognized the Simon-Carves ovens would deal with more coal, yield more coke, and make less ash than beehives. They cost about $1,000 each, or equal to three beehives. The 10 percent extra coke yield would not cover this increased outlay; to be commercially viable the installation must depend on the value of "bi-products." Jacobs proposed to take from them up to 50,000 tons of tar annually for ten years, paying them $5 per ton, which worked out at 20 cents per ton of coal. Lynch recognized there was a difference of opinion on the vital question whether the coke was equal to that from the beehive: "These various views, I judge, represent the interests of the parties holding them as much as anything else." Then he undermined Jacobs's standing: "I think Mr. Jacobs is a very well informed man but he certainly is not a practical coke man and all he knows about coke is what he learned from books. . . . I have read descriptions of [the Simon-Carves oven] and know just as much about it as Mr. Jacobs does." This was an extraordinary claim, and Lynch completely vitiated it on the next page of his letter, "I know nothing at all about the operation of the oven," and ended his report by turning Jacobs's visit into an opportunity to celebrate the excellence of the present situation: "He was very much surprised at the extent of the coke industry here, and our simple, efficient and economical method of handling the coal and leading the coke. The No. 3 Leisenring plant he thought could not be surpassed, but when he saw our Standard plant this morning, as the boys say, he was 'paralized.' He thinks, next to natural gas, the most wonderful thing he ever saw in all his travels is the prompt and economical handling of the coal in the Connellsville Coke Region. This has nothing to do with the new process of making coke, but I like to tell you these things to show you that the immense amount of money you send out here every month is not being wasted, at least in the estimation of the experts you send here."[20]

A business proposal came in a letter from Jacobs three days later. He asked for a commission of $5,000 for his services, which would include providing a competent man to erect the first 100 ovens. His horizons were wide—the coke company would pay $20 per oven for any additional ovens built by them up to 4,000. If they agreed to install at least 250 ovens, he now undertook to buy from them for ten years all the tar and the ammoniacal liquor they produced for $5 per gross ton of tar—the ammonia to be included at no extra cost. He wanted "at nominal price" up to fifty acres near the ovens for plant to deal with the byproducts. If, after examining the matter, they decided not to build closed ovens, he asked $2,000 for expenses he would have incurred, and that they should agree to treat the information he would give them as confidential.[21] His letter was answered within four days of its New York City date, and no more was heard of a proposal that might have made the biggest beehive coke producer the initiator of the new technology that eventually would destroy that industry completely.

Frick showed the same scant interest in innovation the following summer, even though in this instance the proposal was to improve old processes rather than replace them. In 1889 the Adams Coke Oven Company of Mansfield, Ohio, introduced modifications that cut costs by substituting mule power for human muscle in drawing ovens and reduced both heat loss and coking time by means of an oven bottom removable by hydraulic pressure. Lynch pointed out that the initial cost of Adams ovens was "fully" double that of ordinary beehives, but as the ovens made more coke daily and showed improvement over the performance of those already installed at Dunbar by better transfer arrangements to the rail cars, he wrote, "It seems to me it would be worth our while to try a few of them." He asked what his chairman thought of building a few at Leisenring 3. Within three days Frick had rejected the idea in the form of a simple handwritten note at the head of Lynch's letter: "Answered verbally, said not to build."[22]

This apparently almost automatic opposition to new ideas again came out very clearly in 1891 in Frick's reaction to the Simon-Carves byproduct oven. In January Samuel A. Tuska wrote from New York offering the rights to the process for Fayette, Westmoreland, Allegheny, and Indiana Counties, Pennsylvania, for $100,000. Should this arrangement not be acceptable, Tuska asked Frick to name his figure. Not having received a reply, he sent another letter nine days later. On 19 January Frick sent a negative response to both letters, and no more seems to have been heard of Tuska. That same summer W. R. Stirling of Illinois Steel pressed Frick to look into the merits of the Simon-Carves process, only to receive the following response: "I do not think it would be of any value to have Mr. Ramsay look into the development of the Simon-Carves process, or any other similar new method of making coke and utilizing the by products. I am inclined to believe that for Connellsville coal you will never see anything else used but the Bee-Hive oven, and anything that tends to deteriorate the quality of the coke for furnace or foundry use I do not think will ever be adopted in the Connellsville region."[23] Given the fact that this was a statement and not an argument, it seems that emotional involvement and personal wishes may have made as important a contribution to the opinion as logic. Soon after the Solvay Process Company produced the first American byproduct coke, national organizations interested in mineral exploitation pressed ahead with experiments into the new process. Frick's mind still seems to have been closed, so that when Joseph D. Weeks wrote to him to ask for sixty tons of coal to be placed in barrels for dispatch to Gelsenkirchen, there to be tested in Huessener ovens, he added a handwritten instruction when he passed on the letter: "See that this is shipped, soon as it can be without interfering with something of more importance."[24]

In the mid-1890s, as byproduct coking was taken up by a number of companies, Lynch continued to feed Frick with items of news that helped confirm his prejudices. So, for instance, when in November 1895 he met Fulton on a train journey, Lynch reported he had told him that the coke they were making in the new Johnstown ovens was of mixed quality. The following spring he passed on an account of a visit to this plant. The Cambria people had entertained high hopes for it, but were "much humiliated and disappointed" by what they had to show visitors. Coke made from coal mined near Johnstown "was a complete failure, not coked at all and the byproducts equally as great a failure. Got no ammonia and did not have sufficent gas to run the boilers that supplies the plant with steam. Had to fire the boiler with coal." Frick sent Lynch's letter on to Carnegie, who, strangely for him, in turn penciled on it a note that helped reinforce a bias already deeply ingrained: "I have always told you that this was a craze from all that I have learnt. In England the 'wise men' gave it a cold shoulder." A few months later, Lynch claimed to have heard that the Otto-Hoffmann people had not built the Johnstown ovens on their latest and most improved plan.[25]

During summer 1896 Lynch visited both the leading coke district in Britain and the Ruhr. He wrote a full report that generally confirmed what, in the light of their earlier reactions, both he and his principal had wanted to find. Most Durham ovens were similar, though somewhat smaller, than their own and produced a poorer coke—a striking turn about from Bell's experience twenty-one years earlier. There were a few Coppee ovens, but these did not recover byproducts. The Pease and Partners engineer at Crook had told Lynch they had to use the very best coals in the district in their Simon-Carves ovens. Maintenance and repair costs were much higher and overall production costs "more" than with beehives. There had been difficulty in selling byproduct coke for blast furnace use; Lynch formed the impression that they got rid of it "at a cut price." Moving on to the Ruhr, he found the district contained about 220 beehive ovens, some 10,000 retort ovens that did not recover byproducts, and 2,000 ovens that did. Again it seemed that his preconceptions were confirmed. Sixty of the surviving beehives were operated by Krupp to produce foundry coke. It was "the poorest coke plant I saw anywhere," but produced "the best looking coke I saw in Germany," although it ". . . did not look nearly so well as our beehive coke." He visited Albert Huessener, and though there were a few favorable points, his reaction to that expert's operations was generally adverse. Lynch played on a prejudice against professionalism: "Huessener did not impress me as a practical man, or as a solid man. I imagine he is by profession a chemist, or scientific man of some kind. There is no doubt but what he understands the theory of coke making, and the recovery of by-products. . . . I saw a good deal of bad coke on his yard." In summing up his European experiences he wrote: "All I saw and heard while abroad confirmed the conclusion I had already reached: namely, the first cost of making coke per ton with by-product ovens is about 25 cents more than with bee-hive ovens; the best bee-hive coke is 10 per cent. better than the best by-product coke made from the same coal for blast furnace purposes; the value of the by-products per ton of coke at present is not over 40 cents; the cost of making coke in by-product ovens, including interest on the capital invested, is about 25 cents per ton greater than the cost of making coke in bee-hive ovens, leaving a net profit for by-products of 15 cents per ton." Frick was comforted by the report: "It would seem as if we had not had much to fear from the erection of byproduct ovens in this country. I will, however, discuss the matter with you more fully when I see you."[26]

A few weeks after this, Lynch sent on a damning comment on Dunbar byproduct operations and followed this up with a report on another visit to Johnstown that claimed they had not yet made a success of byproduct coking. In turn Frick passed the report and Lynch's comments on it to Carnegie with the note: "Thought this would interest you. Please return."[27] Late in 1897 there was an interesting sidelight on the attitude of Lynch and Frick to evidence. Illinois Steel Company was then endeavoring, without much success, to arrange for the coking of Midwestern coals in byproduct ovens. John W. Gates wrote to Frick referring to talks they had had in the past about "bi-product" and retort ovens and asking him for the loan of reports on these processes. Frick responded promptly, but a few days later Gates was in contact again saying that he and C. H. Foote had read the report from Lynch that Frick had sent, but: "Mr. Brown [W. L. Brown, a member of the Illinois Steel Finance Committee] is under the impression that you have several other reports from people whose position might not be as strongly in favor of the bee-hive oven in the Connellsville district as Mr. Lynch. If you have any of them, I would appreciate very much if you would send me copies."[28]

In fairness to those in charge at H. C. Frick Coke, it must be recorded that skepticism about the new processes was reinforced by an independent Carnegie Steel report on byproduct ovens from Daniel Clemson, one of the partners. To place the Clemson report in context, one must recognize that although he played an important part in organizing Carnegie iron ore transport and their natural gas business, Clemson seems to have had no especial expertise in relation to coke. Presumably, therefore, he had, at least in considerable part, to draw on the reports of others who had. Clemson found that Glassport was getting 50 cents a ton less for the 75 percent of their coke output that was of furnace grade than was then being paid for Connellsville coke (the 1897 average price there was $1.65). A Newcastle furnace reported it got a lower coke rate and higher iron yield with Frick coke than with supplies from Glassport. Clemson reported Cambria was extending its byproduct installation but suggested this was largely because that company's reserves of Connellsville coal were almost exhausted. He concluded: "I have not seen anything in my observations that would lead me to believe that the byproduct ovens have been a success in this part of the country." When it was presented to the Carnegie Board of Managers, Clemson made clear that he felt that coke quality was sacrificed if more gas was obtained. At this point Frick contributed what seemed a clinching, but was in fact a wildly inaccurate, statement: "We have had the gas from our coke ovens analyzed and find it does not contain anything of value." When Lauder expressed the comforting opinion, "It is pretty clear this matter is not in condition for us to take it up now," Frick added, "It is also clear that if the Carnegie Steel Company were to go into it, that action would be an encouragement for other people to take up the manufacture of coke, thus reducing our market."[29]

With his strange, intuitive feeling for the drift of change, Andrew Carnegie was not so readily convinced as some of his leading associates, though as indicated above his opinions varied. Even before the managers discussed Clemson's findings, he was once again mulling over the question of the byproduct process. He wrote on New Years Day 1898 to his cousin George Lauder, who had been involved in their search for coke supplies of their own more than twenty years before: "The by-product coke oven seems to win slowly, especially in Britain. Mr. Frick however tells me that Cambria has been unfortunate and so have the works near Pittsburgh. It seems we had better just watch closely and wait."[30] Three days later Lynch reported to Frick on what he saw as the commercial failure of the Simon-Carves ovens. That company had said it would erect ovens at its own expense and take payment from the cost savings. Other oven makers had said the same, "but, when it came down to business, they invariably—to use a slang expression—fall down." A few weeks later Frick tried to persuade Carnegie that reasonable policies by the beehive industry could check a shift to the new methods of production: "Do not think we have anything that, in the long run, will prove more valuable than Connellsville coal land. As a competitor do not think by-product ovens are 'in it' unless we should advance price of coke too high."[31] That spring Lynch was scathing about a paper by John H. Darby, a British enthusiast for byproduct coking. By now he had recognized that, except in appearance, there need be little or no difference between beehive and retort oven coke, but it was the recovery of byproducts—the very rationale of the cost saving of the new-style ovens—that he argued spoiled the coke for furnace use. Lynch pointed out that in the discussion of the Darby paper, those who testified to the value of the byproducts had said little about that of the coke. He cited experience with the ovens at Latrobe, Dunbar, Johnstown, and Sharon to justify his opinion that, though they might be successful in making gas or other byproducts, their coke was poor. The conclusion of his eight-page letter was predictable, if unexpected as a summary of the views and discussion of the Darby paper: "In my judgement, the weight of testimony produced is favorable to the Bee Hive oven; certainly nothing was adduced to lessen my faith in the Bee Hive oven, from our standpoint as coke manufacturers, or to shake, in the slightest degree, the conclusion we reached, after a careful investigation of the subject, four years ago." His defense impressed Carnegie, who a few days later ended a letter to Lauder, "Lynch's report on byproducts best I have ever seen from him—very able."[32] Even so, Carnegie was by now clearly wavering. On the back of Lynch's report he penciled a note to Lowthian Bell, the ironmaster who had approached him about byproduct recovery sixteen years earlier. He asked Bell to pass it on to the other Nestor of the Middlesbrough iron trade, Bernhard Samuelson, who had installed byproduct ovens near his furnaces, before returning it to him. He pointed out that although the previous year they had made 4.8 million tons of coke, 36 percent of the U.S. total, he was uncertain as to the best line of advance, but as he put it, "Byproduct ovens to make this would cost a penny."[33]

In summer 1899 Lynch spelled out the limited reserves of Connellsville coking coal available. He concluded that as demand for coke grew, "the value of Connellsville coal will continue to increase as surely as effect follows cause." A year before, E. W. Parker, an advocate of improved methods, had written, "It is not to be doubted that men and corporations who have millions of dollars invested in coal lands, mines and coking plants, will employ such methods in their business as will make the best returns."[34] But whatever the short-term gain from preserving the status quo, Lynch would live to see that he had underestimated the effect on the future situation for Connellsville of the new coking processes that he had so consistently denigrated. Quietly but persistently, Carnegie was advocating that they should at least not close their minds to the possibility of investing in plant incorporating the new technology and located in radically different places than those within the old coke districts. Though far away from the scene and primarily acquainted with a different industry, he proved to have better insight into the direction of change than those more intimately involved.

The Progress of Byproduct Coking, 1900–1914

By the end of the nineteenth century, the United States was firmly established as the world's largest producer of steel. In many parts of this business, its practice was acknowledged as the world's best and many widely admitted that some of its producing districts could claim the lowest costs for iron production. It had achieved these distinctions despite obstacles of distance unmatched in the leading steel industries of western Europe. Estimates pointed to the fact that by this time the low cost of coke

Table 5.2 Comparative estimated average production costs per ton of Bessemer pig iron in selected world districts, 1897–1898

Iron district	Iron ore	Coke	Limestone	Labor	Sundries	Total
Pittsburgh, United States	$6.67	$1.45	$0.36	$0.61	$0.24	$9.34
Cleveland, Great Britain	$7.27	$3.20	$0.48	$0.68	$0.36	$12.00
Liege, Belgium	$7.76	$3.52	$0.36	$0.85	$0.36	$12.85
Westphalia, Germany	$7.76	$3.39	$0.36	$0.73	$0.44	$12.68

SOURCE: (London) *Iron and Coal Trades Review*, quoted in *BAISA*, 1 January 1898.
NOTE: Sterling values are converted at £1 = $4.85.

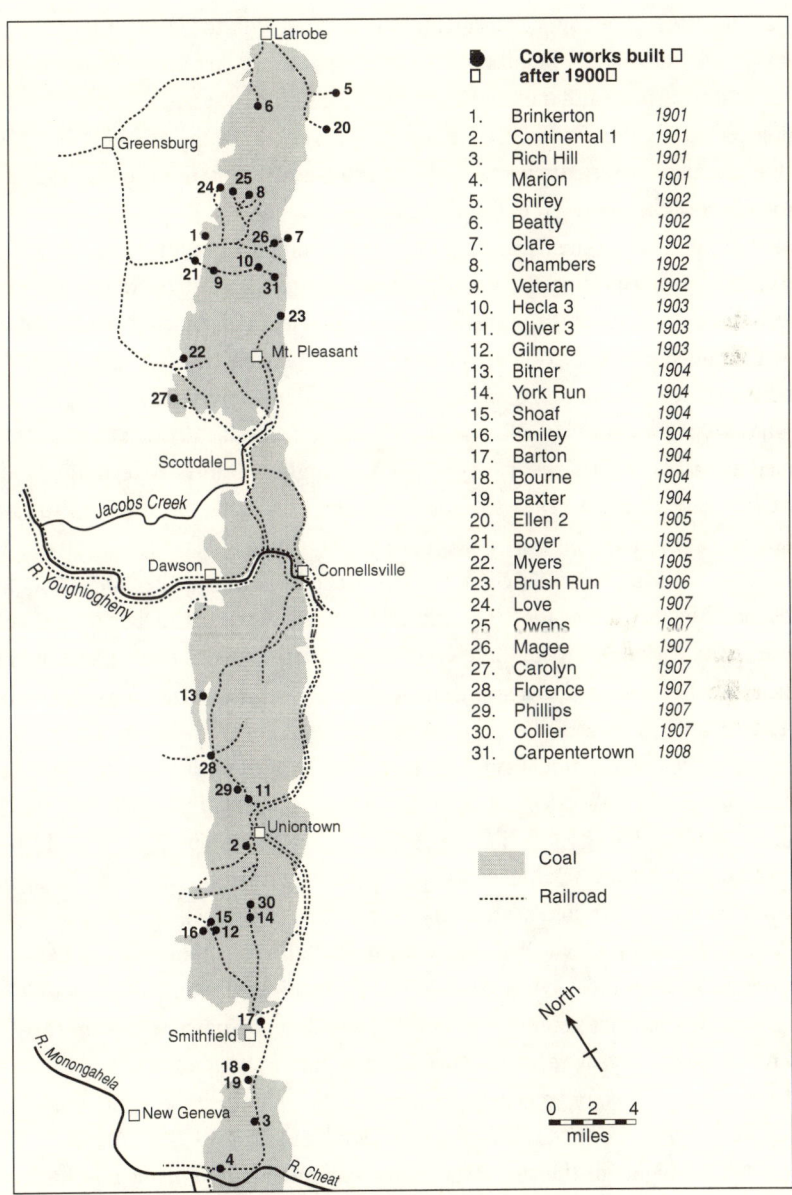

Coke works built in the "old basin" after 1900.

constituted its greatest single advantage as compared with the Old World, although the superbly developed organization of the long distance and now massive flows of Upper Lakes iron ore and mechanization of iron and steel operations, which resulted in low unit-labor costs, were also important. Added to the unquestionable excellence of the product, such cost schedules helped explain why American ironmasters and coke makers alike were slow to desert the beehive oven.

Before 1900 the Connellsville district had undoubtedly become the world's leading center for coke production. County Durham in northeast England, the area from which the technology of the beehive oven had been learned some sixty years before, now contained about 12,500 ovens and in 1902 produced 4.7 million tons of coke. Rhenish Westphalia, centered on the Ruhr coalfield, made 9.1 million tons in 1900. By the end of 1902 the Connellsville and Lower Connellsville districts together contained 26,329 ovens. That year they shipped 14.1 million tons of coke; output could have been higher but a severe shortage of freight cars made it impossible to carry away all the tonnage the furnaces could have consumed.[35] Further expansion lay ahead, so that within another eight years the Coke Region contained almost 50 percent more ovens than in 1902. Output in 1913 was 42 percent higher than that of eleven years earlier. Even so, these years of very large extension were also ones in which the industry faced increasing challenges. They came only in part from other coking coalfields. Indeed, between 1902 and 1913 the Connellsville–Lower Connellsville share of the national output of beehive coke went up slightly, from 58.9 percent to 59.8 percent. West Virginia and the western counties of Virginia, once seen as promising serious rivalry, now faltered, their coke output as a proportion of the beehive total falling from 15.2 percent to 11.2 percent. Probably these figures slightly exaggerate the importance of these states, for though Connellsville tonnages also included output from one byproduct plant at Dunbar, the figures for the mid-Appalachian states involved two, the National Tube installation at Benwood, West Virginia, and a smaller plant built at Pocahontas, Virginia (of which nothing further is known except that it seems to have survived until about 1906). A much more telling indicator of changing circumstances was that Connellsville's share of all the coke produced in the nation fell from 55.7 percent in 1902 to 43.4 percent in 1913. These figures highlight the fact that, despite the opening of a major new field and large expansion in beehive tonnages, the years preceding the outbreak of war in Europe were above all marked by an accelerating increase in the proportion of coke made by product ovens. The record 1913 shipments of 20,098 thousand tons from Connellsville and Lower Connellsville were 99,000 tons greater than those of the previous record year of 1906, but over the same period output of byproduct coke increased by 8 million tons, or almost 200 percent. The changing status of the two

Table 5.3 Coke production, 1900, 1910, and 1913 *(net tons in thousands)*

Method	1900	1910	1913
Total all coke	20,533	41,709	46,299
Beehive	19,458	34,507	33,585
of which Connellsville	10,166	18,690	20,098
Byproduct	1,076	7,139	12,715

processes not only represented a mounting success of modern, scientific, efficiently monitored operations over paleotechnic methods of production but also signaled the beginning of the end for the Connellsville Coke Region.

Even as the new process made its spectacular gains, some of those involved in the Connellsville industry either remained blind to its deficiencies or tried to persuade themselves and others that it was not essential or perhaps even possible to make changes. In the early 1890s this had been the tone in which Thomas Lynch had communicated with Frick about their operations in relation to the new methods of coking. A decade later, Fred Keighley of Uniontown, speaking in Pittsburgh at the winter meeting of the West Pennsylvania Mining Institute, continued to make that argument: "The operations, systems, machinery, safety appliances and general improvements in the Connellsville coke region today are of a character unexcelled by any mining region of the world."[36] There may have been some foundation for the claim, but if so it probably came from the quality of the mining operations, and so far as it applied to coking, it was no more than perfection in the practices of an obsolescent technology. Only a few months afterward a very different assessment was made by an Englishman, Frank Popplewell, in his survey of American iron and steel production, in which he wrote of a technically lagging, traditional coke sector: "In no other part of the industry has increased production exerted so slight an influence on the methods employed, or brought about so little specialisation."[37] Over the next few years, important improvements were at last introduced into beehive operation. These were in large part a necessary response to the challenge from the byproduct oven, a rear-guard action or an attempt to fend off the evil day when the old methods of production would be completely unable to compete commercially with the new. In 1912 William H. Blauvelt, one of the pioneers of the byproduct industry, paid generous tribute to these improvements in technology: "The bee-hive oven has been carried to its highest perfection in this country; drawing and loading apparatus has been applied to it to reduce the arduous labor of the old hand method; and modifications of the original bee-hive shape have been successfully introduced, which add materially to the economy of operation, while maintaining the principles of carbonization as employed in the standard bee-hive."[38] But, whether slightly delayed or not by these improvements, byproduct ovens continued to advance.

In part the gradual eclipse of the old coking methods was due to its now limited resource base. There was a general problem of exhaustion of coking coals best suited to it and the particular difficulty of often inadequate supplies nearby for individual coke works. By the early years of the new century, a number of plants in the older areas of Connellsville were either idle because their coal had been worked out or were being forced to bring supplies in from a greater distance, often from tracts opened to feed other ovens. The latter practice saved on the capital account of the coke companies at the expense of their direct operating costs. Above all, however, the relative decline of the beehive industry was due to the increasing recognition that the byproduct process offered commercial advantages. Greater capital outlay, reflected by higher depreciation and maintenance charges, was more than cancelled out by a higher coke/coal ratio and income from byproducts. This came out well in a cost comparison provided by John Fulton in the 1905 edition of his standard work, *Coke*. Shortly afterward, another comparison suggested even greater advantages for the byproduct oven. The time-honored belief that beehive coke was a better blast furnace fuel was now recognized as untenable. It was on these grounds that Fulton had opposed the new technology in the early 1890s, later to be so fully converted by the evidence that he had to "change his opinion decidedly and to regret his earlier opposition."[39] Any worthwhile comparisons had to take into account overall costs.

As Blauvelt recognized the cost situation of the beehives had been improved by increase in size, other modifications of design and the introduction of labor saving machinery. Early ovens had been only ten feet in diameter. These had increased gradually to twelve-and-a-half feet. Ovens at Oliver No.2 were thirteen feet in diameter, and United States Coal and Coke decided to build all its ovens of this size. Greater use of coke-drawing machinery was expected to lead to a further increase in oven size, and indeed some West Virginian ovens were reported to be as much as twenty-five feet in diameter. As output per oven increased, direct comparison of the size of the industry at different times based merely on the number of ovens became impossible. An even more dramatic change involved the shape of the oven. By 1905–1906, T. C. Mitchell, the Rainey general manager, was building at Mt. Braddock in the southern part of the old basin a new battery of ovens with completely different dimensions—thirty feet in length, forty inches wide at one end and forty-six inches across at the other. It could be opened at both ends to facilitate the handling of the coke. "Rectangular" ovens of this type cut two to five hours from normal coking times as well as saved labor. Overall costs of production were reduced 20 cents a ton. A more general change was that coke was increasingly both loaded and drawn mech-

Table 5.4 Estimated plant and expenditures to produce 118,800 tons of coke annually, beehive and Otto-Hoffman ovens, 1904–1905

	Beehive ovens	Byproduct ovens
Coke yield per ton of coal	65%	72%
Daily output per oven (tons)	2.0	6.0
Number of ovens required	198	66
Cost per oven	$300	$3,000
Byproduct recovery plant cost per oven	n.a.	$2,500
Total outlay per oven	$300	$5,500
Total cost of plant	$59,400	$363,000
Annual maintenance costs (at 5%)	$2,970	$18,150
Depreciation and maintenance (20 years)	$0.050	$0.220
Costs of making coke and saving byproducts	$0.450	$0.400
Total costs	$0.500	$0.620
Value of byproducts	n.a.	$0.220
Value of coal saved	n.a.	$0.132
Ultimate cost of coke per net ton	$0.500	$0.368

SOURCE: Based on J. Fulton, *Coke* (Scranton, N.J.: International Textbook, 1905).
NOTE: Costs shown are those above that of coal used.

Table 5.5 Estimated relative costs of coke made in beehive and byproduct ovens, 1906

	Beehive	Byproduct
Cost per oven	$325	$4,000
Daily output per oven (tons)	2.00	4.25
Ovens required to make 1,000 net tons daily	500	235
Total cost of plant	$162,500	$940,000
Pounds of coke obtained per 100 pounds coal	66	71
Coal cost per $1-net ton of coke	$1.50	$1.41
Operating cost of per net ton of coke, including repairs	$0.46	$0.70
Interest and depreciation per net ton (at 10%)	$0.05	$0.31
Total costs	$2.01	$2.42
Credit for byproducts	n.a.	$1.41
Net cost of 1 net ton of coke	$2.01	$1.01

SOURCE: International Library of Technology, *Surface Arrangements at Bituminous Coal Mines etc.* (Scranton, 1907), 71.

anically. Fulton in 1905 reported the use of electrically driven larries.[40] Drawing coke with the traditional "duck bill" implement was extremely hard labor, which made it difficult to find competent coke drawers, especially during summer months. George T. Wickes, inventor of one of the various machines devised to bypass these problems, recognized the large potential market without fully conveying the urgency of the situation: "Anything which tends to prolong the general life of beehive ovens will be welcome to those who are interested in cheapening the cost of producing coke in such ovens." A Covington Machine Company drawing machine was tried at the Continental 1 works of the H. C. Frick Coke Company in October 1904. Allowing for standing charges, its inventor claimed operating costs of 42 cents per oven as compared with an average of 92 cents with hand-drawn coke. Now, one man with an assistant, two men to water down the oven in advance of them, and another to remove the small amount of coke left after the machine had done its work, could together draw and load over thirty ovens, whereas even under the most favorable circumstances the traditional hand methods required one man for every three or four. As well as higher productivity and solving supply problems with a difficult class of hand labor, the speedier handling of output was claimed to produce a better coke. It reduced its tendency to "burn," which created more ash and thereby blocked the vital pores in the coke. Quicker coke removal also reduced heat loss before the next charge of coal. Savings in time could indeed be dramatic. In the New Salem "Belgian" type longitudinal ovens of the Connellsville Central Coke Company, it was expected that drawing would take only fifteen seconds, and the ovens could be recharged, leveled, closed, and ignited within forty minutes compared with three hours, twenty minutes in ordinary beehives with hand forking and bricking up. Yet mechanization created some problems of its own. As the above suggests, machine drawing worked best with specially designed ovens; some machines were found to damage older ovens. Even so, by 1907 mechanical drawing was becoming general.[41]

Table 5.6 Average annual prices for beehive coke and selected labor costs, 1900–1913

	1900	1905	1910	1913
A. Year's average price per ton	$2.70	$2.26	$2.10	$2.95
B. Costs for mining, leveling, drawing, forking[a]	$3.74	$3.615	$4.005	$4.2425
B as % of A	138.5	159.9	190.7	143.8

SOURCE: *Connellsville Weekly Courier*, May 1914, 12, 30.

a. Includes rate for mining and loading 100 bushels room and rib coal, leveling per oven, drawing coke from 100 bushels charged, and forking cars—50,000 to 60,000 pounds total. In short, this represents a sample of some of the main contributors to the average costs of production at any one time. The rates shown apply respectively to the period after 1 March 1900, 1 March 1905, 16 January 1910, and 1 April 1912.

Despite many improvements, the beehive industry continued to be burdened by inherent deficiencies in technology and by other factors of a mature industry. Two of the latter were the wasting of its resource base and, notwithstanding the progress of mechanization, the inherently labor-intensive nature of its processes. As many plants worked out their coal reserves, not only did their immediate costs rise, but the increasing scarcity also led to an increase in the value of the coal acreages that remained, again pushing up costs. The lack of large blocks of low-cost, unworked coal meant it was impracticable for operators to contemplate installing byproduct plants in the old coke region. In any case, for some, though not for all, their capital resources were unequal to the large outlay such a development would have required. Meanwhile, there was a tendency for labor costs to increase in relation to the price of coke, thereby squeezing profit margins.

All in all, whereas byproduct ovens were equipped with controls that left relatively little to chance, success or otherwise in the beehive process still depended heavily on the skill and care of its workers. The most critical of all their responsibilities was the regulation of the admission or exclusion of air from the oven. Careful management in this respect could raise coke yields per ton of coal by perhaps three or four percentage points. For Oliver Coke Works, Keighley claimed a 67 percent yield. This was probably exceptional, and as Charles Catlett put it, "I venture the assertion that the owners of many plants in the Connellsville region, otherwise well-managed, who complacently accept Mr. Fulton's statement that the yield of the Connellsville coal in coke is 66 percent would be astonished should they ascertain what is their actual yield."[42]

The loss of energy from beehives occurred on a colossal scale. In a few cases efforts were made to recover waste heat. By 1907 in one recently erected plant, heat from fifty beehives was used to produce electricity for mining operations. But generally the loss of energy continued unabated. In 1909 one writer tried to convey its scale in especially vivid terms, claiming the energy lost in unrecovered gas alone could have equaled the power of a Niagara if it been properly utilized in gas engines and dynamos.[43] Meantime, in parts of the northeastern United States, the gas procured from byproduct ovens looked more and more attractive. The rapid advance in open-hearth steel opened up one important outlet for it. As late as 1900, two-thirds of steel tonnage was Bessemer and only one-third open hearth; by 1911 these proportions had been almost exactly reversed.

One uncontestable advantage of the beehive was its simplicity and low first cost, which meant that individual units of plant could be built more quickly or closed down with less loss. In the long run this flexibility would make it ideal marginal capacity to be brought in as a supplement to byproduct-coke production or closed down to keep the process with the higher-standing charges active as long as possible.

But at this time, when confrontation between the two processes was still a keenly fought and as yet unresolved issue, beehive producers sometimes failed to use their powers to juggle capacity and prices wisely. One clear indication of the quick response time possible in the old industry as compared with the new came in summer 1907 when a local firm contracting to build one hundred ovens at Cheat Haven for the Southern Connellsville Coke Company promised to have some of them ready for firing in sixty days. By contrast, barely 50 percent of the byproduct ovens reported as under construction at the end of 1900 had been completed two years later. But the cost advantages of beehives did not apply equally in all situations, as Carl Meissner of U.S. Steel made clear shortly before World War I. He pointed out that Connellsville provided favorable conditions for the older process, but in the Pocahontas region, where more investment in externals—new housing for instance—might be needed, and even more important where in the low-volatile coals the coal/coke ratio was lower than in Connellsville, byproduct coking could offer better costs.[44] As to pricing, a 1910 episode showed Connellsville firms had still not solved the problems that had plagued them a quarter century before, when they had been more able to control the overall supply of coke. Anticipating a large demand, they advanced the price of coke to $3 a net ton at the ovens. Many customers deserted them for other sources of supply. The result was that, though Connellsville increased its share of beehive coke production from 53.8 in 1909 to 54.1 percent, the byproduct coke tonnage increased from 35.2 percent as large as Connellsville to 38.2 percent. In fact, by this time Coke Region producers were losing control of the market. They lowered their prices in 1911, but output fell away by 12.6 percent while that of byproduct ovens went up 9.9 percent. As one critic recognized, the old district had "failed to realize that the day of the byproduct oven has arrived."[45]

Above all, as some of the these features show, beehive coke makers were as much hindered by their old framework of thinking as by material circumstances. In view of the then recent technical improvements, McClenathan and his fellow contributors to the *Centennial History of Connellsville* seemingly were oversimplifying when they summed up local practice in 1906: "Just as Lester Norton dumped the coal into his little crude oven, burned it until he had clarified it of its gases, and then drew it out ready for use, so is coke made in this district at the present time." But although they exaggerated, they had at least identified the strong thread of conservatism. A quarter century earlier, in his history of Westmoreland County, Albert had characterized coke operators as a go-ahead group: "They are approachable people and have not the hard-skull conservatism and secretiveness of older men in an industry of older growth."[46] Now, however, those men had grown old and they or their descendants had become wealthy. A combination of wealth, age, parochialism, and a shrinking natural-resource base did not provide fertile ground for imaginative thinking. Some years before the great European war, A. W. Belden of the U.S. Bureau of Mines was scathing, very much as Koerner had been more than a quarter century before, about the skills and attitudes he found in the Coke Region. Determination of the coking properties of coals was even now generally left to practical coke workers: "The very fact that Connellsville coal produces coke of excellent quality no matter how inefficiently the ovens are handled should preclude the use of such evidence." Nor were things better in operation of the ovens: "To this day the burning of coke, except in a few instances, is left in the hands of unskilled laborers and technical knowledge of coking processes is woefully lacking. Until 1896, when the byproduct coking industry began to grow appreciably, little was heard of any technical study or deep thought being applied to coke making." He deplored the waste of energy, which he attributed to complacency: "The matter of increased yield, even when brought to the attention of those in authority, is most often passed over with the remark: 'We are doing well enough and making money, so why should we make any change?'" Another outsider found that the large investment needed for byproduct plants was advanced as a clinching argument against this new technology, an approach adopted "against all changes and improvements."[47]

The various improvements in beehive coking were far outclassed by those now being made in byproduct works, by which the size of ovens and the number that could be operated per man were both increasing. An evaluation of these lines of improvement made increasingly obvious that there was now an unbridgeable gap between the relative efficiencies of the new and old technologies. Gradually, some of those involved in beehive manufacture were brought, however grudgingly, to recognize this. This was poignantly brought out at a meeting of the Engineers Society of Western Pennsylvania held in May 1912. A paper on byproduct coking was presented by the managing engineer of the Heinrich Koppers Company of Joliet, Illinois. Among the contributors to the discussion that followed was Fred C. Keighley, whose career in the beehive industry had begun in December 1879 and who was then general superintendent of mines for the Oliver and Snyder Steel Company. He testified to a reluctant conversion; hard evidence had finally compelled him to recognize his ignorance of the real drift of circumstances and therefore to let go long-held presuppositions. He still maintained that the yield of the beehive oven was higher than byproduct men reckoned and that the byproduct ovens had an output 7.5 times that of a typical beehive, though they cost twenty times as much, but he admitted that the old criticism that byproduct coke carried excessive amounts of water was probably no longer valid, and recognized that it "possesses all the qualities of beehive coke." This being so, there were only a few final obstacles to adoption of the byproduct process:

"The question of the advisability of replacing beehive with byproduct ovens would hinge solely upon the ability of the coke manufacturers to acquire the large amount of capital required, the location adopted for the profitable disposal of the coke and its byproducts and a coalfield of such magnitude, location and quality that would cover the requirements of the proposition. That is a combination very difficult to find." In making such a qualified statement, Keighley failed to go so far as to recognize, publicly at least, that the triumph of the byproduct oven implied the decline and eventual elimination of the Connellsville Coke Region as an important factor in the trade it had dominated for so long.[48]

Given the fact that the drift of technical change and cost advantage were now unmistakably in the direction of an ultimate replacement of beehive by byproduct ovens, the speed with which this was brought about would be determined by the interplay of a complex of factors, including the general commercial situation, assessments of the immediate and long-term demand for coke and byproducts, and the financial resources and business acumen of the players. The opening and rapid development of Lower Connellsville and the inclusion of its expanding output in the figures for the Connellsville district for many years gave the impression that this region at least was resisting the advance of the new process. In fact, progress in byproduct coking was steady, and though not until after the period under review, Connellsville was to undergo an erosion of its prime status far more rapid than its earlier rise.

The considerations of location involved with beehive and byproduct ovens were radically different. As they made only coke, itself the product of an approximately one-third reduction in the weight of the coal charged into the oven (though an increase in bulk), beehives were only in exceptional circumstances located away from the mine that supplied them. Their coke might be shipped long distances to the furnace, usually by rail, sometimes by water, occasionally by a combination of both. This could mean, as in 1902–1903, that in times of exceptional business activity the railroads were so stretched that coke might pile up at the ovens while furnaces starved for want of fuel. Byproduct coking, in part because a smaller loss of weight occurred in the conversion process but mainly because they produced byproducts, above all large amounts of gas, were most logically located in immediate contact with integrated iron and steel operations; the furnaces using the coke, the rolling mills the gas, and steel works using both gas and tar. Such a concentration might remove uncertainties about fuel supplies at boom times. Blauvelt spelled out the differences more fully. In beehive ovens "coke yields are considerably below the theoretical, and of course all the by-products are wasted. These facts, except in unusual cases, make it impracticable to locate beehive ovens away from the mines." By contrast, although there was a "freedom of location" in the case of byproduct ovens, this meant they were usually at the point of coke consumption "or at some center of distribution."

Although it entails freight charges on from 1.2 to 1.4 tons of coal for every ton of coke produced, yet coal usually carries a lower rate than coke and is more easily transported, not requiring special cars and not being injured by handling. In some cases it can be shipped by water with material saving in freights, and with proper care it can be stored at the plant in almost any quantity without material deterioration. This permits a blast furnace plant having its own coke ovens at the furnace to possess an assured supply of coke, independent of weather or shipping conditions. It is quite common for byproduct coke oven-plants to accumulate a stock of from one to eight months supply of coal. The byproducts are much nearer their market, and the gas is often available for industrial uses or for municipal lighting. The plant is nearer a supply of diversified labor, which is an advantage in the more varied process of byproduct oven operation. An important advantage of locating the oven plant at the point of consumption is that it permits a convenient assembling of several kinds of coal at the ovens. This mixture of coals is often a great advantage, since it permits the best quality of coke to be produced when the coke made from any one of the coals alone might be of inferior quality, or perhaps not at all adapted to the market requirements.[49]

Before 1903 only two integrated iron and steel producers had installed byproduct ovens—Cambria Steel at Johnstown and, some years later, the National Tube Company at Benwood south of Wheeling, West Virginia. Production of both steel and pig iron reached unprecedented levels during 1902, in the case of iron being almost 2 million tons in excess of the previous year's figure, itself a record. The coke suppliers could not meet the demand. Connellsville shipped 14.1 million tons, far more than ever before, and could have delivered still bigger tonnages but for lack of freight cars.[50] At one time throughout U.S. Steel, as many as eleven blast furnaces were idle for lack of fuel, though some 250,000 tons of coke was piled up at the ovens for many weeks. Some other companies were still more badly affected by the coincidence of boom and congestion. At its Lebanon ironworks in eastern Pennsylvania, the Lackawanna Iron and Steel Company had five blast furnaces idle for ten months as a result of fuel shortages.[51] Apart from appeals to the railroads to improve services for the Coke Region, the reaction to this 1902–1903 crisis involved a major expansion of coke-making capacity. By the beginning of 1903, 15,000 new beehive ovens were reported under construction throughout the nation. This astounding figure, representing an increase equal to more than half the number of existing ovens in the Connellsville region, would prove less significant in the long run than the spur given by the crisis to the byproduct coke industry. At the end of 1902 there were 1,663 byproduct ovens in existence, but 3,413 more were reportedly under construction. In fact,

Table 5.7 Byproduct coke ovens by location, 1899–1913

Year	Ovens at iron and steel works making blast furnace coke	Ovens not at iron and steel works
End 1899	415	605
1903, built & building	2,037	1,005
End 1906	2,973	574
End 1913	3,692	1,996

SOURCES: Based on U.S. Geological Survey, *Annual Report, 1899–1900*, part 6 (Washington, D.C.: GPO, 1907); J. Fulton, *Coke* (Scranton, N.J.: International Textbook, 1905); *Connellsville Weekly Courier*, May 1914.

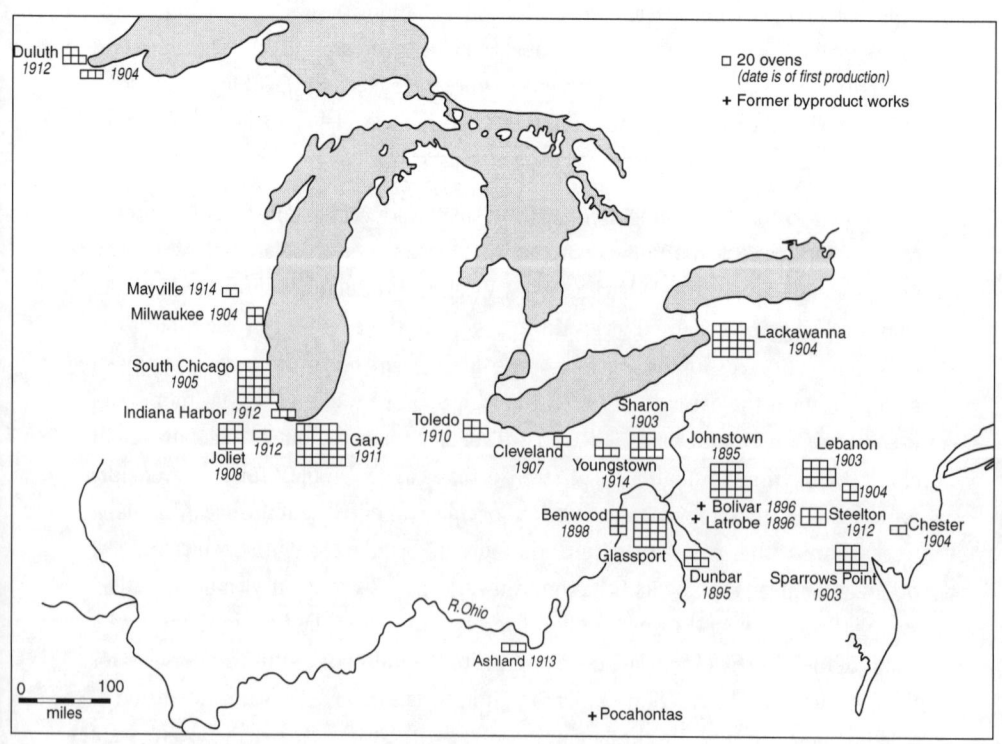

Byproduct ovens making furnace coke, 1914.

the latter figure proved to be an exaggeration; three years later the total number of byproduct ovens was only 3,103. Even so, this period marked a breakthrough for byproduct ovens located at iron and steel works. Then and later, there was also a growth of municipally owned oven plants producing gas for lighting and heating.

The strategy for development by steel companies of coking under the new circumstances of the industry varied widely. This reflected their differing locations and existing coke supplies as well as their perception of the wisest long-term plan. An uneven pattern of growth resulted. Some companies had to disentangle themselves from large involvement in the beehive industry. Into the early years of the new century, Cambria Steel continued to play a leading part. Sixty Otto-Hoffmann ovens had been put into operation there in 1895. Capacity was extended in 1899, 1904, and 1907. By 1914 there were 372 ovens at Johnstown ranking it as the nation's second-largest steel plant installation. As this expansion went on, Cambria Iron ran down its capacity in the Coke Region. In 1901 it still had four beehive oven plants close together north of Dunbar totaling 905 ovens. It chose not to invest in Lower Connellsville, and by 1906 two of its old basin plants with 400 ovens had been abandoned because of the exhaustion of their coal. By the end of 1908, another plant had gone and operations were confined to the Atlas-Anchor works; before 1914 Cambria was wholly out of Connellsville coke.[52]

The situation of leading furnace plants farther east was less straightforward as they were distant from good coking coals. Originally depending on local anthracite, since the 1870s they had been using increasing tonnages of coke and Connellsville was now their main source of supply. But they had little capital invested in coal and coke. Byproduct coking seemed to offer a chance for cost reduction by mixing nearer, poorer, but cheaper coals with the high-quality Appalachian coals on which they had such long hauls and for which freight charges were considerable. In 1908 the average price of merchant coke in the Connellsville district was $1.80; at that time the carload

Table 5.8 Byproduct ovens in major iron and steel centers, 1899, 1903, 1906, and 1913

Year	Chicago	Lake Erie/ Detroit	Valleys	East and Central Pennsylvania and Maryland	Pittsburgh to Midland	Alabama
1899	0	0	25	160	120	120
1903	0	630	237	822	120	320
1906	400	644	235	1,014	120	280
1913	825	237	280	1,016	332	680

SOURCES: Based on U.S. Geological Survey, *Annual Report, 1899–1900*, part 6 (Washington, D.C.: GPO, 1907); J. Fulton, *Coke* (Scranton, N.J.: International Textbook, 1905); *Connellsville Weekly Courier*, May 1914.

freight per net ton to Steelton was $1.80 and to Sparrows Point $2.15. The rate on coal per ton from mines in Clearfield County was only $1.32 to Steelton and $1.60 to Sparrows Point.[53] However, as time would show, the matter of getting the blend of coals right presented problems.

Maryland Steel was a pioneer of the new developments, building 200 byproduct ovens at Sparrows Point in 1903 and a small extension nine years later. In 1903 and 1904, having been sorely troubled by the shortage of rail capacity to bring in Connellsville coke, both Lackawanna Steel and Pennsylvania Steel built byproduct ovens in the Lebanon area near their nonintegrated blast furnace plants. Pennsylvania Steel installed byproduct ovens at its integrated Steelton works in 1907. The most instructive cases were those of the major new Lackawanna Steel plant at Buffalo and the Bethlehem Steel Corporation.

Lackawaana Steel completed its removal from Scranton to a virgin site on the shores of Lake Erie early in the new century. From 1903 it could draw on its own experience of byproduct coking at Lebanon. The next year it announced plans for 564 Otto-Hoffman byproduct ovens at Lackawanna—by far the largest establishment to date—to be supplied with coal from its own mines in Indiana and Cambria Counties, Pennsylvania. Only 188 of these ovens were built.[54] Two factors seem to have been involved in a change of plan. In the first place, notwithstanding the initial announcement, there was dispute about the type of oven to be installed. In April 1904 Fulton received a letter from the metallurgical engineer at Lackawanna, Dr. Rothberg, designer of an oven that received some orders during this decade. He wrote: "We have here 188 Otto-Hoffman ovens and 282 of my type practically finished, and are starting 470 more of my type. The whole plant will have 940 ovens. The first 470 will be started in about a month."[55] Whether or not the dispute about type of oven was a contributing factor, there is circumstantial evidence that byproduct coking at Lackawanna ran into difficulties. In spring 1905 the United States Steel Corporation decided against the opportunity to buy the six-year-old investment of the Ellsworth Coal and Coke Company in Washington County, Pennsylvania. Some time later Lackawanna bought the Ellsworth properties, which then had 75 beehive ovens; in 1909 Lackawanna controlled 278 there.[56]

While the evidence of difficulties with the new process at Lackawanna is indirect but suggestive, at Bethlehem the problem was clear and spectacular, mirroring the early experiences at Cambria over which Lynch had almost gloated. In 1904, with an annual furnace capacity of 200,000 tons, Bethlehem was one of the larger steel companies with no control over coke works. From that year it was under the aggressive leadership of Charles M. Schwab, who from his key role at Carnegie Steel had intimate knowledge of the finest part of the Connellsville industry. By 1910 Bethlehem had decided to install at South Bethlehem four batteries of seventy-five byproduct ovens each, contracting with the Didier Company of Germany for construction. Each battery would process 4,300 tons of coal daily, and ultimately twice as much. A thirty-day coal store would act as security against any risk of interruptions of fuel supplies. The cost of the installation would be $3 million. The ovens were built but then were demolished before making any coke on a routine commercial basis, trials proving that the coals used would generate so much heat as to destroy the ovens. By 1914 construction began on 424 Koppers ovens to replace the failed Didier plant.[57]

As with the East, Chicago had always been penalized by long hauls on Connellsville coke, though in this instance its advantages in access to ore supplies formed an effective counterbalance. By 1900 the Illinois Steel Company was expecting to produce 1.5–1.6 million tons of beehive coke at its own ovens in Pennsylvania.[58] Necessity had made it one of the pioneers in Lower Connellsville. The first byproduct ovens in the Chicago area were built by the Semet Solvay Company on the western edge of Calumet in 1904–1905. Within U.S. Steel, it seemed for a time that byproduct coking might make it possible to use coal mined nearer to Chicago. As shown elsewhere to a large extent these hopes proved unfounded, but byproduct ovens could use mid-Appalachian coal and provide cheaper fuel for open-hearth furnaces. Before these possibilities were realized, top decision takers at USS had to be persuaded that byproduct operations were viable in comparison with Connellsville beehive operations in which they held such a dominating position. Understandably, the first fruits of their conversion to the new technology were located in Chicago.

In 1906 a group of U.S. Steel engineers visited Europe to study coking operations. After receiving a report of its findings, the corporation invited German engineer Heinrich Koppers to the United States for consultation. The outcome was a decision by the USS board in May 1907 to install 275 ovens of Koppers's design at Joliet at a cost of $2.05 million, Koppers to supervise construction. There were modifications to the project, but on 15 September 1908 coke was made from the first forty ovens. Joliet for a time became the American headquarters of the Koppers Company.[59] This led in turn to a much bigger project. In summer 1905 USS decided to build the new Gary works. By early 1907 careful tests were underway both in the United States and in Europe to decide on the best type of byproduct oven to be installed there. At that time about 400 ovens were contemplated.[60] In fact, by 1911 Gary had 490 Koppers ovens. Ninety more were added in 1913 and 1914. As late as 1904 Illinois and Indiana made under 4,500 tons of coke—0.019 percent of the national production of coke from states that accounted for one-tenth of the nation's pig iron. This miniscule output came from minor beehive operations. Eight years later Illinois produced 1.76 million and Indiana 2.62 million tons of byproduct coke, a total of 9.96 percent of United States coke production and 39.4 percent of all made in byproduct ovens. Others followed the USS lead; for instance, in 1912–1913 Inland Steel of Indiana Harbor made its first venture into coke manufacture.

In 1913, James Farrell, the U.S. Steel president, in evidence to the Stanley Committee indicated how successful the Gary and Joliet installations had been. By now, throughout USS it was reckoned that byproduct ovens were saving some 3 million tons of coal that would have been needed if their coke had been made by the older technology. Byproduct tar in some cases had increased the steel output of their open-hearth furnaces by as much as 24 percent compared with operations using producer gas, coal, or other fuel. He even claimed that at Gary the byproduct process made it possible to use as much as 25 percent Illinois coal mixed in with Pocahontas coal, whereas previously the former had never been a source of supply.[61] It seems likely that Farrell put an extremely favorable interpretation on the effects of byproduct coking in both open-hearth use of tar and the contribution of Illinois coal.

With Joliet in 1908, Gary in 1911, and an important installation at Ensley, Alabama, in 1912, USS was now, if belatedly, embarked on large-scale involvement in byproduct coking. In 1909 it produced what was, but for the exceptional trading conditions of 1916, its highest-ever output of beehive coke. That year byproduct coke production within USS was only 14.3 percent as great as its beehive output, yet within three years it was 44.7 percent as large. Even so, there remained a region that, despite its early prominence in the byproduct industry in the 1890s, by 1916 had no major byproduct-oven projects by either the USS or leading independent iron and steel companies. This was the nation's biggest iron-producing district in the upper part of the Ohio Valley. For the East, Lake Erie, and Chicago, distance from the old coke regions, and therefore dependence on long rail-hauls on coke, had justified the introduction of byproduct ovens once they had proved capable of providing a good furnace coke. The situation in the wider Pittsburgh district was more complex. Distances from the coke fields were shorter, and as was gradually being recognized, river transport provided attractive possibilities. Company differences caused variety in the lines of advance.

During 1898 a merchant byproduct coke plant had been constructed at Glassport on the Monongahela some two miles southwest of McKeesport. It sold coke to blast furnaces and for domestic use; gas from it was used for lighting and as an industrial fuel. In the same year the National Tube Company installed byproduct ovens at its Benwood plant south of Wheeling. This was expanded in 1901 to 120 ovens. Benwood was incorporated into USS from its inception. At South Sharon (later known as Farrell) the Sharon Steel Company commissioned 212 Otto-Hoffman ovens in 1903. This company was brought into USS in December 1902 through its purchase of the recently combined Sharon and Union steel companies. Apart from these fairly small and exceptional installations, no byproduct coke ovens existed in the Pittsburgh–Upper Ohio River district until World War I. However, one major local iron and steel firm had, in a rather peculiar manner, prefigured the pattern of development that would later make Pittsburgh a major focus of byproduct coking.

Overshadowed though it was in size and renown by Carnegie Steel, the long-established Pittsburgh operations of Jones and Laughlin (J&L) underwent major expansion at the turn of the century. From 1895 they had been producing open-hearth steel and over the next few years rapidly expanded capacity in this respect. Overall, their steel capacity increased from 650,000 tons in 1898 to over 1,000,000 tons by 1904; by the latter date iron capacity also was over 1,000,000 tons. These increases affected the company's development policy in coke. Under the title of Laughlin and Company, the group had for many years operated the beehive plant at Tyrone on the north bank of the Youghiogheny midway between the Morgan Valley and Hickman Run. But from 1890 J&L had also been shipping coal from the Vesta mine in Washington County, where the company had large properties. By the end of the century, they controlled the enormous area of twenty-seven square miles of coal lands tributary to the fourth pool on the Monongahela. Barging this coal downriver to Pittsburgh could yield considerable cost savings over rail-hauled coal or coke. By 1905–1906 the rail freight on coke from Connellsville to Pittsburgh was about 60 cents a ton; coal could then be shipped down the Monongahela to Pittsburgh for about 3 cents a ton.[62] Gradually, the Tyrone operation was reduced; 141 ovens there in 1894 had shrunk to only 36 seven years later. Sometime afterward, the plant was sold to the Kendall Coal and Coke Company, which itself was soon running out of coal supplies. Meanwhile, as production and river shipments of Vesta coal increased, J&L embarked on an important new departure in coke-oven location. By 1897 they had begun to build beehive ovens in Pittsburgh on the right bank of the Monongahela some distance above their Eliza blast furnaces. They then purchased the old Laughlin estate of Hazelwood nearby and erected more ovens. By early 1898 the plant was being extended from 500 to 700 ovens. With 1,510 ovens, Hazelwood was by 1909 the world's leading coke works. The plant included ten experimental rectangular ovens, and additionally at the so-called Middle Yard J&L had a further 160 beehives for times of peak demand. In this same year they brought into production the first blast furnace at the new Aliquippa works over twenty miles down the Ohio from their Pittsburgh operations. By 1910 they were building coke ovens there. These too were beehives, supplied with waterborne coal in the same fashion as Hazelwood.

Jones and Laughlin tried to make the most efficient use of this huge installation. For a number of years their natural gas supply had been failing and they had installed a producer gas plant, which had proved troublesome and expensive. By 1903, to mix with or supplement natural gas, they were conveying gas from their beehives for storage in a holder from which they were laying pipes to their various open-hearth shops. Naturally, they were asked why they should spend so much on a new beehive plant rather than put in byproduct ovens. Early in the Hazelwood development, Willis King tried to rationalize their decision: "Coke made by the by-product process has hardly proved satisfactory for blast furnace use, although it may be successful when the requirements are not so great. Moreover the prices for tar and ammonia are hardly enough to warrant great expense in adopting the by-product system."[63] Time and experience eventually proved that J&L had been too cautious, but the pattern of coking they had turned to in the almost twenty years leading up to World War I was to provide a model for bigger and more modern schemes of coke production.

6 The Physical and Social Implications of Beehive Coke Manufacture

In February 1886 the American Institute of Mining Engineers met in Pittsburgh. John Peter Lesley, once a minister of religion and after that for many years a leading Pennsylvania state geologist, gave a paper entitled "The Geology of the Pittsburgh Coal Region." A learned address became an unrestrained celebration of the blessings bestowed by nature on this region. For Lesley, it was perhaps, "the most valuable spot on the surface of the planet. . . . A vast community has organized itself by the spirit of the nineteenth century in a thousand forms of intelligence and force. . . . There seems to be no limit to the development of every kind of human life in the region." He envisaged the uplands around Pittsburgh becoming "one of the gardens of the world, populous, prosperous and beautiful to every eye."[1] However, things worked out very differently from this happy vision. In the coal and coke region, there were natural resources in abundance and spectacular growth in both economy and society, but everywhere nature was defiled, and over generations tens of thousands of human beings were exploited and alienated.

Economic and Population Growth

The mining and coke industry had various major impacts on the Connellsville region, its physical environment and landscape, population and settlement patterns, and its general economic and social condition. At the end of the nineteenth century, expansion in the industry was accompanied by a surge in population, though not until the last great extensions in the first twenty years of the next century was the area's share of Pennsylvania's population higher than in the years immediately before coke making began. In short, mineral production and processing did not provide jobs on a scale comparable with manufacturing elsewhere in the state.

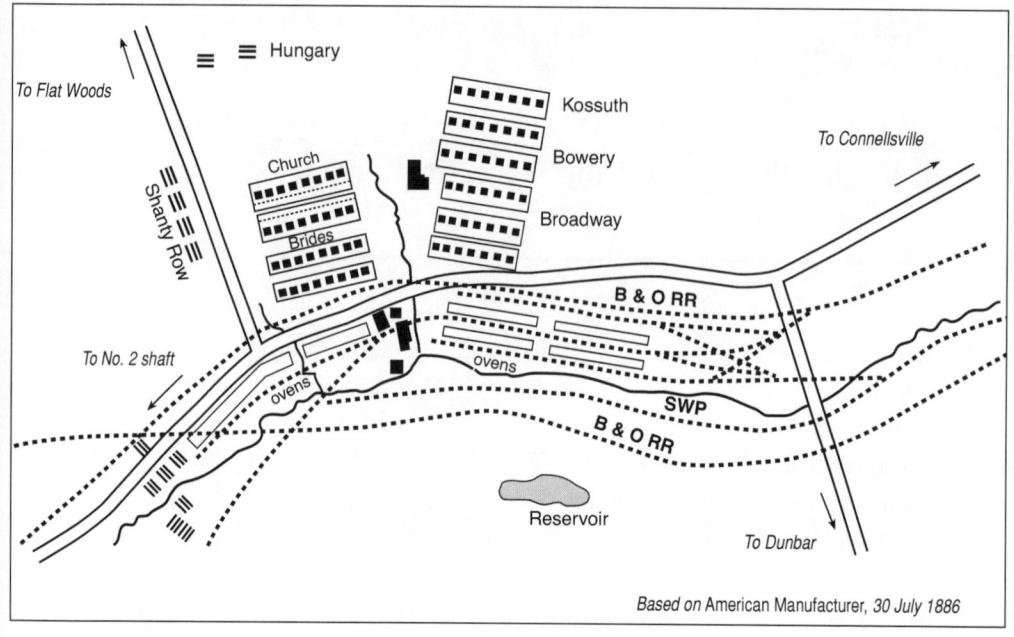

Plan of Leisenring, Fayette County, 1886.

In addition to its need for miners or men at the ovens, the rise of the coke industry had important multiplier effects through other trades—jobs, income, and profits in railroads, brick making, engineering, and equipment manufacture. From coke making and the associated trades alike there came an increased demand for the general services of a modern society. All these related elements of economic growth brought with them population increase and social evolution. Numerically, the growth was on a relatively modest scale. Between 1890 and 1910, the population of the United States increased 46.1 percent. Pennsylvania experienced a rise of 45.8 percent. Over these twenty years Allegheny County, scene of the fastest growth of manufacturing in the state and one of the most rapidly growing urban agglomerations in the nation, grew 84.7 percent. In this critical period, the apogee of the beehive industry, Westmoreland and Fayette Counties, outgrew all others, registering advances of 104.4 percent and 108.7 percent respectively. Though each contained locally important independent activities such as glass manufacture and metal working, it was the whole complex of activities whose foundations lay in the mines and ovens that accounted for most of this exceptional increase. Yet if the two counties had retained their 1840 share of Pennsylvanian population, their 1910 numbers would have been reduced by only 60,000, or 15 percent.

Table 6.1 Populations of Fayette and Westmoreland Counties and Pennsylvania, 1840, 1880–1920

Year	Fayette	Westmoreland	Pennsylvania	Counties as percentage of state
1840	34,000	43,000	1,724,000	4.42
1880	59,000	78,000	4,283,000	3.19
1890	80,000	113,000	5,258,000	3.65
1900	110,000	160,000	6,302,000	4.29
1910	167,000	231,000	7,665,000	5.19
1920	188,000	273,000	8,720,000	5.29

Table 6.2 Foreign-born males in the Coke Region and elsewhere, 1880

Pennsylvania	34.21
Westmoreland County	21.28
Fayette County	17.48
Venango County (oil)	22.19
Schuylkill County (anthracite)	67.13
Luzerne County (anthracite)	98.19
Cambria County (coal/steel)	45.60
Allegheny County (steel and others)	88.44

NOTE: Foreign-born males as a percentage of native-born males (all twenty-one or over).

In the last two decades of the nineteenth century, the coke region gained a colorful and generally bad reputation for the recent immigrants who provided a large part of its workforce. Yet as late as the 1880 Census, the district had been less characterized by immigration than the state as a whole and as compared with some other leading mineral districts.[2] Even after this the district remained less dependent on recent immigrant workers than many industrial or mining areas. This was especially the case in its towns. Foreign-born residents comprised 11.2 percent of the people in Connellsville and 6.1 percent in Uniontown in 1900 compared with 26.4 percent in Pittsburgh and 28.4 percent in Scranton.

The population geography of the region was typical of a coal mining area. Innumerable little clusters of population scattered throughout the region at mine and oven locations were almost wholly dependent on direct employment in either one or other of these occupations. It was difficult to romanticize the coal and coke villages—"patches" as the still smaller settlements were almost dismissively described. The share of recent immigrants here was much larger than in the towns or the counties. Such settlements had little or no function other than to house and in the longer

Ovens at Star Junction, early twentieth century. *Courtesy of Pennsylvania State University, Fayette, Coal and Coke Heritage Center*

term to reproduce the labor force for the nearby mine and ovens. A company store, a school, a church, and in some cases perhaps a small hospital would be the only other activities offering alternative types of regular employment or providing other community services. Many patches were so small that when their mine and ovens closed they might be deserted or demolished. Enman listed 125 villages and smaller settlements for the old basin. He was able to estimate the population of 112 of them for 1910, his calculations being based not on official enumerations but on the number of dwellings and an assumed average of six persons per dwelling. On this basis the total population for the 112 places was 52,166, an average of almost 466 per settlement; 38 contained over 500 residents, 12 exceeded 1,000. The largest, Mount Braddock, held an estimated 1,600. Eighteen were smaller than 100.³

Distinct from this scattered population, some of the main settlements were growing quickly around 1900, though in contrast with Pennsylvania's anthracite coalfield none of them reached anywhere near the status of an important metropolitan area.

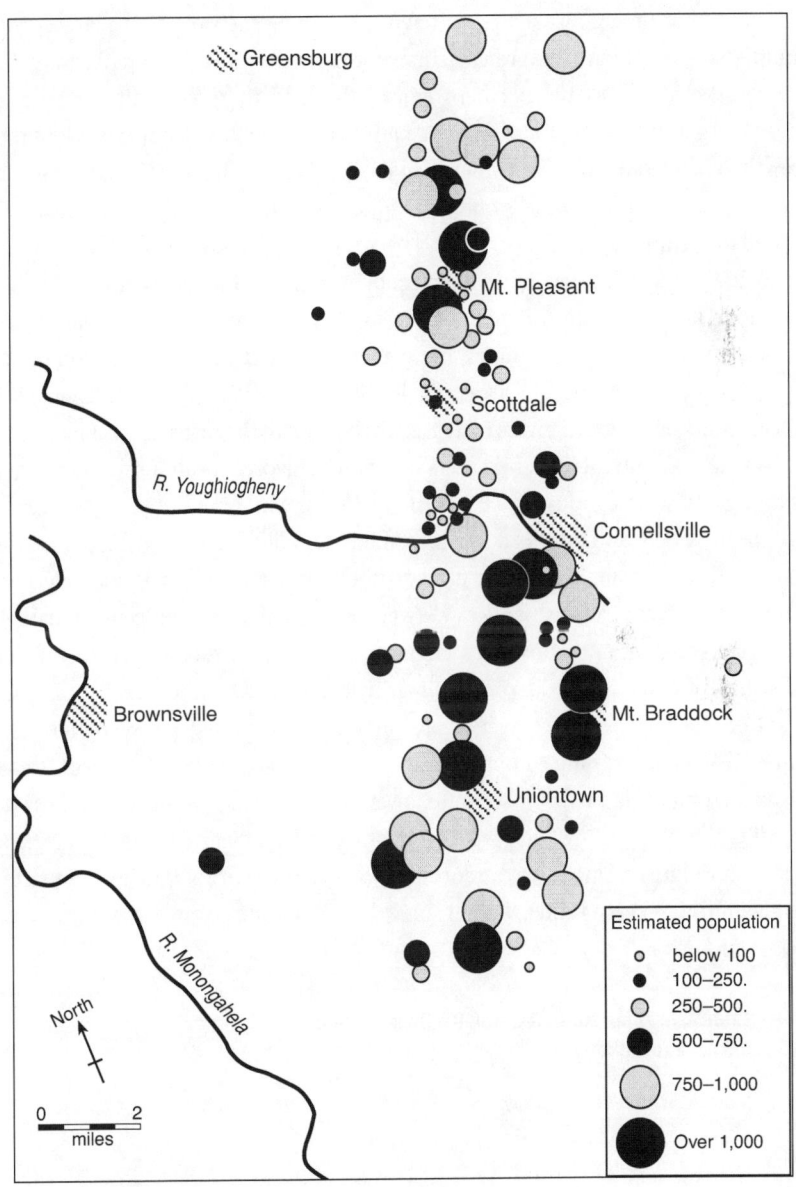

Coke and mine settlements in the "old basin," 1910.

Indeed, at that time no Coke Region town was among the twenty-two largest communities in the state. The growth curve for Scottdale and Mount Pleasant had already leveled off. At the northern end of the field there was rapid increase in Greensburg and Latrobe, but they were peripheral to the district and much of their growth depended on activities other than coal and coke. The most interesting comparison was between Connellsville and Uniontown. Until the 1880s Connellsville, located in the middle of the district, had been the bigger center. Thereafter, developments in the southern part of the field brought more rapid increase to Uniontown. After 1900 it was boosted still more by development in Lower Connellsville, whereas at the same time closure of mines and ovens as a result of the exhaustion of coal reserves was concentrated in areas north and south of Connellsville. Though the process was uneven, both towns increased their share of the district's population.

To a large extent, these main centers became the favored locations for both manufacturing and service industries. Firebrick works, mineral-based enterprises, seem to have been widely spread. Production of mine supplies, including boilers, larries, cages, and tanks came from such firms as the Connellsville Iron Works. Electrical equipment and electricians' services were geared to both mine and general markets. Surveying, sinking, and consultant engineering activities, though present in Connellsville, were before World War I primarily located in Uniontown.[4] Control functions for the industry were even more unevenly distributed between the major centers. Each large mining company had to have a hierarchy of management. Necessarily, each plant had its own separate lower-order managerial functions. Everyday coordination of the H. C. Frick Coke Company was from Scottdale, though its head office was in Pittsburgh. To an extraordinary degree those firms whose headquarters were within the region rather than in some distant manufacturing or finance center chose Uniontown.

Table 6.3 Population of Connellsville and Uniontown, 1840, 1880–1920

Year	Connellsville	Uniontown	Percentage of counties
1840	1,436	1,710	4.08
1880	3,609	3,265	5.01
1890	5,629	6,359	6.21
1900	7,160	7,344	5.37
1910	12,845[a]	13,344	6.58
1920	13,804	15,692	6.40

a. New Haven, with a 1900 population of 1,532, was shortly afterward annexed to Connellsville; the relatively greater 1900–1910 growth of Uniontown was therefore more marked than census figures indicate. The percentage column uses combined figures from Fayette and Westmoreland.

Table 6.4 Range of manufacturing in coke district settlements *(1900 populations)*

Location	Manufacturing
Connellsville/New Haven (8,692)	iron, tinplate, mining supplies, safety lamps, railroad and mine cars, automobiles, and machinery.
Uniontown (7,344)	iron, steel, glass, bricks, carriages, malted liquors
Greensburg (6,508)	engines, nuts and bolts, glass, flour, and others
Mount Pleasant (4,745)	glass, brewing
Latrobe (4,614)	steelworks, brewing, and others
Scottdale (4,261)	iron, tinplate, engines, mining machinery, and cast-iron pipe
Blairsville (3,386)	foundry work, glass, and flour
Dunbar (1,662)	iron, steel, and glass
Brownsville (1,552)	glass, flour, lumber, and alcoholic beverages
Ligonier (1,219)	lumber, woodwork
Fairchance (1,219)	iron
Larimer (1,050)	foundry work
Saltsburg (828)	steel, bottles
Masontown (466)	wine
New Geneva (ca. 375)	stoneware
Millsboro (ca. 350)	distillery products
Oliphant Furnace (n.a.)	powder

SOURCE: *Lippincott's Gazetteer of the World*, 1905.

Table 6.5 Headquarters of coke firms working in the Connellsville and Lower Connellsville regions, 1914

Location	Companies	Controlling Works	Ovens
Pittsburgh	17	79	23,359
(of which H. C. Frick Coke)	(1)	(57)	(18,477)
New York City	1	12	2,552
Ohio	3	5	1,166
Uniontown	35	51	5,760
Connellsville	4	4	303
Scottdale	3	3	466
Greensburg	3	6	917
Mt. Pleasant	2	2	60
Dawson	2	3	1,329
Smithfield	2	2	64
Brownsville	2	2	245
Nine other Pennsylvania sites	9	9	1,810
Totals	83	178	38,031

SOURCE: Based on *Connellsville Weekly Courier*, May 1914.

Not surprisingly, when considering these expanding business centers, some enthusiastic nineteenth-century writers thought, like Lesley, that they could conflate high levels of economic activity and rapid expansion with well-being and even felicity. Writing of their home settlement, the compilers of *Nelson's Biographical Dictionary* were lyrical about the virtues of Uniontown, celebrating growth and seeing romance where others might have recognized environmental degradation. By 1899 they reckoned it held 12,000 inhabitants including the suburbs:

On all sides are evidences of wealth and comfort; "plenty is scattered o'er a smiling land." The coke ovens flame in all directions in the region round about; the very poetry of manufacturing industry is exhibited as their lurid glow sometimes blends with the mellow light of the moon, or the maiden splendor of the evening star. Lines of railway traverse the town, the streets are full of life and energy; the old National Road passing through the heart of Uniontown links the ages that are gone with the living present; the mountains with their soft blue tint and lovely outline girdle it as they do Jerusalem; on all sides are great possibilities, varied development, rich historic associations, a past that is inspiring, a future that is radiant with hope and assured of splendid achievement. Such is the Uniontown of 1899—the Uniontown of the last decade of this most marvelous of centuries.[5]

Eschewing this sort of romanticism, some realized even in the times of expansion the dangerously narrow economic base of the Coke Region. A 1911 editorial in the *Coal and Coke Operator* looked ahead to what might happen when coal was mined out. Serious depreciation of value of commercial and realty interests could be expected unless action was taken: "Is it not about time for the citizens and owners . . . to get busy in efforts to attract manufacturing enterprises to their midst, in order that there may be employment for their inhabitants and to avoid depreciation of property?" It suggested further fabrication of steel and possibly textiles, though the latter demanded "an atmosphere . . . free of smoke and smudge." The most desirable line of development seemed to be the use of currently wasted gases and other products to support a range of industries. These businesses would employ skilled, well-paid workers and support chemical laboratories or perhaps a dyestuffs industry, which at last might make the United States free from the need to import such materials from Europe. The editorial ended: "There is much in this subject that prompts us to commend it to the coke producers for serious examination and consideration, not only as a means of securing a profitable price for their product, but a source of permanent stability to the towns in which so many of them are owners of property."[6] It was a sensible idea at a time when purposeful action might have made some use of it, but instead the industry was soon to surge into its last frantic boom before gradually subsiding into a long decline. With the coal and coke industries went much of the regional economy as well as the population and society that it had supported. Over many years the great expansion had been an unplanned growth; through decades to come its contraction was to follow the same route.

Coke Region Society and Social Relationships

The nature of the region's basic activities, the time at which they developed, the relative isolation of the area from large centers of population, and the scattered distribution characteristic of the operations within it all contributed to exploitative relationships between owners and their workers. It is true that essentially the relations between capital and labor were no different from those in the mill towns along the Monongahela, but what went on in the Coke Region was rather more isolated from the prying eyes of journalists, though less so than in the very isolated coal districts of mid-Appalachia (the appalling conditions of which have been so vividly described by J. A. Corbin).[7] Coke Region development occurred as economic inequalities were increasing in the nation, competition and individualism replacing mutual help. A man's well being and that of his dependents had become his own responsibility. In 1888 the Pennsylvania Department of Internal Affairs published a paper on "the alleviation of distress among working men." It recognized the drift of change: "In the earlier history of our country, the people were nearly on the same plane of industrial advantage. They did not have much beside intelligence, energy, strong arms and faith, and a desire to make their way. . . . [T]here doubtless was a nearer kinship in those days when each man knew those around him, than there is now. No thoughtful person can help seeing that acquaintanceship is becoming more circumscribed and class distinctions more strongly marked."[8] Thirty-five years later the economist J. M. Clark summarized this new socioeconomic regime, by then fully developed: the working man "is, under our social system, a free being, responsible for his own continuous support and that of his family; hence his maintenance is his own burden and not an obligation of industry, except so far as he can exact wages that will cover it."[9] In coke making, subject as it was to powerful pressures from larger consuming industries to lower costs and using large numbers of non-English-speaking immigrants for labor-intensive, generally low-skill production processes, this social philosophy inevitably led to poor employment and domestic conditions.

At work the scales seemed always to be loaded against the common man. There was a general disposition to keep a close eye on employees and to get rid of those whose ideas seemed to threaten the settled order. As Frick put it in a spring 1886 report to Jay Morse on a resumption of work at Morewood: "They withdrew some of their demands and we acceded to some of them. We will have to work along patiently, and I hope, some time in the near future, we will be able to weed out the bad men there and get better control of our own property." Nearly two years later he returned to the same theme. Frick believed they could blow out some South West Coal and Coke ovens, which "will enable us to get rid of some very objectionable characters there who are continually giving us trouble, and have a wholesome effect on the balance of the employees, thus enabling us to very materially reduce the cost." On the other hand, his Chicago partners generally, though not invariably, encouraged what they saw as fair play in relations with their workers. At the time of the 1887 strike, Morse summed up the situation: "I think the trouble you are having is largely due to the fact that the men have not been used honestly in times past,—and the sooner you get on an honest basis the better. When the men have been down, the producers have taken every advantage possible of them, and vice versa. It does seem to me that this 'see-saw' business ought to be stopped and, at least, every precaution should be taken by the producers to have their contracts with the men on an actual basis of facts, so that no question could be raised as to the understanding about coal mined, coke loaded, etc, and that you pay the men for what they do." His colleague, Gray, returning to this theme, stressed, "The men should be required to be honest with us, and our manager should be required to be as equally honest with them."[10]

Inevitably, there were numerous accidents in working coal, most affecting no more than one or two individuals. On such occasions the treatment the injured received from the operators depended on the judgment of its management; sometimes compensation being made in order to avoid the matter coming to possibly embarrassing court proceedings. There were instances of generosity, but whether this was the case or not seems to have been arbitrary. In September 1890 Frick wrote to Morris Ramsay: "I note the accident to the rope rider. As he was a faithful employee, you had better see that his doctor bill is paid, and that good care is taken of him." Six months later he responded to two other accidents: "I have your favor of the 11th and would favor donating Joe Pushcar an artificial limb and I suppose it would be just as well for us to pay the doctor bill of George Reese."[11] Letters from ill or injured men all too often evoked responses that, though not unkindly, were aloof and paternalistic. Early in 1888 F. J. Hall wrote a pathetic letter to Frick from Monongahela City: "Dear Sir, I find that I am improving so very slow. If I should live to get well I will not be able to do any work this winter. Thankful to you for your kindness rendered in the past seven years that I have been in your service. I would like to speak a good word for George who has worked with me the last two years. He is faithful and good tempered. I remain Yours respectfully. . . ." Frick replied promptly, courteously, but stiffly—his letter can scarcely have warmed Hall's heart: "I have your favor of the 22nd inst and regret to hear that you are not improving as fast as you expected. We will give George a trial, and, if he attends to his duties faithfully and well will be glad to continue him in our service. Hoping you may fully recover in a short time, I am yours very truly, H. C. Frick."[12]

Injury to a breadwinner could be a family disaster. Some of the poverty of working people, their dependence on the continuing labor of their menfolk, and the parsimonious attitude of management can be gleaned from the death of a Slav, Joe Tropka, an experienced miner who had worked at the Standard shaft for almost six years before he was killed there on 5 December 1891. Drawing a rib of coal with Joe Newatinie, he knocked out the last post, but as he stepped back out of the way tripped against his companion who was holding the lamp. Before he could get to his feet again the roof fell, killing him instantly. Six days after his death, J. D. McCaleb wrote to Frick from Mount Pleasant, saying that Tropka's widow, Katathrina, had asked him to write to ask for aid. She had three children, was "entirely destitute," and "from what I can learn of all the circumstances, I think it is a matter worthy of the notice and favorable action of the company." Frick inquired of Lynch, who in turn contacted the Standard superintendent, Robert Ramsay. Ramsay outlined the circumstances of Tropka's accident and then, in business-like fashion, went on to consider its implications, in the process managing to raise specters liable to disturb his superiors:

As to his family. There are three children, one daughter married who lives with her husband in the same house, one girl about 11 years and a boy about 9 years of age. The widow looks about 45, and claims to be sickly and not able to earn a living for herself and children. I am unable to satisfy myself as to the circumstances of this family. It has been reported that he was a member of a beneficial society among the Slavs, and that his widow would receive $500.00. She says that it is true he was a member, but only joined it two months before he was killed, and that she would only be entitled to the money after 6 months membership. At this moment, Charlie Newman, a coke drawer here, states that he is a member of this society, and that this woman is entitled to the money, and believes she has already got it. Joe Steffen states that she has been paid $500.00. In view of the conflicting circumstances of this case I would suggest that an effort be made to find out from the headquarters of this society what the facts are. I tried to learn something about it from Newman, but all he seemed to know was that the headquarters is in Chicago. I wonder if this is not the so called Anarchist Society we have heard so much about the last few years? I will try and find out something more satisfactory about this matter, and would suggest caution before you do anything in the way of assistance.

Three days later Lynch returned McCaleb's letter to Frick along with Ramsay's report. He noted that he had taken some practical steps to help and then put the matter into a wider context:

I have made inquiry and found that the Company has not been to any expense in this case, but that the funeral expenses were yet unpaid, and I instructed Standard to notify the undertaker to send his bill to us and we will pay it. As the woman is not in bad circumstances, I would not be in favor of doing anything more in this case. I am opposed to this third party business, having people like McCaleb, Max Schamberg [Austro-Hungarian consul in Pittsburgh], Dunhill at Greensburg and other go-betweens going into cases of this kind. If the parties who want help would come to us themselves, I would feel more like doing something for them. All these go-betweens have axes to grind and are making a living off these people, and when we do give aid after being solicited to do so by these third parties, I am satisfied they give the people to understand that it was through their agency alone that the aid was forthcoming, and leave the people under the impression that they could not have gotten any assistance from us if they had not enlisted their services.[13]

As more shaft mines were added to the smaller slope-and-adit operations of earlier days, there was a new hazard, the threat from gas. The first major disaster caused by this occurred at Leisenring on 19 February 1884 when nineteen men lost their lives in an explosion of fire damp. A few months later a number were killed or injured in a similar explosion at the Youngstown works near Uniontown. Within four or five days, fourteen of the victims had been buried, the company reportedly defraying all expenses and "doing everything possible to relieve the temporary wants of the breaved families." In March 1887 there was a terrible gas explosion at Uniondale that killed several miners. Men at the nearby Morrell, Colvin, Wheeler, Atlas, and Anchor pits had to be ordered out until their mines were cleared of gas.[14] Far worse lay ahead. In 1889 H. C. Frick Coke bought the Mammoth mine, a deep shaft operation at the northern end of the coal basin, from J. W. Moore. In June 1890, immediately after an accident at Hill Farm mine near Dunbar, the company sent a circular to their superintendents warning them, as Thomas Lynch put it, "to be cautious and vigilant in operating the mines." Seven months later 102 men, all "foreigners," were killed at Mammoth. At the inquest the mine inspector of the Fifth Coal District concluded that the fire damp that caused the explosion came from the Redstone seam, seventy-five to eighty-five feet above the Pittsburgh seam, "the great gasometer of this region."[15] The ovens themselves were by no means safe places of work. In 1913 and 1914 at coke ovens throughout the nation, 96 men were killed as well as 644 seriously and 4,059 slightly injured. A high proportion of the accidents were connected with haulage facilities.[16]

The problem of poor, more easily exploitable immigrant labor became serious in the Coke Region in the course of the last twenty years of the nineteenth century. The early workers in the industry had been either native Americans or from western

Europe. Before the depression of the mid-1870s, it was even possible for some to write happily about the situation in the coalfields and retain optimism as to prospects. For instance, the authors of an 1872 atlas of Pennsylvania concluded their account of the quality and location of the state's coal resources with, "Above all, this vast store of latent power is found in a country with a good government, and where the laws protecting men in their rights and property are well and faithfully executed, and inhabited by a Christian, industrious and enterprising people."[17] By the end of that decade, as the industry revived from its depression, things had begun to change. In 1879 the first Slavs were recruited to work at Morewood, and two years later a small party of them came to the White and Sherrick operations in the Morgan Valley. Although many had no dependents with them, long before the end of the century many small settlements were largely made up of these immigrant families, their many different national origins being grouped, however inappropriately, under the name of Hungarians, commonly shortened to "Huns." From the start they met strong ethnic prejudices.

In spring 1882, writing from Morewood, a correspondent of the *Pittsburgh Dispatch* painted a picture of these new workers scarcely calculated to improve relationships with the rest of society. He wrote of them not as fomenters of strikes but rather as tools in the hands of the owners: "Greedy, grasping, covetous, living next door to hunger that they may have a few more dollars to take back with them to Hungary, they do not count the possible far-off benefit of strikes, but reckon them only as causing the loss of so many day's wages. They are thus a convenient lever to the operator's hand, wherewith he regulates the more demanding spirit of his other laborers." He made much of the tendency of their womenfolk to help in the heaviest work, especially in forking coke into railcars. Finally, he revealed his ignorance of the background of those he was writing about: "Many of the early colonists have gone back to the old country, following the fashion of the Chinese, whose cousins they are."[18]

Discrimination built up over the years. When a strike in the region ended early in 1886, Walter Ferguson mentioned reports that the "Huns" were still causing trouble, "which I suppose will only hasten their departure from the region. I certainly would not do much to help those fellows out of prison." Three-and-a-half years later, a leading trade journal, referring to the general end of another strike, focused on a highly emotive aspect of the new immigration: Hungarians "have been on a grand spree, destroying property and abusing men generally. They have finally been pleased to allow American citizens to go to work."[19] In 1887, under a headline "The Hordes of Huns," the *Connellsville Courier* quoted the *Pittsburgh Dispatch* as reporting that "since the importation of foreign labor was commenced in the coke region, nearly 10,000 poverty-stricken foreigners have been dumped among the hills and mountains of Fayette and Westmoreland counties."[20] At about the same time there appeared a Pennsylvania state report, "The Employment of Labor in the Connellsville Coke Region," also unlikely to contribute to local harmony. It noted the first Hungarians had come when there was no strike on the horizon:

Word was sent by them to their friends at home and from that time forth they have come in a steady stream. In Hungary.... [T]he average wage per day is about sixty cents and board. There are coal mines along the Carpathian Mountains and the miners of that region were infatuated with the promise of making from two to four dollars a day in this country. At first a few came over to try their fortunes, and these were so gratified at the chance of saving money, that cheering news was sent to their kinsmen at home. The more provident of them save from $600 to $1,000 with which they either pay off the mortgage held on their property in Hungary by the Jewish, Greek or Armenian creditors, or they buy a tract of ten to fifteen acres in their native country, build a house and become comparatively independent.[21]

Two prominent Americans from very different backgrounds made interesting comment on the labor situation in the western Pennsylvanian coal and coke districts at this time. James M. Swank, born in Westmoreland County before it became a center of coal and coke production, a long-term champion of protection as secretary and then general manager of the American Iron and Steel Association for almost forty years, was also prejudiced against new immigrants. As early as 1884, under the heading "Destitute Italians and Hungarians," he had adopted a very different tone from that of the optimistic atlas makers of twelve years before: "We cannot afford to make this country a lazar-house for Europe.... [The issue] concerns the very foundation of American prosperity, and the whole scope and aim of our republican institutions."[22] A quarter of a century later, and this time in specific reference to the Coke Region, he had not softened his approach: "All over this activity—over all this "black district"—there hangs a black cloud other than that which the coal itself makes when it is converted into coke or is consumed by locomotives and the manufacturing enterprises that it has created. A very large proportion of the population of western Pennsylvania which is engaged in mining coal and making coke is composed of undesirable foreign elements, and with these are associated many undesirable negroes who have been brought from the Southern States. So numerous and oftentimes so lawless are these foreign and negro laborers that the character of whole communities has been radically changed within the last ten or fifteen years."[23]

Swank failed to acknowledge that the relatively simple mining and coke making operations of Connellsville had become dependent on these plentiful supplies of unskilled, cheap, and usually tractable labor. This fact was however recognized by the Harvard economist Frank Taussig, an American-born son of Czech immigrants, who also saw how depressing the results had been. In 1900 he traced some consequences, made interesting comparisons, and showed more compassion as well as more understanding than Swank: "A bitter competition has intensified the evil social conditions which must emerge where great masses of ignorant laborers are congested in out of the way places. Truck-shops, low wages, semi-feudal conditions, cheap coal, have meant a cheap man. At the iron mines the conditions seem to have favored the better mode of securing cheapness,—vigorous and intelligent labor, using highly elaborated machinery. ... But at the very foundation of the industry, at the coal mine and the coke oven, we have a social sore."[24] A few years later he filled out this account:

> Such nationalities as the Italians, the Bohemians, the so-called Huns and Polaks ... supplied the men for heavy and dirty work. ... The nature of the operations caused cheapness to be attained at the coal mines and coke ovens, partly indeed by machinery and organization, but largely by cheap labor. The mining of coal is mainly pick-and-shovel work, requiring little handicraft skill or trained intelligence; and this is still more true of the work at the coke ovens. ... [M]ultitudes of newly arrived immigrants have been drawn to the mines, partly through deliberate arrangement by the employers, partly by the silent adjustment of supply to demand. There they have huddled,—inert, stolid, half-enslaved. ... In times of activity their condition is passable. In the periods of depression which recur in the iron trade, the price of coke sinks, production is restricted, wages fall, and the barest living is all that the miners and coke workers can secure,—sometimes not even this. The American or Americanized laborers met a disheartening situation and tried in vain to stem the tide of falling wages and half-employment, with its attendant misery, strikes, [and] bloodshed.[25]

The Slavs came into the Coke Region as a poor workforce; their experience there marginalized them still more. One aspect of this came out in the aftermath of the explosion at Mammoth on 27 January 1891. Two weeks later Lynch described the reaction of some of their workers: "Father Lambing was telling me today that the Bohemians and Huns refused to sign receipts for the relief fund distributed yesterday for fear it would compromise their rights of legal action against the company." A long-term effect of such calamities was to drive newer immigrants into riskier mining situations. By May the company had a great many applications from English-speaking men for work in drift mines but not at the shafts because, Lynch believed, they feared gas in that type of mine. Five pit bosses had recently left their employment, mostly because of the gas threat. Some had taken jobs at considerably lower rates of pay. The majority of workers in shaft mines were Slavs, Hungarians, and Poles.[26]

As well as the onerous ordinary conditions of work and the ever-present dangers of injury or sudden death, living conditions in the Coke Region were for a majority of

Leisenring No. 1 Mine, ovens, and settlement, *circa* 1893. *Courtesy of Frick Art and Historical Center, Frick Archives*

men and their families hard and bleak. Mining and coke making were located in what had previously been sparsely populated farming areas, and in order to make possible ready access to the place of work, the companies found it necessary to provide accommodation. By 1899 the H. C. Frick Coke employed more than 12,000 men and owned 3,500 dwellings. For many years the general quality of housing was low and conditions of tenancy precarious; on the companies' part, possession of these properties was viewed as an additional source of income for owners as much as an essential service for workers. In 1911 W. J. Lauck of the United States Immigration Commission produced an unimpassioned but deeply depressing survey of conditions in the western Pennsylvanian coal districts. He found that the houses were normally of two stories, uniform style, and made from cheap materials: These were

box-like frame buildings of eight, ten or twelve rooms, designed to accommodate two families, one on each side of the building. Some of the houses are plastered and well finished inside. A few companies light their villages with electricity from their power plants, but as a rule oil lamps or other means of lighting must be furnished by the tenants. Water for all purposes must be carried by the housewife from a distance of a few feet to several hundred yards. In some villages drain troughs or pipes are constructed to carry away waste water, but in the majority of cases it is emptied into the gutters or yards. The houses are rented for a fixed monthly amount, usually $1.50 per room, the cost for the house varying with the number of rooms. The investment is very profitable. The tenement houses of one company, which cost $1,100 each to construct, rent for $156 a year; at another mine, houses of similar construction have an annual rental of $168.[27]

Many years later an elderly woman recalled her childhood in coke-company housing at more or less the same time as that of Lauck's survey. Her memories were briefly recorded but colorful with the insights of direct childhood experience: "I personally know of the horrible housing provided by Frick and Rainey. Houses without inside finish of walls, houses with doors so poorly fitted that an inch of light was plainly visible at both the top and the bottom, were common. A large shelf built across one wall of the upstairs room served as the bed for an entire family." Nor were outside conditions any better: "Trenches were dug on each side of the road between the rows of houses for the purpose of dumping slop jars and other sewerage."[28]

Lauck vividly depicted the typical coke village at the end of the first decade of the century, as the region reached its highest-ever levels of production. Most communities consisted of fifty to one hundred red or gray square-frame dwellings.

At one end of the village a large building is found in which the company store is located, and at the other end of the main street there are, as a rule, a church or churches and a public school house. In some villages there are sidewalks of coke, ashes or slate from the mines; in others there are none of any description. In wet weather boards of various lengths and widths may be laid end to end part of the way by some of the inhabitants, but generally the tenants step directly from their houses into the streets. Open drainage is everywhere, and the street gutters are usually shallow ditches unless the hillside upon which the village is located slopes sharply, in which case the gutters soon become deep gullies. Rubbish, household garbage, and other discarded articles commonly litter the gutters, streets and yards. In some places near Uniontown the villages are laid out on such steep hillsides and the drainage is so defective that the houses lower down are flooded and uninhabitable in rainy weather and receive the refuse and waste water from those above even under favorable conditions. In some towns the lots around the houses are fenced off and there is space for a garden in the rear and flower beds at the front. In a few villages there are shade trees. In the majority the streets and yards are covered with coke ashes. Living conditions as a rule are exceedingly insanitary. Toilets are in all cases dry, with ground vaults, and are often located near the dwellings. Some mining communities near the larger cities use the city water supply; others draw their water, which is usually filtered, from company reservoirs. In many cases the inhabitants of the villages depend upon wells sunk at regular intervals. Wells or hydrants are placed about 200 yards apart, one for every ten or twelve families.[29]

Lauck's descriptions might be regarded as the questionable impressions of a member of a new brand of social investigators; Mrs. Nicolay's description as the colored recollections of a now-distant childhood, but there is sufficient contemporary evidence to confirm the general truth of their accounts. This evidence also makes clear that the provision of housing was a profitable rather than charitable undertaking. When he was trying to interest others in a share in South West Coal and Coke in 1885, Frick made much of the houses that company owned. He told Mellon they had already built six "brick double dwelling houses" and "over 100 frame dwelling houses." At that time only 60 percent of their ovens were running, but income from houses was $1,000 a month. To Morse he explained, "We figure that houses pay us about 15 percent annually on their costing."[30] Lynch is generally credited with doing much to improve conditions for Frick tenants, but he was clearly conscious of the need for economy of expenditure and of the fact that housing could pay so well. In June 1895 he suggested to Frick that they should spend $600-800 repairing the best houses at Jimtown so as to see them through the two- to four-years life expectancy of its ovens before the coal ran out. After that he thought they could sell a number of the houses, especially "a row on the public road leading to the Dawson cemetery, a nice location and plenty of ground there." That year the company should build ten blocks of houses at Leisenring 3 and ten at Mammoth, both plants being in rather isolated locations: "It is difficult to get men when the works in the region generally are running full, because of the scarcity of houses. The only way we have been able to get along was to crowd in the single Hungarians." He was planning to tear down some houses at Mammoth, which Moore had built before they bought the mine and ovens, that were in very bad shape. He did not favor putting up large or expensive properties, proposing an outlay of about $600 per block rather than the $800-900 spent in recent years: "Apart from the necessity of these houses to shelter the men and their families at the works, I believe our experience has been that they are a good investment in themselves." An inventory of H. C. Frick Coke at the end of 1898 showed it owned housing for 3,388 families yielding an annual revenue of $200,000.[31]

In the coal and coke settlements, dangers and nuisances were rife, some of which represented family disasters. In 1890 Frick wrote to Morris Ramsay: "Very much regret to hear of the drowning of that child. Do you think we can possibly be held responsible in any way? You should investigate occasionally and see whether there

Physical and Social Implications 213

Leisenring No. 2 Mine, ovens, and pollution. *Courtesy of Frick Art and Historical Center, Frick Archives*

are any holes of that kind. If so they should be filled up." Though much less cataclysmic, smoke was a perennial and apparently inescapable annoyance. Lauck pictured the horror of the general situation:

Some towns are built far enough away from the coke ovens to be but little affected by the smoke, but others are only a few yards distant and are very smoky and dirty. . . . The smoke and gas from some ovens destroy all vegetation around the small mining communities. . . . [T]he ovens are usually located along the base of the hill opposite the village, and the intervening valley is filled with smoke through which arises in semi-obscurity the iron frame of the coal tipple and the engine-house, whence come the incessant rattle of the coal as it is dumped into the ovens and the screech of the coke-drawing machines as they discharge the finished product. In the constant noise and din each alternate oven sends forth sheets of flame, and columns of dark brown smoke which darkens the sky and drifts over the village and through the houses on the opposite side of the hill.[32]

Specific examples show how complicated the situation could be. In 1885 a church in the little settlement of Smithton, a small community well down the Youghiogheny River between Jacobs Creek and West Newton, obtained a judgment of $450 for damages caused by smoke from the ovens of the Waverley Coal and Coke Company. The company made preparations to use the ovens again and another suit was expected.[33] For plants in the heart of the region, anonymity and possible security from complaint could be found from the sheer number of possible offenders. Much more important, wholly dependent communities could not normally afford the luxury of complaining against pollution, the existence of which resulted from the work of their menfolk. An extraordinary instance of coke company power and arrogance in relation to the public involved W. J. Rainey. In 1892 this firm wanted to build ovens at Sedgwick. The plant would be on the street and within two feet of housing. The matter was taken to litigation, where the company endeavored to find refuge in confusion: "The argument of the defense is that there is no town laid out and no such street as Front Street. . . . The plan of the lots was never recorded and is now lost and the question as to whether the place is a village or not depends upon individual proof." Later, in some cases at least, the attitude to the impact of work on living conditions was more enlightened, so that in 1912 the Oliver and Snyder Steel Company decided to move twenty-two blocks of houses at Oliver No.1 coke works "to a more desirable location where they would be out of the smoke etc."[34]

A continuing source of discontent was the role of company stores. Even before these were established some operators in isolated places issued their own "scrip," which was used in place of currency in hotels, saloons, eating-houses, and other company establishments. The early Frick company seems to have taken some delight in the artistry of its own substitute for United States banknotes.[35] The initial reasons for the stores was similar; and in principle at least, as rational; mines, ovens, and their dependent communities were often so far away from established settlements that for everyday purchases it would be convenient if retail facilities could be available on the spot. Purchases could be made without cash by use of a check—a printed slip—obtained from the pay office of the coal or coke company. On payday the total amount of these checks was deducted from the man's earnings. It all seemed straightforward, but the price at which items were sold, the freedom or otherwise to purchase elsewhere, and the fact that company stores proved highly profitable investments raised serious controversy. For Lauck the fully developed system was "one of the worst of the general conditions of employment. . . . The system is an evasion of the law and a frequent means of exploiting employees." Though stores had to be owned by a nominally independent company, they were in fact integral parts of the coke operations and in some cases "the most profitable part of a company's busi-

Tenements at Valley works, *circa* 1893. *Courtesy of Frick Art and Historical Center, Frick Archives*

ness." Another objectionable aspect of the system was that it gave the company insight into the ways in which their employees spent their nonworking time, a potentially dangerous power over individual freedom. An instance of this came in response to an 1885 plea for financial help from a former Morewood worker, Adam Bachman. He ended a letter to Frick on a plaintive note: "I beg of you for god sake and My Dear children sake do help me." When Frick asked Lynch what he felt about Bachman's request, he received the reply: "I really don't know how to advise in this matter. The man seems to be an innocent sort of a fellow." His greatest fault seemed to be drinking: "Never saw him drunk but get a good many of his checks from the saloon keepers." It was alleged that trade by the company stores was protected both by excluding competition from the community, including debarring the entry of hucksters and peddlers of meat, vegetables, and fruit, and by removal of employees who did not patronize the store. In fact, because of the store system as well as deductions for rent, fuel, and "smithing" (sharpening of work tools), workers often did not receive much more than half their earnings in cash.[36]

216 Physical and Social Implications

Superintendents' houses at Trotter, *circa* 1893. *Courtesy of Frick Art and Historical Center, Frick Archives*

The evidence is mixed but generally seems to support the critical conclusions to which Lauck was drawn. In December 1884 a leading Coke Region newspaper recognized the role of the company store in the weak bargaining position of the workers—in midwinter, and after wages had been cut by one-third, "nine out of ten had little or nothing coming to them on pay day after their store bill and house rent had been deducted. They had been compelled to live a sort of hand to mouth life, and are in no condition to strike or offer any resistance to the reduction were they ever so willing."[37] There has long been dispute as to whether prices for everyday commodities were higher or lower than in independent retail outlets or whether, as seems more likely, some items were cheaper, others more expensive. In fact, efficient operation could produce both low prices and high profits. At the end of October 1885, the H. C. Frick Coke Company became associated with the Chicago and Connellsville Coke Company. Lynch looked into their new associate's store operations and wrote to Frick about stocktaking by the store manager there, a Mr. Turnbull: "He is not well and doesn't want to start until he feels better. He may be a good store keeper but his store don't show it." The Chicago and Connellsville payroll was $10,000 a month, but Turnbull's sales had been only $3,000. "His net profits run from 10 to 15%; you know what ours average. His prices average 10% higher than ours." To back his claim that they were not charging unreasonably high prices, Lynch produced not only figures but also sworn affidavits from men employed by the Union Supply Company, nominally independent but in fact an effective part of the H. C. Frick Coke Company. Their employees remained unconvinced. One of the demands of the strikers in 1886 was the abolition of company stores. They alleged they were commonly required to spend at least twenty dollars a month there. Though the men were unsuccessful in their aim, outsiders now often saw what operators could or would not. During next year's dispute, Morse at least showed that he realized that psychological as well as commercial considerations should be taken into account: "It don't make any difference whether you charge your men for articles at a less price than they can buy them for elsewhere. The men feel a lack of independence even if they are not obliged to buy from you. That irritates them. A man, if he earns say $50, would rather have it in his hands and pay it out himself than have the amount deducted from his pay. I recognize the fact that there is some profit to the Store and Coke Companies directly but, indirectly, I think there is a positive loss. I have never seen it otherwise. Your business is making coke, and I don't believe it is well to mix merchandising with it."[38]

Profitability rather than the convenience of employees and their families had indeed been a key consideration. In spring 1890 Lynch looked into the possibility of building a store at Stonerville. At this time they were selling to people employed there about $800–1000 worth of goods each month; if they put up their own store in the village they could not hope to increase sales by more than $600 a month, would have to keep a delivery wagon, and all in all would make no profit. Consequently, Lynch could not see "that it would pay at the present time to have a store at that point," and instead they should extend their Tarr store. As with housing, the profits made from company stores were by no means negligible. In the fourteen months to the end of February 1883, net earnings in stores controlled by the H. C. Frick Coke Company were $32,841, equal to 16.86 percent of the value of their sales and 8.7 percent as large as profits on coke. In January 1898 as a postscript to a letter to Carnegie, Frick spelled out the success of this side of their business over the sixteen years since they first became partners: "Union Supply Company has this day declared a dividend of 100 percent, your share being $31,914.00. It is earning at the rate of 350 percent per annum on its capital at present. Has made almost $2 million dollars on its capital of $75,000 since its formation in 1882." In light of such figures, it is understandable that a few years later some critics were suggesting that one reason why owners were slow to mechanize coke-making operations was that they did not wish to reduce the clientele for their stores. Finally, it is important to note that though John Enman in a 1974 study of Union Supply's Buffington store concluded that it did not exploit employees, he recognized that it set prices at levels competitive with those in outlying areas of western Pennsylvania, whereas bulk purchase meant costs were lower.[39]

The bigger settlements of the region, though not very large, presented an appearance very different from the drab, relatively simple villages next door to the mines and ovens. Connellsville and Uniontown in particular were important service centers, containing the general offices of coal and coke companies, banks, a range of commercial and retail provision, and various independent manufacturing operations. To a lesser extent there were similar activities in the next tier of towns, Mount Pleasant, Scottdale, and also Masontown, which expanded rapidly in the early twentieth century. From the outlying "camps" or villages the entire population would come into town for important purchases of food and clothing as well as for recreation. Lauck was impressed by the distinctive atmosphere created by the breadth of functions in these places: "On Saturday or "pay day" evenings the stores, amusement places, saloons, and even the principal streets of the urban centers are filled with a heterogeneous collection of races and tongues. Each of the important centers in the coal and coke producing territory is indeed a diminutive Pittsburgh, and the Saturday and pay night scenes on its principal streets are a replica on a small scale of what may be observed on Fifth Avenue and other downtown sections of Pittsburgh proper."[40] Yet for a long time even these places lacked adequate cultural facilities. In spring 1893, writing to Andrew Carnegie, J. C. Kurtz of the Youghiogheny Bank, Connellsville, outlined his aim to establish a YMCA in his town, whose population had increased by 56 percent in the 1880s and was still growing rapidly. He summarized the cultural poverty of the wider area: "The people here, generally, are poor, and as the entire coke region is made up very largely of workmen who have never enjoyed opportunities of education, it is a deplorable fact that the lack of such refining influences as public libraries [of which there was at that time not one in the entire Coke Region] exert is sadly reflected in the people of the larger towns." The H. C. Frick Coke Company had located its general offices for the region in Scottdale. Not far away was Everson, where in the mid-1890s the company established shops to make steel coke cars. As a result, one local paper pointed out, Scottdale and its neighborhood was largely peopled by Frick superintendents and employees, a concentration that meant "the greatest interest of Mr. Frick in the advancement of the town." Whether because of this, from shame at the contrast between his own wealth and opportunities and the local public deprivation, or from genuine philanthropy, Frick began to respond to the needs of this cultural desert. After donating an observatory

Union Supply Store at Summit Station. *Courtesy of Pennsylvania State University, Fayette, Coal and Coke Heritage Center*

to Mt. Pleasant in 1895, he provided Scottdale with a music hall suitable for concerts and charity gatherings.[41]

Gradually, the industry, generally led by H. C. Frick Coke, began to improve the living conditions of their working people. As early as 1899 the press was reporting that with few exceptions most Frick employees "reside in comfortable houses . . . surrounded by plots of ground, where gardens abound. . . . [T]he firm has spared neither pains nor expense to establish pleasant and desirable homes for its workmen." House rents were from two to four dollars a month, which included free coal and water.[42] This was to put a very favorable gloss on conditions in the region. Moreover, not all the philanthropy, even if popular, was well conceived—it was for instance reported at Christmas 1910, "As per custom the H. C. Frick Coke Company distributed 25 tons of confectionary to the children of its employees." But undoubtedly there were signs of progress. At this time the company donated a 557-acre farm seven miles from Uniontown for a "Childrens' Home, Insane Asylum, and Workhouse," the unmined coal beneath it to pay for the erection of the buildings. Two years later it

Workers and supervisors outside the Leith Mine in 1893. *Courtesy of Pennsylvania State University, Fayette, Coal and Coke Heritage Center*

was establishing dairy farms near its settlements to supply workers' families with fresh milk. By 1915 the paternalism was extending even into other fields: "Each year the H. C. Frick Coke Company, in order to promote the cultivation of vegetable and flower gardens by its employees at all its coke plants in the Connellsville region, furnishes fertilizer, and in a number of instances, plows the ground and furnishes seed."[43] It was at this time that *Iron Age* frankly recognized that labor in the coke field was the hardest to handle in the whole industry and that improving living conditions had been a way of tackling this problem. When Henry Clay Frick died in 1919, one of his obituary writers, Robert A. Walker, was eloquent about the improvements Frick had brought about. He spoke of the "ideal environments" and "ideal conditions existing today." Walker continued: "After giving their employees good, comfortable homes, various forms of recreation and opportunity for wives and mothers to learn the domestic arts were provided, and they also showed their employees how to go about cultivating to high degree flower and vegetable gardens, which are a part of nearly every home in the Connellsville region in which a Frick employee lives. The employees were taught the advantage of the better things of life, were given free medical attention, low rents, cheap coal; in fact, a careful study was conducted and is still being made, for steadily improving the surroundings of these men."[44] No doubt there was some truth in this, but it was at best a romanticized presentation of reality and essentially a description of the higher price that now had to be paid for dependency, or in attempts to buy compliance from working men.

Landscape Impacts, Resource Waste, and the Life Expectancy of the Coke Industry

Massive development of the coal and coke industries eventually brought about dramatic change to the physical environment of an area that had until then been opened and settled by farmers. One effect of large-scale mineral working was summed up in an 1884 description of the northern edge of the coal region along the main line of the Pennsylvania Railroad in Westmoreland County. West of Greensburg the railroad passed over "a land of broad acres of good farms." The description of the Irwin area was less encouraging: "The surface is fertile. . . . [T]he coal mines do not permit of a great amount of cultivation, though some good farming is done."[45] In the Coke Region this usurpation of the land was taken to an extreme, the intensity of development of a mineral-based economy meant that agriculture for a time was almost overwhelmed. There were two main reasons for this: the greater profit possible from turning farmland over to mineral extraction and processing, and the direct and baneful effect of those activities on the land remaining in cultivation.

At the peak of the development process, an economic survey recognized the various ways in which for more than thirty years the district's farming had been either squeezed out or degraded: "The development of the coke industry in the decade between 1870 and 1880 marked a transition to the poorer agriculture in South West Pennsylvania. Farmers found it more profitable to engage in the production of coal and coke than to raise crops. Many of them made fortunes. Tenants took the place of owners and the farms steadily deteriorated." Smoke from ovens destroyed natural vegetation and crops alike, there were problems with subsidence, and soil water often failed. It was sometimes possible to win compensation that might be costly to the coke companies. In the 1890s Fayette County juries often imposed fines of $20 or so an acre for damage to the surface of farms, including removal of their water supply. On one farm Lynch estimated a fine for damages would amount to over $5,500. Apart from damage to crops, farmers found it hard to retain laborers when they could earn more in coal workings or coke yards. Indeed, even for the farmer himself it might be more profitable to use his labor and horses in these operations than in agriculture. Less tenuous, but very important, was the psychological impact of the intrusive new economy: "The farmer seeing the great wealth made in coal, oil and gas, becomes disatisfied with the comparatively small returns from his hard labor on the farm."[46]

In 1884 there were 3,231 farms in Fayette County with a total estimated value of $20,270,000. Their annual production was worth $1,758,000, providing an 8.7 percent return on capital. At that time there were 10,543 coke ovens in the entire region, including Westmoreland County. At $300 each, the ovens alone represented an investment of some $3,163,000. A large part of their coal was procured from slopes or adits, whose development involved fairly small outlays. The value of coke shipped in this relatively depressed year was $3,607,000. It is impossible to be precise, but such figures suggest the prospect of making a considerably greater return on capital by investing in coal and coke than in farming.[47]

Bit by bit, the transfer of land from agricultural use into coal workings, coke ovens and yards, railroad sidings, or town sites went on through the purchase of farms. This conversion in land use often enabled the owner to realize a considerable capital sum; sometimes it involved haggling with those wanting the minerals under the fields but occasionally it was a case of flight from an increasingly intolerable situation. William Thaw (1818–1889) of Pittsburgh had made a fortune in steamboat freight transport on the Ohio River and in railroads before he turned to Connellsville coal. By the early 1880s he owned some land in the Pleasant Unity district at the northern end of the field, an area then believed to be on the eve of development. He also acquired a bigger tract south of Uniontown, running roughly east-west and extending from near the western outcrop, across Beeson's Run and the local branch of the South West Pennsylvania, and almost to that railroad's main line. At the beginning of 1889 he purchased the 160-acre farm of Dr. Walker near Uniontown for the modest price of $6,200, or $38.75 an acre. Sometimes movement from agriculture to mining was eased for the mutual benefit of farmer and developer. In June 1891, for example, Frick instructed J. Thompson of Uniontown to close an option with Isaac S. Brown, "at reduction of $1,000 and give him this year's crop." On other occasions farmers felt impelled to get out, as was shown in an ungrammatical but eloquent and anguished letter sent to Frick some months before his negotiations to purchase Brown's land: "Under the pressure of circumstances, I desire to change my location and therefore wish to sel my farm and think the coke company should buy it. They have smoked me badly on one side and to treat me fare should buy me out. I hope you will give it some attention and let me know the result, Yours, S. C. Wakefield."[48]

In some instances the outcome of bargaining was that even powerful coke companies were frustrated. In 1871 ovens were built at Mt. Braddock along the line of the Fayette County Branch. Northward from there and extending halfway to Dunbar were coal lands owned by W. and J. K. Beeson. In 1890, when coke prices were exceptionally high, H. C. Frick Coke bought land of the "Beesun" tract from two of the major outside holders of coal land, J. V. K. Thompson and Andrew Mellon. In June a member of the Beeson family wrote from "JK Beeson Dry Goods and Groceries, 510 and 512 Main Street, Uniontown," in connection with Frick's wish to purchase an interest in Mt. Braddock Farm, some of whose coal had been sold to his old partner, E. M. Ferguson, eighteen years before. Beeson tried to negotiate a good price but was rather out of his depth. He pointed to the fact that coal had appreciated in value and would advance still more in the future—the very reason Frick wanted his land: "The condition that the coal market is already worked into, i.e. the absolute scarcity of coal now remaining outside the hands of operators, will certainly make Furnacemen and other Investors lively bidders in the near future." He offered a compromise from his original price: "Instead of the cash payment being $30,000 I will accept $22,000 cash and $1,400 each year for seven years on 5 percent per annum." Frick seems to have replied immediately, for only two days later Beeson wrote again: "I do not wish to appear obstinate in this matter. I only feel as though my property is worth *fully* all I ask for it, and I have no desire to make a sacrifice. If Mr. Frick was the owner, I am sure that he would ask more than my price is."[49] Perhaps it is not surprising that the Beeson deal probably was not completed.

Three months later Frick tried to obtain some coal in the north of the region. Morris Ramsay undertook the negotiations but was given instructions that reveal the complications and possibly annoying minutiae involved: "Ascertain just what you can buy that 4 acres of surface from Fox for, with the old loghouse, and let me know. I would purchase the half acre of coal from David Baer. In taking deed for it, however, see that it states that we have right to remove all the coal, without liability for his house or anything therein." Ramsay acted promptly and a week later Frick wrote: "John Fox asks certainly too much money for his land. I would leave him keep it." At the same time another case indicated that as well as a right price and persuasiveness, secrecy too could be an important factor in dealing with local landowners. "It might be well for you to find John Warden, and get from him the very best proposition you can for his father's coal. A long time and low rate of interest would be important, but you must do this all very quietly, as I should not like that we should be used to assist him in making sale to some body else; that is if any one else thought we are figuring in earnest for the property, they might go right in and buy."[50]

Waste was a prime characteristic of the coke industry, much of it on an appallingly large scale. There was first the loss of coal as a result of inefficiency in mining, a feature characteristic of an age that judged success by short-term balance sheets rather than by taking into account long-term costs of destruction of irreplaceable fossil fuels. In the mid-1880s, in his wholesale attack on the state of the industry, Koerner reckoned that from 30 to 40 percent of coal was left behind as pillars in the workings. Responding, Fulton argued that with panel-plan mining, involving the eventual withdrawal of the pillars, as little as 5–10 percent of the coal remained unworked. But such a high rate of extraction was exceptional, and as late as the eve of World War I it was admitted that as much as 14 percent of the coal was normally left behind in the mine.[51] In oven practice, waste of all the products except coke resulted in an industrial landscape marked above all by smoke and the universal dirtiness it caused. Gas and "noxious fumes" were unavoidable constituents of the great clouds of pollutants that poured from the ovens and rolled uncheckable over the Coke Region. The problem was made worse by the tremendous concentration of capacity in a relatively small area—by the 1890s the Mt. Pleasant Branch of the Baltimore and Ohio Railroad passed an almost continuous row of ovens, "one block beginning where the last ends."[52] To some extent the smoke nuisance was exacerbated by the distinctive American drive to maximize production. As a member of the Pease family of coke makers from Durham, England, once explained to a commission of inquiry there, it was common in Connellsville to draw the coke more quickly than in their own practice. This "green" state meant more volatiles were left in the coke, and it was this that caused the thick black smoke when the coke was drawn.[53]

Naturally, these conditions appalled conservationists and waste-conscious scientists alike. In 1910, President Charles Richard van Hise of the University of Wisconsin, a geologist who had become concerned with conservation and social issues, drew the attention of his readers to this aspect of local mining and coke making: "I do not know how many of you have traveled through the Connellsville coal region. If you have done so and have happened to look out of the window of the train, you have seen long rows of beehive ovens from which flame is bursting and dense clouds of smoke issuing, making the sky dark. By night the scene is rendered indescribably vivid by these numerous burning pits. The beehive ovens make the entire region of coke manufacture one of dulled sky, cheerless and unhealthful."[54] He described the general environmental and human consequences of waste; others spelled out some of the details. A 1911 editorial in *The Coal and Coke Operator* drew attention to the effects of gases on vegetation, houses, and stores, "to say nothing of the extra labor entailed to women and others by the smudge and smoke emitted." The article mentioned that it had been shown in Saxony that the sulfurous gases rather than the smoke emitted had damaged trees and other vegetation; "the defilement and defacement that is caused to the landscape and towns by the solid particles in the smoke are equally a reproach, as testifying to our uneconomic methods of manufacture." The present situation was particularly insupportable because better methods of coking would bring commercial gain to the producer as well as environmental benefit to the whole community. Others emphasized this material loss to the industry. As early as 1891 a paper to the Franklin Institute had pointed out: In the Coke Region "every one of the brilliant fires bears witness that we are wasting the richness of our land in order to pay the wiser European coke manufacturer, who saves his ammonia and sends it to us in the form of sulfate of ammonia; and who also saves his tar, which, after passing through the complex processes of modern organic chemistry, reaches our shores in the form of aniline dyes, saccharin, nitrobenzol etc."[55]

Not only was the public generally unaware or undisturbed by this loss, but even some of those engaged in the coke industry had no real idea of its magnitude. Twenty years after the Franklin Institute paper, a company manager from Bulger in the new coal areas of Washington County illustrated this in striking fashion at a meeting of the Engineers' Society of Western Pennsylvania: "Three or four years ago while travelling with the chief engineer of the H. C. Frick Coke Company, I made the statement that in every 24 hours 35,000 tons of volatile matters was being discharged into the atmosphere by the coke ovens in the Connellsville coke region. He laughed at the statement and said it was ridiculous; that the quantity was far less than that. He figured it, and told me when he had finished that my statement was wrong; that I should have made it 40,000 instead of 35,000."[56] When Theodore Roosevelt called the state governors, other interested parties, and experts to a conference on conservation in the White House in spring 1908, the opening address on ores and related minerals was direct in its description of the wastefulness of coke manufacture and radical in suggesting solutions: "Much of our coke-making is still extravagant; some ovens use the gases, and all should do so without delay—if necessary under State regulation, since the people have some rights both in the preservation of their heritage and in maintaining the purity of the air they breathe." The White House audience applauded, but it is not known what reaction Connellsville coke makers generally, or old colleagues in particular, made to this keynote speech, delivered by Andrew Carnegie. Another speaker suggested that words used nearly fifty years before by the London *Times* in commenting on United States expenditures in the early stages of the Civil War were also appropriate to the issues they were discussing: "What strength, what resources, what vitality, what energy there must be in a nation that is able to ruin itself on a scale so transcendent and magnificent."[57]

The known spatial limits to the prime resource of Connellsville coking coal and waste in its mining and coking directed attention to the long-term availability of coal to produce a given level of coke and of income. This brought up the question of its life expectancy as an important mineral district. As output increased this would inevitably be shortened, though the operators long consoled themselves with the thought that what coal remained would increase in value. In 1884 Fulton estimated that current levels of production exhausted a square mile of coal land every year. Given his very generous figure of the area of the field, two hundred square miles, this would wholly exhaust it in two hundred years. Four years later the *Connellsville Courier* presented a much shorter timescale—exhaustion in forty years.[58] An official 1891 assessment was that not much less than one-third of the area of coking coal in the "Blairsville trough," defined as extending some forty-two miles southward from just below Latrobe, had already been worked out. Output in 1900 was three times as high as when Fulton had made his 1884 projection, and demand was rising rapidly. The following year, in evidence to the Industrial Commission, Schwab suggested that if national steel consumption went up in the future as in the past, Connellsville would be exhausted in thirty years, a timespan roughly coinciding with that projected by the *Courier* a decade before, though at a time of very different levels of production.[59] A few years later maps of operations in the older parts of the Coke Region already indicated large areas of worked-out coal, but by this time Lower Connellsville coke had been accepted and the resources of that region added to the longevity expected of Connellsville "proper." There remained considerable variation in the projections being made. By the middle of the first decade of the new century, some estimates put the area of unmined coal in the older field at from 30,000 to 40,000 acres and in Lower Connellsville from 40,000 to 50,000; others reckoned on 40,000 in each. On the basis of these figures and at current rates of working, both fields would be exhausted in twenty-five years or less. The Latrobe, or Upper Connellsville, and the Greensburg basins would scarcely last as long as the other two. Some disagreed with the opinion that there was any doubt about the extent of the coal remaining. J. W. Boileau of Pittsburgh went so far as to assert: "The old region has been so thoroughly covered by mines that the physical properties and characteristics of the coal bed are definitely known, and every acre of coal can be accounted for." By 1912 his own projections and those of another authority of the working life ahead—in Fayette County alone—ranged from fourteen to sixteen years for the older field. For Lower Connellsville there was a rather longer range of possibilities, from twenty to thirty-one years. Even in the latter area, according to Boileau's calculations 58 of the 88 coke oven plants existing in summer 1914 would have exhausted their coal in 20 years. H. C. Frick Coke would manage rather better than independent operators, having a life expectancy of 14 years in the older region to their 10; in Lower Connellsville the respective figures were 31 and 18.[60] Increase in output—such as was called for over the next few years because of war-stimulated activity—would naturally shorten these perspectives.

Some saw still wider implications from the expected demise of the Connellsville

An early company town, or "coal patch." *Courtesy of Pennsylvania State University, Fayette, Coal and Coke Heritage Center*

Union-organizing parade with "coal patch" in the background. *Courtesy of Pennsylvania State University, Fayette, Coal and Coke Heritage Center*

coke industry. Though most were perhaps unconscious of the predictions that had been made seventy years before, there now threatened a reversal of the processes of spiraling economic growth throughout western Pennsylvania based on the area's superb mineral endowment. The 1908 Conference of Governors was told of the manufacturing eminence of Allegheny County, but it was suggested that, "If the wasteful methods of the past are to continue; if the flames of 35,000 coke ovens are to continue to make the sky lurid within sight of the city of Pittsburgh, consuming with frightful speed a third of the power and half of the values locked up in her priceless supplies of coking coal, the present century will see the termination of this supremacy."[61] The speaker who mooted this possibility was by no means a disinterested party, for he was the state geologist of West Virginia. However, apart from the expected gain for other beehive coke regions, he had failed to recognize that a technological revolution was already far advanced in coke manufacture. Decline in the Connellsville region would still be contemplated with concern by various interests, from companies and workers to innumerable ancillary and general service occupations, but from the perspective of the manufacturing situation of Pittsburgh and the long-term health of the iron and steel industry, the further advance of the byproduct oven offered an escape from the consequences of decades of frightful waste of an incomparable natural resource. Some realized the possibility that industrial America could survive and even thrive without Connellsville coke.

7 Peak and Decline

The Climax of the Old and the Triumph of the New Coking Processes, 1914–1919

In the last days of 1914, sixty-year-old Thomas Lynch, president of the H. C. Frick Coke Company, the United States Coal and Coke Company, and director of the United States Steel Corporation, died. Almost exactly five years later, his long-time chief and mentor, Henry Clay Frick, also passed on. The short period between their deaths was marked by a dramatic transition in the beehive industry, from the status of the dominant to that of a dwindling and secondary source of supply for the nation's steel industry. In 1914 beehive ovens produced 67 percent of the nation's coke; 1919 national coke production was 9.6 million net tons greater than in 1914, but the share of beehives was only 43 percent. Between those two years, beehive coke output fell 4.3 million tons, while production of byproduct coke increased by almost 14 million tons, or well in excess of 100 percent.

Although 1914 was a year of depression in iron and steel, the proponents of the new coking technology were still busily arguing for its superiority. In May William Blauvelt of Semet Solvay and Carl Meissner, chairman of the U.S. Steel Coke Committee, spoke at the New York meeting of the American Iron and Steel Institute about recent progress in byproduct ovens. Blauvelt emphasized their advantages in cost savings from recovering byproducts and of a higher coal-to-coke yield. In 1912 the average combined value of coke and byproducts produced per oven had been $1,019 for beehive and $11,265 for byproduct ovens. The value of byproducts recovered in the coke industry was $16 million; if they had been recovered from the coal used in beehive ovens as well as from that processed by other ovens, the total value would have amounted to $80 million. The average coal-to-coke yield in beehives was 64.7 percent, from byproduct ovens 75.3 percent.

Early byproduct ovens at Dunbar, *circa* 1905. *From* Surface Arrangements at Bituminous Mines

Blauvelt hammered home the conclusions after careful consideration of these figures: "If this difference had been added to the production of beehive coke, it would have added to the wealth of the country 5,390,000 tons of coke if the same coals had been coked in byproduct ovens, in addition to the above value of the byproducts. This loss is equivalent to the absolute destruction of about 6,800,000 tons of our coal supply during the year." He also summarized the transformation of the byproduct coke industry over the twenty years it had operated in the United States. At the beginning average oven capacity was 4.4 tons a day, and a crew of men handled twenty-five ovens; daily capacity in the most recently built ovens was 20 tons, and mechanical progress meant the same-sized crew could handle fifty or sixty ovens. Before, 110 tons had been dealt with daily; as much as 1,000 or even 1,200 tons was handled now.[1]

By World War I, designers, builders, and operators of byproduct ovens in the United States were claiming the same sort of leadership in the industry worldwide as they had gained at an earlier date in other major manufacturing sectors. As long ago as 1902, Atwater, reviewing progress in the main industrial countries, had anticipated this would happen. At that time the proportion of United States coke made in byproduct ovens had been only just over one-eighth that in Germany: "In the early stages of the industry the ovens adopted were direct copies of those which had proved successful abroad. This was, of course, the natural thing to do in the transplanting of so expensive a process. As the industry developed it began to receive individuality from its new environment, and developed on lines somewhat different from those followed in its place of origin. As has been with the blast-furnace, the rolling-mill, the Bessemer converter, and the open-hearth furnace, so it has been with the by-product coke oven."[2] A decade later Blauvelt believed this technical superiority had now been won: "As might be expected, America now leads Europe in output of plant, size of oven and rate of coking. . . . [Because of the] introduction of more machinery and more efficient design the number of ovens handled per man is also increased greatly. The rate of coking is one point in which American practice has gone ahead of Europe."[3] In fact, it was during World War I, at a time of larger than ever expansion of capacity and progress in other directions, that American supremacy was firmly established. Ovens were not only commonly bigger than those in Europe, but the use of silica-brick linings—made from the quartzite of the Medina and Oneida formations in Huntingdon and Blair Counties, Pennsylvania—permitted higher oven temperatures and thereby shortened coking times. As compared with twenty-four hours or more in Europe, the best American practice now had coking times of only about sixteen-and-a-half hours.[4] Again, as it was so often over previous years, it was Blauvelt who summed up the advances, putting the situation in its wider context:

The superiority of American by-product ovens over those of Europe, from the view point of metallurgical practice, is due to the larger units and larger output per unit, the more extensive use of labor-saving machinery, and the use of silica refractory material which permits of higher heats and shorter coking time. The modern oven will carbonize more than 20 tons per day. In order to meet the requirements for a metallurgical fuel, it is agreed that the coke must be hard, must be resistant to attrition and oxidation, must have an open-cell structure, that is cells of good size and approximately 50 percent of cell space, and must be highly combustible. The by-product oven, with its variable mixtures of coal, variable heats, coking time, width of oven, fineness of coal charged, and other controlling factors, not only permits such a control of coke but also allows the use of many coals which would not be suitable with the beehive oven. As the best coals are being progressively exhausted, this latter point becomes more important.[5]

In the light of the circumstances that Blauvelt continued to emphasize, one could expect that byproduct ovens would make continuing, even accelerating, gains at the expense of beehives. Spurred by war-inflated demand for steel, there occurred a veritable explosion in the plant installed, the so-called "practical" capacity of byproduct

Table 7.1 Output of beehive and byproduct coke in peak pig iron production years, 1907–1920 *(net tons in thousands)*

Year	Beehive	Byproduct
1907	35,172	5,608
1913	33,585	12,715
1916	35,464	19,069
1918	30,481	25,998
1920	20,511	30,834

SOURCE: Based on U.S. Department of the Interior, *Minerals Yearbook* (Washington, D.C.: GPO) for each year.

ovens increasing from 15.7 million tons in 1914 to 34.4 million five years later. During the same period and throughout the nation, 10,500 beehives, or 12.1 percent of the total, went out of existence, and the "practical" capacity of this section of the industry fell from 46.9 to 41.2 million tons. In the Connellsville fields the shrinkage was smaller.

During the war beehive ovens were unable to meet the increase in demand, partly because of a lack of suitable first-rate coal and partly because their overall costs were increasingly less competitive with those of the byproduct industry. Only in 1915 did national output of beehive coke exceed that of 1910. For the Connellsville region, 1912 and 1913 were successive record years, but 1916 output far exceeded that of any preceding year.

In short, high activity in the national economy through large-scale extension in the iron and steel industry called forth not only a major extension of coke-making capacity but also accelerated the wholesale shift from one mode of production to another. National effective blast-furnace capacity increased by 5.5 million tons, or almost 11 percent, during these years. Also relevant to the changing relative attractiveness of the two coking processes was the greatly increased extension in steel capacity, from 44.4 million net tons of steel at the end of 1914 to 60.2 million five years later. Most of this expansion was in open-hearth furnaces and therefore created an increased demand for gas, tar, and other furnace fuel. As a supplier of these, the byproduct oven looked increasingly attractive at a time of sharply rising fuel costs. At the end of the war, Blauvelt pointed out that the gas surplus to that required for heating the ovens themselves, as well as the tar obtained from production of a ton of coke, would together furnish the necessary energy to produce a ton of ingots from an open-hearth furnace, or 10–15 percent more iron from a blast furnace than when heated with producer gas.[6] A final, major factor tilting the balance of advantage

Table 7.2 Beehive coke works and ovens, Connellsville and Lower Connellsville districts, 1914 and 1919

	Connellsville		Lower Connellsville	
Year	Works	Ovens	Works	Ovens
1914 (May)	91	20,690	88	17,341
1919 (November–December)	69	18,891	83	17,087

SOURCES: *Connellsville Weekly Courier*, May 1914, 18 December 1919.

against the beehive was the increase in value of the other byproducts of coking, some of which had been of negligible importance during peacetime.

Gas, tar, and sulfate of ammonia, all became more important as the war-stimulated economy expanded, took certain new directions, and in some instances replaced formerly imported supplies, now unobtainable. In the case of sulfate of ammonia, for example, 1914 imports at 89,158 net tons had amounted to almost one-third of consumption. Yet at that time, the possible amount recoverable from the coal then being made into coke in the United States was not far short of three times the national demand. By 1918 home production had more than doubled.[7] Even more dramatic changes occurred with two previously less well-known chemicals, benzol and toluol. In 1913 only one of the many coke-making firms recovered these two products. As hostilities cut off imports of coal-tar chemicals from Germany, the traditional source of supply, benzol, used in making the high explosive picric acid, doubled in price almost overnight. Toluol, base material for the manufacture of TNT, sold in 1913 for $0.29 a gallon; by 1916 it averaged $2.85. (Over the same three years the average value of byproduct coke went up only from $3.83 to $3.95 a ton.) Together with the greatly increased demand for coke, the changes in the importance of byproducts brought about the extension of existing plants and the building of new ones. Long a laggard, U.S. Steel now made important headway. In June 1917 its finance committee voted $2.9 million to build benzol and toluol plants at its coke ovens at Lorain, Cleveland (AS&W), and the new Duluth works.[8] In 1913 throughout the nation, beehive ovens had made more than twice as much coke as byproduct ovens; in 1917 their shares were 60 percent and 40 percent respectively; on 2 November 1918, byproduct ovens for the first time produced over half the total coke tonnage in the United States.[9]

It was during this period that the Koppers oven established its lead in the industry. Heinrich Koppers had been invited to the United States after U.S. Steel engineers visited Germany in 1906. In 1910 the twenty-three-year-old Joseph Becker was sent out by their Essen headquarters to take charge of the laboratories in Joliet. In the latter part of 1914, Koppers sold the American patents of his oven and a controlling

Table 7.3 Byproduct ovens at major iron and steel centers, 1914 and 1920

Location	1914	1920
East and central Pennsylvania and Maryland	988	1,686
Lake Erie and Detroit	237	1,552
Chicago	991	1,651
Valleys	212	745
Pittsburgh and upper Ohio	120	1,288
Alabama	400	1,081
All byproduct ovens	5,809	10,881

SOURCE: Based on U.S. Department of the Interior, *Minerals Yearbook* (Washington, D.C.: GPO) for these years.

interest in that branch of his company to Andrew Mellon for a sum alleged to have been as little as $300,000. The headquarters were moved from Joliet to Pittsburgh. When the United States entered the war, remaining German interests in the company were taken over by the Alien Property Custodian and eventually passed from this organization to American investors. Meanwhile, Becker and his team of workers became deeply involved in a huge expansion program. During the war years, under his overall direction of design and construction, Koppers installed 3,378 ovens—a number equal to 59 percent of all those existing in the United States at the end of 1913—at twenty-two different plants. By the end of 1918, Koppers ovens made up 52 percent of all those in existence; at the end of 1920, when the programs begun in the war were nearing completion, their share reached 55 percent. Within twenty years the Koppers Company was worth $130 million.[10]

Another result of World War I expansion was a major shift in the geographical distribution of coke-oven capacity. There were major developments on the shores of the Great Lakes, coke plants at Indiana Harbor, Dearborn, and the McKinney works in Cleveland being constituents of completely new iron and steel complexes. Until 1922 the South Chicago works of USS continued to use some beehive coke, but the Chicago area was no longer dependent on long hauls of coke from Pennsylvania but on rail or combined rail and water shipments of coal to be locally carbonized in byproduct ovens. This was accompanied by a shift in the source regions for coking coal. By the year the United States entered the war, West Virginia and to a lesser degree Kentucky had supplanted Pennsylvania as suppliers of fuel for Chicago furnaces.

The Fairfield ovens were part of the new works that the Steel Corporation built to supplement the older iron and steel works at Ensley. Most dramatic of all, in this short period byproduct ovens for the first time made big inroads into the area more

Table 7.4 Source of coal used in Illinois and Indiana byproduct ovens, 1917

State	Coal (th. tons)
Illinois	434
Indiana	448
Kentucky	1,765
Pennsylvania	431
Virginia	91
West Virginia	4,878
All coal	8,050

SOURCE: Based on *Non Metals*, part 2 of *Mineral Resources of the United States* (Washington, D.C.: GPO, 1917).

immediately tributary to the Connellsville Coke Region—Pittsburgh, the Valleys, and the Upper Ohio Valley. In 1914 these areas contained under 6 percent of the byproduct ovens in America; by 1920 they had nearly 19 percent. Although already declining in relative standing within the nation's steel industry, large wartime extensions, mainly open hearth, were made to many of the plants in this section of the industrial belt. At the same time the main areas of natural gas production were shifting away from the northern Appalachians. (Between 1908 and 1924 Pennsylvania's proportion of the value of U.S. natural gas production fell from 35 percent to 20 percent.)

The model for Jones and Laughlin's development lay in their huge Hazelwood beehive plant. By 1920 the Koppers ovens they installed there at the end of the war were capable of coking 5,000 tons of coal daily. Six years later they built their first byproduct battery at Aliquippa. Crucible Steel added a smaller battery to the integrated works it had begun to build at Midland in 1911. These projects—indeed all coke plants built to this time—were dwarfed by U.S. Steel's first installation in the area. In 1914 subsidiary companies of USS made 7.1 million tons of beehive coke and 4.1 million tons of byproduct coke. Already the corporation had acquired large tracts of coal lands west of the Monongahela; during the war years it added more. In summer 1914 Frick emphasized to Gary how impressed he was with prospects for Greene County coal; he recommended they should buy 50,000 acres of it. Four years later he urged Gary to buy 60,000 acres from J. V. K. Thompson, a tract Frick reckoned contained the only unsold coking coal in that county. The price was $500 an acre, or about 50 cents a ton. This coal was highly attractive in other respects as well: "A compact body of that size averaging 8 feet in thickness, situate on the Monongahela River, thereby saving over 40 cents per ton in transportation charges alone to our works on the river, is something that cannot be duplicated in all the world." Gary was persuaded by such an enthusiastic endorsement.[11] In this way and at this critical time the man who more than any other had personified the power of the beehive coke trade helped lay the firmest of foundations for Pittsburgh area water-based transport of coal and the expansion of byproduct coking, which proved that the days of the Connellsville Coke Region were ending.

In mid-October 1915 the U.S. Steel Finance Committee resolved to build a 200-oven byproduct plant north of its Clairton iron and steel works. The site was large, though, given local relief conditions, it was inevitably elongated along the Monongahela (the dimensions were 5,200 by 1,800 feet). Spending was approved for river craft to deliver coal to this plant from USS mines mostly tributary to the sixth pool.[12] Gradually, the project grew in size, causing the abandonment of some other expansion schemes. Three months after the initial Clairton plan, the finance committee approved expenditure of $3.15 million for a 210-oven plant at Carnegie Steel's Ohio works, Youngstown, and $2.36 million for 150 ovens at Newcastle in the Shenango Valley.[13] Almost immediately plans for Clairton were revised upward to provide for 640 ovens. The committee approved $850,000 for a pipeline to carry surplus gas from the ovens to Homestead, Edgar Thomson, and Duquesne steel works. By summer 1917 the estimated cost at Clairton had doubled to $25 million. That autumn, three towboats and a fleet of coal barges were almost ready for use. More funds were authorized to provide for napthalene recovery and concentrated ammonia plants. In view of the size of these outlays—at a time when major extensions were being made in many other departments of USS business—it was decided to "lay on the table" the Youngstown and Newcastle projects. Initially, this was only a deferment, but in

Table 7.5 Annual changes in total coke production and that by the beehive and byproduct processes, 1913–1920

Year	Total coke production	Beehive output	Byproduct output
1913	+5.3	+2.2	+14.4
1914	−25.4	−30.5	−11.8
1915	+20.3	+17.9	+25.4
1916	+33.1	+28.9	+35.5
1917	+2.0	−6.5	+17.7
1918	+1.6	−8.1	+15.9
1919	−21.8	−37.5	−3.3
1920	+16.2	+7.7	+22.7

SOURCE: Based on *Minerals Yearbook* (Washington, D.C.: GPO) for these years.
NOTE: Output as percentage of that of the previous year.

A battery of the Clairton coke works, *circa* 1930. *Courtesy of U.S. Steel Corporation Archives*

spring 1918 the finance committee resolved not to recommend the building of ovens at the two works unless government contracts were secured for sale of toluol on a basis that would result in a net total cost of not more than $20,000 for each of the planned 400 ovens. A few weeks later the federal government decided not to make any further such contracts for the time being, resulting in abandonment of the projects.[14] The implications of the Clairton venture for the Coke Region were serious. Planned coke output from the whole 640-oven installation was 2.74 million net tons, equal to the produce of something like 4,650 beehive ovens, one-quarter of all the ovens controlled by H. C. Frick Coke in Connellsville and Lower Connellsville in 1914.

The first Clairton battery was at work in 1918. By the following year it was using 12,500 tons of high volatile (33–35 percent) coal a day, hauled on average forty-seven miles from the mine by a fleet of 120 barges powered by seven towboats. Nine miles of forty-inch-diameter gas mains had been laid to the local steel works.[15] Already, the corporation planned to double the initial plant, and by 1923–24 Clairton contained 1,134 ovens in eighteen batteries. By 1928 there were 1,482 ovens, representing a coke capacity some 40 percent as large as that of the whole Connellsville region at its peak just before the war.[16]

Until World War I the beehive coke industry had still been making changes in hopes of staving off its challenger. A summary of innovations made in it during the early stages of the war has about it the ring of a half-despairing stop-gap measure, a brave but hopeless attempt to stem a tide by tinkering with details. In the words of one account: "Improvements in United States beehive coke ovens are outlined, including the McMurray door, the Stauft coke extractor and Campbell's plastic clay for filling and daubing coke-oven doors." As the war ended, one patentee even went so far as to claim an ability to transform the older technology into the new, making beehives convertible into ovens from which all byproducts could be collected, adding, "The plant does not need to be dismantled or destroyed."[17] All such efforts were vain. Within U.S. Steel in the good year of 1915, byproduct coke production was only 55 percent as large as the output from beehive ovens; 1919 was a year of recession, but USS overall coke tonnage was considerably larger than four years earlier. Its byproduct ovens now made almost 61 percent more coke than its beehives. Nationally, too, there had been a dramatic change. In periods of general expansion, the byproduct oven produced proportionately more coke than beehives; when there was a slight fall back, it either continued its advance or declined much less than the older ovens. Both the old technology, and Connellsville as its chief exponent, were becoming marginal. Soon they would be in wholesale decline.

New Patterns of Coal Transportation and Coking

In the mid-twentieth century, the Lake Superior ore trade was transformed by a technical change that made it practicable to work "taconite," the low metal-content country rock from which the high-grade ores of the iron ranges of that district had been derived. As a result the dominance of flows of ore to the blast furnaces in the lower Lakes region by unprocessed "direct shipping" ores was replaced by that of high iron content "pellets" produced in the mineral district by large capital-intensive installations. More than a quarter century earlier, the triumph of the byproduct coke oven had brought about even more radical, but in some ways reverse, changes in fuel supply. In this section of the vast iron, steel, and mineral complex, the processing plant, in the form of beehive ovens, had traditionally been located at the source of the mineral and the finished product, coke, was shipped. Now, economies to be derived from fully integrated iron and steel works, having the best overall heat balance and efficiency, meant that batteries of byproduct ovens were located at and functioned as integral parts of the iron and steel making and rolling-mill complex and unprocessed coal, not coke, was transported. In short, the changes in coking practice resulting from the introduction of the byproduct oven were accompanied by new locations for the production of both coal and coke and, consequently, new geographies of the industry's movement of energy.

New sources of coal were now acceptable because the large capacity and blending facilities of the byproduct plants, as well as their more adaptable technology, made it practicable for the first time to make excellent blast-furnace fuel from coals that previously had not been regarded as capable of producing metallurgical-grade coke. Even now (as considered earlier), the changes in coking did not yet make it possible to use, for instance, large tonnages of Illinois coal in the byproduct ovens that were constructed at Chicago-area iron and steel plants. But the fact that there were lower rail charges on coal than on coke meant it was generally commercially attractive to move the raw material even over long distances rather than the finished product, the former being heavier but less bulky than the latter. Given the geographical build of the northeastern industrial region of the United States, most of the coal traffic, like that of coke, was moved by the railroads from mine to coke-oven stockyards, but conditions of mineral movements to the Upper Lakes, including at least some of those to Chicago, modified this somewhat. The possibility of shipping coal for part of its journey by water, as in the southward flow of iron ore—and indeed often using the holds of ore boats returning to Upper Lake ports—meant that combined rail/water movement occurred. The sometimes keen competition for business between railroads in the wide area between the Appalachian Plateau and the Lake Erie shore, in fact, brought about a wide variety of patterns of movement.[18] In marked contrast with this wider picture, for the metallurgical centers of the Ohio Valley, above all in its upper parts, there was a wholesale transfer of the movement of fuel for the blast furnace from rail to water.

Though it was only fully developed in the era of byproduct coking, water transfer had a long history in this region. It may be divided into three phases: the movement of coke from coalfield beehive ovens, transfer of coal to beehive ovens located at the ironworks, and coal shipments to feed byproduct ovens. At each stage, water carriage offered lower haulage costs. In the first phase, the wish to avoid damage to coke as well as the greater speed and convenience of direct movement by rail brought an end to water movement. In the second, there was a gradual recognition of still greater possible economies, which brought about the establishment and, very quickly after that, a predominant third phase. The full development of the old basin had depended on the construction of a network of railroads. In the opening of Lower Connellsville too, rail access played a central role, involving not only a mesh of lines over the coalfield but also main lines along its western edge following the Monongahela. Soon afterward, barge movements down that river became of major impor-

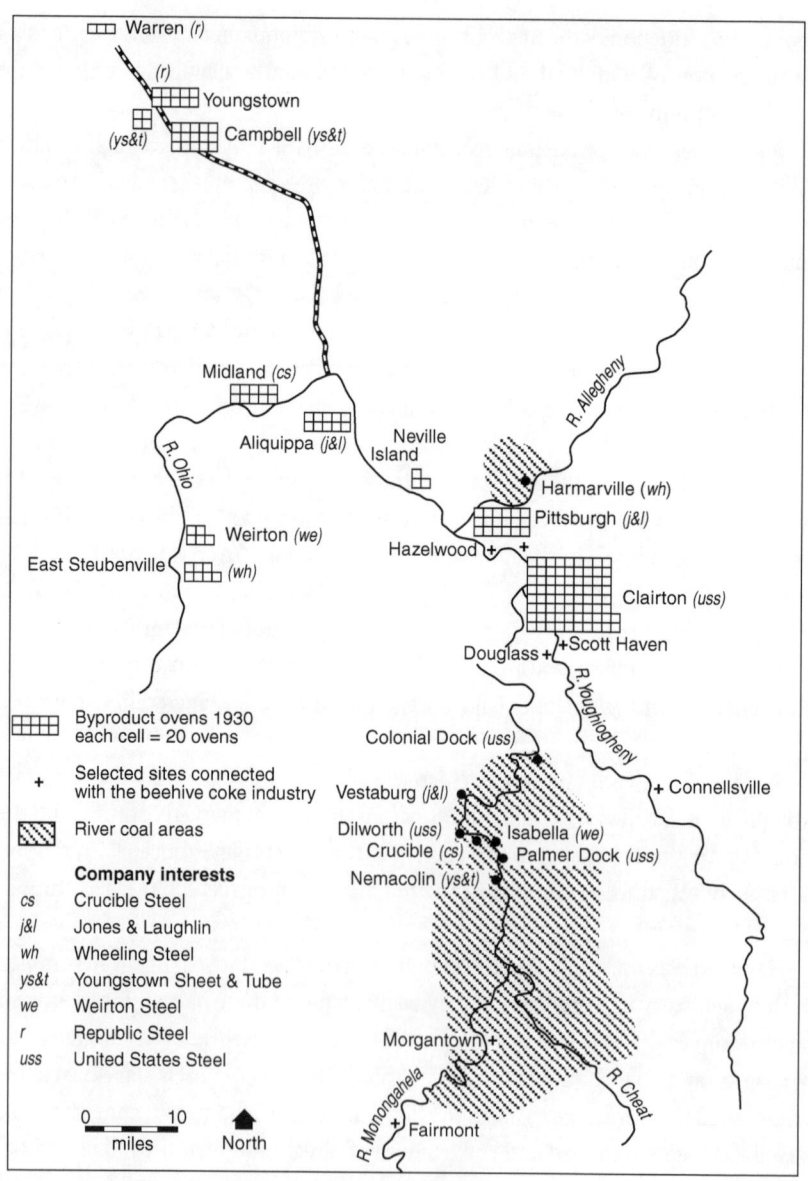

The new pattern—river coal and byproduct coking.

tance as well. This flow would be dominated by coal, not coke. In this way the changing geography of coal output, innovations in modes and routes for movement, and a new technology of coke production were closely interrelated.

The seam of coking coal found in the Connellsville basin and in slightly modified form in Lower Connellsville continued, uninterrupted, dipping westward below the Monongahela into Greene County and the southern parts of Washington County. By the early twentieth century it had been recognized that, at least on the eastern edges of these two counties, their coal was of coking quality. As Boileau put it in 1907: "All that is needed to make Greene County coal into the best of coke is intelligent application and consideration of the coal being dealt with."[19] In fact, there were three additional requirements; acceptance, capital, and improved physical access. Gradually, producers realized that forthcoming changes in the relationship between mushrooming demand from the iron works and the ability of existing coking coal areas to satisfy that demand would provide an increasingly strong spur for development of the areas west of the Monongahela. Early in 1907 the *Connellsville Courier* acknowledged that almost all the coal land in the Connellsville and Lower Connellsville fields had been taken up and at present rates would be worked out in twenty-five years or less. The smaller Upper Connellsville and Greensburg fields would scarcely last as long. On the other hand, Greene County contained a vast reserve of coking coal stretching westward almost as far as Wheeling.[20] Five years later, and after iron production had reached new high levels, another authority gave the old basin an average expectation of life of twelve to fifteen years. The implications were daunting, involving by the end of that time the loss of some 24,000 ovens, "leaving about 16,000 ovens and about 40,000 acres of coal in the Klondike region to supply the demand which increases at an annual rate of 1,510,000 tons of coke in markets tributary to the Pittsburgh district." In order to replace that capacity during the next twelve years, one observer wrote, "there must be developed a productive yearly tonnage of 20,000,000 tons of coking coal, or, making allowance for increasing consumption, perhaps twice as much as that. It might also require the building of 6,000 new beehives or 4,000 rectangular ovens *each year.*"[21] These were wildly dramatic figures, but the course of real events was disturbing enough. For example, during 1912 only 166 new ovens were built in the old basin, while 1,528 ovens were torn down. Additionally, three small coke-making establishments, having 298 ovens, were abandoned.[22]

In Lower Connellsville, although exploitation had begun so recently, production had been on such a rapidly mounting scale that by 1912 forecasts predicted that the coal there would be largely exhausted in about fifteen years. Boileau now put the expectation of a working life for the old basin at slightly over sixteen years and of Lower Connellsville at less than twenty. Looking beyond, one commentator expected that "the coke region will shift to the west in Greene and Washington counties and to the West Virginia district."[23] The prognosis of inevitable decline in the older coke regions proved to have been broadly correct, as was the direction from which replacement tonnages might come. The only mistake was to assume that the coalfields west of the Monongahela would become major coke districts. Instead, almost all the coking coal mined there was used in byproduct ovens. This meant new locations for coke making, distant from the coalfield, the link between made by major changes in transportation.

Not until after World War I was Washington County a coal producer on anything approaching the scale of Westmoreland and Fayette Counties; Greene County took even longer. Even so, the first important steps in their development had begun at the same time as the opening of Lower Connellsville. In autumn 1899 James W. Ellsworth bought 13,000 acres of coal land near Bentleyville, Washington County, with plans to market 6,000 tons of coal a day from the following year.[24] Development had not yet begun in Greene County. A decade later the acquisition of coal there was well underway, though production increased only slowly. One of the pioneers of the new district was the long-term speculator in coal lands Josiah Van Kirk Thompson. By 1907 his holdings in Greene County were mostly east of Waynesburg and well placed for access to the then-proposed Uniontown and Wheeling Short Line. Coal lands west of the Monongahela were relatively cheap, though there were marked variations from place to place as well as increases over time. Their wide range was shown in two of Thompson's 1909 transactions. Early that year he bought the coal under two farms on Muddy Creek, Jefferson Township, 301 acres in all, for $300 an acre. Four months later he sold 2,998 acres of coal land, said to be some of the best in the county, for $1,667.80 an acre.

Others too were busy building up their holdings. At the beginning of 1911, Thompson received $1.7 million from Andrew Mellon for 5,885 acres in Perry Township in southern Greene County. After this, Mellon controlled 15,000 acres in the county. Even so, Thompson far exceeded all others, by early 1914 possessing title to coal in seventeen of the county's eighteen townships, in all 120,000 acres worth on average probably $200 an acre.[25] He was in a position to sell to the big steel companies, which had now recognized the value of coal across the Monongahela. Though it was emphatically not to become a prominent feature, there had also been some growth of coke production in these western Pennsylvania counties.

The pioneer Ellsworth coal operation was acquired in the middle of the first decade of the century by Lackawanna Steel. As well as building byproduct ovens at both Lebanon and its new plant on Lake Erie, Lackawanna also erected a large number of beehives at or near Ellsworth. They produced excellent coke, low in ash, sulfur,

Table 7.6 Production of bituminous coal in southwestern Pennsylvania counties, 1900–1920 *(net tons in thousands)*

Year	Fayette	Westmoreland	Washington	Greene
1900	15,055	14,980	4,856	n.a.
1907	29,261	28,917	14,536	158
1913	32,608	33,259	18,309	317
1920	30,742	24,510	23,321	2,079

SOURCE: G. H. Ashley, *Bituminous Coalfields of Pennsylvania* (Harrisburg, 1928).

and phosphorus.[26] A little later, the Bessemer Coke Company, which had begun with interests in the old basin before building ovens in Lower Connellsville, sold its Martin works there to Republic Iron and Steel shortly after paying Thompson $800,000 for 1,105 acres of Greene County coal. This property was subsequently connected with the track of the Monongahela Division of the Pennsylvania Railroad. Bessemer built 100 ovens on Ten Mile Creek and a railroad down to Millsboro on the west bank of the river. Well to the north, in 1911 the H. C. Frick Coke Company was reported to be considering exploiting 3,200 acres of coal near Charleroi, sinking two shafts and building coke ovens at Dunlevy. By 1912 there were also developments up river into West Virginia. The Monongahela Railroad built an extension from Martin across the Monongahela and southward through the eastern fringe of Greene County and on to Rivesville in the Fairmont district of West Virginia. At Rivesville this track connected with the Buckhannon and Northern Railway. It opened a large coal tract. Near the mouth of Dunkard Creek, the Poland Coal and Coke Company began to construct what was anticipated to be a 400-oven coke works. As the commercial press hopefully reported about this project, "others will no doubt follow in rapid succession." By summer 1913 Reliance Coal and Coke Company was building what was said to be a 400-oven plant across the river from Brownsville at Denbo, Washington County.[27] In fact, these plants west of the river either did not materialize—as in the case of Frick Coke at Charleroi—or were smaller than first expected. There was no great influx of either existing or new coke makers such as had occurred a decade earlier in Lower Connellsville. Development of coal districts west of the Monongahela and further expansion of coking-coal production on either side of the river would be associated above all with coke making located elsewhere. This involved new technologies and new patterns of production. For these, there had long been precedents, however incomplete or shadowy.

Before the opening of the Pittsburgh and Connellsville Railroad in 1855, the very small tonnages of Connellsville coke had to be shipped down the unreliable Youghiogheny River. McCormick and his colleagues had carried their coke all the way to Cincinnati by water; slightly later, shipments through to the Ohio may have been carted downriver to the head of more reliable navigation before being loaded into boats. Thirty years later the possibilities inherent in their location on the main river highway to Pittsburgh were explored by the most imaginative iron and steel business in that city. In the 1870s the Carnegie interests looked for coke supplies to support their expanding iron capacity at the Lucy and Edgar Thomson furnaces. Early in March 1880 George Lauder and Tom Carnegie were taken by a Mr. Davidson to inspect his coal lands on the Cheat River, the main right bank tributary of the Monongahela. A few days later Tom wrote to his brother about costs of transport from there. By slackwater navigation on the Monongahela, he reckoned they could move coke for 15 cents plus another 5 cents for extra handling from the river, giving a total transport cost for the coke, delivered into the stockhouse at Edgar Thomson, of 20 cents as compared with 81.66 cents by rail. For their Lucy furnaces or markets down the Ohio River, the advantage over rail would be greater.[28] Although two years later the Carnegies linked their fortunes to those of Henry Clay Frick, in various guises the pattern of development they had briefly considered in 1880 gradually took shape. Other companies played an important part.

An important step was the establishment of coke capacity in Pittsburgh, even though it used coal from the established coking-coal fields. One example was the Carrie furnaces across river from Homestead works; indeed, in the late 1890s, it was absorbed by Carnegie Steel to supply Homestead with molten iron. Before this, the Carrie furnaces were controlled by the Fownes interests. At the beginning of 1890 the Carrie Furnace Company bought 600 acres of coal near Uniontown. It was expected to build about 225 ovens there to make its own coke but instead put up a smaller battery and located it near its blast furnaces. The Carrie ovens coked slack brought to them from mines along the Youghiogheny.[29] A much larger example of this pattern of development (considered more fully elsewhere) was the Jones and Laughlin construction of ovens at Hazelwood to coke coal shipped from their Vesta mines west of the Monongahela. Again, however, it was Carnegie Steel that gradually felt its way toward the pattern of supply that would dominate in the twentieth century.

In 1887 the Carnegies announced that they would build 150 ovens along the Pittsburgh, McKeesport, and Youghiogheny Railroad near Scott Haven on the Youghiogheny River. They would use slack and refuse from Scott's mines. For some reason there was a delay in going ahead, and when in 1891 their Youghiogheny coke works was built, it was located nearer to Douglass. By the end of the 1890s, annual capacity there was 100,000 tons coke, though even in the boom conditions of 1899 it was operating far below this level. Even so, its location seems to have inspired

Andrew Carnegie to envisage the next major stage of development, the placing of byproduct coke ovens near the area's iron and steel plants. In December 1897 he took the initiative in a letter to jog Frick's memory: "Any developments in by-product ovens? I sent you offer of a party in Sweden to build plant and take half of savings for a number of years, then we own it. Might let them try experiment on Liberty property. [Apparently Liberty southwest of and across the lower Youghiogheny from McKeesport.] We can get cheap coal by river now that it is free and I suppose that Patterson Cheat River coal would do—plenty of it. We would have no investment. I thought well of this.—How did it strike you?" Frick replied promptly. Although still writing rather slightingly about byproduct coke, he was open-minded in other respects: "Before we build any more ovens in Connellsville region, we should certainly consider question carefully whether it would not be well to build a plant on Liberty farm, in order to know exactly what can be done. Gas, of course, from ovens, could be utilized at Homestead."[30] It was to be almost twenty years before these patterns of coal supply, transport, and coking briefly outlined at that time were realized in a major installation built a few miles south from Liberty.

The opening and subsequent mushroom growth of Lower Connellsville reduced the urgency of this new framework of thinking for a few years. The time at which the old prescriptions for coal production, transport, and coking were clearly seen to be no longer valid can be roughly dated as 1909–1910. In 1908 U.S. Steel reportedly invited and began receiving bids for as many as ten new coke works in Lower Connellsville. Next year, Jones and Laughlin, though they had a major beehive installation inside the built-up area of Pittsburgh, contracted with the Thompson-Connellsville Coke Company for 30,000 tons of coke a month for three years and agreed to help finance the necessary expansion of its plant. Yet this was the year in which USS was believed to have taken the decision not to build any more beehives, except to round out existing works. In 1909 it purchased the River Coal Company and two years later the Pittsburgh Coal Company's large Colonial works, but the corporation decided not to go ahead with a number of proposed new oven plants. Its new Ralph mine was not provided with ovens, coal from there being sent instead to docks on the Monongahela from which it was barged to Pittsburgh.[31] Plans for a railroad across Greene County, begun and then abandoned by the Baltimore and Ohio in the 1880s, proposed again to run from the little town of Monongahela farther north across Washington and Greene Counties to Wheeling in 1895, were once more mooted during World War I as a means of cutting freight rates on coke and of opening vast new coking-coal reserves.[32] Once more the proposed line failed to materialize. In the middle of World War I, U.S. Steel took the major decision to build Clairton coke works. After that, the flow of coal from the mine to the Monongahela and thence by barge

Table 7.7 Production of leading Appalachian coking-coal counties, 1906 and 1920 *(tons in thousands)*

County	1906		1920	
	Coal production	Coal made into coke at mine	Coal production	Coal made into coke at mine
Pennsylvania				
Fayette	27,044	18,608	30,742	14,319
Westmoreland	27,537	9,006	24,510	5,872
Washington	12,714	189	23,321	1,345
Greene	n.a.	n.a.	2,079	83
West Virginia				
McDowell	8,708	2,528	16,819	869
Fayette	8,260	1,000	9,015	625
Virginia				
Wise	3,041	1,977	6,062	1,622

SOURCE: *Mineral Resources of the United States* (Washington, D.C.: GPO) for these years.

downriver to Pittsburgh gradually became a dominant feature in the economic geography of energy in western Pennsylvania. As well as Greene County operations, the Filbert and Gates mines were among others in Lower Connellsville that began to send coal to Palmer dock and on to the new, and soon rapidly expanding, byproduct plant. As this went on, other large iron and steel companies were also gaining a footing in the region and investing in smaller versions of the same sort of production-transport-consumption system.

Early in the century Selwyn M. Taylor had formed a coal and local railroad company to acquire and develop a 7,500-acre tract of Freeport coal near Harmarville along the Allegheny River twelve miles northeast from downtown Pittsburgh. In 1907 after Taylor's death, J. V. K. Thompson and J. P. Brennen acquired a majority interest. In 1918 the Wheeling Steel Corporation bought the mine and coal holdings and began sending coal in their own barges down the Allegheny and Ohio to byproduct ovens at East Steubenville.[33] This Wheeling development was exceptional, for far and away the main sources for coal were along the Monongahela. In the 1920s Youngstown Sheet and Tube Company gained control of the Lower Connellsville properties of the Brier Hill Coal Company. They electrified the mine but abandoned the coke ovens. Through the Buckeye Coal Company, they also owned mines at Nemacolin, west of the Monongahela, from which coal was shipped to be coked at Youngstown.[34] The new pattern became more firmly established during the course of the 1920s as byproduct plants were built at the Jones and Laughlin Pittsburgh works in 1919–1920, by Crucible Steel at Midland in 1920, and at the end of that decade by

J&L at Aliquippa. By 1923 coke traffic on the Monongahela was 385,000 tons, but movements of coal amounted to 18.7 million tons.[35] By this time there had been a marked change in relationship between coal and coke tonnages in the various counties of western Pennsylvania, and in some of those of neighboring states as well. It was noteworthy that only Westmoreland County, excluded from the great new river axis of transportation, had already suffered a fall in coal output.

Coke Production after 1920

The 1920s

During the Great Depression, the Brookings Institute published a far-reaching survey entitled *America's Capacity to Produce.* Systematically, it analyzed the immense resources on which the nation could call as well as the current near-prostration of some of them. The manufacture of coke was singled out for special comment: "The coke industry offers perhaps the best illustration of a mass of obsolescent capacity slowly being displaced by a newer and more efficient process."[36] This had largely occurred in the midst of the general prosperity of the 1920s, though the decline already so obvious was to be long and drawn out.

For many years existing coke plants had been able to supply far more coke than was required. Though a record year, 1910 capacity was still 45 percent in excess of consumption. Even during the war national coke capacity was 25 percent above the new and unprecedented peaks of demand. It was under such conditions that the byproduct oven now all but completed its replacement of the older process. Between 1915 and the end of the 1920s, the astounding total of 40 million tons of new byproduct capacity was built. By 1928, 85 percent of the byproduct capacity was in plant installed since August 1914. In the face of this onslaught, the beehive coke industry collapsed. Whereas over the 1920s the capacity of byproduct ovens increased by 50 percent, that of beehive ovens fell by almost two-thirds; vast expenditure on the former was accompanied by the wiping out of about $100 million invested in the older process. As early as the boom year of 1920, 2,421 beehives were abandoned throughout Pennsylvania; under the severely depressed conditions of the following year, 5,044 more went the same way. This rundown continued at an uneven pace from year to year. For example, 1927 was a fairly average year for the decade in both iron and coke production, but another 2,338 beehive ovens were abandoned in Pennsylvania, leaving at the year's end 32,135 in operation throughout the state. Apart from the fact that the business interests involved in the extension of the one process and the decline of the other were to a considerable extent separate, an economic rationale for this wholesale substitution was found in the fact that in 1929, byproducts recovered from the new-style ovens were equal to 19 million tons of coal and had a gross value

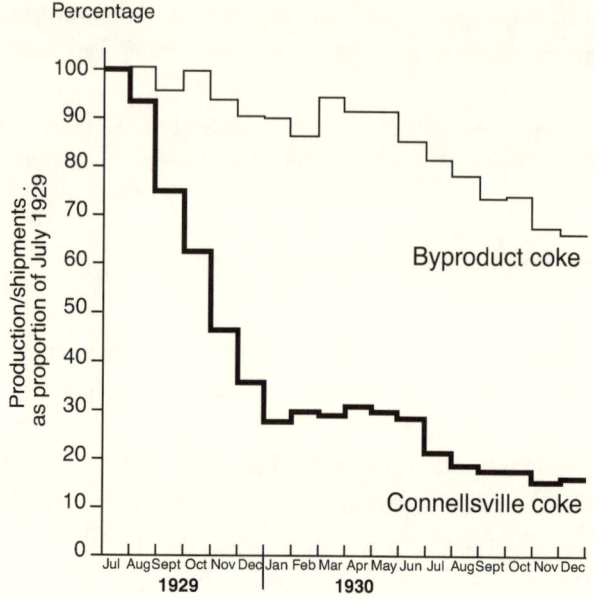

Indices of monthly output of byproduct coke and shipments of Connellsville coke, July 1929 to December 1930.

of $192 million.[37] During the same year pig iron shipments were far higher than ever before, and it was a very good year for the steel industry. Coke production was at an unprecedented 59.9 million tons, but whereas in 1920, an earlier good year, beehive coke made up 39.9 percent of production; in 1929 its share was 10.8 percent, and despite the high activity in industry, 44 percent of the beehives were idle compared with only 0.8 percent of byproduct capacity.[38] But as had been anticipated in the experience of 1921, the shrinkage of the older technology in prosperous years was less impressive than its near collapse in times of adversity. Iron shipments in 1930 were 13 million tons below the previous year's figures. Output of byproduct coke fell 15.4 percent, while beehive tonnage was down 57.1 percent. In short, under the new conditions, not only was there a collapse of the older technology, but it was more apparent than before that it had become a marginal capacity, laid off in times of depressed trade only to be partially reactivated at times of peak demand. Once built, byproduct ovens were cheaper to use than beehives: labor costs were less and, in relation to value of products, consumption of coal was much lower. The latter situation was well illustrated by some figures brought out some years later by a new federal agency.

The marginality of beehive coke was now explicitly recognized. In a 1924 text, *Coal Carbonization,* Horace Porter devoted over two hundred pages to byproduct technology and merely four-and-a-half pages to "Primitive methods of coal car-

Table 7.8 Capacity and output of the beehive and byproduct coke industries, 1910–1930
(net tons in thousands)

Year	Capacity of all ovens		Rated capacity of operating plants		Practical capacity of working ovens		Output of working ovens	
	beehive	byproduct	beehive	byproduct	beehive	byproduct	beehive	byproduct
1910	59,100	8,600	52,000	8,460	49,400	8,037	34,570	7,139
1915	55,000	18,400	48,700	18,375	46,300	17,456	27,508	14,072
1920	46,500	41,200	40,100	41,200	38,100	39,140	20,511	30,834
1925	34,900	47,500	24,600	46,315	23,400	43,999	11,355	39,912
1930	15,900	61,000	9,900	60,749	9,400	57,712	2,776	45,196

SOURCE: E. G. Nourse, et al., *America's Capacity to Produce* (Washington, D.C.: Brookings Institution, 1934), 552–53.
NOTE: Practical capacity deducts 5 percent from rated capacity of working ovens for repairs and "plant disability."

bonization—the Beehive oven." A continuing place for the older process depended on the fact that, despite its waste of coal and byproducts, beehives were cheap, simple, and flexible; ideal standby capacity. (More than a decade later, Sweetser described a rather similar situation in unintegrated ironmaking plants: "Only under special conditions is it now possible for a blast furnace to be profitably operated unless it is directly connected with a by-product coke plant having a satisfactory market for its coke-oven gas. The few blast furnaces now in active condition in this country not so connected are only 'marginal' plants and can only run in prosperous times." At the beginning of 1929, there had been 119 merchant blast furnaces; eight-and-a-half years later only 46 survived.)[39] Both merchant iron industry and beehive ovens retained their marginal functions on a progressively diminishing scale for another half century.

Connellsville continued to lead in beehive coke production throughout the interwar years, though its position can be traced much more definitely in the 1920s than in the 1930s. At the end of 1927, it contained 80.5 percent of all Pennsylvania beehive ovens. Its share of production was lower—77.2 percent in 1925 and 72 percent in 1930. During this decade its mines became more important as sources of coal supply to byproduct ovens located outside the Coke Region than for beehives within it. In 1927, 64.46 million tons of coal were used throughout the United States to make byproduct coke; 15.37 million tons of this came from the Connellsville district. At the then average coal:coke ratio of 72 percent, this would yield about 11.1 million tons of coke. Production of beehive coke from the old basin, Lower Connellsville, and Upper Connellsville together amounted to 4.96 million tons in 1927.[40]

The new Clairton oven complex, whose first batteries were in production by mid-1918 and which was extended with new major new units commissioned in 1924 and 1927, dominated H. C. Frick changes in the area, its rapid expansion providing the

Table 7.9 Byproduct and beehive coke industries, 1939

Oven type	Total value of products (tons)	Bituminous coal used (tons)	Coal used per $1,000 value of products
Byproduct ovens	$342,197,000	61,464,000	179.6
Beehive ovens	$4,781,000	1,349,000	282.2

SOURCE: National Resources Planning Board, *Industrial Location and National Resources* (Washington, D.C.: GPO, 1943).

biggest destination for Connellsville coal and acting as a major factor in the decline of the region's old ovens. During the 1921 depression H. C. Frick Coke blew out all its beehives for four months, shipping all its coking coal to Clairton. The subsequent spring there was a strike in Connellsville, and Clairton turned to West Virginia and Kentucky for its supplies. Gradually, facilities for delivering its coal were improved. Conveyor-belt connections were made from mines to two docks on the Monongahela from which the coal was shipped downriver to byproduct ovens. In spring 1919 H. C. Frick Coke acquired a site on the Monongahela between Brownsville and Fayette City. Five years later the company opened a conveyor-belt connection from the Colonial field to a new Colonial dock, shipping the product from there by barge to Clairton. In late 1920 the U.S. Steel Finance Committee approved the purchase of equipment for hauling 600 tons of coal daily from Lambert mine to Palmer, and by 1928 Palmer dock was sending on coal brought by conveyor belt not only from the local mine but also from Footedale, Buffington, Filbert, Lambert, and Ralph. Over the years other Lower Connellsville mines were connected to the docks of their riverside neighbors—for example, Edenborn to Gates, and Leckrone to Ronco—and the two main conveyor-belt systems were extended to draw on a wider range of mines. Cross-river investment from the start was geared to water shipment to Clairton. Coal reserves near Rice's Landing were bought in 1916, and large expenditures were made there in the early 1920s to develop the Dilworth mine complex, first with shipments of 2,000 tons a day as the target, soon to be increased to 5,5000 tons.[41] By the late 1920s, the 1,482 ovens at Clairton were capable of carbonizing 30,000 tons of coal a day and of producing annually about 7.7 million tons of coke. Average annual output from all the beehive ovens in the Coke Region in 1927–1929 was half as much.[42]

Though supplying outside byproduct plants as well as the beehives still active within its bounds, Connellsville was now of declining importance as a source of coking coal. To some extent this was due to exhaustion or drowning (flooding). Of the original tonnage of Pittsburgh Bed coal in Westmoreland County, it was calculated that 62.4 percent had been worked out by the late 1920s, at which time Washington County had worked out only 10.9 percent of its coal and Greene County a mere 1 per-

Table 7.10 **Mines and coal outputs of selected Appalachian coking-coal districts, 1923 and 1929** (output, net tons in thousands)

District	1923		1929	
	Mines	Output	Mines	Output
Connellsville, Pa.	312	37,882	140	36,647
Fairmount, W.Va.	309	22,882	136	23,739
Pocahontas, W.Va./Va.	107	16,481	81	22,738
Harlan, Ky.	75	8,752	57	14,340
Combined output		85,997		97,464
Connellsville share		44.0%		37.6%

SOURCE: Based on U.S. Bureau of Mines statistics for each year.

cent.[43] West Virginia, Virginia, and eastern Kentucky were of rapidly increasing importance as coal suppliers. As late as 1916 Pennsylvania produced 61.0 percent of the 81.6 million tons of coal charged into coke ovens of all types; ten years later consumption was only slightly up, to 82.9 million tons, but the state's share had fallen to 52.2 percent. The shift to the mid-Appalachian fields was largely caused by favorable differentials in rail freight charges and their lower mine wages.[44]

The Great Depression and Years of Uncertain Revival

During the 1920s the advance of the byproduct oven, consequent new patterns of coal procurement and movement, and the working out or flooding of large areas of its own reserves caused a large shrinkage in the Connellsville coal and coke industries. Some thirty-nine of its beehive coke plants closed, and the number of ovens fell from 35,678 to 25,828.[45] All this had happened as the national economy boomed. The Great Depression brought the collapse of an already dwindling industry. By 1931 the number of ovens in the region had fallen by another 10,000 units, and coke production was less than 600,000 tons—under one-sixth 1929 output (compared with 60.7 percent for byproduct ovens) and only a little more than one-quarter the level of fifty years before. The tally of working wage earners in Fayette County coke that year averaged only 614.[46]

Year after year through the first half of the 1930s, most beehives lay idle, with many crumbling into dereliction. In place of the blazing, smoking batteries of earlier years, one observer noted: "Thousands of ovens are dead, cold and falling into ruins." Some plants were deliberately destroyed to avoid taxation, whereas others were taken over as temporary homes by unemployed workers and their families needing to establish legal residences in order to qualify for relief checks. Then in late

Table 7.11 Pig iron shipments and coke output, 1936–1940
(net tons in millions)

Year	Pig iron shipments	Coke output Byproduct	Beehive	Share of beehives in coke output
1936	34.5	44.6	1.7	3.7%
1937	39.4	49.2	3.2	6.1%
1938	20.4	31.7	0.8	2.5%
1939	35.9	42.9	1.4	3.2%
1940	47.0	54.0	3.1	5.4%

SOURCE: Based on *Historical Statistics of the United States* (Washington, D.C.: GPO, 1957), 365; *Minerals Yearbook* (Washington, D.C.: GPO, 1948).

summer 1936, a revival in steel and an accompanying acute shortage of scrap sparked a sudden increase in demand for iron and consequently for coke. The byproduct coke industry could not cope with the unexpected turn of events. Koppers, which had not built a single new byproduct oven for four years, was now pressed with orders for new capacity, but this could not be commissioned soon enough to meet the needs of the times. The older ovens could be much more quickly rehabilitated and fired. By late September demand had already pushed the price for beehive coke up from a mere $.50 to $3.80 a ton. Ovens at Mt. Hope, Continental No.1, and the Keister works were among those rapidly put back into operation.[47] Nationwide, 1936 beehive coke output was not far short of twice that of the previous year; in 1937 it almost doubled again. Then the recession of 1938 proved that the revival had been only a temporary blip on a downward course; output that year was even lower than in 1935. There was then another strong recovery, but even so the beehive share of national output was lower than in 1937.

Although the H. C. Frick Coke Company continued to dominate the region's coal and coke industry, its patrimony was conspicuously diminishing. It closed many coke plants, dismantling them and salvaging what it could of their facilities and equipment. For instance, in spring 1936 it was authorized by the U.S. Steel Finance Committee to dismantle unsound or obsolete equipment at eleven plants with an estimated return from salvage of $11,885 and a $3,994 savings in taxes. In other cases, coke works were leased to other producers or property was sold to developers. In November 1937, Frick Coke decided to sell plant and townsites at Bittner, Juniata, Leith, and part of Standard mine, which it hoped to sell for $77,976. As far as coal production was concerned, H. C. Frick Coke very noticeably favored operations in Lower Connellsville, nearer to the shipping points, than in old basin mines. In January 1937 it owned forty mines in the old basin and twenty in Lower Connellsville. Of the former, eight were leased to others, twenty-nine were idle, and only three

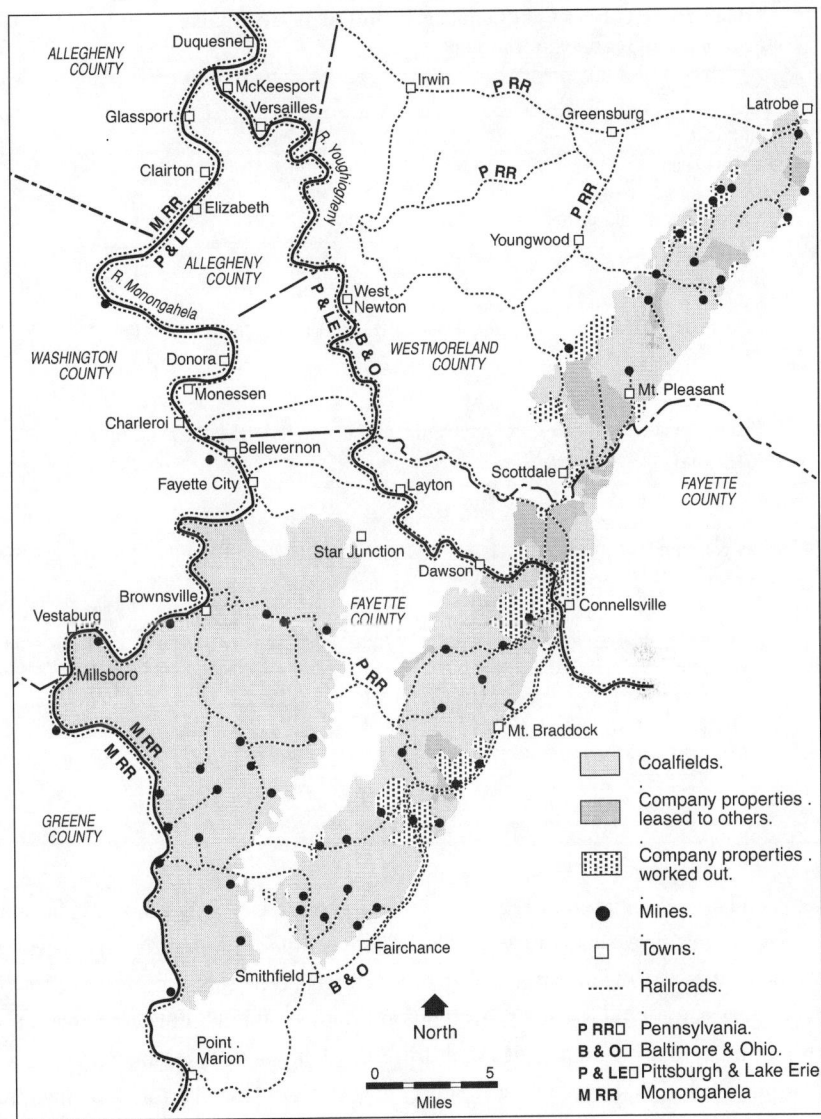

The H. C. Frick Coke Company in the Connellsville region, 1937.

Table 7.12 H. C. Frick Coke Company in the Connellsville Coke Region, 1910, 1920, 1930, and 1938

	1910	1920	1930	1938
Coke plants	64	51	27	8
Beehive ovens	20,857	18,290	9,324[a]	1,722
Coal operations not connected with coke plants	7	10	27[b]	n.a.

SOURCE: U.S. Steel Corporation, annual reports for 1910, 1920, 1930, and 1938, U.S. Steel Corporation Archives.
a. Of these beehive ovens, 3,960 were inactive.
b. Twelve other operations were large shippers of coal as well as suppliers for the beehives.

Table 7.13 United States, Pennsylvania, and Connellsville coke production, 1915–1940 *(tons in thousands)*

	1915	1920	1925	1930	1935	1940
U.S. coke total	41,581	51,345	51,267	47,972	35,141	57,072
Byproduct coke						
United States	14,073	30,834	39,912	45,196	34,224	54,014
of which Pennsylvania	3,092	7,730	9,853	12,529	n.a.	14,862
Beehive coke						
United States	27,508	20,511	11,355	2,776	917	3,058
of which Pennsylvania	22,531	15,908	9,574	2,011	n.a.	2,550
of which Connellsville	17,921	10,750	7,395	1,258	n.a.	n.a.

remained active; in the latter region, no mines were leased out, seven were idle, and thirteen were active. Of its thirty-six idle mines, twenty-four were allowed to become flooded, and were already largely dismantled. By this time some 70 percent of Frick coal reserves were in Greene or Washington Counties, though they contained only two mines, both idle. Even so, it was at this time that work began on another major new project designed as a long-term source of coal supply for Clairton. Robena mine was developed between 1937 and the late 1940s. When completed, it was claimed to be the world's largest and most mechanized mine, capable of shipping 20,000 tons of coal daily.[48]

Unfortunately for the regional economy, the decline in its coke industry coincided with a general contraction in manufacturing and downturn in local agriculture. Outmigration now brought an end to the spiraling population growth that had characterized the area for many decades. Between 1900 and 1920 Fayette County population had increased by 77,700 persons, or 70.4 percent, whereas the increase for

Pennsylvania had been only 38.4 percent; over the next twenty years, the county's population went up by 6.8 percent while the state increase was 13.5 percent. With the exception of Uniontown, the main urban centers in the Coke Region had ceased to grow. The depressing dereliction of abandonment was spreading at the expense of the grime, noise, and darkened buildings of activity. From Youngwood toward Scottdale, as the writers of the American Guide volume on Pennsylvania found, there now stretched a "rugged, scrub-covered terrain . . . broken occasionally by coal workings or by clusters of abandoned beehive ovens. . . . Between Everson and Connellsville blighted growths cover the rolling land."[49]

The Last Phase: 1940 to the 1970s

World War II brought a last major surge to the beehive coke industry, though it is unfortunately impossible to be precise about output in the Connellsville fields. Throughout the nation in 1942, beehive ovens produced 8.3 million tons of coke, more than in any year since 1926, but even so much less than one-quarter their World War I peak. The next year beehives provided 12 percent of all the coke consumed in blast furnaces.[50] When the emergency associated with war-induced levels of demand began, the Coke Region was a sorry picture of abandoned plants. Now at last some long-idle mines and coke ovens were reactivated. Eighty hand-drawn ovens were put back in production at Acme works. H. C. Frick Coke reopened the Buffington mine as well as the mines and ovens at Youngstown and Shoaf. Leisenring No. 2 and No. 3 had been out of action for fourteen years when work on their rehabilitation began in 1941. By 1944 they shipped about 500,000 tons of coke, and because their mines were producing more coal than could be coked locally, the Colonial conveyor-belt line was extended to enable them to make shipments out of the region. These wartime exertions quickly extinguished the remaining reserves at some of the revived operations: the coal at Crossland (Atlas), Davidson, Leith, Lemont, and Phillips was exhausted between 1940 and 1945. Buffington mine was closed in 1946.[51]

After World War II the overall cost significance of the supply of coke to the iron and steel industry declined as large economies were made in its consumption. Production of pig iron in 1959 was almost identical with that of 1948 at 60 million tons, but about 10 million fewer tons of coke were required in the furnaces that produced it. The savings continued—blast furnaces consumed about the same tonnage of coke in 1978 as in 1960 but produced 20 million more tons of iron. These reductions were the result of a variety of factors. In the 1950s, use of pelletized and sintered ore, some utilization of other fuels (such as natural gas and oil) as supplementary sources of energy in the blast furnaces, and further increases in furnace-blowing volumes helped bring about a marked improvement in the coke rate. Consumption of coke

Leisenring No. 1, *circa* 1946. *Courtesy of Frederick A. Hetzel*

per ton of iron averaged 0.906 net tons in 1953 and 0.785 tons six years later. The promise of further reductions was realized after the 1950s as richer imported ores or high-grade pellets made from the taconites of the Lake ranges came to dominate the iron material charged to the furnaces. There was also continued progress in the use of alternative fuels so that by 1963 it was reckoned that injection of powdered coal could provide around 17 percent of a furnace's total fuel requirement, every ton of coke replaced by coal reducing costs by $2–3. From 1930 to 1957 coke consumption per ton of iron had fallen 6.74 percent; in the following twenty-seven years the decrease was 37.42 percent. By 1967 the coke rate was already down to 0.631 tons; in the mid-1980s iron was being made with half as much coke as at the end of World War I.[52]

The byproduct oven had long been the normal coke-making technology. In the 1950s, as major extensions were made to iron and steel capacity, the companies also invested in new ovens, with the material assistance of a federal program of accelerated depreciation. It eventually became clear that a long-term effect of this great surge in expansion was that much of the capacity would become obsolete at the same time.

In the 1970s and 1980s the combination of recession and pressing needs for investment in new steel-making technology diverted attention away from coke ovens. The beehive industry had been notorious for waste of natural resources and pollution. In an age increasingly concerned about environmental standards, even the byproduct batteries now became targets not only for criticism but also for savage restrictive action; the commercial logic that had located them at steelworks made them particularly obnoxious to the urban populations that surrounded them. The fluid state of oven technology and the high cost of new units were other factors helping push the question of investment in new coking capacity into the background. By this time the industry was aging badly, which worsened both commercial results and environmental acceptability. The normal effective life of a byproduct coke oven battery is twenty-five to thirty years. At the beginning of 1947, 22.3 percent of the byproduct ovens in the United States had been between twenty-eight and thirty-five years old; forty-one years later the proportion over thirty years of age was 49.1 percent. "As they get older they tend to incur serious maintenance problems from leaking doors and seals. Stays and other structural parts . . . deteriorate. The wear and tear . . . can result in environmental control problems making it almost impossible to meet established legal guidelines. Eventually operating efficiency and coke quality are adversely affected." By 1990 twenty out of the thirty-three coke-oven plants in the United States had no desulfurization system, which meant that together they could "belch out 300,000 tons of sulfur dioxide annually."[53] Although still extraordinarily well endowed with high-grade coking coal, the United States began to import considerable tonnages of coke, not infrequently made in ovens that coked American coal but that were newer, bigger, and more efficient than those at home. Altogether over recent decades, there has been a dramatic fall in coke-making capacity, from about 71 million metric tons in 1960 to only 26–27 million by 1989: coke output was 64.5 million tons in 1955, under 52 million by 1975, and 25 million tons by 1989.[54]

Despite the large economies in the use of coke and the overwhelming predominance of the byproduct oven, a small beehive industry managed to survive far into the postwar years. Though dwindling, it was still dominated by Connellsville. As for so long, what remained of it could be rapidly activated as a supplement in times of high demand and readily closed when the peaks had passed, meaning it followed an oscillating, though generally downward, course. There was a sharp recession in 1949, but the outbreak of the Korean War the next year brought a new surge, increasing 1950 iron production by 11 million tons over 1949 figures. Total coke production grew 14.3 percent, but byproduct coke output rose only 11.1 percent. This meant another call on the depleted resources of Connellsville. In December 1949 2,035 beehive ovens had been at work; a year later there were well over 8,000. Some units idle since as far back as 1929 were now brought back into production. Where possible, old-time coke workers were recalled, and for the last time there were the outward signs of something approaching a boom: "thousands of flaming jets billowing thick clouds of smoke throughout the Uniontown-Connellsville district." When the emergency needs passed, the region quickly reverted to lesser levels of activity. In the early 1950s Leisenring Nos. 1 and 2 were closed. Shoaf too ceased at this time, though it was to be reopened later under different management. Despite the decline in tonnages produced, as late as 1957 national beehive capacity was 1.75 million tons; 100,000 tons of this was at the Utah mine of Kaiser Steel, the rest was divided between eight coke works in southwestern Pennsylvania, of which five belonged to U.S. Steel.

Although the beehive industry was adversely affected by the federal government's encouragement of investment in new byproduct capacity, throughout the generally prosperous 1950s and early 1960s its provision of marginal capacity was clearly visible in the course of yearly production figures. In the first half of the 1960s, beehives generally benefited from new markets in the foundry trade and even in the chemical industry, whereas at this time byproduct coking was suffering from the loss of some of its business to petrochemical firms. Eventually, however, the fact that they discharged all products except coke into the atmosphere or onto the earth's surface caused the beehive ovens to fall foul of a new generation of much more exacting environmental standards.[55] Meantime, more of the resource base of the Connellsville region was failing.

Despite the long persistence of a small coke industry, most coal produced in southwestern Pennsylvania continued to be shipped out of the region. Riverboats pushing tows of sometimes six barges, each holding 7,000 to 10,000 tons of coal, had long been a characteristic feature of the Monongahela valley scene. In one year at the end of World War II, 68.5 million tons of coal were shipped from operations in Fayette, Westmoreland, Greene, Washington, and Allegheny Counties; over 25 million tons of this was loaded onto barges on the Monongahela. As late as the early 1970s, U.S. Steel, developing a new mine in Greene County, was planning to send its annual output of 4 million tons of metallurgical coal downriver to Clairton. As this indicates, the emphasis was increasingly on production from areas farther west, while in the old basin and Lower Connellsville the last of the mines as well as the coke plants were failing. In the course of 1960 and 1961, U.S. Steel closed mines at Leisenring No. 3, Maxwell, Colonial No. 3, and Bridgeport on grounds of depletion of reserves; retired the Leisenring No. 2 coke plant and the Colonial dock and terminal yard; and resolved to dismantle their facilities. By 1974 only two large operations were left in Fayette County, the Isabella mine of the National Mines Corporation and U.S. Steel's Mount Braddock mine.[56]

The remains of the Allison ovens, 1982. *Courtesy of Eugene Levy*

Improvements in mining technology, westward movements in coal production, and decline in the beehive industry were accompanied by a continuing downward drift in workforces in the old coke region. Westmoreland County has increased in population through most of the postwar period, but Fayette County suffered a fall of almost 24 percent between 1950 and 1990. In the 1950s, decline was largely confined to rural areas and smaller mine and coke settlements, but the population of Connellsville fell 3.6 percent and Uniontown over 12 percent. Outmigration could not fully compensate for economic contraction. By early 1958 unemployment was 23.5 percent in the Uniontown-Connellsville area; in Pennsylvania it averaged 10 percent. Many miners were already traveling seventy-five to one hundred miles a day for work to avoid having to relocate.[57]

After a peak in 1970 and reasonably high levels in 1973 and 1974, national coke production fell away sharply. By 1979 coal consumption in coke production by steel companies was 69.4 million tons, only 79.6 percent the 1970 level. During the 1980s the iron and steel industry went through a crisis of unprecedented severity and pushed through draconian rationalization programs, its companies cutting back on coal and coke production. In 1984 U.S. Steel sold its Dilworth-Robena coking-coal mining and shipping operations along the Monongahela, until so recently a complex that had been a prized corporate asset. By the mid-1990s USS no longer possessed any coal-mining operations in Pennsylvania. Production in Fayette and Westmoreland Counties had now ceased except for a few strip mines supplying electric-utility companies.

Long before these storms of the crisis of America's basic manufacturing, the old-style beehive coke industry had quietly expired. The last working ovens, those at Shoaf in the southwestern portion of the old basin, closed in March 1972. Henceforward the only material expressions of the once great Connellsville industry would be found in relic settlements and in its many lines of mute, dead, and rapidly decaying ovens scattered forlornly across the landscapes of a region that, in its heyday, the companies had exploited and peopled and had finally laid waste.

Appendix A Statistical Tables

A1. Coke Production for the United States, Connellsville, West Virginia, and Virginia, 1880–1930 *(net tons in thousands)*

| Year | United States | | Connellsville | West Virginia | Virginia |
	Beehive	Byproduct			
1880	3,338	n.a.	2,206	139	n.a.
1881	4,114	n.a.	2,639	187	n.a.
1882	4,793	n.a.	3,043	230	n.a.
1883	5,465	n.a.	3,552	257	25
1884	4,874	n.a.	3,192	223	64
1885	5,107	n.a.	3,096	260	49
1886	6,845	n.a.	4,180	264	122
1887	7,612	n.a.	4,147	442	167
1888	8,540	n.a.	4,955	532	149
1889	10,258	n.a.	5,930	608	146
1890	11,508	n.a.	6,464	833	166
1891	10,353	n.a.	4,761	1,009	167
1892	12,011	n.a.	6,329	1,035	148
1893	9,465	13	4,806	1,062	125
1894	9,187	16	5,454	1,194	180
1895	13,315	18	8,244	1,285	245
1896	11,706	83	5,412	1,650	268
1897	13,027	262	6,915	1,473	354
1898	15,753	294	8,460	1,925	531
1899	18,762	906	10,130	2,278	619
1900	19,458	1,076	10,166	2,358	685
1901	20,616	1,180	12,610	2,284	907
1902	23,998	1,403	14,139	2,516	1,124
1903	23,392	1,882	13,345	2,708	1,176
1904	21,053	2,608	12,427	2,283	1,102
1905	28,769	3,462	17,896	3,400	1,499
1906	31,843	4,558	19,999	3,713	1,578
1907	35,172	5,608	19,029	4,113	1,545
1908	21,832	4,201	10,700	2,637	1,162
1909	33,060	6,255	17,786	3,944	1,347

(table continues)

A1. *(continued)*

Year	United States Beehive	United States Byproduct	Connellsville	West Virginia	Virginia
1910	34,570	7,139	18,690	3,804	1,494
1911	27,704	7,848	16,334	2,291	910
1912	32,868	11,115	20,001	2,466	968
1913	33,585	12,715	20,098	2,473	1,304
1914	23,336	11,220	14,076	1,428	781
1915	27,508	14,073	17,921	1,391	630
1916	35,464	19,069	21,654	2,521	1,242
1917	33,167	22,439	17,806	3,350	1,304
1918	30,481	25,997	16,138[a]	3,320	1,234
1919	19,043	25,138	10,255	1,414	930
1920	20,511	30,834	10,750	1,828	1,028
1921	5,538	19,749	3,572	398	280
1922	8,573	28,550	5,675	920	379
1923	19,380	37,598	13,114	1,763	775
1924	10,286	33,983	6,668	1,328	485
1925	11,355	39,912	7,395	1,546	422
1926	12,489	44,376	8,342	1,713	371
1927	7,207	43,885	4,682	1,923	317
1928	4,493	48,313	2,605	1,799	248
1929	6,472	53,412	3,981	1,928	315
1930	2,776	45,196	1,258	1,901	220

SOURCES: *Connellsville Courier* and *Mineral Resources Yearbook*.
 a. Shipments to and including 1917; afterward production only.

A2. Ovens in operation, coke shipments, and average prices of Connellsville coke, 1880–1931

Year	Ovens	Shipments (th. net tons)	Avg. price ($)	Year	Ovens	Shipments (th. net tons)	Avg. Price ($)
1880	7,211	2,206	1.79	1908	37,842	10,700	1.80
1881	8,208	2,639	1.63	1909	39,158	17,786	2.00
1882	9,283	3,043	1.47	1910	39,137	18,690	2.10
1883	10,176	3,552	1.14	1911	38,904	16,334	1.72
1884	10,543	3,192	1.13	1912	38,884	20,001	1.92
1885	10,471	3,096	1.22	1913	39,067	20,098	2.95
1886	10,952	4,180	1.36	1914	37,965	14,076	2.00
1887	11,923	4,147	1.79	1915	38,986	17,921	1.80
1888	13,975	4,955	1.19	1916	38,362	21,654	2.58
1889	14,458	5,930	1.34	1917	38,110	17,806	6.25
1890	16,020	6,464	1.94	1918	37,061	16,139[a]	7.25
1891	17,204	4,761	1.87	1919	35,758	10,255	4.70
1892	17,256	6,329	1.83	1920	35,678	10,750	8.30
1893	17,513	4,806	1.49	1921	35,473	3,572	4.07
1894	17,834	5,454	1.00	1922	35,042	5,675	7.15
1895	17,947	8,244	1.23	1923	34,611	13,114	5.90
1896	18,351	5,412	1.90	1924	33,070	6,669	3.85
1897	18,628	6,915	1.65	1925	26,809	7,395	3.67
1898	18,643	8,460	1.55	1926	26,142	8,342	4.19
1899	19,689	10,130	2.00	1927	25,878	4,682	3.78
1900	20,954	10,166	2.70	1928	25,878	2,605	3.41
1901	21,575	12,610	1.95	1929	25,828	3,981	3.38
1902	26,329	14,139	2.37	1930	22,755	1,258	3.29
1903	28,092	13,345	3.00	1931	15,660	574	3.20
1904	29,119	12,427	1.75	1932	9,935	303	2.98
1905	30,842	17,896	2.26	1933	9,249	436	2.99
1906	34,059	19,999	2.75	1934	9,457	436	4.10
1907	35,697	19,029	2.90				

SOURCE: *Connellsville Courier*
NOTE: From 1900, figures include Lower Connellsville.
a. For 1918 and all following years, figures represent production, not shipments.

A3. Coke shipments of Connellsville "proper" and Lower Connellsville, 1900–1930
(net tons in thousands)

Year	Connellsville "proper"	Lower Connellsville	Year	Connellsville "proper"	Lower Connellsville
1900	10,021	386	1918	9,502	7,761
1901	10,236	1,116	1919	6,844	4,933
1902	10,418	1,899	1920	7,135	5,008
1903	9,102	2,329	1921	2,219	1,645
1904	8,883	2,887			
1905	11,365	3,871	1924	3,639	3,168
1906	12,058	5,188	1925	4,291	3,372
1907	13,089	6,311			
1908	6,808	3,892	1929	1,428	2,710
1909	11,517	6,269	1930	272	1,145
1910	10,880	8,000			
1911	9,665	6,669			

A4. Coal used in coke production in United States, in selected Coke Region districts, and in byproduct ovens, 1900–1929 *(net tons in thousands)*

Year	United States	Connellsville "proper"	L. Connellsville	Greensburg, Irwin, U. Connellsville	Byproduct ovens
1900	32,113	14,947	580	1,467	n.a.
1905	49,331	16,980	5,667	2,325	n.a.
1910	63,088	17,206	12,130	2,373	9,529
1915	61,833	14,540	11,931	2,357	19,554
1920	76,191	10,744	7,593	2,084	44,205
1925	74,533	6,471	5,058	1,244	57,110
1929	86,786	2,242	3,986	753	76,759

SOURCES: H. N. Eavenson, "The Pittsburgh Coal Bed: Its Early History and Development," *TAIME* (1938); *The First Century and a Quarter of American Coal Industry* (Pittsburgh: Privately published, 1942), 579–80.

A5. Beehive and byproduct coke production by United States Steel Corporation, 1907–1935 *(tons in thousands)*

Year	Beehive	Byproduct	Year	Beehive	Byproduct
1907	12,716	829	1922	3,432	9,805
1908	7,591	579	1923	7,143	11,695
1909	11,896	1,694	1924	3,266	11,142
1910	11,641	2,008	1925	3,290	13,011
1911	9,491	2,629	1926	3,823	13,513
1912	11,555	5,164	1927	1,816	12,691
1913	11,062	5,601	1928	448	15,545
1914	7,093	4,081	1929	987	16,368
1915	9,702	4,799	1930	51	13,062
1916	12,479	6,423	1931	16	7,025
1917	11,177	6,284	1932	1.6	2,965
1918	9,962	7,795	1933	9.4	4,871
1919	5,933	9,530	1934	5.1	5,377
1920	6,125	10,083	1935	n.a.	7,328
1921	1,698	8,127			

SOURCE: Annual reports of U.S. Steel Corporation.

A6. Annual average prices for Connellsville coke and Pittsburgh Bessemer-grade pig iron, 1886–1912 *(dollars per ton)*

Year	Connellsville price	Bessemer pig iron	Coke price as percentage of iron price	Year	Connellsville price	Bessemer pig iron	Coke price as percentage of iron price
1886	$1.36	$18.96	7.2	1900	$2.70	$19.50	13.8
1887	$1.79	$21.37	8.4	1901	$1.95	$15.90	12.3
1888	$1.19	$17.38	6.8	1902	$2.37	$20.65	11.5
1889	$1.34	$18.00	7.4	1903	$3.00	$19.00	15.8
1890	$1.94	$18.85	10.3	1904	$1.75	$13.75	12.7
1891	$1.87	$15.95	11.7	1905	$2.26	$16.35	13.8
1892	$1.83	$14.37	12.7	1906	$2.75	$19.55	14.1
1893	$1.49	$12.87	11.6	1907	$2.90	$22.85	12.7
1894	$1.00	$11.38	8.8	1908	$1.80	$17.10	10.5
1895	$1.23	$12.72	9.7	1909	$2.00	$17.40	11.5
1896	$1.90	$12.14	15.6	1910	$2.10	$17.20	12.2
1897	$1.65	$10.13	16.3	1911	$1.72	$15.70	10.9
1898	$1.55	$10.33	15.0	1912	$1.92	$15.95	12.0
1899	$2.00	$19.03	10.5				

SOURCES: For coke, *Connellsville Courier;* for iron, F. Taussig, *Some Aspects of the Tariff Question* (Cambridge, Mass.: Harvard University Press, 1915), 160.

A7. Major new byproduct coke-oven plants (100 or more ovens) located at blast furnaces, 1914–1920

Location and company	Ovens	Date built
East		
Maryland Steel, Sparrows Point, Md.	300 Koppers	1914–1919
Rainey-Wood, Swedeland, Pa.	110 Koppers	1919
Bethlehem Steel, Bethlehem, Pa.	424 Koppers	1915–1916
Lake Erie/Detroit		
Ford, Dearborn, Mich..	120 Semet-Solvay	1919
A. S. and W., Cleveland, Ohio	180 Koppers	1918
McKinney, Cleveland, Ohio	204 Koppers	1916
National Tube, Lorain, Ohio	208 Koppers	1918
Donner, Buffalo, N.Y.	150 Koppers	1920
Chicago		
S. and T. of America, Indiana Harbor, Ind.	120 Semet-Solvay	1919
Pittsburgh, Upper Ohio, and Valleys		
Carnegie, Clairton, Pa.	768 Koppers	1918–1919
J. and L., Pittsburgh, Pa.	300 Koppers	1919–1920
Crucible, Midland, Pa.	100 Koppers	1920
Republic, Youngstown, Ohio	143 Koppers	1914–1915
Y. S. and T., Youngstown, Ohio	306 Koppers	1916–1918
Other districts		
T.C.I., Fairfield, Ala.	434 Koppers	1912–1920
C.F.I., Minnequa, Colo.	120 Koppers	1918
Solvay Coke, Portsmouth, Ohio	108 Semet-Solvay	1917
S. and T. of America, Mayville, Wisc.	108 Otto-Hoffman	1914–1917
Cambria, Johnstown, Pa.	250 Cambria	1918–1920

SOURCE: Based on *Mineral Resources of the United States* (1921).

Appendix B Biographical Notes

Boileau, John (1873–?). b. Athens County, Ohio. Pittsburgh-based geologist and coal expert. From 1897 specialized in handling coal lands. Played an important part in attempts to rationalize the independent sector of the industry in the early twentieth century.

Boyle, John D. (1832–?). b. Fayette County. Involved in politics and eventually mayor of Washington, Pa. Later involved in opening coal in Westmoreland County. As Boyle and Hazlett, built first ovens in Westmoreland County at Mt. Pleasant. Withdrew from business ca. 1895.

Brennen, John P. (?–1917). General superintendent of McClure Coke Company until its incorporation in H. C. Frick Coke. Examined and proved Lower Connellsville coking coal. Manager of Eureka Fuel Company for Federal Steel and built Buffington, Footedale, and Leckrone pioneer ovens. When these were brought into United States Steel, Brennen managed Sharon Coke Company for Sharon Steel until it too was absorbed in USS. He then joined J. V. K. Thompson and built and operated plant for Thompson Connellsville Coke Company.

Brown, William H. (?–1873). Associated with both Schoonmaker and M. M. Cochran enterprises in coke.

Brown, W. Harry (1856–1921). b. Brown's Station, Pittsburgh, son of William H. Brown. Became one of world's largest producers and shippers of coal. Along with the Cochrans, began major coking coal and coke operations as Washington Coal and Coke Company. Also operated Nellie mine near Connellsville and Alicia mines 1 and 2 on Monongahela near Brownsville, the last two mines together supplying a large coke plant at Brownsville.

Clingerman, Walter H. (1869–?). In 1885 started work in Pennsylvania Railroad workshop, and in 1895 built Everson car shops for H. C. Frick Coke. By 1898 assistant general superintendent and in 1904 general superintendent for H. C. Frick Coke. Lynch delegated powers to him, and in January 1915 he succeeded Lynch as president.

Cochran, James (1823–1894). b. Tyrone, Fayette County, of Scotch-Irish descent. Employed in carrying sand, rock, and cinders down the Monongahela River to Pittsburgh before entering the coke trade at what later was known as the Fayette coke works in 1842. Afterward also had large interests in Spring Grove. Jimtown works given name in his honor.

Cochran, Mordecai (1797–1880). Pioneer of the Connellsville coke trade.

Cochran, Mark Mordecai (1854–?). b. Lower Tyrone. In 1890 became associated with the Dawson coke business of his cousin, James Cochran. Organized Washington Coal and Coke Company in 1893. President of Washington Run Railroad Company, and in 1899 formed Cochran Coal and Coke Company, which was later merged into Washington. Organized Cochran Coal and Coke Company of West Virginia in 1902.

Davidson, Daniel R. (1820–1884). Promoter in Pittsburgh and Connellsville Railroad, later interested in coke.

Dravo, John (1819–1905). b. West Newton. Entered coal-shipping business on his own, operating Youghiogheny riverside mines. Organized and became general manager of Pittsburgh Gas, Coal, and Coke Company in 1868. Overhauled and extended the Davidson coke plant on the outskirts of Connellsville.

Ferguson, E. M. (1838–?). b. New York City. With his younger brother, Walter, in 1878 joined H. C. Frick in a partnership that provided finances to allow the latter to extend his interests in coal and coke.

Frick, Henry Clay (1849–1919). b. West Overton, Westmoreland County, grandson of a flour and whisky maker, Abraham Overholt, and son of a small-scale farmer. Joined Tinstman and Rist in the coke trade in 1871. Within ten years controlled the largest coke company and subsequently in association with Carnegie continued to expand so that the H. C. Frick Coke Company became the controlling force in the whole industry.

Fulton, John (?). Mining engineer associated above all with the Cambria Iron Company. Author of a number of important articles on the Connellsville coke industry and of the textbook *Coke* (1905).

Hill, Alexander M. (?–1863). A tanner before investing in one of the first coke plants in the region in 1844.

Hutchinson, A. A. (?) b. Pittsburgh. Prominent in the development of the coke industry in the 1870s and early 1880s.

Leisenring, Edward (1845–1894). Son of John, he succeeded his father as chairman of the Connellsville Coke and Iron Company, which in 1889 he sold to H. C. Frick. Afterward involved in Virginia coal and coke developments.

Leisenring, John (1819–1884). b. Philadelphia. After long involvement in railroad operations and coal production in the anthracite region, led the group of eastern capitalists who in 1880 established the Connellsville Coke and Iron Company beginning the development of major coal reserves and large-scale coke production.

Lesley, J. Peter (1819–1903). b. Philadelphia. From 1838 until 1841 assistant to Henry D. Rogers in First Geological Survey of Pennsylvania, and became a Presbyterian and Congregational minister, 1844–1851. Subsequently professor of geology and mining at University of Pennsylvania. In 1859 produced the remarkable *Iron Manufacturer's Guide to the Iron Works and Iron Ore Mines of the United States* for the American Iron Association, and in 1863 reported to Pennsylvania Railroad Company on Bessemer process. After 1874, state geologist of Pennsylvania and supervisor of the Second Geological Survey.

Lynch, Clay F. (1880–?). b. Dunbar. During vacation worked at H. C. Frick Coke, 1898; shipping clerk at Mammoth, 1902–1903; superintendent at Brinkerton, 1903, and at Calumet, 1904; assistant to general superintendent of H. C. Frick Coke, 1905–1909; general superintendent of Bunsen Coal Company, Illinois, 1909–1915; and general superintendent H. C. Frick Coke, 1915.

Lynch, Thomas (1854–1914). b. Uniontown. Entered employment of Dunbar Iron Company as store clerk and worked as clerk for other companies. In 1875 was store clerk in Frick Broadford works and by 1877 superintendent of Valley coke works and store when leased by Frick. Superintendent of all H. C. Frick Coke operations throughout Connellsville region, 1882; general manager, 1890; and president, 1896. A U. S. Steel director and president of U. S. Coal and Coke Company of West Virginia. From 1892 associated with safety programs and with schemes for improved welfare of mine and coke-oven families.

McCormick, Provance (1799–1887). b. near Connellsville. Early life, a teamster for goods between Philadelphia and Pittsburgh. In 1841 pioneer of the coke trade in the Coke Region.

Mellon, Andrew (1855–1937). Member of distinguished banking family. Key figure in establishment of many industrial enterprises. Also invested largely in coal lands in southwest Pennsylvania, in the old basin, Lower Connellsville, and farther west. From 1913 played important part in organization of the Koppers Gas and Coke Company.

Moore, J. W. (1837–1893). b. Tyrone, Westmoreland County. In 1873 moved from stock dealing into coke production at Summit works near Broadford, the coal under the family farm providing the basis for a start. By 1879 withdrew from this venture to start Redstone coke works near Uniontown. Later transferred to Mt. Pleasant–area Mammoth works. Purchased Wynn coke works near Uniontown, 1889. August 1889 sold out to H. C. Frick Coke.

Morgan, Algernon S. M. (ca. 1831–1914). Opened Morgan mines wholly for coke production.

Rainey, William J. (1834–1900). b. on farm at Martin's Ferry, Belmont County, Ohio. Produced and traded in Ohio coal. Moved to Cleveland, which thereafter remained his home. Started to trade in coke in 1877 and began production of beehive coke in 1879. At time of death owned eight coke works with 2,231 ovens.

Ramsay, Morris (1848–1892). b. near Dunfermline, Scotland. Family to United States 1853 but later returned to Scotland. Began work as a machinist near Dunfermline but returned to United States and hauled coal in Monongahela River mines, 1870; to Latrobe and became superintendent for Loyalhanna Coal and Coke Company, 1872; to Mt. Pleasant as mining engineer for Morewood Coke Company, 1886; head of engineering corps at H. C. Frick Coke; and then returned to Morewood as superintendent for the South West Coal and Coke Company.

Ramsay, Robert (1840–1899) b. near Dunfermline, Scotland. started work at Hays mine on Monongahela above Pittsburgh, 1863. By 1865 hoisting engineer at Shafton, Westmoreland County, the first shaft mine west of the Alleghenies. Engaged by Carnegie, Phipps and Company to operate Monastery coke works, 1881. When this was merged into H. C. Frick Coke in 1883, moved to Mt. Pleasant as superintendent of all that company's mines. In late 1880s superintendent of Standard ovens and mine, claimed to be the largest coal-producing shaft mine in the world.

Rist, Joseph (?). b. Westmoreland County. Farmed before entering the coal and coke trade as a partner with Tinstman and Frick.

Schoonmaker, James S. (1842–?). b. Pittsburgh. In 1872 in association with his father-in-law, W. H. Brown, entered the coke business. In 1879 gained complete control of company. Also involved with Redstone Coke Company.

Strickler, Stewart (1812–?). b. New Salem, Fayette County (later a service center for the Lower Connellsville coke trade). In 1864–1865 sold Sterling ovens to Graff, Bennett and to Shoenbergers and moved to Tennessee.

Taylor, Selwyn (1864–1904). b. Allegheny, Pa. Mining engineer prominent in design of coal mines and coke works who played an important part in the opening of Lower Connellsville while contractor to the Illinois Steel Company for Buffington, Footedale, and Leckrone coke works.

Thompson, Jasper M. (?–1889). A cattle farmer and buyer, in 1864 set up First National Bank of Uniontown and by the 1870s investing Uniontown capital in coal lands.

Thompson, Josiah V. K. (1854–1933). b. Menallen Township, Fayette Company, son and successor of J. M. Thompson at First National Bank of Uniontown. Became a major owner of coking coal lands in Fayette County, later entering the coke trade in the Thompson-Connellsville, Tower Hill, and Rich Hill coke companies. Acquired and sold very extensive holdings of coal lands west of the Monongahela. By 1913 the largest individual owner of coking coal in the United States with tracts in Fayette, Greene, Washington, and Allegheny Counties, Pa.

Tinstman, Abraham (1834–?). b. Huntingdon Township, Westmoreland County. Cousin of H. C. Frick. Managed the Broadford flour and whisky business of their grandfather Abraham Overholt before becoming interested in coal and coke production. Later a dealer in coal lands.

Whyel, Harry, and George (twins, 1863–?). b. Pittsburgh. Harry was superintendent of operations for H. C. Frick Coke at Leith for fourteen years. In 1884 George opened the Smock mine. The brothers established Whyel Coke Company, 1902. Another joint venture was the Consolidated Connellsville Coke Company.

Notes

Abbreviations used in the Notes and Bibliography

ACLC	Andrew Carnegie Papers, Library of Congress
AISA	American Iron and Steel Association (American Iron and Steel Institute after 1908)
AISI	American Iron and Steel Institute
BAISA	*Bulletin of the AISA*
BP	Bethlehem Papers, Hagley Library
CSCP	Carnegie Steel Company Papers, U.S. Steel Corporation Archives
EMJ	*Engineering and Mining Journal*
FCCP	H. C. Frick Coke Company Papers, U.S. Steel Corporation Archives
FP	Frick Papers, Frick Art and Historical Center
ISCP	Illinois Steel Company Papers, U.S. Steel Corporation Archives
JISI	*Journal of the Iron and Steel Institute*
LP	Leisenring Papers, Hagley Library
TAIME	*Transactions of the (American) Institute of Mining Engineers*
USX	U.S. Steel Corporation Papers, U.S. Steel Corporation Archives

1. The Foundations of the Industry

1. J. D. Weeks, *Report on the Manufacture of Coke*, a special report prepared for the Tenth Census of the United States, vol. 10 (Washington D.C.: GPO, 1884).

2. C. K. Hyde, *Technological Change in the British Iron Industry, 1700–1870* (Princeton, N.J.: Princeton University Press, 1977).

3. American Philosophical Society, "Essay on the Manufacture of Iron with Coke on the Juniata Canal near Hollidaysburg as compared with Merthyr Tydfil" (Lewiston, Pa.,1836), 4; F. Overman, *Manufacture of Iron* (Philadelphia: H. C. Baird, 1850), 170, 175; H. N. Eavenson, *The First Century and a Quarter of American Coal Industry* (Pittsburgh: Privately published, 1942), 380–81; P. Temin, *Iron and Steel in Nineteenth Century America: An Economic Enquiry* (Cambridge, Mass.: MIT Press, 1964), 70, 73; H. M. Jenkins, *Pennsylvania: Colonial and Federal* (Philadelphia: Pennsylvania Historical Publishing Association, 1904), 4:197.

4. Overman, *Manufacture of Iron*, 174.

5. Rev. T. Fleming quoted in W. G. Smeltzer, *Homestead Methodism, 1830–1933* (Homestead, Pa., 1933).

6. Thaddeus Harris quoted in R. Brown, *Historical Geography of the United States* (New York: Harcourt Brace, 1948), 185.

7. *Connellsville Tribune* quoted in *Iron Age*, 21 June 1888, 1013.

8. Jenkins, *Pennsylvania: Colonial and Federal*, 176–78; *Pittsburgh Gazette*, 23 April 1796.

9. E. C. Pechin, "The Minerals of South West Pennsylvania," *TAIME* 3 (1874–1875): 400.

10. J. Birkibine, "The Produce of Charcoal Iron Works," *TAIME* 7 (1878–1879): 150.

11. K. Warren, *The American Steel Industry 1850–1970* (Pittsburgh: University of Pittsburgh Press, 1988), 12, 16, 17.

12. J. Birkibine, "The Charcoal Iron Industry of the United States," *BAISA* (22 October 1879): 266.

13. R. Brownlee, *The Connellsville Coke Region*, Report of the Pennsylvania Bureau of Mines (Harrisburg: State of Pennsylvania, 1898), xxi.

14. J. P. Lesley, *The Iron Manufacturer's Guide* (New York: John Wiley, 1859), 90.

15. S. P. Hildreth, "Observations on the Bituminous Coal Deposits of the Valley of the Ohio," *American Journal of Science* (1836).

16. G. Mellen, *A Book of the United States* (New York, 1839), 321.

17. Hildreth, "Observations on the Bituminous Coal Deposits," 79–86.

18. K. Warren, *Mineral Resources* (Newton Abbott, Devon, Eng.: David and Charles, 1973).

19. G. H. Ashley, *Bituminous Coalfields of Pennsylvania*, vol. 1 (Harrisburg, 1928).

20. J. Fulton, "Coal Mining in the Connellsville Coke Region of Pennsylvania," *TAIME* 13 (1884–1885): 333; *EMJ*, 16 April 1881, 279; *BAISA*, 23 November 1881; *American Manufacturer*, Coke Supplement, November 1886; Pittsburgh Chamber of Commerce, "Pittsburgh and Western Pennsylvania" (Pittsburgh Chamber of Commerce, 1885); E. B. McCormick, "Labor in the Connellsville Coke Region," in *Annual Report of the Secretary of Internal Affairs* (Harrisburg: State of Pennsylvania, 1888), F3–F4; H. C. Frick Coke Company, "Connellsville Coke" (Np: privately printed, 1892).

21. *Iron Age*, 1 July 1911, 16; *Surface Arrangements at Bituminous Mines* (Scranton, Pa.: International Library of Technology, 1907), 38; *EMJ*, 24 February 1883, 101–2.

22. *Coal and Coke*, 6 October 1899, 11–12; The construction and operation of beehive coke ovens is fully considered in Appendices A and B of F. Quivik, *Connellsville Coal and Coke Region*, Historic American Engineering Record (Washington, D.C.: Department of the Interior, 1995), 139–49.

23. H. C. Frick to M. Ramsay, 26 January 1891, FP.

24. *Coal and Coke*, 6 October 1899, 12.

25. *BAISA*, 20 November 1895; T. Lynch to H. C. Frick, 29 March 1899, FP; F. C. Keighley, "Coke Manufacture for Profit," *Coal and Coke*, 2 December 1898, 15.

26. *Pittsburgh Mercury*, 8 April 1813; J. Fulton, *Coke* (Scranton, N.J.: International Textbook, 1905), 131.

27. J. C. McClenathan, et al., *Centennial History of the Borough of Connellsville, Pennsylvania, 1806–1906* (Connellsville: Centennial Historical Committee, 1906), 266.

28. Fulton, "Coal Mining in the Connellsville Coke Region," 333–34; Fulton, *Coke* (1905), 132; *BAISA*, 23 August 1876, 228; *Iron Age*, 21 June 1888, 1013; *BAISA*, 4 December 1889.

29. *Frank Cowan's Paper*, quoted in *BAISA*, 23 July 1873.

30. *BAISA*, 19 April 1893, 114; *Frank Cowan's Paper*.

31. State of Pennsylvania, *Industrial Statistics*, part 2 of the *Annual Report of the Secretary of Internal Affairs* 15, no. 12, F3.

32. *Frank Cowan's Paper*.

33. *Connellsville Weekly Courier*, May 1914, 26.

34. J. M. Swank, *History of the Manufacture of Iron in All Ages* (Philadelphia: AISA, 1892), 477.

35. Ibid., 113; McCormick, "Labor in the Connellsville Coke Region," F3–F4.

36. L. Hunter, "The Heavy Industries before 1860," in *The Growth of the American Economy*, ed. H. F. Williamson (Englewood, N.J.: Prentice Hall, 1944), 214.

37. A. Hewitt, December 1849, quoted in Swank, *Iron in All Ages*, 435.

38. J. P. Lesley quoted in Fulton, *Coke* (1905), 133.

39. *Pittsburgh Daily Gazette*, 5 September 1853.

40. M. E. Sheppard, *Cloud by Day: The Story of Coal and Coke and People* (Chapel Hill: University of North Carolina Press, 1947. Reprinted, Pittsburgh: University Press, 1991), 34–35.

2. The Maturing Industry

1. W. W. Rostow, *The World Economy: History and Prospect* (London: Macmillan, 1978), 52–53.

2. *BAISA*, 14 May 1874; Swank, *Iron in All Ages*, 371.

3. Eavenson, *First Century and a Quarter of American Coal Industry*, 579; Fulton, "Coal Mining in the Connellsville Coke Region," 334.

4. Review of Klupfel articles in *BAISA*, 28 June 1871, 341–42.

5. I. L. Bell, *Notes of a Visit to the Coal and Iron Mines and Ironworks in the United States* (Newcastle upon Tyne, 1875), 15; idem, "Report on the Iron Manufacture of the United States and a Comparison of it with that of Great Britain," *Iron*, 13 October 1877, 454.

6. *Frank Cowan's Paper*, quoted in *BAISA*, 3 September 1873.

7. *Iron Age*, 6 February 1873, quoted in H. R. Mussey, *Combination in the Mining Industry: A Study of Combination in Lake Superior Iron Ore Production*, (New York: Columbia University, 1906), 58–59.

8. *AISA Report 1874*, 63; *JISI* (1873): 476; (1874): 453–54; *Iron*, 8 April 1876, 462.

9. *BAISA*, 5 March 1875; 12 March 1875; 2 April 1875; Fulton, *Coke* (1905), 342; V. S. Clark, *History of Manufactures in the United States*, 3 vols. (New York: McGraw-Hill, 1929), 2:250–51; Pennsylvania 1875, 386.

10. *BAISA*, 28 May 1874; 7 May 1875.

11. J. Fulton, "Bituminous Coal, Coke, and Anthracite Coal in Ironmaking," *BAISA*, 27 June 1877, 170.

12. Clark, *Manufactures in the United States*, 2:251; *BAISA*, 11 July 1877; J. G. Butler, *Fifty Years of Iron and Steel* (Cleveland: Penton Press, 1923); Sweetser in *Iron Age*, 30 December 1943, 32.

13. G. Harvey, *Henry Clay Frick: The Man* (New York: Charles Scribners, 1928), 51.

14. Bell, *Notes of a Visit*, 15.

15. F. Platt, *Special Report on the Manufacture of Coke in the Youghiogheny River Valley*, Second Geological Survey of Pennsylvania (Harrisburg: Board of Commissioners, 1876).

16. *EMJ*, 18 September 1875, 281; and 17 June 1876.

17. *BAISA*, 21 May 1879, quoted in *Philadelphia Public Ledger;* Harvey, *Henry Clay Frick*, 66.

18. *EMJ*, 8 March 1879, 163; *Republican Standard* quoted in *EMJ*, 2 August 1879, 79; *EMJ*, 29 November 1879, 407; *Connellsville Weekly Courier*, May 1914; McCormick, "Labor in the Connellsville Coke Region," F4; Fulton, "Coal Mining in the Connellsville Coke Region."

19. C. S. Wardley, "'The Early Development of the H. C. Frick Coke Company': Address Delivered at the Frick Centennial Meeting of the Westmoreland-Fayette Historical Society, 18 June 1949," *Western Pennsylvania Historical Magazine* 32 (1949): 80; *EMJ*, 2 August 1879, 79; G. D. Albert, *History of the County of Westmoreland* (Philadelphia: Everts, 1882), 407–10.

20. *BAISA*, 3 September 1873; *EMJ*, 17 June 1876.

21. Frick and Company, Day Book, July 1876, FP.

22. *Iron Age*, 11 May 1899, 27.

23. U.S. Bureau of the Census, *Census of Manufactures 1905*, Bulletin 78 (Washington, D.C.: GPO, 1905), 20, table 8.

24. AISA, "Report for 1887" (Philadelphia: AISA), 18; idem, "Works Directory" (Philadelphia: AISA, 1892); Butler, *Fifty Years of Iron and Steel*.

25. *EMJ*, 1 September 1883, 125; and 3 November 1883, 278; Fulton, *Coke* (1905), 326–27.

26. H. S. Perloff, et al., *Regions, Resources, and Economic Growth* (Baltimore, Md.: Johns Hopkins University Press, 1960), 211, based on W. Isard, "Some Locational Factors in the Iron and Steel Industry since the Early Nineteenth Century," *Journal of Political Economy* 56 (1948).

27. *EMJ*, 4 August 1882, 62.

28. *EMJ*, 30 August 1884, 146.

29. F. Ellis, *History of Fayette County* (Philadelphia: Everts, 1882), 231, 246.

30. 37th Annual Report of the Pennsylvania Railroad.

31. *New York Railroad Gazette* quoted in *BAISA*, 12 August 1885, 210.

32. *Engineering*, 26 January 1883, 89.

33. H. C. Frick to M. H. Twombly, 5 February 1883, FP.

34. H. C. Frick to M. H. Twombly, 13 July 1883, FP.

35. *EMJ*, 3 November 1883; 29 December 1883, 393; 12 January 1884, 19; and 12 April 1884, 287.

36. J. F. Wall, *Andrew Carnegie* (Pittsburgh: University of Pittsburgh Press, 1989), 511. Wall put the figure at $5 million.

37. Wall, *Carnegie*, 511; *EMJ*, 26 April 1884, 322.

38. Wall, *Carnegie*, 513–15.
39. *BAISA*, 10 July 1895.
40. Wall, *Carnegie*, 779–80.
41. *EMJ*, 5 December 1885, 389.
42. McCormick, "Labor in the Connellsville Coke Region," F2.
43. Albert, *History of the County of Westmoreland*, 407–10; *Iron Age*, 11 May 1899, 29; *BAISA*, 23 January 1901; *Connellsville Weekly Courier*, May 1914, 48.
44. *Connellsville Weekly Courier*, May 1914, 52.
45. Quoted in *Iron Age*, 19 June 1913, 1497.
46. Wall, *Carnegie*, 508; *Iron Age*, 21 April 1887; *BAISA*, 18 March 1891, 74.
47. Vice President King, Baltimore and Ohio Railroad, to A. Carnegie, 26 October 1885; M. H. Twombly to Carnegie Steel, in minutes of directors, 27 November 1900, CSCP; A. Moreland to A. Carnegie, 8 March 1900, ACLC.
48. *EMJ*, 28 June 1913, 1306.
49. *EMJ*, 16 April 1881, 279; *Iron Age*, 21 July 1881, quoted in *JISI* 2 (1881).
50. *EMJ*, 26 May 1883, 295; 9 June 1883, 329; and 22 December 1883.
51. H. C. Frick to A. Carnegie, 24 October 1883, FP; *EMJ*, 12 January 1884, 19; minutes of the H. C. Frick Coke Company, FP; *EMJ*, 23 May 1885, 357.
52. *EMJ*, 22 December 1883, 379; 12 January 1884, 19.
53. H. C. Frick to E. B. Leisenring, 9 January 1884, FP.
54. *EMJ*, 9 February 1884, 114; 8 March 1884, 190; 29 March 1884, 339.
55. *EMJ*, 6 December 1884; 20 December 1884, 413; 14 February 1885, 111.
56. *EMJ*, 3 May 1884, 339; 17 May 1884, 377; 10 January 1885, 27; 7 February 1885, 92; 14 February 1885, 111; 23 May 1885, 196, 357; 6 June 1885, 391; 22 May 1886, 377; 25 September 1886, 225.
57. *EMJ*, 5 April 1884, 266; 20 December 1884.
58. *EMJ*, 17 July 1886, 47; 21 August 1886, 136; 5 November 1887, 336; 5 February 1887, 103; 26 February 1887, 156; 5 March 1887, 174; 27 August 1887, 156.
59. E. B. Leisenring to J. K. Taggart, 8 December 1887 and 9 January 1888, LP; *Connellsville Weekly Courier*, May 1914.
60. *Iron Age*, 26 June 1888, 1013; E. B. Leisenring to J. K. Taggart, 30 October 1888, LP.
61. *BASIA*, 15 January 1890; H. C. Frick to J. Morse, 13 March 1889, FP.
62. H. C. Frick to E. B. Leisenring, 6 March and 15 May 1889, FP; *Connellsville Weekly Courier*, May 1914, 7.
63. *EMJ*, 28 December 1889, 574; H. C. Frick to J. Morse, 17 July 1889, FP.
64. *Iron Age*, 27 November 1890, 261.
65. *EMJ*, 5 October 1889, 301.
66. H. C. Frick to A. Carnegie, 29 October 1895, FP; *BAISA*, 10 November 1895; "Report by C. M. Schwab on visit to coke region made on 13 July 1898," in minutes of Board of Managers of Carnegie Steel Co., undated, CSCP; Brownlee, "Connellsville Coke Region," xxix.
67. *BAISA*, 10 October 1896; A. Carnegie to H. C. Frick, 25 January and 18 September 1896, FP.
68. Temin, *Iron and Steel in Nineteenth Century America*, 284.
69. J. G. Butler to H. C. Frick, 11 October 1890, FP.
70. Temin, *Iron and Steel in Nineteenth Century America*, 277.
71. McClenathan, *Borough of Connellsville*, 274.
72. S. H., Heald, ed. *Fayette County, Pa.: An Inventory of Historic Engineering and Industrial Sites*, Historic American Engineering Record (Washington, D.C.: National Parks Service, 1990), 124; *EMJ*, 18 April 1885, 266.
73. H. C. Frick to Cambria Iron Company, 8 July 1884, FP; J. Fulton, *Coke*, (Scranton, N.J.: International Textbook, 1895), viii; Fulton, *Coke* (1905), iv; *EMJ*, 5 April 1884, 266; 7 February 1885, 92; 28 November 1885, 374; and 5 December 1885, 389; *BAISA*, 2 December 1885.
74. H. Phipps to A. Carnegie, 1 January 1880; G. Lauder to A. Carnegie, 25 February 1880; D. Stewart to A. Carnegie, 6 March 1880; A. Carnegie to W. J. Rainey, 4 March 1881; and H. Phipps to A. Carnegie, 4 January 1882, CSCP.
75. H. C. Frick to T. M. Carnegie, 6 April 1883, FP.

76. "H. Oliver" in *The Iron and Steel Industry in the Nineteenth Century: Encyclopedia of American Business History and Biography*, ed. P. Paskoff (New York: Facts on File, 1989), 260.

77. Heald, *Fayette County, Pa.*, 97; *EMJ*, 9 January 1886, 25; 10 January 1887, 438.

78. *BAISA*, 15 July 1899, 122.

79. G. Lauder to A. Carnegie, 14 November 1883, ACLC; H. C. Frick to A. Mellon, 28 October 1885, FP; K. Warren, *Triumphant Capitalism: Henry Clay Frick and the Industrial Transformation of America* (Pittsburgh: University of Pittsburgh Press, 1996), 36; H. C. Frick to J. Morse, 19 September 1885; W. R. Stirling to H. C. Frick, 4 November 1885; and H. C. Frick to J. Morse, 17 June 1889, FP.

80. H. C. Frick to O. Potter, 8 September 1886, FP.

81. W. R. Stirling to H. C. Frick, 21 June 1888; H. A. Gray to H. C. Frick, 18 December 1888; and T. Lynch to H. C. Frick, 8 March 1888, FP.

82. H. C. Frick to M. Ramsay, 19 April 1889; H. C. Frick to W. R. Stirling, 27 May, 14 June, and 5 July 1889; and H. C. Frick to J. Morse, 6 July 1889, FP.

83. W. R. Stirling to H. C. Frick, 20 August 1888; and F. W. Haskell to H. C. Frick, 11 February 1889, FP.

84. H. C. Frick to M. Ramsay, 11 July 1889, 17 September, 20 November, and 9 December 1890; and H. C. Frick to H. S. Smith, 9 December 1890, FP.

85. H. C. Frick to J. Morse, 18 January and 8 June 1886, FP.

86. J. Morse to H. C. Frick, 17 September, 23 November, and 17 December 1886, FP.

87. J. Morse to H. C. Frick, 12 and 13 July 1887; and W. R. Stirling to J. Morse, 12 July 1887, FP.

88. H. A. Gray to E. M. Ferguson, 20 September 1887, FP.

89. AISA annual statistics, 1887.

90. H. C. Frick to A. Carnegie, 9 August 1889, FP.

91. H. C. Frick to J. Morse, 19 December 1885; J. Morse to H. C. Frick, 29 November 1887, 3 April, and 30 April 1888; and H. A. Gray to H. C. Frick, 25 April 1888, FP.

92. H. C. Frick to F. Thomson, 17 June 1889; and H. C. Frick to H. A. Gray, 18 June 1889, FP.

93. J. Morse to H. C. Frick, 9 and 18 April 1888, FP.

94. H. C. Frick to J. Morse, 3 August 1889; J. Morse to H. C. Frick, 3 May 1888; H. C. Frick to H. A. Gray, 7 November 1889; and H. C. Frick to J. Morse, 16 October 1889, FP.

95. H. C. Frick to J. McCrea, 4 May 1892; H. C. Frick to H. A. Gray, 4 May 1892; and H. C. Frick to J. Morse, 26 May 1892 and 22 February 1893, FP.

96. Illinois Steel Company minutes, 21 June 1893, ISCP.

97. H. C. Frick to J. Morse, 20 September 1894, FP.

98. Illinois Steel Company minutes, 17 December 1897, ISCP.

99. H. C. Frick to J. W. Gates, 19 December 1895; and H. C. Frick to Illinois Steel Company, 20 November 1896, FP; Illinois Steel Company minutes, 29 December 1896, ISCP; H. C. Frick to F. Thomson, 17 June 1889, FP; Illinois Steel Company minutes, 17 December 1897; H. C. Frick to A. Carnegie, 19 February 1898; and T. Lynch to H. C. Frick, 21 November 1898, FP.

100. H. C. Frick to A. Carnegie, 5 March and 13 January 1890, FP.

101. A. Carnegie to H. C. Frick, 25 January 1896, FP.

102. H. Phipps to H. C. Frick, 25 June 1897; and A. Carnegie to H. C. Frick, 9 October 1897, FP.

103. H. C. Frick to A. Carnegie, 22 and 30 November 1897; A. Carnegie to H. C. Frick, 1 December 1897; and A. Carnegie to G. Lauder, 1 January 1898, FP.

104. H. C. Frick to A. Carnegie, 17 and 20 January 1898, FP.

105. H. C. Frick to A. Carnegie, 2 December 1897; and H. C. Frick to F. Thomson, 23 December 1897, FP.

106. Carnegie Steel, minutes of Board of Managers, 26 April and 12 May 1898, CSCP; A. Carnegie to H. C. Frick, 5 February 1898, FP; Carnegie Steel, minutes of Board of Managers, 14 November 1898 and 25 June 1900, CSCP.

3. Organization in the Coke Trade

1. Platt, *Manufacture of Coke in the Youghiogheny River Valley*; McCormick, "Labor in the Connellsville Coke Region," F2, F5.

2. Ibid.
3. Sheppard, *Cloud by Day*, 42.
4. McCormick, "Labor in the Connellsville Coke Region," F6.
5. Ibid.
6. *Connellsville Courier*, May 1914, 28; C. Erickson, *American Industry and the European Immigrant, 1860–1885* (Cambridge, Mass.: Harvard University Press, 1957), 117.
7. *Connellsville Courier*, 4 December 1884.
8. *Connellsville Weekly Courier*, May 1914.
9. *Pittsburgh Commercial Gazette*, 10 February 1886, quoted in *BAISA*, 17 February 1886; T. Lynch to H. C. Frick, 21 January 1886, FP.
10. *EMJ*, 16 August 1884, 108; and 25 October 1884, 287; D. F. Brestensky, ed., *The Early Coke Worker* (Connellsville: South West Pennsylvania Heritage Preservation Commission, 1994), 87–95.
11. *American Manufacturer*, 19 February 1886, 10; *EMJ*, 13 February 1886, 105; T. Lynch to H. C. Frick, 21 January 1886, FP; *EMJ*, 24 April 1886; *American Manufacturer*, 26 February 1886, 10; H. C. Frick to J. Morse, 18 January 1886, FP.
12. H. C. Frick to J. Morse, 13 May 1886, FP.
13. *EMJ*, 1 January 1887, 10; and 19 February 1887.
14. *EMJ*, 7 May 1887, 334.
15. *EMJ*, 14 May 1887, 352; and 28 May 1887, 387; *Pittsburgh Times*, 1 June 1887; Harvey, *Henry Clay Frick*, 83.
16. R. Ramsay to H. C. Frick, 31 May 1887, FP.
17. T. Lynch to H. C. Frick, 2 June 1887, FP.
18. E. B. Leisenring to H. C. Frick, 19 May 1887, FP.
19. *EMJ*, 9 July 1887, 28.
20. *EMJ*, 23 July 1887, 64; and 6 August 1887, 100.
21. *EMJ*, 27 August 1887, 154; *Connellsville Weekly Courier*, May 1914, 28.
22. *EMJ*, 3 September 1887, 172; 10 September 1887, 193; and 5 November 1887, 336.
23. *Connellsville Weekly Courier*, May 1914, 28.
24. M. Ramsay to H. C. Frick, 9 April and 30 August 1888, FP.
25. *Connellsville Weekly Courier*, May 1914, 28.
26. Note 1538, USX.
27. *EMJ*, 3 August 1889, 102; and 10 August 1889, 124.
28. Harvey, *Henry Clay Frick*, 90–91; H. C. Frick to A. Carnegie, 2 August 1889, FP.
29. A. Carnegie to H. C. Frick, 7 August 1889, FP; Harvey, *Henry Clay Frick*, 91–92.
30. H. C. Frick to A. Carnegie, 2 February 1891, FP; *Connellsville Weekly Courier*, May 1914, 30; *BAISA*, 8 April 1891.
31. *Connellsville Courier*, 13 February 1891; and 20 February 1891.
32. Ibid., 13 February 1891.
33. Ibid., 20 February 1891.
34. H. C. Frick to A. Carnegie, 17 March 1891; A. Carnegie to H. C. Frick, 21 March 1891; and H. C. Frick to G. Lauder, 28 March 1891, FP.
35. H. C. Frick to J. Morse, and Frick to W. R. Stirling, 26 March 1891, FP.
36. *1891 Strikes and Lockouts*, Report L-19 (Harrisburg: Pennsylvania Department of Internal Affairs, 1892); H. C. Frick to J. Morse, and W. R. Stirling, 30 March 1891, FP.
37. H. C. Frick to A. Carnegie, 1 April 1891, FP.
38. Report sent from Morewood to the Executive Chamber, Harrisburg, 2 April 1891. See also E. Pulay, *The Shots Fired at Morewood* (Mount Pleasant: Southwestern Pennsylvania Heritage Preservation Commission, 1996).
39. Confirmation telegram, H. C. Frick to J. Morse, 2 April 1891, FP.
40. H. C. Frick to M. Ramsay, 2 April 1891, FP.
41. H. C. Frick to M. Ramsay, 4 April 1891, FP.
42. R. J. Linden to H. C. Frick, 5 April 1891; M. Ramsay to H. C. Frick, 13 and 5 April 1891; T. Lynch to H. C. Frick, April 1891; and H. C. Frick to M. Ramsay, 15 April 1891, FP.

43. *1891 Strikes and Lockouts*, 12D.
44. "Dispatch from Scottdale," 20 April 1891, quoted in *BAISA*, 22 April 1891; R. J. Linden to H. C. Frick, 15 and 19 April 1891; and H. C. Frick to J. Morse, 23 April 1891, FP.
45. H. C. Frick to A. Carnegie, 21 April 1891; and H. C. Frick to J. Morse, 21 April 1891, FP.
46. A. Carnegie to H. C. Frick, 22 April 1891, FP.
47. H. C. Frick to A. Carnegie, 28 April 1891, FP; Pulay, *Shots Fired at Morewood*, 25; M. Ramsay to H. C. Frick, 4 May 1891, FP.
48. M. Ramsay and R. Ramsay to H. C. Frick, 29 April 1891; and H. C. Frick to M. Ramsay, 30 April 1891, FP.
49. *1891 Strikes and Lockouts*, 12D; untitled translated article by C. M. Parker, FP.
50. T. Lynch to H. C. Frick, 29 April and 9 May 1891, FP.
51. M. Ramsay to H. C. Frick, 15 May 1891, FP.
52. T. Lynch to H. C. Frick, 18 May 1891; H. C. Frick to J. Morse, 20 May 1891; and J. Morse to H. C. Frick, 23 May 1891, FP.
53. *1891 Strikes and Lockouts*, 12D.
54. H. C. Frick to A. Carnegie, 25 May 1891, FP.
55. H. C. Frick to M. Ramsay, 24 June 1891, FP.
56. *1891 Strikes and Lockouts*, 13.
57. *New York Tribune* quoted in *BAISA*, 8 April 1891.
58. *BAISA*, 11 April 1894.
59. M. J. Welsh in *Pittsburgh Times*, 14 April 1894.
60. *Connellsville Courier*, 6 April 1894; *BAISA*, 11 April 1894; *Pittsburgh Times*, 14 April 1894.
61. *Pittsburgh Times*, 14 April 1894; H. C. Frick to W. Ramsay, 2 May 1894; and C. E. Dunn to H. C. Frick, 11 May 1894, FP.
62. R. S. Laws to J. B. Bosworth of H. C. Frick Coke Co., 30 August 1894, FP.
63. *BAISA*, 10 November and 20 April 1895.
64. H. C. Frick to J. W. Gates, 11 September 1895; and T. Lynch to H. C. Frick, 11 September 1895, FP.
65. *Connellsville Courier*, 4 October 1895, quoted in *BAISA*, 10 October 1895; T. Lynch to H. C. Frick, 9 October 1895, FP.
66. *Connellsville Courier*, 8 January 1897, quoted in *BAISA*, 20 January 1897.
67. Carnegie Steel Company minutes, 5 and 12 March 1900, CSCP.
68. *BAISA*, 25 July 1902; McClenathan, *Borough of Connellsville*, 286 (emphasis added).
69. T. Lynch to H. C. Frick, summer 1899, FP.
70. *EMJ*, 4 January 1908, 75; *BAISA*, 1 December 1907, 141; and 1 January 1908, 1.
71. *EMJ*, 11 January 1908, 126; *Encyclopedia Britannica Year Book, 1913*, 900.
72. *American Manufacturer*, 13 February 1880, 10.
73. Quoted in Ellis, *History of Fayette County*, 411.
74. *Coal and Coke*, December 1915, 688.
75. "The Connellsville Coke Region of Western Pennsylvania," *EMJ*, 8 March 1879, 163; *EMJ*, 23 January 1886, 57.
76. Deed to coal holdings, 11 June 1886, FP.
77. H. C. Frick to T. Lynch, 25 November 1882; and H. C. Frick to R. Ramsay, 28 May 1886, FP.
78. *EMJ*, 23 May 1885, 357.
79. *Connellsville Weekly Courier*, May 1914, 10.
80. H. C. Frick to J. G. A. Leishman, 6 July 1886, FP.
81. USS Finance Committee minutes, 11 and 25 September 1906.
82. Deed to coal holdings, 11 June 1886.
83. H. C. Frick Coke Company minutes, 19 May 1890, FCCP.
84. J. Boileau, *Coalfields of South Western Pennsylvania* (Pittsburgh, 1907), 57.
85. *Coal and Coke*, 5 February 1914, 87.
86. *Western Pennsylvania* (Pittsburgh: Western Pennsylvania Biographical Association, 1923), 515.
87. Sheppard, *Cloud by Day*, 76ff; *Coal and Coke*, 5 March 1914, 158.
88. H. C. Frick to E. H. Gary, 12 June 1914, FP.

89. *Coal and Coke,* October 1915.
90. Sheppard, *Cloud by Day,* chapter 7.
91. *EMJ,* 16 January 1915, 166; J. N. Boucher, *Old and New Westmoreland* (New York: American Historical Society, 1918), 288–90; *National Cyclopedia of American Biography* 16 (1918), s.v. "T. Lynch"; Quivik, 159.
92. T. Lynch to H. C. Frick, 25 December 1885, FP.
93. *Coal and Coke,* 28 January 1909; *EMJ,* 30 January 1915, 256.
94. Quivik, *Connellsville Coal and Coke Region,* 160; H. C. Frick to J. Farrell, 31 January 1916, FP; *National Cyclopedia of American Biography* 21 (1931), s.v. "Clingerman."
95. *EMJ,* 24 January 1885, 57; 8 June 1889, 530; *National Cyclopedia of American Biography* 31 (1944), s.v. "Ramsay, Robert."
96. H. C. Frick to M. Ramsay, 16 April 1891, FP.
97. H. C. Frick to M. Ramsay, 13 November 1890, FP.
98. H. C. Frick to M. Ramsay, 23 May, 20 June, and 21 July 1892, FP.
99. *Scottdale Independent,* 27 October 1892; H. C. Frick to R. Ramsay, 1 November 1892; and memo of payment made, 4 November 1892, FP.
100. *Pittsburgh Dispatch,* 30 December 1892; *Mt. Pleasant Journal,* 3 January 1893; *Scottdale Independent,* 5 January 1893.
101. H. C. Frick to J. Morse, 3 January 1893, FP; *Scottdale Independent,* 12 January 1893.
102. H. C. Frick to W. Ramsay, 24 March, 28 March, 4 April, 30 April, 3 May, 7 May, 22 May, 3 July, 25 September, 12 October, 24 October, 4 December, 6 December, 11 December, and 19 December 1894, FP.
103. H. C. Frick to W. Ramsay, 4 June 1895; and W. Ramsay to H. C. Frick, 14 November 1895 and 28 December 1896, FP.
104. W. Ramsay to H. C. Frick, 1 June 1897; F. W. Haskell to H. C. Frick, 2 June 1897; H. C. Frick to W. Ramsay, 3 June 1897; and W. Ramsay to H. C. Frick, 19 February 1899, 4 October 1900, and 28 May 1901, FP.

4. New Districts

1. *EMJ,* 29 July 1899, 140.
2. *EMJ,* 21 April 1900, 480; and 28 April 1900, 492.
3. *BAISA,* 1 October 1899; 1 November 1899; and 1 January 1900; *Coal and Coke,* 8 February 1901, 288; Geological Survey, annual reports for 1902 and 1903.
4. *EMJ,* quoted in *BAISA,* 15 October 1900, 171.
5. *EMJ,* 14 October 1899; and 8 December 1900.
6. N. P. Hyndman in *Coal and Coke,* 15 January 1903, 7; Boileau, *Coalfields of South Western Pennsylvania,* 58; *EMJ,* 19 January 1889; and 26 October 1889, 367; *BAISA,* 15 January 1890, 11.
7. *BAISA,* 15 October 1900, 171; *Coal and Coke,* November 1900, 171.
8. Boileau, *Coalfields of South Western Pennsylvania,* 42; T. Lynch to H. C. Frick, 26 November 1895, and 4 May 1896, FP.
9. *Encyclopedia Britannica,* 10th ed., s.v. "iron and steel"; T. H. Burnham and G. O. Hoskins, *Iron and Steel in Britain 1870–1930* (London: Allen and Unwin, 1943), 145.
10. F. C. Keighley quoted in Boileau, *Coalfields of South Western Pennsylvania,* 56.
11. Boileau, *Coalfields of South Western Pennsylvania,* 41; Heald, *Fayette County, Pa.,* 18; Quivik, *Connellsville Coal and Coke Region,* 23; *Colliery Guardian,* 16 October 1900, 1044.
12. Boileau, *Coalfields of South Western Pennsylvania,* 57; Heald, *Fayette County, Pa.,* 123; Warren, *Triumphant Capitalism,* 249; *EMJ,* 2 November 1889, 393.
13. *BAISA,* 1 October 1899; and 15 February 1900.
14. Boileau, *Coalfields of South Western Pennsylvania,* 58.
15. *Coal and Coke,* 19 May 1899, 14; and 11 August 1899, 15; *EMJ,* 7 April 1900; *BAISA,* 1 November 1899.
16. United States Steel Corporation, Executive Committee minutes, 19 June 1901, 76; *BAISA,* 25 October 1902; *Coal and Coke,* 1 July 1901; 1 January 1902, 10; and 15 July 1908, 19.

17. *Coal and Coke*, 15 January 1903, 7.
18. McClenathan, *Borough of Connellsville*; Boileau, *Coalfields of South Western Pennsylvania*, 42; *Coal and Coke*, 21 November 1912, 322.
19. McClenathan, *Borough of Connellsville*; J. B. Hogg, *New Map of the Connellsville Coke Region and Adjacent Fields, showing all Coke Works* (N.p., 1909); G. Porter, *Industrial Map of the Connellsville Coke Region* (N.p., 1907).
20. McClenathan, *Borough of Connellsville*, 284–85.
21. *EMJ*, 18 May 1907; *Coal and Coke*, 15 May 1906, 17.
22. *EMJ*, 26 January 1907; and 16 February 1907, 355; *Connellsville Weekly Courier*, May 1914.
23. Heald, *Fayette County, Pa.*, 55; *Coal and Coke*, 1 January 1906; *BAISA*, 1 December 1908, 134; *Coal and Coke*, 1 March 1908.
24. *Coal and Coke*, 15 April 1906, 17; *EMJ*, 2 November 1907, 845.
25. *Coal and Coke*, 15 January 1902, 11; and 15 April 1908.
26. *Coal and Coke*, 9 February 1911, 93; H. C. Frick to E. H. Gary, 12 June 1914, FP.
27. *Coal and Coke*, 15 July 1908, 19; and 1 August 1908, 14.
28. *Coal and Coke*, 1 January 1908, 14; and 14 January 1909, 36.
29. *Coal and Coke*, 28 January 1909, 72; W. R. Ingalls, *The Mineral Industry in 1909: Its Statistics, Technology, and Trade* (New York, 1910), 136; A. Cotter, *United States Steel: A Corporation with a Soul* (New York: Doubleday Page, 1921), 310.
30. H. C. Frick Coke Company minutes, 26 June 1911, FCCP; USS Finance Committee minutes, 23 May 1911, USX; *Iron Age* quoted in *Coal and Coke*, 1 July 1911, 16.
31. McClenathan, *Borough of Connellsville*; *Connellsville Weekly Courier*, May 1914.
32. Temin, *Iron and Steel in Nineteenth Century America*, 268–69.
33. C. M. Schwab, "Testimony to the United States Industrial Commission," in United States Industrial Commission, *Reports*, vol. 13 (Washington, D.C.: GPO, 1901), 464.
34. *TAIME* 4 (1875–1876): 99–101.
35. *TAIME* 16 (1887–1888): 581–93.
36. T. S. Reynolds on the St. Louis Ore and Steel Company in P. Paskoff, ed., *The Iron and Steel Industry in the Nineteenth Century: Encyclopedia of American Business History and Biography* (New York: Facts on File, 1989), 300–301.
37. Fulton, *Coke* (1905), 9.
38. *Iron Age*, 13 January 1898, 15; United States Geological Survey, *Annual Report for 1899–1900*, part 5 (Washington, D.C.: GPO, 1900), 574; G. Thiessen, et al., *Coke from Illinois Coals*, Bulletin 64 (Illinois State Geological Survey, 1937), 49–50; *Blast Furnace and Steel Plant*, May 1963, 358–64.
39. Fulton, *Coke* (1905), 177, 358–64; USGS, *Annual Report for 1899–1900*, 599, 611.
40. *BAISA*, 10 June 1899.
41. *Encyclopedia Britannica*, 9th ed., s.v. "Pennsylvania."
42. *BAISA*, 18 September 1889.
43. J. D. Weeks, "The Elk Garden and Upper Potomac Coalfields of West Virginia," *TAIME* 24 (1894): 351–64; Fulton, *Coke* (1905), 44.
44. *Encyclopedia Britannica*, 9th ed., s.v. "West Virginia."
45. J. R. Smith, *North America* (London: Bell, 1924), chapter 11, especially, 214–28.
46. S. E. Morris, "The New River Coalfield of West Virginia," *TAIME* 8 (1879–1880): 261–68; C. R. Boyd, "The Mineral Resources of South West Virginia," *TAIME* 8 (1879–1880): 338–48. On the new coke areas generally, see J. H. Allen, "Coal and Cokes of East Kentucky," *TAIME* 21 (1892–1893): 53–60.
47. *Encyclopedia Britannica*, 9th ed., s.v. "Virginia."
48. *EMJ*, 25 September 1886, 225.
49. H. A. Gray to H. C. Frick, 6 January 1888; H. A. Gray to J. Morse, 6 April 1888; J. Morse to H. C. Frick, 6 April 1888; and H. A. Gray to H. C. Frick, 6 June 1888, FP; *BAISA*, 30 May 1888.
50. J. Morse to H. C. Frick, 6 September 1889; and H. C. Frick to J. McRea, 13 May 1892, FP.
51. *Pittsburgh Commercial Gazette*, quoted in *BAISA*, 5 and 12 July 1893.
52. "Anon, from Parkersburg" to J. M. Drill of Buffalo, 18 June 1894, FP.
53. K. Warren, "The Leisenring Venture," *Pittsburgh History* 78, no. 1 (spring 1995): 34–44.

54. J. M. Hodge, "The Big Stone Gap Coalfield," *TAIME* 21 (1892–1893): 922–38.
55. USGS, *Annual Report for 1899–1900*, 598.
56. United States Industrial Commission, *Reports*, 13:506.
57. E. H. Gary quoted in *BAISA*, 10 January 1902.
58. *BAISA*, 25 July 1904; E. W. Parker, *United States Geological Survey Annual Review of Coke Industry for 1907*, 266–78.
59. *Iron Age*, 14 April 1904, 38; *Coal and Coke*, 17 February 1910, 110; and 4 July 1912, 425.
60. Ingalls, *Mineral Industry in 1909*, 122.

5. New Technology

1. J. Fulton quoted in *BAISA*, 10 November 1896; C. A. Meissner, notes on coke manufacture, June 1911, USX.
2. D. A. Fisher, *The Epic of Steel* (New York: Harper and Row, 1963), 200.
3. *JISI* (1876), volume 1; (1882) 2:241; (1884), 1:700; *EMJ*, 5 November 1881, 304; Fulton, *Coke* (1905), 202.
4. *EMJ*, 31 January 1885, 71; and 14 March 1885, 176–77.
5. F. Koerner, "The Manufacture and Cost of Coke," *EMJ*, 29 October 1886, 291; 4 December 1886, 399; 5 February 1887, 93.
6. *EMJ*, 6 November 1886; 11 December 1886, 421–22; and 23 April 1887, 291.
7. J. Winslow in *EMJ*, 30 October 1886; H. M. Howe in *EMJ*, 26 November 1886, 362.
8. *EMJ*, 26 November 1886, 362.
9. *Pittsburgh Post*, 29 July 1892.
10. *BAISA*, 12 September 1894; and 17 October 1894; *Colliery Guardian*, 19 October 1894, 202.
11. *BAISA*, 14 November 1894.
12. *BAISA*, 20 November 1895.
13. *BAISA*, 15 December 1898; *TAIME* 28 (1898): 874; *BAISA*, 1 December 1897; T. Lynch to H. C. Frick, 29 April 1896, FP.
14. *Iron Trade Review*, 4 October 1894, quoted in *BAISA*, 17 October 1894; E. W. Parker quoted in *BAISA*, 15 December 1898; Illinois Steel Company, director's minutes, 10 December 1895 and 21 May 1896, ISCP; *Iron Age*, 14 March 1895, 550; *BAISA*, 20 October 1897.
15. *TAIME* 28 (1898): 874.
16. *BAISA*, 20 November 1895; O. W. Kennedy to T. Lynch, 25 February 1897, FP.
17. W. King in *Pittsburgh Dispatch*, quoted in *BAISA*, 15 September 1899.
18. F. Taussig, "The Iron Industry in the United States," *Quarterly Journal of Economics* 14 (February 1900): 167; E. W. Parker quoted in *BAISA*, 15 December 1898.
19. I. L. Bell to A. Carnegie, 28 November 1882, FP.
20. T. Lynch to H. C. Frick, 20 November 1889, FP.
21. Jacobs to H. C. Frick Coke Company, 23 November 1889, FP.
22. *EMJ*, 20 April 1889, 376; T. Lynch to H. C. Frick, 17 July 1890, FP.
23. S. A. Tuska to H. C. Frick, 6 January and 15 January 1891; H. C. Frick Coke Company to S. A. Tuska, 19 January 1891; and H. C. Frick to W. R. Stirling, 22 June 1891, FP.
24. J. Weeks to H. C. Frick, 6 June 1896, FP.
25. T. Lynch to H. C. Frick, 25 November 1895, 29 April 1896, and 9 September 1896, FP.
26. T. Lynch to H. C. Frick, 9 September 1896; and H. C. Frick to T. Lynch, 11 September 1896, FP.
27. O. W. Kennedy to T. Lynch, 12 October 1896; T. Lynch to H. C. Frick, 24 October 1896; O. W. Kennedy to T. Lynch, 25 February 1897; and T. Lynch to H. C. Frick, 25 February 1897, FP.
28. J. W. Gates to H. C. Frick, 24 and 29 December 1897, FP.
29. Report from D. Clemson to Carnegie Steel Board of Managers, 4 January 1898, CSCP.
30. A. Carnegie to G. Lauder, 1 January 1898, ACLC.
31. T. Lynch to H. C. Frick, 3 January 1898; and H. C. Frick to A. Carnegie, 19 March 1898, FP.
32. T. Lynch to H. C. Frick, 23 May 1898, FP; A. Carnegie to G. Lauder, 9 June 1898, ACLC.
33. A. Carnegie to I. L. Bell, note on letter of T. Lynch to H. C. Frick, 23 May 1898, ACLC.

34. T. Lynch, memorandum of summer 1899, ACLC, 65; E. W. Parker quoted in *Iron Trade Review*, 8 September 1898, 8.

35. *Iron Age*, 12 March 1903, 6; *JISI* (1905), 2:597.

36. F. C. Keighley quoted in *BAISA*, 1 March 1905.

37. F. Popplewell, *Some Modern Conditions and Recent Developments in Iron and Steel Production in America* (Manchester: Manchester University Press, 1906), 27.

38. *Coal and Coke*, 12 December 1912, 272.

39. "Retort and Beehive Coke Ovens," *EMJ*, 4 February 1911, 251–52.

40. *JISI* (1906) 4:769; *Chemical Abstracts* (1907) 1:1058; *JISI* (1907), 1:411; Fulton, *Coke* (1905), 362–63; *EMJ*, 8 December 1906, 1074. For an earlier scheme for mechanical drawing, see *Connellsville Courier*, 19 August 1892.

41. *TAIME* 32 (1902), quoted in *Review of American Chemical Research* 9 (1903): 158; *JISI* (1905), 2:594; *Iron Age*, 10 August 1905; *TAIME* 36 (1906): 353; *Chemical Abstracts* (1907), 1:1058; *Coal and Coke*, 1 January 1908, 10; and 15 April 1908; W. M. Judd, "Coke Oven Construction," *EMJ*, 10 November 1906, 877. For a review of various types of machine, see Macfarren to Engineers Society of Western Pennsylvania, quoted in *JISI* (1908), 1:272–73; and Quivik, *Connellsville Coal and Coke Region*, 40–52.

42. *JISI* (1901), 2:384–85; *TAIME* 33 (1902): 273.

43. *Chemical Abstracts* (1907), 1:635; and (1909), 2:2500–2501.

44. *Coal and Coke*, 15 August 1907, 10–11; *BAISA*, 25 November 1903; C. A. Meissner, "The Modern By-product Coke Oven," quoted in F. H. Wagner, *Coal and Coke* (New York: McGraw Hill, 1916), 302–3.

45. *Chemical Abstracts* (1910): 1362; *EMJ*, 26 October 1912, 772.

46. McClenathan, *Borough of Connellsville*, 283; Albert, *History of the County of Westmoreland*, 407.

47. A. W. Belden quoted in Wagner, *Coal and Coke*, 298–99; and Belden quoted in *History of Iron and Steel Making in the United States* (New York: American Institute of Mining, Metallurgical, and Petroleum Engineers, 1961), 40–41; *EMJ*, 4 February 1911, 251–52.

48. *Coal and Coke*, 1 August 1912, 68.

49. *Coal and Coke*, 12 December 1912, 272–73.

50. *Iron Age*, 12 March 1903, 6.

51. *Iron Age*, 29 January 1903, 37; 26 February 1903, 27; and 19 March 1903, 26.

52. *Coal and Coke*, 8 February 1901; McClenathan, *Borough of Connellsville*; G. Porter, *Industrial Map of the Connellsville Coke Region* (N.p., 1907); *Connellsville Weekly Courier*, May 1914.

53. Note, 1908, FP.

54. *Connellsville Weekly Courier*, May 1914; Warren, *American Steel Industry*, 115.

55. Fulton, *Coke* (1905).

56. *Coal and Coke*, December 1909.

57. *Connellsville Weekly Courier*, May 1914, 38, 40.

58. E. H. Gary, "Testimony to the United States Industrial Commission," in United States Industrial Commission, *Reports*, vol. 1 (1900), 985.

59. Fisher, *The Epic of Steel*, 201; U.S. Steel minutes, 28 May 1907, USX.

60. *EMJ*, 23 February 1901, 387.

61. Quoted in *Iron Age*, 22 May 1913, 1242.

62. Popplewell, *Modern Conditions and Recent Developments*, 39.

63. *JISI* (1909), 1:536; Fulton, *Coke* (1905), 310.

6. The Physical and Social Implications of Beehive Coke Manufacture

1. *TAIME* 14 (1885–1886): 618–19.

2. *Connellsville Weekly Courier*, May 1914, 13.

3. J. A. Enman, "The Relationship of Coal Mining and Coke Making to the Distribution of Population Agglomerations in the Connellsville (Pa.) Beehive Coke Region" (Ph.D. diss., University of Pittsburgh, 1962).

4. See advertisements in *Connellsville Weekly Courier*, May 1914. For a full survey see Quivik, *Connellsville Coal and Coke Region*, 120–27.

5. S. G. Nelson, *Nelson's Biographical Dictionary and Historical Reference Book of Fayette County* (Uniontown, Pa.: S. G. Nelson, 1900), 485. On national origins of employees in and outside mines in 1912, see Quivik, *Connellsville Coal and Coke Region*, 72–73; Enman, "Relationship of Coal Mining and Coke Making," 450–53.

6. Editorial in *Coal and Coke*, 13 April 1911, 236.

7. D. A. Corbin, *Life, Work, and Rebellion in the Coal Fields: The Southern West Virginia Miners, 1880–1922* (Urbana: University of Illinois Press, 1981).

8. State of Pennsylvania, *Industrial Statistics*, part 2 of *Annual Report of the Secretary of Internal Affairs* 15, no. 12 (Harrisburg, 1888).

9. J. M. Clark, *Studies in the Economics of Overhead Costs* (Chicago: University of Chicago Press, 1923), 81.

10. H. C. Frick to J. Morse, 13 May 1886 and 21 February 1888; J. Morse to H. C. Frick, 1 June 1887 and 18 April 1888; and H. A. Gray to H. C. Frick, 4 September 1888, FP.

11. H. C. Frick to M. Ramsay, 24 September 1890 and 12 March 1891, FP.

12. F. J. Hall to H. C. Frick, 22 January 1888; and H. C. Frick to F. J. Hall, 24 January 1888, FP.

13. J. D. McCaleb to H. C. Frick, 11 December 1891; R. A. Ramsay to T. Lynch, 16 December 1891; and T. Lynch to H. C. Frick, 19 December 1891, FP.

14. *EMJ*, 23 February 1884, 150; 1 November 1884, 303; and 13 March 1886, 197.

15. *Connellsville Courier*, 13 February 1891; *BAISA*, 10 August 1902.

16. *Coal and Coke*, June 1915, 602.

17. H. F. Walling and O. W. Gray, *Historical Topographical Atlas of Pennsylvania* (Philadelphia: Stedmon, Brown, and Lyon, 1872), 27.

18. *Pittsburgh Dispatch* quoted in *BAISA*, 29 March 1882.

19. W. Ferguson to H. C. Frick, 22 February 1886; *EMJ*, 17 August 1889, 148.

20. *Connellsville Courier*, 8 July 1887.

21. *Frick v. Stevens*, quoting Pennsylvania official documents, 1887–88, 60.

22. *BAISA*, 1 October 1884.

23. J. M. Swank, *Progressive Pennsylvania* (Philadelphia: Lippincott, 1908), 228.

24. Taussig, "The Iron Industry in the United States"; A. A. Marchbin, "Hungarian Activities in Western Pennsylvania," *West Pennsylvania Historical Society Magazine* 23, no. 3 (September 1940): 133–145.

25. F. Taussig, *Some Aspects of the Tariff Question* (Cambridge, Mass.: Harvard University Press, 1915), 137–38.

26. T. Lynch to H. C. Frick, 13 February and 27 May 1891, FP.

27. *Iron Age*, 11 May 1899, 28–29; W. J. Lauck, "The Bituminous Coal Mines and Coke Works of Western Pennsylvania," *Survey*, 1 April 1911.

28. H. H. Nicolay to the Court, 29 July 1966, *H. C. Frick v. Stevens*.

29. Lauck, "Bituminous Coal Mines and Coke Works of Western Pennsylvania," 38–40.

30. H. C. Frick to A. Mellon, 28 October 1885; and H. C. Frick to J. Morse, 26 September 1885, FP.

31. T. Lynch to H. C. Frick, 10 February 1895 (2 letters), FP; entry of 1 November 1898, ACLC, 56.

32. Lauck, "Bituminous Coal Mines and Coke Works of Western Pennsylvania."

33. H. C. Frick to M. Ramsay, 18 April 1890, FP; *EMJ*, 21 March 1885, 196.

34. *Pittsburgh Post*, 31 August 1892; minutes of meeting, Oliver and Snyder Steel Company, 16 December 1912.

35. Harvey, *Henry Clay Frick*, 55–57.

36. Lauck, "Bituminous Coal Mines and Coke Works of Western Pennsylvania," 41. See also P. S. Foner, *History of the Labor Movement in the United States* (New York: International Publishers, 1955), 21; A. Bachman to H. C. Frick, 27 April 1885; H. C. Frick to T. Lynch, 30 April 1885; and T. Lynch to H. C. Frick, 1 May 1885, FP.

37. *Connellsville Courier*, 5 December 1884.

38. T. Lynch to H. C. Frick, 28 January 1886; H. C. Frick to T. M Carnegie, 6 April 1883; and T. Lynch to H. C. Frick, 9 November 1885, FP; *Connellsville Weekly Courier*, May 1914, 28; J. Morse to H. C. Frick, 1 June 1887, FP.

39. T. Lynch to H. C. Frick, 1 April 1890; H. C. Frick to A. Carnegie, 17 January 1898, FP; J. Enman quoted in Quivik, *Connellsville Coal and Coke Region*, 65.

40. Lauck, "Bituminous Coal Mines and Coke Works of Western Pennsylvania," 38.

41. J. C. Kurtz to A. Carnegie, 5 April 1893, ACLC; *Greensburg Press* quoted in *BAISA*, 20 December 1895.

42. *Coal and Coke*, 6 October 1899, 13.

43. *Coal and Coke*, 5 January 1911, 15; and 3 July 1913, 227; *Iron Age*, 6 August 1915, 470.

44. Obituary of H. C. Frick, *Iron Age*, 11 December 1919, 1213.

45. House of Commons, "Account of the Pennsylvania Railroad," *British Parliamentary Papers, 1884*, vol. 88, p. 74.

46. T. Lynch to H. C. Frick, 1 May 1896, FP; J. T. Holdsworth, *Report of the Economic Survey of Pittsburgh* (N.p., 1912), 146.

47. Pittsburgh Chamber of Commerce, *The Mercantile, Manufacturing, and Mining Interests of Pittsburgh* (Pittsburgh Chamber of Commerce, 1884); *Connellsville Weekly Courier*, May 1914, 6.

48. *EMJ*, 19 January 1889, 73; J. H. Campbell, *Map of the Connellsville Coal and Coke Region* (N.p.: J. H. Campbell, 1883); H. C. Frick to J. Thompson, 20 June 1891; and S. C. Wakefield to H. C. Frick, 19 February 1891, FP.

49. J. K. Beeson to H. C. Frick, 17 and 19 June 1890, FP.

50. H. C. Frick to M. Ramsay, 17 and 24 September 1890, FP.

51. *EMJ*, 29 October 1886, 291; 6 November 1886; *Connellsville Weekly Courier*, May 1914, 38.

52. Nelson, *Biographical Dictionary*, 255.

53. R. E. Pease, "Evidence," in United Kingdom Board of Trade, Committee on Industry and Trade, *Report* (1925), 2:1091.

54. C. R. Van Hise, *The Conservation of the Natural Resources of the United States* (New York: Macmillan, 1910), 28.

55. *Coal and Coke*, 13 April 1911, 236; B. Terne quoted in *Mining* (1961): 47.

56. Quoted in *Coal and Coke*, 1 August 1912, 68.

57. *Proceedings of a Conference of Governors at the White House, May 1908* (Washington, D.C.: Government Printing Office, 1909), 22, 423.

58. J. Fulton in *TAIME* 13 (1884–1885), 330, 334; quoted in *Connellsville Weekly Courier*, May 1914, 36.

59. State of Pennsylvania, *The Connellsville Coke Region*, Report of Pennsylvania Bureau of Mines (Harrisburg, 1891), xx; Schwab, "Testimony to the United States Industrial Commission," in United States Industrial Commission, *Reports*, vol. 13 (Washington, D.C.: GPO, 1901), 464.

60. *EMJ*, 9 March 1907, 500; *BAISA*, 9 March 1907; *Connellsville Weekly Courier*, May 1914, 26.

61. *Conference of Governors at the White House*, 33.

7. Peak and Decline

1. AISI, "Report of 6th Annual Meeting," 22 May 1914.

2. C. G. Atwater, "The Development of the Modern Byproduct Coke Oven," *TAIME* 33 (1902): 763.

3. *Coal and Coke*, 12 December 1912, 373.

4. On silica bricks, see *Chemical Abstracts* (1915), 2805; on coking times, see C. E. Underwood of Northampton Coke Works, "Bethlehem in 1919," BP, 1770.

5. W. H. Blauvelt to American Institute of Mining Engineers, 1918, summarized in *Chemical Abstracts* (1919), 258.

6. Ibid.

7. W. H. Childs, "Byproducts Recovered in the Manufacture of Coke," paper presented at the meeting of the AISI, 26 May 1916, 11; United States Department of the Interior, *Minerals Yearbook* (Washington, D.C.: GPO, annually), 1913 and 1917 editions.

8. U.S. Steel Finance Committee minutes, 19 June 1917, USX.

9. Department of Interior, *Minerals Yearbook*, 1913 and 1917 editions; *Chemical Abstracts* (1919), 258.

10. "Joseph Becker" in B. E. Seeley, *Iron and Steel in the Twentieth Century: Encyclopedia of American*

Business History and Biography (New York: Facts on File, 1994), 35; *Non Metals*, part 2 of *Mineral Resources of the United States* (Washington, D.C.: GPO, 1920), 398–99.

11. H. C. Frick to E. H. Gary, 12 June 1914, 12 August 1918, and 29 August 1918, FP.
12. *EMJ*, 10 November 1917, 835.
13. U.S. Steel Finance Committee minutes, 15 October 1915, 18 January and 7 March 1916, USX.
14. Ibid., 14 March 1916, 24 July 1917, 30 October 1917, 16 April 1918, and 14 May 1918, USX.
15. *Iron Age*, 3 January 1918, 83; *Blast Furnace and Steel Plant*, June 1919, 257.
16. H. C. Porter, *Coal Carbonization* (New York: Chemical Catalogue, 1924), frontispiece; *Industrial and Engineering Chemistry* (November 1928): 1139; AISI, *Yearbook 1928*, 89.
17. *JISI* (1915), 1:514; B. Zwillinger patent quoted in *Chemical Abstracts* (1918): 2683.
18. G. J. Miller and A. E. Parkins, *Geography of North America* (New York: Wiley, 1923), 228; H. H. McCarty, *The Geographic Basis of American Economic Life* (New York: Harper, 1940), 261.
19. Boileau, *Coalfields of South Western Pennsylvania*, 54.
20. *Connellsville Courier* quoted in *BAISA*, 9 March 1907.
21. *Coal and Coke*, 21 November 1912.
22. *Coal and Coke*, 11 September 1913, 437.
23. *Coal and Coke*, 26 December 1912, 403; and 21 November 1912, 322.
24. *BAISA*, 1 November 1899.
25. *BAISA*, 9 March 1907; *Coal and Coke*, 14 January 1909, 31; 8 April 1909, 257; 26 January 1911, 65; and 5 February 1914, 87.
26. Boileau, *Coalfields of South Western Pennsylvania*, 57.
27. *BAISA*, 9 May 1908, 981; and 1 December 1908, 134; *EMJ*, 5 August 1911, 278; *Coal and Coke*, 21 November 1912; and 12 June 1913.
28. G. Lauder to A. Carnegie, 2 March 1880; and T. M. Carnegie to A. Carnegie, 8 March 1880, ACLC.
29. *EMJ*, 11 January 1890, 68; Carnegie Steel minutes, 3 May 1898, CSCP.
30. *EMJ*, 5 November 1887, 336; *Iron Age*, 11 May 1899, 30; W. B. Dickson, *History of the Carnegie Veterans Association* (Montclair, N.J.: Mountain Press, 1938), 29; A. Carnegie to H. C. Frick, 1 December 1897; and H. C. Frick to A. Carnegie, 13 December 1897, FP.
31. *Coal and Coke*, 1 August 1908, 14; Ingalls, *Mineral Industry in 1909*, 135–36.
32. *BAISA*, 1 July 1895; *Iron Age*, 8 June 1916, 1419.
33. *EMJ*, 16 February 1907, 355; and May 1945, 291–92.
34. *Fifty Years in Iron and Steel* (Youngstown Sheet and Tube Company, 1950), 60.
35. State of Pennsylvania, *Coal Analyses* (Harrisburg: Department of Forests and Waters, 1928), 10.
36. E. G. Nourse, et al., *America's Capacity to Produce* (Washington, D.C.: Brookings Institution, 1934), 62; *Mineral Resources of the United States* (Washington, D.C.: GPO, 1928), 638.
37. Nourse, *America's Capacity to Produce*, 62, 69–70.
38. Ibid., 65, 67.
39. Porter, *Coal Carbonization*, 56; R. H. Sweetser, *Blast Furnace Practice* (New York: McGraw-Hill, 1938), 126–27, 335.
40. *Mineral Resources of the United States* (Washington, D.C.: GPO, 1927); Enman, "Relationship of Coal Mining and Coke Making," 437–38.
41. Heald, *Fayette County, Pa.*, 21–22; U. S. Steel Finance Committee minutes, 9 November 1920, 11 November 1920, and 8 November 1922, USX; H. C. Frick Coke, "Historical Tabulation," 1928, FCCP.
42. G. Ashley, *Bituminous Coalfields of Pennsylvania* (1928), 1:218.
43. Ibid., 1:96.
44. *Mineral Resources of the United States* (1927), 625.
45. Heald, *Fayette County, Pa.*, 22; AISI annual reports.
46. State of Pennsylvania, Department of Internal Affairs, *Report on Production Industries, Public Utilities, etc. for 1931* (Harrisburg, 1933); E. W. Miller, "Connellsville Beehive Coke Region: A Declining Mineral Economy," *Economic Geography* 29 (1953): 144–58.
47. R. T. Wiley, *Monongahela: The River and Its Region* (N.p.: privately published, 1937); *The Bulletin Index* 1 (October 1936).
48. U. S. Steel Finance Committee minutes, 28 April 1936 and 16 November 1937, USX; "Ford, Bacon,

and Davis Report 99," November 1937, FCCP, 1, 2, 21–23; *Mining Congress Journal* (October 1946); U. S. Steel, "Report to Stockholders," 5 May 1947, USX.

49. *Pennsylvania: A Guide to the Keystone State,* American Guide Series (New York: Oxford University Press, 1940), 570–71.

50. *Iron Age,* 4 May 1944, 146.

51. Heald, *Fayette County, Pa.,* 48, 61, 125; Enman, "Relationship of Coal Mining and Coke Making," 333.

52. Isard, "Some Locational Factors"; AISI annual statistical reports; W. T. Hogan, *Economic History of the Iron and Steel Industry in the United States,* 5 vols. (Lexington, Mass.: D. C. Heath, 1971), 1130; Heald, *Fayette County, Pa.,* 90–91; *Iron and Steel Engineer* (January 1963): 168; N. Anderson, *North American Coke Today* (Southport, Conn.: privately published, 1990), 12.

53. Quoted in *Times Review of Industry,* March 1948, 68; Anderson, *North American Coke Today,* 20, 50, 101.

54. W. T. Hogan, *Global Steel in the 1990s* (Lexington, Ky.: D. C. Heath, 1991), 132–33; *Steel,* 19 December 1966, 46; Anderson, *North American Coke Today,* 4–5.

55. State of Pennsylvania, Bituminous Division, Bureau of Mines, *Annual Report, 1950; Mineral Resources of the United States; Pittsburgh Press,* 26 November 1950; Heald, *Fayette County, Pa.,* 92, 96, 121; Anderson, *North American Coke Today.*

56. C. L. Potter, "The Preparation of Coal and Coke for Coke Ovens and Blast Furnaces," *AISI Yearbook* (Philadelphia, 1946), 11; *Wall Street Journal,* 5 January 1972, 28; *Connellsville Courier,* 28 December 1960; *Uniontown Herald,* 12 March 1974; U. S. Steel Executive Committee minutes, 14 March and 11 April 1961, USX.

57. U.S. Army Corps of Engineers, *Comprehensive Survey of the Ohio River Basin* (Washington, D.C.: GPO, 1964); D. J. Bogue and C. L. Beale, *Economic Areas of the United States* (New York: Free Press, 1961), 972–74; U.S. *Congressional Record* (13 March 1958), 4201; (15 August 1958), 17875.

Bibliography

Archives

Bethlehem Papers. Hagley Library, Wilmington, Delaware.
Carnegie Papers. Library of Congress, Washington, D.C.
Carnegie Steel Company Papers. U.S. Steel Corporation, Pittsburgh, Pennsylvania.
Frick Papers. Frick Art and Historical Center, Pittsburgh, Pennsylvania.
H. C. Frick Coke Company Papers. U.S. Steel Corporation, Pittsburgh, Pennsylvania.
Illinois Steel Company Papers. U.S. Steel Corporation, Pittsburgh, Pennsylvania.
Leisenring Papers. Hagley Library, Wilmington, Delaware.
U.S. Steel Corporation Papers. U.S. Steel Corporation, Pittsburgh, Pennsylvania.

Government and Other Documents

1891 Strikes and Lockouts. Report L-19. Harrisburg: Pennsylvania Department of Internal Affairs, 1892.
Belden, A. W. *Metallurgical Coke.* Bureau of Mines Technical Paper 50. Washington, D.C.: GPO, 1913.
Brownlee, R. *The Connellsville Coke Region.* Report of the Pennsylvania Bureau of Mines. Harrisburg: State of Pennsylvania, 1898.
Heald, S. H., ed. *Fayette County, Pa.: An Inventory of Historic Engineering and Industrial Sites.* Historic American Engineering Record. Washington, D.C.: National Parks Service, 1990.
McCormick, E. B. "Labor in the Connellsville Coke Region." In *Annual Report of the Secretary of Internal Affairs.* Harrisburg: State of Pennsylvania, 1887.
Parker, E. W. United States Geological Survey annual review of coke industry.
Pease, R. E. "Evidence." In United Kingdom Board of Trade, Committee on Industry and Trade. *Report.* Vol. 2. 1925.
Pittsburgh Chamber of Commerce. "The Mercantile, Manufacturing, and Mining Interests of Pittsburgh." Pittsburgh Chamber of Commerce, 1884.
———. "Pittsburgh and Western Pennsylvania." Pittsburgh Chamber of Commerce, 1885.
Platt, F. *Special Report on the Manufacture of Coke in the Youghiogheny River Valley.* Second Geological Survey of Pennsylvania. Harrisburg: Board of Commissioners, 1876.
Proceedings of a Conference of Governors at the White House, May 1908. Washington, D.C.: GPO, 1909.
Quivik, F. *Connellsville Coal and Coke Region.* Historic American Engineering Record. Washington, D.C.: Department of the Interior, 1995.
Sisler, J. D. *Detailed Descriptions of Coalfields in Pennsylvania.* Bituminous Coal Fields of Pennsylvania. Harrisburg, 1932.

State of Pennsylvania. *The Manufactures and Manufacturers of Pennsylvania of the Nineteenth Century.* Philadelphia: State of Pennsylvania, 1875.

———. *The Employment of Labor in the Connellsville Coke Region.* Report 15. Harrisburg: Pennsylvania Bureau of Industrial Statistics, 1888.

———. *Industrial Statistics.* Part 2, *Annual Report of the Secretary of Internal Affairs.* Vol. 15, no. 12. Harrisburg, 1888.

———. *The Connellsville Coke Region.* Report of Pennsylvania Bureau of Mines. Harrisburg, 1891.

———. *Coal Analyses.* Harrisburg: Department of Forests and Waters, 1928.

———. *Coal Resources of the Bituminous Coalfields of Pennsylvania.* Harrisburg: Department of Forests and Waters, 1928.

———. *Report on Production Industries, Public Utilities, etc. for 1931.* Harrisburg: Department of Internal Affairs, 1933.

———, Bituminous Division, Bureau of Mines. *Annual Report, 1950.* Harrisburg, 1950.

United States Army Corps of Engineers. *Comprehensive Survey of the Ohio River Basin.* Washington, D.C.: GPO, 1964.

United States Bureau of Census. *Report of Thirteenth Census.* Vol. 10, *The Coke Industry.* Washington, D.C.: GPO, 1910.

United States Department of the Interior. *Minerals Yearbook.* Washington, D.C.: GPO, annually.

United States Geological Survey. *Annual Report.* Part 5. Washington, D.C.: GPO, 1899, 1900.

United States Industrial Commission. *Reports.* 13 vols. Washington, D.C.: GPO, 1899–1901.

Weeks, J. D. *Report on the Manufacture of Coke.* A special report prepared for the Tenth Census of the United States. Vol. 10. Washington D.C.: GPO, 1884.

Books, Articles, and Other Texts

Ackerman, R. L. *A Short History of Andrico, a Coal Patch.* New Alexandria, Pa.: privately published, 1998

Albert, G. D. *History of the County of Westmoreland.* Philadelphia: Everts, 1882.

Allen, J. H. "Coal and Cokes of East Kentucky." *TAIME* 21 (1892–1893): 53–60.

AISA. *Bulletin (BAISA).* Philadelphia: AISI, 1866–1912.

AISI. *Yearbook.* Philadelphia: AISI, annually.

Anderson, N. *North American Coke Today.* Southport, Conn.: privately published, 1990.

Ashley, G. H. *Bituminous Coalfields of Pennsylvania.* Vol. 1. Harrisburg, 1928.

Atwater, C. G. "The Development of the Modern Byproduct Coke Oven." *TAIME* 33 (1902). As reported in *Review of Chemical Research* 9 (1903): 158.

Bell, I. L. *Notes of a Visit to the Coal and Iron Mines and Ironworks in the United States.* Newcastle upon Tyne, 1875.

———. "Report on the Iron Manufacture of the United States and a Comparison of it with that of Great Britain." *Iron,* 13 October 1877, 454.

Birkibine, J. "The Produce of Charcoal Iron Works." *TAIME* 7 (1878–1879): 149–50.

———. "The Charcoal Iron Industry of the United States." *BAISA,* 22 October 1879, 266.

Bogue, D. J., and C. L. Beale. *Economic Areas of the United States.* New York: Free Press, 1961.

Boileau, J. *Coalfields of South Western Pennsylvania.* Pittsburgh: privately published, 1907.

Boucher, J. N. *History of Westmoreland County.* New York: Lewis, 1906.

———. *Old and New Westmoreland.* New York: American Historical Society, 1918.

Boyd, C. R. "The Mineral Resources of South West Virginia." *TAIME* 8 (1879–1880): 338–48.

Brestensky, D. F., ed. *The Early Coke Worker.* Connellsville: South West Pennsylvania Heritage Preservation Commission, 1994.

Brown, R. *Historical Geography of the United States.* New York: Harcourt Brace, 1948.

Burnham, T. H., and G. O. Hoskins. *Iron and Steel in Britain 1870–1930.* London: Allen and Unwin, 1943.

Butler, J. G. *Fifty Years of Iron and Steel.* Cleveland: Penton Press, 1923.

Casson, H. N. *The Romance of Steel.* New York: A. S. Barnes, 1907.

Childs, W. H. "Byproducts Recovered in the Manufacture of Coke." Paper presented at the meeting of the AISI, 26 May 1916.

Clark, J. M. *Studies in the Economics of Overhead Costs.* Chicago: University of Chicago Press, 1923.

Clark, V. S. *History of Manufactures in the United States*. 3 vols. New York: McGraw-Hill, 1929.
Corbin, D. A. *Life, Work, and Rebellion in the Coal Fields: The Southern West Virginia Miners, 1880–1922*. Urbana: University of Illinois Press, 1981.
Cotter, A. *United States Steel: A Corporation with a Soul*. New York: Doubleday Page, 1921.
Dickson, W. B. *History of the Carnegie Veterans Association*. Montclair, N.J.: Mountain Press, 1938.
D'Invilliers, E. V. "Estimated Costs of Mining and Coking and Relative Commercial Returns from Operating in the Connellsville and Walston-Reynoldsville Districts, Pennsylvania." *TAIME* 35 (1905): 44–59.
Eavenson, H. N. *The Pittsburgh Coal Bed: Its Early History and Development*. TAIME, 1938.
———. *The First Century and a Quarter of American Coal Industry*. Pittsburgh: Privately published, 1942.
Ellis, F. *History of Fayette County*. Philadelphia: Everts, 1882.
Enman, J. A. "The Relationship of Coal Mining and Coke Making to the Distribution of Population Agglomerations in the Connellsville (Pa.) Beehive Coke Region." Ph.D. diss., University of Pittsburgh, 1962.
Erickson, C. *American Industry and the European Immigrant, 1860–1885*. Cambridge, Mass.: Harvard University Press, 1957.
Essay on the Manufacture of Iron with Coke on the Juniata Canal near Hollidaysburg as compared with Merthyr Tydfil. Lewiston, Pa.: American Philosophical Society, 1836.
Fifty Years in Iron and Steel. Youngstown, Ohio: Youngstown Sheet and Tube Company, 1950.
Fisher, D. A. *The Epic of Steel*. New York: Harper and Row, 1963.
Foner, P. S. *History of the Labor Movement in the United States*. New York: International Publishers, 1955.
Fulton, J. "Bituminous Coal, Coke, and Anthracite Coal in Ironmaking." *BAISA*, 27 June 1877, 170–71.
———. "Coal Mining in the Connellsville Coke Region of Pennsylvania." *TAIME* 13 (1884–1885): 330–37.
———. *Coke*. Scranton, N.J.: International Textbook, 1905.
Gates, J. K. *The Beehive Coke Years*. Uniontown, Pa.: Privately printed, 1990.
Gresham, J. M. *Biographical and Portrait Cyclopedia of Fayette County, Pa*. Chicago: J. M. Gresham, 1889.
H. C. Frick Coke Company. "Connellsville Coke." N.p.: privately printed, 1892.
Harvey, G. *Henry Clay Frick: The Man*. New York: Charles Scribners, 1928.
Hildreth, S. P. "Observations on the Bituminous Coal Deposits of the Valley of the Ohio." *American Journal of Science and Arts* 29 (1836).
History of Iron and Steel Making in the United States. New York: American Institute of Mining, Metallurgical, and Petroleum Engineers, 1961.
Hodge, J. M. "The Big Stone Gap Coalfield." *TAIME* 21 (1892–1893): 922–38.
Hogan, W. T. *Economic History of the Iron and Steel Industry in the United States*. 5 vols. Lexington, Mass.: D. C. Heath, 1971.
———. *Global Steel in the 1990s*. Lexington, Mass.: D. C. Heath, 1991.
Holdsworth, J. T. *Report of the Economic Survey of Pittsburgh*. N.p., 1912.
Hopkins, G. M. *Atlas of the County of Fayette and State of Pennsylvania*. Philadelphia: G. M. Hopkins, 1872.
Hyde, C. K. *Technological Change in the British Iron Industry, 1700–1870*. Princeton, N.J.: Princeton University Press, 1977.
Ingalls, W. R. *The Mineral Industry in 1909: Its Statistics, Technology and Trade*. New York, 1910.
Ingham, J. N. "Reaching for Respectability: The Pittsburgh Industrial Elite at the Turn of the Century." In *Collecting in the Gilded Age*, edited by DeCourcy E. McIntosh. Pittsburgh: Frick Art and Historical Center, 1997.
Isard, W. "Some Locational Factors in the Iron and Steel Industry since the Early Nineteenth Century." *Journal of Political Economy* 56 (1948): 203–17.
Jenkins, H. M. *Pennsylvania: Colonial and Federal*. Vol. 4. Philadelphia: Pennsylvania Historical Publishing Association, 1904.
Judd, W. M. "Coke Oven Construction." *EMJ*, 10 November 1906, 877.
Keighley, F. C. *History of the Connellsville Region*. Uniontown, Pa.: privately published, 1900.
King, C. D. *Seventy-Five Years of Progress in Iron and Steel: Manufacture of Coke, Pig Iron, and Steel Ingots*. New York: AIME, 1948.
Koerner, F. "The Manufacture and Cost of Coke." *EMJ* (29 October 1886): 291; (4 December 1886): 399; (5 February 1887): 93.
Lauck, W. J. "The Bituminous Coal Mines and Coke Works of Western Pennsylvania." *Survey*, 1 April 1911, 34–51.

Lesley, J. P. *The Iron Manufacturer's Guide*. New York: John Wiley, 1859.
———. "The Geology of the Pittsburgh Coal Region" *TAIME* 14 (1885–1886): 618–19.
Levy, E. D., and D. P. Demerest. "A Relic Industrial Landscape: Pittsburgh's Coke Region." *Landscape* 29, no. 2 (1986): 29–36.
McCarty, H. H. *The Geographic Basis of American Economic Life*. New York: Harper, 1940.
McClenathan, J. C., et al. *Centennial History of the Borough of Connellsville, Pennsylvania, 1806–1906*. Connellsville, Pa.: Centennial Historical Committee, 1906.
Marchbin, A. A. "Hungarian Activities in Western Pennsylvania." *West Pennsylvania Historical Society Magazine* 23, no. 3 (September 1940): 133–45.
Marquand, F. F. "The by-product coke plant at Clairton, Pennsylvania." AISI May meeting.
May, E. C. *Principio to Wheeling, 1715–1945*. New York: Harper, 1945.
Mellen, G. *A Book of the United States*. New York, 1839.
Miller, E. W. "Connellsville Beehive Coke Region: A Declining Mineral Economy." *Economic Geography* 29 (1953): 144–58.
Miller, G. J., and A. E. Parkins. *Geography of North America*. New York: Wiley, 1923.
Moore, J. *Clayton, the Pittsburgh Home of Henry Clay Frick: Art and Family*. Pittsburgh: Helen Clay Frick Foundation, 1988.
Morris, S. E. "The New River Coalfield of West Virginia." *TAIME* 8 (1879–1880): 261–68.
Mussey, H. R. *Combination in the Mining Industry: A Study of Combination in Lake Superior Iron Ore Production*. New York: Columbia University, 1906.
Nelson, S. G. *Nelson's Biographical Dictionary and Historical Reference Book of Fayette County*. Uniontown, Pa.: S. G. Nelson, 1900.
Nourse, E. G., et al. *America's Capacity to Produce*. Washington, D.C.: Brookings Institution, 1934.
Overman, F. *Manufacture of Iron*. Philadelphia: H. C. Baird, 1850.
Paskoff, P., ed. *The Iron and Steel Industry in the Nineteenth Century: Encyclopedia of American Business History and Biography*. New York: Facts on File, 1989.
Pechin, E. C. "The Minerals of South West Pennsylvania." *TAIME* 3 (1874–1875): 399–409.
Pennsylvania: A Guide to the Keystone State. American Guide Series. New York: Oxford University Press, 1940.
Perloff, H. S., et al. *Regions, Resources, and Economic Growth*. Baltimore, Md.: Johns Hopkins University Press, 1960.
Popplewell, F. *Some Modern Conditions and Recent Developments in Iron and Steel Production in America*. Manchester: Manchester University Press, 1906.
Porter, H. C. *Coal Carbonization*. New York: Chemical Catalogue, 1924.
Pulay, E. *The Shots Fired at Morewood*. Mount Pleasant: Southwestern Pennsylvania Heritage Preservation Commission, 1996.
Rogers, H. D. *The Geology of Pennsylvania*. 2 vols. Harrisburg: Commonwealth of Pennsylvania, 1858.
Rostow, W. W. *The World Economy: History and Prospect*. London: Macmillan, 1978.
Sanger, M. F. S. *Henry Clay Frick: An Intimate Portrait*. New York: Abbeville Press, 1998.
Seeley, B. E. *Iron and Steel in the Twentieth Century: Encyclopedia of American Business History and Biography*. New York: Facts on File, 1994.
Sheppard, M. E. *Cloud by Day: The Story of Coal and Coke and People*. Chapel Hill: University of North Carolina Press, 1947. Reprinted, Pittsburgh: University Press, 1991.
Shinn, W. P. "Pittsburgh: Its Resources and Surroundings." *TAIME* 8 (1879–1880): 11–26.
———. "Pittsburgh and Vicinity—A Brief Record of Seven Year's Progress." *TAIME* 14 (1885–1886): 667–74.
Smeltzer, W. G. *Homestead Methodism 1830–1933*. Homestead, Pa., 1933.
Smith, J. R. *North America*. London: Bell, 1924.
Special Historical and Statistical Number. Connellsville Weekly Courier, May 1914.
Surface Arrangements at Bituminous Mines. Scranton, Pa.: International Library of Technology, 1907.
Swank, J. M. *Introduction to a History of Iron Making and Coal Mining in Pennsylvania*. Philadelphia: AISA, 1878.
———. *History of the Manufacture of Iron in All Ages*. Philadelphia: AISA, 1892.
———. *Progressive Pennsylvania*. Philadelphia: Lippincott, 1908.

Sweetser, R. H. *Blast Furnace Practice.* New York: McGraw-Hill, 1938.
Taussig, F. "The Iron Industry in the United States." *Quarterly Journal of Economics* 14 (February 1900): 143–70.
———. *Some Aspects of the Tariff Question.* Cambridge, Mass.: Harvard University Press, 1915.
Temin, P. *Iron and Steel in Nineteenth Century America: An Economic Enquiry.* Cambridge, Mass.: MIT Press, 1964.
Thiessen, G., et al. *Coke from Illinois Coals.* Bulletin 64. Illinois State Geological Survey, 1937.
Thurston, G. H. *Directory of the Monongahela and Youghiogheny Valleys.* Pittsburgh: G. H. Thurston, 1859.
Van Hise, C. R. *The Conservation of the Natural Resources of the United States.* New York: Macmillan, 1910.
Wagner, F. H. *Coal and Coke.* New York: McGraw-Hill, 1916.
Walkinshaw, L. C. *Annals of South Western Pennsylvania.* New York: Lewis, 1939.
Wall, J. F. *Andrew Carnegie.* Pittsburgh: University of Pittsburgh Press, 1989.
Walling, H. F., and O. W. Gray. *Historical Topographical Atlas of Pennsylvania.* Philadelphia: Stedmon, Brown, and Lyon, 1872.
Wardley, C. S. "'The Early Development of the H. C. Frick Coke Company': Address Delivered at the Frick Centennial Meeting of the Westmoreland-Fayette Historical Society, 18 June 1949." *Western Pennsylvania Historical Magazine* 32 (1949): 79–86.
Warren, K. *Mineral Resources.* Newton Abbott, Devon, Eng.: David and Charles, 1973.
———. *The American Steel Industry 1850–1970.* Pittsburgh: University of Pittsburgh Press, 1988.
———. "The Leisenring Venture." *Pittsburgh History* 78, no. 1 (spring 1995): 34–44.
———. *Triumphant Capitalism: Henry Clay Frick and the Industrial Transformation of America.* Pittsburgh: University of Pittsburgh Press, 1996.
Watkins, H. M. *Coal and Men: An Economic and Social Study of the British and American Coalfields.* London: Allen and Unwin, 1934.
Weeks, J. D. "The Elk Garden and Upper Potomac Coalfields of West Virginia." *TAIME* 24 (1894): 351–64.
Western Pennsylvania. Pittsburgh: Western Pennsylvania Biographical Association, 1923.
Wiley, R. T. *Monongahela: The River and Its Region.* N.p.: privately published, 1937.
Williamson, H. F., ed. *The Growth of the American Economy.* Englewood, N.J.: Prentice Hall, 1944.

Maps

"A Topographical and Geological Map of the Coal Measures, etc. of the Valley of the Ohio." *American Journal of Science and Arts* 29 (1836).
Campbell, J. H. *Connellsville Coal and Coke Region from Latrobe to Fairchance.* 1883.
———. *Map of the Connellsville Coal and Coke Region.* N.p.: J. H. Campbell, 1883.
Coke Works of the Connellsville Coke Region. Coke Supplement of the *American Manufacturer* (November 1886).
Coke Works of the Connellsville Coke Region. N.p.: Pennsylvania Railroad, 1890.
"The Connellsville Coke Region of Western Pennsylvania." *Engineering and Mining Journal,* 8 March 1879, 163.
Connellsville Coke Region and Adjacent Fields. Westmoreland-Fayette Branch of the Historical Society of Western Pennsylvania, 1940 (originally drawn in 1926).
Hogg, J. B. *New Map of the Connellsville Coke Region and Adjacent Fields, Showing All Coke Works.* N.p., 1909.
Lesley, J. P. "Map showing the positions of the furnaces and rolling mills of Western Pennsylvania etc." In *The Iron Manufacturer's Guide.* New York: American Iron Association, 1859.
Lee, A. Y. *Map of the Industries of Western Pennsylvania.* No. 1. 1884.
———. *Map of the Connellsville Coke Region.* Pittsburgh, 1894.
Map of the Connellsville Coke Region and Adjacent Fields. Connellsville Weekly Courier, May 1914.
Paddock, J. H. *Topographic Map of the Connellsville Coke Region from Surveys by the H. C. Frick Coke Co.* New York: Julius Bier, 1893.
Porter, G. *Industrial Map of the Connellsville Coke Region.* N.p., 1907.
Topographic Map of the Connellsville Coke Region from Surveys of the H. C. Frick Coke Company. N.p., 1893.

Index

Accidents in coal and coke industries, 204–6; in mine settlements, 212; mine disasters, 206
Adams oven, 171
Anthracite, use in iron smelting, 5; falls behind in 1870s, 31; in late 19th century, 38, 141
Associations and pools in coke, 30, 34, 36, 46–52
Atwater, C. G., on American innovations in byproduct coking technology, 230–31
Austro-Hungarian investigation of Coke Region conditions 1895, 101

Baltimore and Ohio Railroad, and the coke field, 69
Beal, J., 1813 advertisement about coking technology, 18
Becker, Joseph, and advance of Koppers oven during World War I, 233–34
Beehive coke ovens, technology, 15–16; improvements in practice in early 20th century, 179–82; as marginal capacity after 1920, 247–49
Bell, I. Lowthian, on American coking 1874, 29
Bessemer process and the coke trade, 24
Bethlehem Steel Corporation, early experiences with byproduct coking, 190–91
Birkibine, John, on charcoal iron industry, 9–10
Blast furnace, coke in, 2; productivity with various fuels, 6
Blauvelt, W. H., on beehive and byproduct coking 179, 186–87, 229–32
Boileau, John, on life-expectancy of Connellsville coke district, 226
Brady's Bend Ironworks, coke used in during 1830s, 5
Brennan, John P., and opening of Lower Connellsville, 112, 131–32, 135
Butler, Joseph G., on coke supplies for Valleys furnaces, 58–59
Byproduct coking and retort ovens, Klupfel on 1871, 29; Lynch and, 113; and mid-Appalachian coals, 155; early American designs, 158; experiments in U.S.A. before 1890, 160; first ovens built, 165; capacity expansion 1915–1929, 247

Cambria Iron Company, early use of coke, 21; in 1880s 52, 54, 59; purchases coal near Cheat River, 124: pioneers byproduct coke ovens at steel works, 165, 167–68, 172, 189
Carnegie, Andrew, on coking methods 175; on waste of oven gases, 225
Carnegie associates, interests in coke, 61, 62, 67; early idea of shipping via Monongahela River, 244
Carnegie Steel Company, plans for own railroad to Coke Region, 73–76
Charcoal, as furnace fuel, 2–3; difficulties in procuring sufficient, 4; in southwestern Pennsylvania, 9–10, in local economic growth, 9–10; in late nineteenth century, 37, 141
Chemists, and coke quality, 65–66
Chicago steel interests, and Connellsville coke, 62–73; in mid-Appalachian coking coals, 150–152; and byproduct coke ovens, 191–2
Clairton byproduct ovens, 111, 235–38; expansion of, 249, 250
Clemson, Daniel, 1898 report on byproduct coking, 174
Coalbrookdale, Shropshire, England, and first coke smelting, 3
Coal/coke yields in Connellsville ovens, 183
Coal land, value of, 24, 110; in Lower Connellsville, 132–33; purchase of, 222–23
Coal mines and coke works: Acme, 255; Adelaide, 103, 107, 121; Alice, 63, 91; Allison, 136, 259; American, 63; Anchor, 36, 189; Atcheson, 135; Atlas (Crossland), 189, 255; Bessemer, 123; Bittner, 252; Bourne, 145; Bridgeport, 138, 258; Broad Ford Station, 24; Brookins, 20; Buckeye, 35, 54; Buffington, 132, 250, 255; Calumet, 52, 121; Colonial, 258; Colvin, 51; Continental, 252; Davidson, 23–24, 26, 28, 61, 255; Dearth, 137; Dickerson, 20; Dillinger and Tarr, 63; Dilworth, 250, 260; Edenborn, 132, 250; Ellsworth, 190; Fairchance, 123; Filbert, 137, 250; Footedale, 132, 250; Fort Hill, 54, 89, 90; Foundry, 36; Frick, 36, 123; Gates, 137, 250; Grace, 54; Griffin, 131; Harmarville, 246; Hazelwood, 193; Hazlett, 35, 122; Henry Clay, 36, 90; Herbert, 134; Isabella, 258; Jackson, 26, 123; Jimtown, 20, 90; Juniata, 252; Keister, 252;

294   Index

Lambert, 132, 137, 250; Larimer, 61, 145; Leckrone, 132, 137, 250; Leisenring (1., 2., & 3.), 52, 90, 94, 96, 101, 206, 255, 258; Leith, 62, 90, 252, 255; Lemont, 54, 255; Low Phos, 134; Mahoning, 52, 54, 59, 60; Mammoth, 51–52, 113, 206; Martin, 135; Maxwell, 258; Monastery, 61; Morewood, 36, 63, 82, 90–94, 207; Morrell, 60, 121, 123; Mt. Braddock, 180, 222, 258; Mt. Hope, 252; Mullen, 36, 54; Mutual, 90, 121; Nellie, 51, 89; Nemacolin, 246; New Geneva, 20; Oliver, 62, 121, 214; Painter, 93; Paul, 54, 89, 121; Pennsville, 88, 123; Phillips, 137, 255; Rainey, 54; Ralph, 137, 245, 250; Redstone, 52; Robena, 254, 260; Ronco, 137, 250; Royal, 136; Scott Haven, 87; Sedgwick/Fayette, 19, 26, 59; Shamrock, 131; Shoaf, 140, 255, 258, 260; Smithton, 214; Spring Grove, 121; Stambaugh, 59; Standard, 35, 49, 61, 88, 91, 107, 252; Sterling, 23, 59, 121; Tip Top, 36; Trotter, 49, 101; Tyrone, 59, 193; Uniondale, 123, 206; Valley, 36; Vesta, 193; Warden, 63; West Overton, 35, 121; Wheeler, 26, 54, 60; White, 36, 90, 207; Wynn, 52; York Run, 137; Youngstown, 206, 255
Cochran family in coke trade, 20
Coke, nature and qualities of metallurgical, 1, 2; technology, 15–16; early use of, 4; rapid advance from late 1850s, 5; experiments in making and use, 18
Coke oven gas, recovery of byproducts from, 225
Coke ovens, number in Connellsville region, 1845 and 1855, 20; 1860 and 1870, 25; 1873–1880, 25
Coke Producers' Association in 1880s, 51
Coke rate, reduction in 38, 256
Coke Region, general features of, xv–xvii; physical conditions, 12, 13
Coke Syndicate in 1880s, 50
Coke, tonnages produced in Connellsville region, 28
Coking coal in Virginia and West Virginia, 55, 70, 71
Colonial Coke Company, 138
Company stores in coke region, 81, 214–18; at Rainey works, 99
Connellsville, economic structure of town, 201; as social and cultural center, 218
Connellsville area, first developments in, 7, 8; iron industry in, 8–10; locational advantages of, 14; compared with European coke districts c.1900, 178
Connellsville coking coal and coke, characteristics of, 13, 14, 16

Darby, A., first use of coke in iron smelting 1709, 3
Davis, L. R., labor leader, 87
Dealings and speculation in coal lands, 105–12
Depression of 1870s, 30
Diversification of economy in coke region, 202
Docks on Monongahela River, 245–46, 250
Dunkard Creek, Greene County, coal, 111

Durham, England, coke production compared with Connellsville, 29, Lynch on 1896, 173

Edgar Thomson steel works and the coke trade, 48, 61
Elk Garden coking coal district of West Virginia, 147
Entrepreneurs in coke, 14–15
Environmental conditions and environmental impacts in Coke Region, 202, 219, 221–28
Eureka Fuel Company in development of Lower Connellsville, 132
Evictions of families in times of strikes, 93–94, 97
Expectation of life of Connellsville coking coal reserves, 141, 225–28

Fairmont coking coal, West Virginia, 146
Farming, effects on of coal mining and coke making, 221–23
Federal Steel Company and Lower Connellsville, 132
Female labor in coking, 81
Ferguson, E. M., joins H. C. Frick 1877, 36
Ferguson, W., on immigrants in coke region 1886, 207
Franklin Institute, encouragement of technical innovation, 3–4
Freight cars for coke, 44
Freight rates and the coke trade, 23; to eastern iron centers, 31, 44–46, 69, 70–72, 189–90
Frick, Henry Clay, 35–36; negotiations for coal lands, 106–7; and development of coal shipments down Monongahela River, 235–36; achievements, 220, 229
Frick, H. C. Coke Company, and predecessor companies, 36; growth in 1880s 53–54; financial interests in during '80s, 62; efficiency of in 1890s, 56; attitude to byproduct coking, 169–76
Frostburg basin, Maryland, early coke iron industry in, 5
Fulton, John, and Connellsville coke, 60; in 1880s controversy over coking methods, 162–63; advises in opening of Lower Connellsville, 131; compares beehive and byproduct coking early 20th century, 180–81: forecast of life expectancy of Connellsville coking coal, 226
"Furnace" ovens, 58

Gates, J. W., at Illinois Steel, 72, 108
Gebhart, Judge, and first commercial sales of Connellsville coke, 19
Gompers, S., visits coke region during 1891 strike, 96
Graff, Bennett and Company pioneer use of coke in Pittsburgh smelting, 22
Gray, H. A., on coke quality, 65; commends West Virginian coking coal, 150
Great Depression and the coke industry, 248, 251

Greene County, coking coals in, 110–11, 235; 20th century developments in mining, coal shipments and coke making, 241–43
Guffey, J. M., refuses to grant U.S. Steel options on West Virginia coal, 108

Hillman, J. H., with J. C. Neff acquires first large coal holdings in Lower Connellsville, 131
Hostetter-Connellsville Coke Company, 138
Hot blast and use of mineral-based furnace fuels, 3–4
House rentals as a source of income in coke region, 211–12
Housing conditions in Coke Region, 101, 210–12
Huessener, A., and byproduct ovens 158; Lynch on, 173
Hunter, L., comments on early relationship between coal and iron industries, 20–21
Hutchinson, A. A., coal lands and ovens, 107
Hyndman, E. K., and organization of Leisenring venture, 106

Illinois and Indiana, coals and coking, 143–44; possibilities for byproduct coking, 166–67, 174
Immigration and quality of workers discussed 1891, 97; in early 20th century, 104; prejudices against, 207–9
Iron industry, growth of after 1820 and demand for fuels, 4; scales of operation and use of coke in 1840s and to 1860, 21–22; 1870s, 30; 1880–1900, 37
Iron and steel companies and increasing control of coke business, 47, 51–52, 57–76
Irwin-Greensburg coke district, 145; strike in 1910–1911, 105

Jones and Laughlin, blast furnaces, 26; interests in coke, 59; on coking coals, 153; on byproduct coking, 168; coke manufacture next to iron and steel operations, 193–94; late purchases of beehive coke, 245; developments in byproduct coking, 235, 246–47

Keighley, Frederick. C., eulogy for Connellsville coal, 126; on coking practice in the Coke Region, 179; concedes superiority of byproduct coking, 185–86
Kennedy, O., becomes H. C. Frick Coke Company general superintendent, 114
Kentucky, coking in eastern, 148, 150
Klondike coke region. *See* Lower Connellsville
Klupfel, G., comments on 1870–1871 coke production in United States, 29
Knights of Labor, in coal and coke, 80, 82, 85, 87, 89
Koerner, F., comparison of Connellsville beehive with byproduct coking in mid-1880s, 161–64
Koppers, Heinrich, and the American byproduct coke industry, 191, 233–34

Labor, in coke manufacture, 15, 65
Labor conditions and relations in Coke Region, 67–68, 77–105
Lackawanna Steel Company, investments in beehive and byproduct coking, 190
Lambing, Father M. A., 81, 96
Lauck, W. J., on housing and social conditions in the Coke Region in early 20th century, 210–12
Leisenring interests, 50, 53, 106; venture in Virginia, 152
Leishman, John G. A., negotiations with Frick over coal lands, 107–8
Liberty as a possible situation for Carnegie Steel byproduct coke plant, 245
Little Juniata River, Pa., charcoal and coke use in iron smelting in 1830s, 4–5
Loar, Captain, of National Guard and Morewood shootings 1891, 91–92, 97
Location of coke manufacture, xv; locational considerations for beehive and byproduct ovens, 186
Lower Connellsville, development of areas within, 134
Lynch, Thomas, character and role, 112–14; comparison of H. C. Frick Coke and South West Coal and Coke companies, 73; opinion of M. A. Lambing, 81; discussions with labor leaders 1887, 85; in 1891 strike, 91, 96; nervousness after 1894 strike, 101; on coking coals beyond the "old basin", 125–26; attitude to byproduct coking, 169–71, 175; death, 229

McClure Coke Company, 50, 54, 56
McCormick, Provance, with others in pioneer coke venture at Sedgwick Station 1841, 19
Meissner, Carl A., on beehive and byproduct coke processes, 184
Mellon, Andrew, and rail route into Coke Region, 74–75; purchases control of Koppers company, 234; purchases in Greene County, 242
"Merchant" ovens, 58
Mid-Appalachian coking coal districts, 146–56, 251
Miners' and Laborers' Amalgamated Association in Coke Region, 80, 82, 87
Mitchell, T. J., and the rectangular oven, 112, 180
Monongahela River, early trade, 7; and early coke operations, 22; coal and coke traffic in 20th century, 247
Monongahela Southern Railroad, 74
Moore, J. W. and P. H., and Coke Syndicate, 51; operations acquired by H. C. Frick Coke Company, 53; possible developments south of Uniontown, 124
Morgan, A. S., in early coke trade, 35
Morse, Jay C., opinions on coke region operations, 67–72; thoughts on company stores, 217
Mullen, William, labor leader in 1887 strike, 84–85

New River coal district, West Virginia, 69, 147–49

Oliphant, F. H., use of coke in smelting at Fairchance 1837, 18
Oliver, Henry, iron, coal and coke interests, 62
Over-expansion in coke capacity in early 1880s, 46

Paddock, J. H., killed in 1894 strike, 100
Parker, C. M., of United Mine Workers of America, in 1891, 95
Pennsylvania, coke districts of, 69, 124, 145
Pennsylvania Railroad and the Coke Region, 28, 69, 70
Pinkerton National Detective Agency, in coke strike of 1887, 86; of 1891, 89, 93
Pittsburgh, Bessemer and Lake Erie Railroad, 73–75
Pittsburgh iron trade and Connellsville coke, 22
Platt, Franklin, geological and economic survey of the Coke Region 1875, 34
Plumsock Ironworks, use of coke 1818, 18
Pocahontas coke district, West Virginia and Virginia, 137, 147, 149; costs compared with Connellsville, 184
Potter, Orrin W., on coke quality, 64

Rail production, early, effects on fuel consumption, 4, 21
Railroads in opening of mid-Appalachian coking coal, 148–49, 153, 155
Railroads in southwestern Pennsylvania: Baltimore and Ohio, 28, 44; into Lower Connellsville, 130; branch lines, 43–44; Connellsville Central, 133; Fayette County, 23; Ligonier Valley, 41; Monongahela, 131; Mount Pleasant and Broadford, 28; Pennsylvania (South West Pennsylvania), 28; into Lower Connellsville, 130; Pittsburgh and Connellsville, 23; Pittsburgh and Eastern, 43; Pittsburgh, McKeesport and Youghiogheny, 40; Redstone Branch, 40, 138; South Pennsylvania, 41, 43; Vanderbilt system, 39; into Lower Connellsville, 130; Western Maryland, 43; Youghiogheny Northern, 40
Rainey coke interests, 50, 54–55; in Lower Connellsville, 135–36
Ramsay, Morris, 65, 87; in and after 1891 strike, 92, 95, 114–17
Ramsay, Robert, in 1887 strike, 83, in 1891 strike, 92, 95, 114–15
Ramsay, William, 117–19
Rectangular coke oven, 112, 180

Schoonmaker, James S., coke interests, 50; acquired by H. C. Frick Coke, 53; and 1887 strike, 85
Schwab, Charles M., and coke workers in 1900,102–3; on life expectancy of coking coal field, 226
Scott Haven coke project of Carnegie Steel, 244
Settlement pattern in Connellsville region, 197–201

Sherrick coal lands, 106–7
Smoke nuisance, 213–14, 224
Social relations, social provision and paternalism in Coke Region, 203, 218–21
South West Coal and Coke Company, 63–73; Frick sells interests in, 72–73
Stirling, W. R., on coke quality, 65
Strickler, Stewart, enters coke business in mid-1840s, 20
Strike breakers, in 1891, 94–95; in 1894, 101
Surveillance of labor attitudes in Coke Region 1895, 102, 114
Syracuse as location for first United States byproduct coke plant, 165

Taylor, Selwyn M., advises on Lower Connellsville, 131–32; and coking coal in lower Allegheny River valley, 246
Technological conservatism in Coke Region, 161–64, 184–85
Technology transfer, and American iron smelting, 3; modification in course of transfer illustrated by construction and operation of the byproduct coke oven, 230–31
Thaw family coal holdings and purchases, 123, 222
Thompson-Connellsville Coke Company, 110
Thompson, J. V. K., 108–12; in Lower Connellsville development, 110; and Greene County, 242; negotiations with United States Steel Corporation, 111, 235
Tinstman, Abraham O., in coke industry in 1860s and 1870s, 35; and origins of the Leisenring project, 106
Tower Hill Connellsville Coke Company, 110

Uniontown, economic structure, 201; as a center for coke district, 218
United Mine Workers of America, and 1891 strike, 93; targets Coke Region 1894, 98
United States Steel Corporation, and development of mid-Appalachian coking coal, 153–54; early operating experience with byproduct coke, 192; builds byproduct coke works, 233, 235–36; plans for installations at Newcastle and Youngstown works, 236
Upper Connellsville district, 123

Valleys district, use of raw coal and coke in smelting, 28, 32, 38; iron companies and investment in Connellsville area coke ovens, 59; in Lower Connellsville, 135
Van Hise, Charles R., on waste in Coke Region operations, 224
Verona (lower Allegheny River valley) coking coal, 145
Virginia, coking coal in south western, 108

Wage scales, Frick company scale 1887, 86; deficiencies of 1894, 99, 101; after 1894, 101–2

Waste, in coal mining, 223–24; in coke manufacture, 224
Weeks, J., 1880 Census Report on Coke, 3
Welsh, Matthew J., on the grievances of working men 1894, 98–99
Westphalian coke making compared with early Connellsville industry, 29; Lynch on 1896, 173
West Virginia, coking coals, 108
Wharton, Joseph, coke operations, 145
Wheeling Steel Corporation, and Harmarville coking coal, 246
Wise County, Virginia, coking coal, 147
Wise, Peter, labor organizer, 81
Working-out of coal, 250

Youghiogheny River, early coke trade, 19, 22–23
Youngstown Sheet and Tube Company, buys Greene County Coal 1913, 110; cokes coal from areas along Monongahela River, 246